THE CIVIL WARS EXPERIENCED

Britain and Ireland, 1638–61

Martyn Bennett

London and New York

For Deborah

First published 2000
by Routledge
11 New Fetter Lane, London EC4P 4EE

Simultaneously published in the USA and Canada
by Routledge
29 West 35th Street, New York, NY 10001

Routledge is an imprint of the Taylor & Francis Group

© 2000 Martyn Bennett

Typeset in Baskerville by Taylor & Francis Books Ltd
Printed and bound in Great Britain by Biddles Ltd, Guildford and Kings Lynn

British Library Cataloguing in Publication Data
A catalogue record for this book is available from the British Library

Library of Congress Cataloging in Publication Data
A catalog record for this book has been requested

ISBN 0–415–15901–6 (hbk)
ISBN 0–415–15902–4 (pbk)

Stars blazed, protazoa coupled, apes levered themselves upright, generations of men and women lived and died, and like them all I, Joan, have made history.

(Kate Grenville, *Joan Makes History*, 1988)

CONTENTS

ACKNOWLEDGEMENTS

There are many people to thank for their help with this work. I must thank the Faculty of Humanities at Nottingham Trent University for the time, money and space to work on this book. The Faculty as a whole and the History Section of the Department of International Studies has been unfailingly supportive and considerate. In particular I must thank the members of the research group, Forward, and the early modern women's manuscripts project, Perdita: Angela Brown, Victoria Burke, Elizabeth Clarke, Marie-Louise Coolahan, Ken Gibson, Stuart Jennings, Veronica Lawrence, Linda Lees, Kirsteen Macpherson, for their suggestions, and information given when they have heard parts of this book as papers. I must also record the similar debt due to the late Dr Anne Mitson, our much-missed colleague. I also offer thanks to two former students in particular, Sam Ratcliffe who worked on the Dublin Cess Book and Bryn Coldrick who provided me with information about his native Meath for me. I also extend my thanks to my students past and present who discuss all of these issues with me on a weekly basis.

Thanks are due to the Scouloudi Foundation for enabling me to work on the 1641 Depositions with the aid of a grant towards the purchase of microfilm copies.

It goes without saying that the fifty-odd archive and record offices and libraries consulted and referred to in the bibliography are due a huge debt of gratitude. It seems churlish to single any out in particular, because they have all together made this work possible. So I hope that the principal archivists and archival assistants who made my work easier take this as a very grateful thank you.

I must also thank the organisations which had heard parts of the work in progress as papers. Forward has already been mentioned, but alongside it stands the Cromwell Association, *Midland History*, which published an earlier draft of Chapter 4 as a conference proceeding entitled ' "My Plundered Townes, My Houses Devastation": The Civil War and North Midlands Life, 1642–1646', *Midland History* 22 (1997) and the Seventeenth Century Studies Centre at Durham University.

INTRODUCTION

I have worked on the mid-seventeenth century for almost twenty years. In the optimism of my youth I harboured hopes that the mid-seventeenth century history of the British Isles was the history of revolution. However, my Civil War education coincided with the onset of two conservative impulses: Margaret Thatcher's twentieth-century Conservative 'revolution' and the publication of Robert Ashton's important work on the mid-seventeenth century, *The English Civil War: Conservatism and Revolution*. In the wake of both of these potent forces my optimism about the progressive nature of the Civil War period began to dissipate. During my post-graduate years I became convinced, just as several of my slightly older colleagues were, that a Royalist victory, whether in 1646, in 1648 or even 1651 could have involved some degree of political or even social change too. Many Royalist activists were as much outsiders as some of Cromwell's russet-coated soldiers. I worked on the small Royalist army of the North Midlands led by Lord Loughborough. The vast majority of the 350 officers under his command were relative political, social and economic nonentities, in the world beyond their parish boundaries. Had these men been on the winning side then it was not beyond possibility they may have demanded some part of the spoils? They would certainly have benefited financially, as many of their opponents were to do after the war, and they would have weeded out and replaced the petty and middling parliamentarian officials in the local county. Perhaps, if their service had been exemplary they may have been rewarded with positions of national importance. However, it would always remain true that the Royalist victors would have wanted a place in the *status quo* rather than any part in a brave new world. Whilst many parliamentarians would have also desired nothing more than this for themselves, the fact is that some of their number forced major changes upon the four nations in the wake of victory in 1648. There were limits to the notion of the conservative revolution. Even if the revolution of December 1648 to March 1649 was in any way conservative, the resulting political consequences, the restructuring of British and Irish polity were radical.

The tide of the twentieth-century Conservative revolution also reached the high water mark. For all of Margaret Thatcher's confidence, much of the brash revolution of the 1980s was revealed in the wake of a deeply flawed economic upturn to be little other than vindictive swipes at societal structures created since the Second World War (and sometimes much earlier) and the social responsibilities imposed by the Welfare State. This attack diminished into a confused, corrupt structureless ragbag of anti-radicalism.

The decline of the Conservative impulses became coupled with the realisation that much work on the period, including my own, had largely excluded all women and most men whilst at the same time effectively ignoring three of the four nations of the British Isles. In some ways this was the legacy of the county-study background which also informed my earlier work. I set out to make a small attempt to offset some of these failings in my 1997 work *The Civil Wars in Britain and Ireland 1638–1651*. By embracing the holistic view of the conflict and struggles in the four nations the inescapable conclusion was that I was looking at not one, but a series of revolutions each devouring its predecessor. It renewed my optimism in the hope or belief that the progressive will eventually supersede the retrograde and the reactionary in any century if not always directly, but by leaving indelible traces for future societies to find, re-enact and re-use. But this new belief in the revolution left some lingering doubts. In many ways the revolution of the mid-seventeenth century did not advance the lot of the vast majority of the people of the four nations. So, having now, after twenty years of studying the Civil Wars period, set out in print how I think the revolution may have occurred and having looked at how some ordinary people were dragged into the war, I decided that it was about time to consider this latter perspective more thoroughly.

This book is then an account or series of accounts of the experiences of a range of people across the British Isles. In it are narratives of segments of lives affected by the Civil Wars. There is little here of the grand narrative in the sense that it is always in the background rather than always to the fore. Some of the characters in this book, like Robert Baillie or Archibald Johnston of Wariston are relatively well known. Indeed in a work which has some similarities with this one, David Stevenson's excellent *For King or Covenant?* includes both these men. Others like Lady Ann Halket may be familiar. Others, including for instance, Mr John Clopton, are largely unknown. Some people here are represented in their own words, because they were literate. Some of them wrote diaries, journals or memorials. Other people here are accounted for by ministers, clerks, constables and some collected information from those who could not write but had narratives of their own to tell, because they had suffered, mentally, spiritually, financially or physically the wars and revolutions in the four nations. Theirs are alternative histories in some ways; they themselves, their stories and experiences do not always appear in the general narratives of the period: in some cases their narratives do not allude to the general narrative at all. Yet these narratives do not simply offer some challenge to the general history much beloved by post-modernist critics. Instead. they strengthen the narrative, give it new form and vigour, for whether these people alluded to it directly or not their narratives are of the Civil War period and instead of weakening the case for history they give it validity and strength by enriching our impressions. Moreover, these narratives return history to the people to whom it belongs, those who made it, endured it and lived it, without stealing it from anyone else.

Snippets or flashes of light have often occurred to reveal people who do not shine in the firmament of history, but largely there is a shroud of darkness. I originally wanted to name this book after Mr Clopton, because his diary exemplified many things about this period. He was obsessed with the weather, concerned to develop his house and land, keen to record the histories of those people around him that he cared about. He knew that the world outside his home was changing rapidly, he was involved at the fringes and he had a friend in the parliamentarian administration of Suffolk. He was also possibly frightened. It is well known that Samuel Pepys codified his diary because he was frightened that it might one day be seized and used in evidence against him: he may also have balked at writing explicit sexual language. Pepys invented a code. Clopton also did so, in his case it was a code of silence, or more realistically, of referring to many important events second hand. He did not use Walter Powell, the Welsh diarist's technique of compiling the diary later as a chronological list. Clopton was less direct, recording the time he heard about the event. Thus the news of the impending death of Charles I is recorded after the king was dead and the execution was recorded on the day the news was well on its way to Edinburgh, never mind just over the Suffolk border. Fear, personal concern and personal priorities dictated many peoples' lives and Clopton clearly shows this. For other people in this book the Civil Wars and revolutions provided a very personal vehicle. For Alexander Jaffray of Aberdeen they conveyed him from one set of religious or cosmographical certainties, through soul-searching questions and sect-hopping to Quakerism's inner light. Fortunately for him they did not, as they were to do for Archibald Johnston, lead from an outward appearance of certainty to a very evident revelation of internal uncertainties. For Elizabeth Jekyll the war was one more danger on the road to spiritual confidence in her salvation, and she was not alone in this. For others, Mary Hammond of Tuam, the Gonne family of Connacht, or the family of Gruffydd ap Stephen, the journey was more physical than mental, involving the destruction of family, friends and home. Nevertheless, they were all swallowed up in the Civil War and revolutions of the mid-seventeenth century, whatever they themselves made of them.

The book opens with a discussion of one point at which the decline into conflict was challenged. In 1638 the scholars of Aberdeen University raised objections to the National Covenant then being signed across Scotland. They were concerned to challenge on valid grounds the establishment of what they clearly saw as a new heterodoxy being forced on the country at the expense of religious unity. That these academics were sidelined along with their objections raises several issues. Their defeat almost obscured their role in the developing narrative of the wars in the four nations, but conversely opens the possibility of counter-factual history and for a consideration of the roles of alternative narratives of the sort presented throughout this book.

Martyn Bennett, Nottingham Trent University, April 1999

TIME LINE

1625	Death of James VI and I and accession of Charles I
	War with Spain
	Charles's first English Parliament
	Charles announces a sweeping revocation in Scotland
1626	Charles's second English Parliament
	A forced loan is imposed by the king in England and Wales
1627	War with France
1628	Charles's third English Parliament meets
	English Parliament's Petition of Right condemns non-parliamentary taxation and other royal policies
	William Laud is appointed Bishop of London
1629	Charles's third English Parliament is dissolved
	Personal Rule begins
	Peace with France
1630	Peace with Spain
1631	Wentworth is appointed lord deputy of Ireland
1633	Charles visits Scotland to be crowned
	Wentworth crosses to Ireland
	William Laud is appointed Archbishop of Canterbury
1634	Ship Money is imposed on maritime counties of England and Wales
1635	Ship Money is levied on all counties of England and Wales; it becomes an annual levy down to 1639
	Trial and condemnation of Lord Balmerino in Scotland
1636	New book of canons is imposed in Scotland
1637	Severe punishment of Burton, Bastwicke and Prynne for publishing anti-episcopal pamphlets
	Imposition of new prayer book in Scotland; encounters great opposition

1637–8		Trial of John Hampden for refusal to pay Ship Money; judges find against Hampden
1638	February	National Covenant is signed in Scotland
	November	General assembly of the Scottish Church meets in Glasgow
1639		First Bishop's War between England and Scotland
	May	English army gathers around Berwick
	June	English troops march to Kelso but retreat; Scots line the Tweed
		Truce of Berwick
	September	Wentworth visits London to advise Charles
	October	Scottish Parliament and general assembly meet
1640	March	Wentworth, Earl of Strafford, briefly returns to Ireland to oversee a meeting of the Irish Parliament
	April	Charles's fourth English Parliament (the Short Parliament) meets, so ending the Personal Rule
	May	Charles's fourth English Parliament (the Short Parliament) is dissolved
	Summer	Scottish Parliament reassembles and passes legislation severely curbing the power of the crown in Scotland
	August	Scottish army crosses the Tyne, throws back English troops around Newburn and occupies much of northern England
	October	Treaty of Ripon
	November	Charles's fifth English Parliament (the Long Parliament) meets
		Impeachment proceedings begin against Strafford and Laud
		Root and Branch petition attacks episcopacy
1641	February	English Triennial Act is passed
	March	Impeachment proceedings against Strafford begin
		Alleged first Army Plot
	May	Act against the dissolution of the Long Parliament without its own consent is passed
		Strafford is condemned by Act of Attainder and executed
		Alleged second Army Plot
	June	Act declaring that customs duties (tonnage and poundage) could be levied only with parliamentary consent is passed
		Ten Propositions are drawn up by English Parliament as the basis for negotiations with the king
	July	Acts abolishing the courts of star chamber and high commission are passed

	August	Act abolishing Ship Money is passed
		Act limiting the boundaries of royal forests is passed
		Act abolishing knighthood fines is passed
		Charles leaves to visit Scotland and ratify the treaty of London
		Scottish army withdraws from northern England
		Alleged plot, 'the Incident', in Scotland
	October	Irish rebellion
		Charles leaves Scotland
	November	News of Irish rebellion reaches London
		Ormond is appointed by Charles lieutenant-general of forces in Ireland
		Grand Remonstrance passes the Commons by narrow majority
	December	Militia Bill is introduced
1642	January	Charles tries but fails to arrest five MPs
		Charles leaves London
	February	Clerical Disabilities Act is passed
		Impressment Act is passed
		Small English army arrives in Dublin
	March	Militia Bill, having passed both Houses, is issued as Militia Ordinance
	April	Charles tries but fails to seize Hull
		Scottish army begins crossing to Ireland to restore order in Ulster
	May	Irish Catholic leaders meet at Kilkenny; agree confederation of Kilkenny
	June	Nineteen Propositions drawn up by Parliament as hardline basis for negotiations with the king
		King and Parliament begin raising armies
	July	Charles again tries but fails to seize Hull
		Earl of Essex is appointed commander-in-chief of parliamentarian armies
		Sporadic violence in England as newly raised troops and recruiting agents clash
	August	Charles raises his standard at Nottingham
		English Civil War formally begins
	October	Battle of Edgehill, Warwickshire – indecisive
		First Confederate general assembly meets at Kilkenny
	November	Charles's march on London is halted at Turnham Green
		Charles retires to Oxford and establishes his HQ there
1643	February	Peace negotiations open in Oxford

	April	Oxford peace negotiations collapse
		King orders Ormond to open negotiations with confederate Irish Catholics
	Summer	Royalist advances in south, Midlands and north of England
	June	Battle of Adwalton Moor, Yorkshire – Royalist victory
		Royalists besiege Hull
	July	Battle of Lansdown, Somerset – Royalist victory
		Battle of Roundway Down, Wiltshire – Royalist victory
		Royalists take Bristol
		Westminster Assembly begins meeting to discuss future religious settlement of England and Wales
	August	Royalists besiege Gloucester
	September	Parliamentarians relieve Gloucester
		First battle of Newbury, Berkshire – indecisive
		Charles I concludes a truce with the Confederate Irish Catholics
		Parliament concludes an alliance with the Scots
	October	Battle of Winceby, Lincolnshire – parliamentarian victory
	November	King appoints Ormond lord lieutenant of Ireland
	December	Death of John Pym
		Troops from Ireland land near Chester to fight for the king in England
1644	January	Scottish army enters England to fight for Parliament
		The royalists' alternative 'Parliament' meets in Oxford
		Parliament's Executive Committee of Both Houses expanded to include Scots and renamed the Committee of Both Kingdoms
		Battle of Nantwich, Cheshire – parliamentarian victory
	March	Parliamentarian army is mauled and captured outside Newark, Nottinghamshire
		Battle of Cheriton, Hampshire – parliamentarian victory
	April	Scottish and English parliamentary armies converge on York to lay siege to the Royalists' northern capital
	June	Battle of Cropredy Bridge, Oxfordshire – Royalist victory
		York tightly besieged
		Prince Rupert leads Royalist army north to relieve siege of York

	July	Battle of Marston Moor, Yorkshire – parliamentarian victory
		Inchiquin declares for Parliament and resumes hostilities against the Confederate Irish Catholic forces in Munster
		Antrim's Irish forces, under MacDonald, land in western Scotland
		Parliamentarians take York
	August	Essex leads parliamentarian army into the south-west
		Essex's army is mauled around Lostwithiel, Cornwall
	September	Essex's army surrenders at Fowey, Cornwall
		Battle of Tippermuir, near Perth – Montrose defeats Covenanter forces
	October	Second battle of Newbury, Berkshire – indecisive, despite parliamentarian advantages
	November	Performance of parliamentarian armies and senior officers strongly criticised in Parliament
	December	Self-Denying Ordinance is introduced in Parliament
1645	January	Archbishop Laud is executed
		Peace negotiations open in Uxbridge
		Parliament begins considering recommendations of Westminster Assembly; approves a new Directory of Worship
	February	Battle of Inverlochy – Montrose defeats Covenanter forces
		Ordinance is passed to reorganise parliamentarian forces and establish a new model army
		Uxbridge peace negotiations collapse
	April	Self-Denying Ordinance passed
		Sir Thomas Fairfax replaces Essex as commander-in-chief of the parliamentarian armies; many other senior officers are replaced
	May	Battle of Auldearn, near Nairn – Montrose defeats Covenanter forces
		Royalists capture and sack Leicester
	June	Battle of Naseby, Northamptonshire – parliamentarian victory
		Earl of Glamorgan arrives in Ireland
	July	Battle of Alford – Montrose defeats Covenanter forces
		Battle of Langport, Somerset – parliamentarian victory
		Parliamentarian armies begin mopping up remaining Royalist pockets in Midlands, south-west and Wales

	August	Parliament begins making provision to establish presbyterian-type churches in England and Wales
		Battle of Kilsyth – Montrose defeats Covenanter forces
		Glamorgan reaches a secret deal with the Confederate Irish Catholics
	September	Parliamentarians take Bristol
		Battle of Philiphaugh, near Selkirk – Montrose defeated by Covenanter forces
		Battle of Rowton Moor, Cheshire – parliamentarian victory
	October	Major royalist stronghold of Basing House, Hampshire, is stormed and captured by parliamentarians
		Rinuccini arrives in Ireland
	December	Secret deal between Glamorgan and the Confederate Irish Catholics is revealed; it is repudiated by the king and Glamorgan is briefly imprisoned
1646	February	Parliamentarians take Chester
		Battle of Torrington, Devon – parliamentarian victory
		Ordinance abolishing the Court of Wards is passed
	March	Further Ordinances are passed to set up Presbyterian churches in England and Wales
		Royalist army in the south-west surrenders near Truro, Cornwall
	Spring	Negotiations between Ormond and Confederate Irish Catholics
	April	English Parliament appoints Viscount Lisle lord lieutenant of Ireland
	May	Charles surrenders to the Scottish army besieging Newark, Nottinghamshire
		Royalist Newark surrenders
	June	Battle of Benburb, County Tyrone – Confederate Irish forces defeat the Scottish Ulster army
		Royalist Oxford surrenders
		Effective end of the Civil War of 1642–6
	July	Parliament draws up Propositions of Newcastle as basis for settlement with the defeated king
	August	Rinuccini renounces proposed Confederate Irish Catholic deal with Ormond and the king
	September	Existing Confederate Irish Catholic truce with the king is to end and hostilities to be resumed
1647	January	Parliament pays off the Scottish army, which

		withdraws from Newcastle back over the border, leaving Charles a prisoner of Parliament
	February	Parliament plans drastic reductions in size of the army
		Viscount Lisle arrives in Ireland
	March	Disquiet in parliamentary armies; the New Model Army around Saffron Walden, Essex, begins a series of meetings
		Lisle leaves Ireland
	May	Parliament presses ahead with plans for large-scale disbandment
		Dungarvan falls to Inchiquin
	June	Parliamentarian army refuses to disband and begins making broader political demands
		Army seizes the king
		English parliamentarian army under Michael Jones lands near Dublin
		Ormond hands Dublin over to English parliamentarian control
	July	Army debates future plans at Reading, Berkshire
		Heads of the Proposals are introduced at General Council of the army
		Presbyterian mob harasses independent MPs
	August	Army enters London to restore order
		Battle of Dungan Hill, near Trim – English parliamentarian forces under Jones defeat Confederate Irish Catholic army
		Negotiations with the king on the basis of the Heads of the Proposals
	September	Cashel falls to Inchiquin
	October	Discontent within the army leads to wide-ranging debates about future plans at Putney, London; radicals present the Agreement of the People
		Battle of Knocknanuss, near Mallow – Inchiquin defeats Confederate Irish Catholic army
	November	Putney debates ended
		Charles escapes from Hampton Court
		Charles in renewed captivity at Carisbrooke Castle, Isle of Wight
		Army mutiny at Ware, Hertfordshire, is crushed and order restored
	December	Charles concludes an alliance with the Scots
1648	January	Parliament breaks off negotiations with Charles
	March	Anti-parliamentarian rising in south Wales

	April	Riot in Norwich, Norfolk
		Hardening attitude towards Charles in parliamentarian army
		Border towns of Berwick and Carlisle fall to English Royalists
	May	Welsh Royalists are defeated at St Fagan's, Glamorganshire, and retreat into Pembrokeshire
		Royalist rising in Kent
		Truce between Inchiquin and the Confederate Irish Catholics
	June	Parliamentarian forces under Fairfax capture Maidstone, Kent
		Kentish Royalists cross into Essex and occupy Colchester
		Fairfax besieges rebel-held Colchester
		Cromwell besieges rebel-held Pembroke
		Sporadic riots and minor risings in other parts of England and Wales
	July	Cromwell takes Pembroke
		Scottish-Royalist army enters England
		Cromwell marches north to engage Scottish-Royalist army of invasion
	August	Battle of Preston, Lancashire – Cromwell defeats the Scottish-Royalist army
		Fairfax takes Colchester
	September	Parliament reopens negotiations with Charles at Newport, Isle of Wight
		Ormond returns to Ireland
		Anti-Royalist covenanters regain control of Scottish government
	October	Cromwell visits Scotland
	November	Growing army discontent at Parliament's willingness to reach a deal with Charles; army moves closer to London
	December	Army enters London
		Army purges the House of Commons
		Preparations for the trial of the king
		Charles brought to London
1649	January	Purged House of Commons authorises the trial of the king
		Ormond concludes treaty with Confederate Irish Catholics
		Charles tried and executed
	February	House of Commons resolves to abolish monarchy in

		England, Wales and Ireland and to abolish the House of Lords
		Scots proclaim Charles, Prince of Wales, king of Great Britain and Ireland
		Rinuccini leaves Ireland
	March	Acts passed to abolish monarchy and House of Lords
	May	Army mutiny crushed at Burford, Oxfordshire
		Act declaring England to be a free Commonwealth is passed
	June	Forces of Irish-Royalist alliance capture territory and threaten Dublin
	August	Battle of Rathmines – Irish-Royalist army defeated by English parliamentarian forces under Michael Jones
		Part of the English army under Cromwell sent to restore English control of Ireland
	September	Cromwell captures Drogheda
	October	Cromwell captures Wexford and New Ross
	November	Death of Owen Roe O'Neill
		Cromwell captures Carrick and besieges Waterford
1650	February	Cromwell captures Fethard and Cahir
	March	Cromwell captures Kilkenny
	April	Montrose's pro-Royalist campaign in northern Scotland ends with defeat at Carbisdale
	May	Montrose is executed
		Cromwell captures Clonmel
		Cromwell leaves Ireland; is replaced by Henry Ireton
	June	Fairfax resigns; Cromwell becomes commander-in-chief of the parliamentarian army
		Charles II takes the covenants in order to secure Scottish support
		Battle of Scarrifhollis, near Letterkenny – parliamentarian forces defeat native Irish Ulster army
	July	Part of the English army under Cromwell launches an invasion of Scotland
	August	Charles II repudiates Ormond's treaty with the Confederate Irish Catholics in order to confirm Scottish support
	September	Battle of Dunbar – Cromwell defeats Scottish-Royalist army
		Cromwell enters Edinburgh
	October	Some Covenanters issue a remonstrance opposing Scottish support for the king
		Cromwell enters Glasgow

	November	Covenanter forces of south-west Scotland are defeated outside Hamilton
	December	Pro-Royalist Covenanters issue a resolution to allow old Royalists to serve in the Scottish army; strict Covenanters protest
1651	January	Charles II crowned at Scone
	July	Battle of Inverkeithing – part of Cromwell's army defeats part of the Scottish-Royalist army
		Much of Cromwell's army crosses the Firth of Forth
	August	Scottish-Royalist army enters England, reaches Worcester and is surrounded there
	September	Battle of Worcester – parliamentarian victory effectively ends the series of internal British wars
	October	Limerick falls to Ireton after a long siege
	November	Death of Henry Ireton
1652	April	Galway falls to English troops
	August	Act for the Settlement of Ireland is passed
1654	April	Ordinance for the Union of England and Scotland is passed
1654	September	Glencairn Rising defeated
		First Protectorate Parliament
1655	January	Parliament dissolves
	March	Penruddock's Rising
	August	Major Generals appointed to administer England and Wales
1656	September	Second Protectorate Parliament
1657	January	Rule of the Major Generals ends
	May	Cromwell refuses to accept Crown offered by Parliament
1658	January	Parliament resumes
	February	Parliament dissolves
	September	Oliver Cromwell dies. Institution of Protectorate of Richard Cromwell
1659	January	Richard's first Parliament opens
	April	The army expells Parliament and ends the Protectorate
	May	The remaining members of the Long Parliament recalled
	August	A Royalist rising led by George Booth is defeated
	October	Long Parliament expelled by the army
	November	George Monck and the army in Scotland declares its support for the Long Parliament and begin to march to England
	December	The Long Parliament resumes sitting

1660	February	Monck arrives in London. Excluded MPs are invited to join the Long Parliament
	March	Parliament dissolves itself
	April	Convention Parliament meets and invites Charles II to return
	May	Charles returns to claim the crowns of England, Ireland and Scotland
	August	Act of Free and General Pardon, Indemnity and Oblivion
	December	Convention Parliament dissolves
1661	January	Venner's Rising. Scottish Parliament assembles
	March	Act Recissory revoked all legislation passed since 1633
	May	Westminster Parliament meets
	June	Parliament in recess

MAPS

Principal places in the text

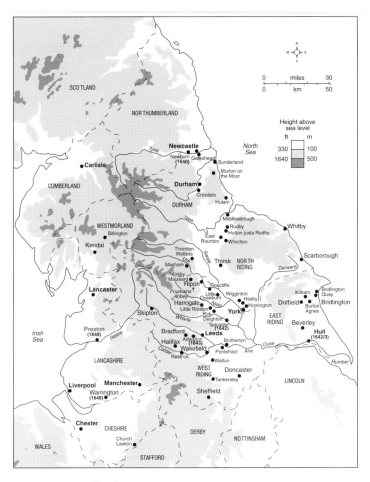

Map 1   Northern England

Map 2 Ireland

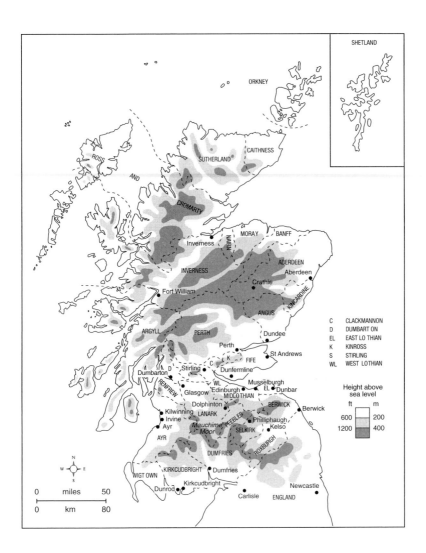

Map 3 Scotland

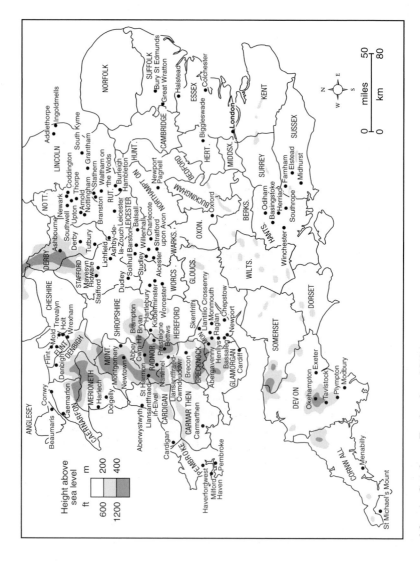

Map 4 Southern England and Wales

1

THE ABERDEEN DOCTORS AND HISTORY

This first chapter is an attempt to examine the relationship between people and history; more particularly when a group of people come up against one of the apparent main strands of history. In this case this chapter looks at a group of academics who strove to discuss the nature of Protestantism with some degree of professionalism even though they realised that the issue was crucial and central to the survival of Protestant worship. It is necessary to set out something of the background to this debate.

The 1637–40 rebellion of the Scottish people was based on the genuine concern that their Kirk was to be overthrown by a king with little interest in them or their culture and distinct Church. Unlike that of England, Wales and Ireland, the Scottish Church had been formed without the leadership of a monarch. Moreover, it had aimed at a modern existence, separate from the civil administration. This had been imperfectly achieved. When he reached maturity James VI had sought to influence Church structure and had successfully re-implanted bishops into the system, but even so, he had failed to make the Kirk an Episcopal Church. At times the bishops functioned as superintendents of the Kirk, rather than acting in the manner of an English or Welsh bishop. To the Scots in 1637 it would have appeared that this compromise was under threat. Charles had no interest in unique qualities: he sought imperial control over his churches. The Church of Ireland, which had different articles of faith and no guiding canons, and the Scottish Kirk with its elected hierarchy, had to be brought into line with the English and Welsh Church. The Anglican Church and the Church in Wales were also were being brought to a new obedience by an authoritative Archbishop of Canterbury, William Laud. Laud was a product of the Church of England. He was of obscure origin, his father was a clothier in Reading and as the Church had been the sole source of his rise in status, he and the Church were bound as one and the restitution of the fortunes of the Church and the desire to impose a secure foundation of faith and order became his life. Laud disliked the doctrine of double predestination favoured by the Calvinists and found in the Churches of the four nations. Instead he favoured the choice promised by the bible, which relates the role of the individual in his or her own salvation by good works and adherence to the rituals of the sacraments. To

Calvinists, who believed that before the creation of the earth an omniscient God, to whom the past, present and future were one, had ordained which souls would be saved (the elect) and which were damned (the reprobate), the notion of sacraments and free will were popish superstitions. To introduce them into the thus far reformed Church was clearly the work of those preparing the ground for the reintroduction of Roman Catholicism. Given the background of the victories being won by the Catholic powers on the continent, this became a tangible sweat-generating fear. The women and men in St Giles identified the Book of Common Prayer as a standard bearer for the counter-reformation, in other words, the popish anti-Christ.

In Scotland Charles I's succession heralded religious and political changes which steadily alienated first, sections of the nobility, the legal profession and finally a growing section of the population. Charles had removed significant sections of the judicial system from the government and placed new members of the nobility in their place. It was perhaps the attack on the Kirk which excited most of the ire. Charles was really only continuing his father's attempts to elevate the importance of the episcopacy at the expense of the elective structure of the Kirk, but he did it in a far less subtle manner. His Scottish coronation in 1633, which he used as a showcase for the re-modelled episcopacy, had the related and no less objectionable theme of demonstrating the English Church as the role-model for the Scots to follow. Whether or not Charles deliberately sought to portray the Kirk as inferior, or just to use the English Church as a model for an ordered Church in all of his three kingdoms, the effect was to suggest the forth-coming Anglicisation of Scotland. The final straw came four years later when Charles sought to impose a prayer book, similar to the Book of Common Prayer in use in England and Wales, but adapted to suit the Scottish Church.

In Edinburgh at St Giles cathedral, people later believed that a woman called Jenny or Jenet Geddes was first to rise. She hurled her small portable cutty stool at the dean of the cathedral in his pulpit. Jenet Geddes may not have thrown this stool, although such a person did live in Edinburgh and some twenty-two years later held a luckenbooth in the market outside the west face of the cathedral, but there is no contemporary evidence that it was her. References to her were only made some time after the event. Even so she had become a potent revolutionary figure. In the cathedral today a sculpture of the 'Cutty Stool' by Merilyn Smith stands on the north side of the nave 'dedicated to Jenny Geddes 1637 by Scotswomen'. Nearby, a few yards from the pulpit, a plaque reads:

> Constant oral tradition affirms that near this spot a brave Scotchwoman Janet Geddes on 23 July 1637 struck the first blow in the great struggle for freedom of conscience which after a conflict of half a century ended in the establishment of civic and religious liberty.

There seems to be little doubt that women were involved in the stool-throwing that day, although Archibald Johnston of Wariston says only this of the rioters:

> At the beginning thairof their rayse sik a tumult, sik ane outcrying
> quhat be the peoples murmering, mourning, rayling, stoolcasting, as the
> lyke was never seien.[1]

On the other hand, an all male presence was suggested by non-written
evidence, as the best known woodcut of the event shows only men on their feet
throwing stools. Yet there is compulsive evidence that women were central in the
early opposition to the religious policies of Charles I in Scotland. David, 2nd
Earl of Wemys, says clearly:

> which buck was so filthy polutted with the treue Rittes and radgs of
> Rome that sum Religius men and women of all sortes did so heat itt
> that they would not permitt itt to be read in Edinburgh and first att the
> ridding of the sead bouk the good religius wimen did rise up to the
> ridder and flange ther bouks ther stoulles att him and did rive all the
> service Bouk a peisses and the Bishop if Edinburgh called Mr. David
> Lindesy quho was sitting in the Kirk that caused reide itt was so stoned
> with the wifes and knocked that he was forsed to flie to ane steare
> benorth the crosse and did wine up otherways they head killed him.[2]

Henry Guthrie, Bishop of Stirling, asserted that women were involved in the
planning of the rebellion as well as in its execution. His explanation of events
was as follows:

> that the work might be done in St Giles' Kirk with the greater solem-
> nity, the bishop of Edinburgh came there himself from Holyroodhouse
> to assist at it. No sooner was the service begun, but a multitude of wives
> and serving women in the several churches rose in a tumultuous way,
> and having prefaced awhile with despightful exclamations, threw the
> stools they sate on at the preachers, and thereafter invaded them more
> nearly, and strove to pull them from their pulpits, whereby they had
> much ado to escape their hands, and retire to their houses ... This
> tumult was taken to be but a rash emergent, without any predelibera-
> tion; wheras the truth is, it was the result of a consultation at Edinburgh
> in April, at which time Mr. Alexander Henderson came thither from his
> bretheren at fife, and Mr. David Dickinson from those in the west
> country; and those two having communicated to my lord Balermino
> and Sir Thomas Hope the minds of those they came from, and gotten
> their approbation thereto, did afterwards meet at the house of Nicholas
> Balfour in the Cowgate, with Nicholas, Eupham Henderson, Bethia
> and Elspa Craig and several other matrons, and recommended to them,
> that they and their adherents might give the first affront to the book,
> assuring them that the men should afterwards take the business out of
> their hands.[3]

Whilst his 1928 editor suggests that Guthrie was being impartial in his account, he had drifted towards royalism after 1644 and his account of the conspiracy may be an attempt to explain that his earlier pro-Covenant response may have been as the victim of conspiracy. Nevertheless, the implication that Edinburgh women were involved at the upper levels is important and supported elsewhere.

The riotous day at St Giles was followed by a series of noisy protests in the streets of the capital and other burghs. The Scottish Privy Council, largely in sympathy with these disturbances, received petitions from the Scottish people and in turn petitioned the king for redress. Both sets of petitioners wanted the prayer book removed. The king was obdurate and would not withdraw, insisting that the prayer book was not a step on the road to popery and professing to believe that if only his council could or would convince his Scottish subjects of that fact then the trouble would pass. Because the strictures of a monarchical government allowed only limited means of influencing a king, the council could not simply tell the king to remove the book. Saved from this form of directness the king could simply resort to telling the council to get on with imposing his wishes on Scotland. By October the frustration of the people of Scotland had inspired the drafting of a *Supplication and Complaint*. This was presented to the council and blamed the Scottish bishops for imposing the prayer book. Even outside the immediate framework of monarchical government a direct demand or accusation could not be directed at the main agent at fault. Only the lieu-tenants could be blamed.[4] The presentation of the *Supplication* prompted more demonstrations and the king ordered the arrest of the so-called Supplicants. The king's chief minister in Scotland, the Earl of Traquair, returned to London to impress upon the king the need for careful management of the situation, only to find himself marginalised by a king determined to impose his will by force. He had taken some of the advice offered by the Earl of Nithesdale and began to prepare the royal castles in Scotland for war. He ignored Nithesdale's other suggestion that the drive to impose the prayer book across the country be slack-ened, and went for direct confrontation, pressing for the arrest of the Supplicants throughout the winter of 1637–8. In February 1637 the king tried to outflank his opponents. Traquair was sent back to Scotland with a proclamation which first offered to forgive the Supplicants if they stopped their opposition to the prayer book. The second strand of the proclamation was to finally declare that the king alone was responsible for ordering the prayer book. This it would have been hoped would prevent any more attacks on the supposed originators as to do so would entail an attack on the king himself. Instead the Supplicants responded with a public reaffirmation of the relationship between the Scottish people and their God. Archibald Johnston and Alexander Henderson, a minister from Leuchars in Fife, drafted the National Covenant. This was in part based on a confession of faith drawn up by James VI and his Kirk in 1581, known as the Negative Oath, and sworn by people of all ranks. The new Covenant also went further, suggesting that some of the acts passed in the General Assemblies since 1581 had been taken under duress. By referring to the need for a free General

Assembly the Covenant suggested that some of the more recent legislation, the Episcopalian policies of James VI and Charles I, were unconstitutional. Henry Guthrie recorded the Archbishop of St Andrews as saying 'Now all that we have been doing these 30 Years past is thrown down at once.' Most of the bishops fled, but three, including Guthrie, stayed on and gave up their titles, whilst one, John Guthrie Bishop of Murray, stayed in place suffering excommunication and imprisonment.[5]

Over the next months and years as attitudes and postures hardened Johnston became embroiled in the oppositionist cause, influenced or comforted greatly by a prophetess, Margaret Mitchel or Mitchelson, 'ane poore damaseil', who gave Johnston the 'best prognostication we could learne for our business'. Johnston recorded two visits to hear Mitchelson during the autumn of 1638, before she went to his house on 23 October where 'hir presence [was] useful to me and myne'. It is possible that Mitchelson was not unique in Edinburgh during that period: Johnston refers to 'sum uthers' who were proving the confidence in God's will which the Covenanters required.[6] On 28 February 1638 at St Giles the first signatures were appended to the Covenant. On the following day it was signed by civil and religious representatives of the burgh at Tailor's Hall on Cowgate; a day later it was made available to all the people of Edinburgh. After that copies were dispersed around the country to be signed by as many people as possible.

The journeying of the Covenant around Scotland in 1638 came to an abrupt halt at the two universities of Aberdeen. Some of the academics took the Covenant into consideration and the result of their debate was of widespread consequence within Scotland and England. Moreover, it set the tone for a good number of the attempts at reaching a median way during the next five years. At King's College in Old Aberdeen, the old Kirktown of the Bishops of Aberdeen, the decade following the accession of Charles I had been absorbed by the continued rounds of a battle over the constitution of the university and the nature of the duties to be performed by the academics there.[7] In essence these debates centred on the validity of the Old Foundation, the precepts under which the university had been founded by Bishop of Aberdeen, William Elphinstone, with papal authority in the 1490s as a college of the Catholic Church. Following the Estates session of 1578 the college had been reconstituted as a Protestant institution, but James VI seems to have been relatively ambivalent to this New Foundation. Further doubt on the validity of the New Foundation was cast in 1617 when James ratified the privileges of the university conferred at its foundation without making it clear which foundation was being referred to. For the next twenty years the battles between the rival factions dominated the university's relationship with central government; for the foundations meant jobs, chairs, scholarship and personal prestige, in other words inter and internecine departmental warfare – the stuff of academic life. When the National Covenant was drafted in Edinburgh, attention in Aberdeen shifted from internal warfare to what seemed to be a national theological and academic debate, in which scholars had a very public role. King's College was not the only university there. During the frustrating wait for the New Foundation to be confirmed, Presbyterians had encouraged George Keith, Earl Marischal, to found a college down the road in New Aberdeen. The Aberdeen doctors, who were principal theologians from King's College, Marischal College and from the town, found that they could not support the aims of the men who drafted the Covenant. Aberdeen was not isolated in its hostile reaction to the Covenant, north-east Scotland as a whole was less enthused by the Presbyterian reaction to the king's religious policy than the southern lowlands and King's College's current patron, the Marquis of Huntly, was opposed implacably to the Covenant.

The men known as the Aberdeen doctors were, from Old Aberdeen, the King's College principal, William Leslie; the professor of Divinity, John Forbes; and the minister of St Machar's Cathedral, Alexander Scoggie. From New Aberdeen they were from Marischal College Robert Baron, Professor of Divinity; James Sibbald, minister of St Nicholas' Kirk; and minister Alexander Ross.[8] These men were all essentially moderate Kirkmen who sought to maintain the widest interpretation of the Protestant faith to avoid any dissent and division which might weaken the Kirk in the face of Roman Catholic aggression. Apart from a kernel of Protestant tenets, they believed that there had to be room for some differentiation in forms of worship within the Kirk. They did not accept the rigidity of the Covenant, but neither did they accept the Episcopalian stance of Charles I. Episcopacy itself they accepted because they could find biblical justification, but they recognised that Melvillian Presbyterianism also had merits and biblical sanction. The king was recognised by the doctors as the fountain of power and authority who had the right to direct the form of the Kirk. They saw only unimportant differences between the stances of the two opponents when compared with the threat posed by Roman Catholicism. Although the doctors recognised that the authority of the king, ironically their own theological stance was not acceptable to Charles himself. When confronted by the controversy the doctors tended to direct their arguments towards the relationship between the National Covenant and the king's power. In the doctors' opinion the National Covenant of 1638 had no royal authority. Whilst their sympathies lay with neither side, their obedience to earthly power meant that they appeared to agree with the king. Nevertheless their stance offered grounds for debate and potentially compromise; they themselves sought to be convinced rather than to overturn the Covenant.

This latitudinarian stance adopted by the doctors, earlier in the decade, had already alarmed Samuel Rutherford who, before the Covenant was drafted, saw their genuine desires for unity within the Protestant world as betrayal of the cause, but he was also angered by Forbes' defence of the Five Articles of Perth. By April 1638 the doctors' first discussions of the issues were made in a spirit of compromise if not sadness over the polarity which had rapidly developed since the previous July. The king, wilfully or not, misread their cautious approach as support for his position and commended the university. The public appearance of the doctors' position came with the circulation of Professor Forbes' manuscript paper A Peaceable Warning, which alerted its readers to the dangers of following the Covenanter lead. Forbes had kept aloof from the college's internal wrangles, and only slowly entered the debate over the Covenant. Within the academic milieu, and then from the pulpit, and then in manuscript, Forbes began to warn of the Covenant's inappropriateness as a means of uniting the Kirk because of its lack of royal authority. The manuscript was ill-received. Regardless of any merit in Forbes' warning, the paper was, possibly deliberately, read as an attack on the nobles leading the Covenanting movement and the serious issues Forbes had raised were thus side-stepped and the discussion re-focused on the apparent personal attacks. In the face of these accusations, Forbes made grovelling apologies to those whom he was alleged to have impugned. Even so he re-wrote the tract and this time published it in print, to try and demonstrate that he was not attacking the Covenanters personally but simply pointing out the dangers of polarisation.

When the delegation of Covenanters – Andrew Cant, minister of Pitsligo, David Dickson, minister of Irvine, and Alexander Henderson – arrived on 20 July, the two groups were already almost irreconcilable. Forbes led the doctors. There were now six men who had remained steadfast in the face of Covenanter attacks. One of the original seven, a minister from New Aberdeen, William Guild, had by July signed the Covenant. The two groups never actually met. By the time the group arrived one of the doctors, probably Robert Baron, had drawn up fourteen queries entitled *General Demands Concerning the Late Covenant*, which to the annoyance of the delegation had been printed and published. It set forth the principal tenet of the doctor's argument: the Covenant was illegal, forbidden by an act of the estates in 1585 which forbade bands of mutual defence, which the Covenant could be defined as. Moreover, the Covenant also appeared to be a step towards taking up arms against the king, and third, it appealed to the Negative Oath and implied that some subsequent General Assembly acts were illegal. This of course meant that the Articles of Perth which Forbes had defended, and the re-invigorated episcopacy, were illegal. The Covenanters had wanted to persuade the doctors to accept the Covenant in private debate but were now forced to reply in the public arena with *The Answers of those Reverend Brethren*, in which they tackled the issue of bands. The 1585 act related to manrent, the tenancy relationships by which military service could be expected of renters. Further, the act was established to prevent rebellious forces being called together to 'disturb the peace' and could not be taken to refer to the defence of the national Church. On the second issue, the perceived steps towards war, the Covenanters were forced to circumvent discussion, claiming that it was too complex a problem to be debated in this arena. On the third issue, the implied illegality of Episcopal legislation, the doctors had a valid point and the Covenanters could only respond that the doctors were mistaken in their belief in the most general terms.

The *Answers* were met by the doctors with a printed response, the *Replies* which in turn the Covenanters responded with *The Second Answers*, only to again be met with the *Duplies*. This latter publication ended the debate. Each pamphlet was quickly republished in Edinburgh and London. The Covenanters, on shaky ground, had to acknowledge privately that their arguments were not wholly secure and that the doctors' writings were demonstrating this and furthermore the debate was drawing the gaze of the four kingdoms upon the issue. David Stewart places the arguments in the context of the wider debate over whether power descended from God, or ascended from the people, with the Aberdeen doctors accepting the first principle and the Covenanters the second.[9] The Covenanters further believed that there should exist, as Andrew Melville had believed, a separation of Church and state, which would prevent the monarch being involved in Church affairs, except as a member of the Kirk. Between the two sides the gulf was wide. It could be defined as the difference between the doctors' belief that the Articles of Perth and the episcopacy were beneficial, and the Covenanters who wanted these things swept away; or between the doctors' belief that the monarch must be obeyed and only diverted from a course of action by being swayed by debate, and the Covenanters' belief that a monarch could and in some cases should be defied by force of arms.

The delegation left Aberdeen, and the doctors were the clear victors on paper. Yet, whilst their arguments may have been a moderate intellectual and tolerant stance, based on the *de facto* as much as the *de jure* position of government, their victory had the effect of enhancing the immovable nature of two sides which had adopted polarised opposites. The doctors hoped to use reason and debate to answer each of the Covenanters' points, but the Covenanters had constructed their legal points only as a framework to cover their more developed political and religious aims. There was no way that they could or would argue in the same way as the doctors; to use modern parlance, the Covenanters had entered into a non-negotiable discourse, whilst the doctors failed to perceive that. To enter into flexible discourse would have seen some defeats for the Covenanters, as the doctors' arguments were intellectually and legally stronger. That could not happen.

The Aberdeen doctors were not malefactors in any real sense. They were balanced, moderate and earnest. They wanted discussion, debate, or as Sir Winston Churchill was later to call it, 'jaw-jaw', not 'war-war'. They came up against formidable men. Alexander Henderson, who was amongst the delegates, had, with Archibald Johnston, drafted the National Covenant, and the doctors had won the argument. Their opponents were convinced men, men for whom debate, rather than division, had become a sign of weakness or a chink in their armour by which the devil or the Pope could divorce Scotland from God.

It was not that Johnston or Henderson had not themselves debated this issue. They had done so, often at night, in the cold dark hours, naked (metaphysically and perhaps actually), cold and alone before their God. In a more secular age many of us would suggest that these battles or discussions were in their own minds as they struggled to think through the dangerous line of argument which would lead them to challenge their king politically and militarily. These men heard God calling them in the night and strove to interpret his messages. Convinced that they were doing his bidding these men put on a united and determined face when challenged by unbelievers. This may appear to be macho posturing, a male obsession with appearing certain in public whilst really being plagued by bad dreams and sleepless nights. It certainly worked sometimes. The general principal that there was a bond between the Scots and their God was the core of a political position which had no alternative but to crush the Aberdeen debate and leave it meaningless. This basic principal became a steam-roller or locomotive of history. The Covenanters could not stand still, they had to be constantly in motion in case any pause let in the devil or the Pope.

Aberdeen remains a place where the possibilities of history met with immovable forces and could be seen as a launch-pad for what used to be called counter-factual history, but has recently had a new lease of life under the computer-generation inspired name of virtual history. Niall Fergusen has argued that counter-factual history has an important role in helping us to perceive the past through the eyes of the participants because it allows us to understand their perspectives on the range of possibilities open to them.[10] This he sees as a weapon against determinism because it enhances the role of chance and accident in the process of history.[11] However, virtual history can lead us, as well as the contemporary observers, down cul-de-sacs. In his essay on England without Cromwell, John Adamson launches a series of speculations on the state of England if Charles I had won the war against Scotland in 1639. Adamson justifies this initial speculation by asserting that many contemporaries believed that the English and Welsh army could have won the war.[12] Yet some of the confidence he cites was more hopeful optimism than real confidence, the Trained Bands marching gloriously out of York comprised the same sort of men who were rampaging through several counties looting when not under the watchful eyes of the king. Adamson is right to stress the catastrophes which befell the more ambitious plans for amphibious landings in Scotland, but to disassociate them from the failings of the English forces is disingenuous. Post-dated confidence which infected some parts of the king's court in the wake of the Pacification of Berwick was not related to the true state of affairs, and this is clearly revealed by the war in 1640. It is dubious to suggest that the king could have won in 1639; the army was not as good as observers claimed it was. More important is that the king did not win the war, he lost, through a combination of factors of which his loss of heart after Kelso was a part. More than this, Charles' loss of heart was not unfounded, it was clearly related to his circumstances and was part and parcel of his mode of government and his personality.[13] The war was lost and any speculation on the course of the 1640s falls to the ground. The debates at Aberdeen may have been a more poignant position from which to launch a counter-factual argument as here there was apparently a debate which could have led to compromise and not to war. Except of course for the problem that the debate could not really exist because there were forces moving which stultified any chance of debate just as surely as there were forces moving which prevented the king's military victory later. Compromise could not and did not exist.

History is not open to endless reformation, there are finite possibilities. Imaginative re-casting of the past is not truly possible in any meaningful sense. To argue that virtual history presents us with the scope for examining the range of possibilities which participants could have expected has limited range. The participants may have had an open mind to these possibilities, but they did not, or could not act on them for many reasons, such as the stance of the Covenanters when faced with the doctors' dissent. Once these possibilities are given narrative form they lose all relevance to history and become fiction. They did not happen; there is no scholarly or academic means of assessing their historicity.

Neither the historian, nor narrative, creates history. Writers can manipulate the past as it existed, but they have no truly creative function in history: historians are the means of, and narrative is one mode of, expression. Narrative can be used to exemplify, explain, to misdirect and mislead, but it cannot entirely create. History is what has been and no matter how much we like, dislike or fear it, it has been and cannot be undone, no matter how skilful the historian is at telling a tale, for bad history is always flawed and those flaws are exposed through the scholarly apparatus used to support the work, either through what they contain or more often, through what they do not contain. Misunderstandings, lapses and gaps are corrected and filled in by those who come later. Historians, even if they are working to the dictates of contemporary politics or some adaptations of nineteenth-century historical and economic theory, cannot but attempt to tell a truth. Of course that truth is not pure and no serious historian believes otherwise, only the 'straw men' characterisation of historians conjured by post-modernists really believe that they can achieve it. There are two factors which militate against reaching this holy grail. First, the nature of historical debate and focus shifts as time passes. For instance, we are not all any longer obsessed with the political élites which once dominated historical enquiry, whether they be monarchs, oligarchs or the 'establishment' in a 'liberal democracy'. We do not centre our discussions on the natural progress of society, recognising that progress and change are not synonymous, and that societies in the past were not there simply as preparatory states for future constructions, i.e. our present. We are still trapped by many shibboleths: we may still focus on men more than women, white rather than black, heterosexual rather than homosexual, the west not the east, hemispherical history rather than global, yet there are developments even here which shift us out from hard and fast positions. In this current study the shift in focus is from the English Civil War to something which more suitably encompasses the full context of the wars in Britain and Ireland between 1637 and 1661. I suspect the last place that the title 'English Civil War' dies will be England; it will hang on to the last gasp justifying itself by the 'fact' that as part of the conflict there was a Civil War in England and that was English in nature. Well, no it was not: the conditions and circumstances of the Civil War were similar in Wales too; at the very least, the war which began, arguably at Nottingham in the summer of 1642 and finished at Harlech in March 1647 was the First English and Welsh Civil War.

The second barrier to complete truth is the historian her- or himself. Like the majority of Arthur's knights, we are no longer innocent. We are all born with acquisitive natures, desiring to learn to assimilate from parents, friends and the social and political structures which cocoon us. At whatever age we become historians we are no longer innocent, we have made tentative or firm decisions on what the world is and go forth accordingly. Then we accumulate the baggage of previous historians, following their routes as if they were some scholarly Arne Saknussemm. Then we reach the goal, the primary source – that gateway to the past – only to find that we have been so loaded with preconceptions of the newly dead that we find not a land where they do things differently, but one in which we appear to be able to interpret their every move. A world which is strikingly familiar, except for the 'fancy dress'. Here we return to the postmodern debate, for it is this quality of historical study which provides some of the basis for the postmodernists' arguments about the 'creative' function of historical narrative. By arguing that narrative creates rather than reflects, postmodernists can turn history into a branch of fiction. Keith Jenkins has argued that we can never know the past, only the versions of the past created by historians, effectively suggesting that we do not study a period of history, we only go to libraries to read what others have said about it.[14] History as a text, he argues, is the product of the political societies from which it derived and if it has any real function then it is to create a 'myth of origin' to serve the interests of the 'élite' in that particular present: it has no role in telling us about the 'real' unrecoverable 'past'.[15] We might argue that Jenkins is really writing about historiography, but he believes that for history to mature, this has to be accepted as a 'truth': we should study historians and their work as history is not accessible. On the other hand many still do argue that historiography is not a means to study history itself: many of those who believe otherwise are not always practising historians, but those who work in fields which have adopted literary criticism techniques in turn adopted from psychological theory, some of which, such as Lacanian discourse, had been discredited in its home base. Jenkins and others dismiss the 'scientific approaches of history', on the easy grounds that there is no one single agreed scientific approach; they presumably dismiss archaeology too, although they do not refer to it, being, it seems, too bound up in the notion that history is only a text or discourse, because for theories derived from literary criticism text has to be central. Ideas incorporated wholesale from another discipline do not here have complete relevance. Postmodernist criticism denies that a past had any role which was entire of itself, or if it did then this is irrelevant as the historian cannot 'recover' that past. It is an argument which downgrades the study of primary sources. Yet to truly study a period we go past the words of historians direct to the material generated at the time: to the words of those living through it, trying through a scholarly and versatile protean approach to work beyond the limits imposed by the initial familiarities, which are often chimeras in any case, and beyond the interpretations of other historians.[16] Contrary to the assumption of the postmodern historian, history is about those involved.

Even if for a moment we allow that history is all text, the texts turned up by historical study cannot all be read as if they are all works of creative literature. The ranges of intentions behind their creation are different to those of writers of fiction, poetry, drama and literary criticism. To depend upon the texts generated by the Aberdeen debate would entirely mislead the reader; the reality of the argument lay elsewhere, in meetings, at Kirk doors where the only text was a signature, in debates at the Glasgow General Assembly. Yes, the Aberdeen debate was a 'shifting problematic discourse', but those shifts and problems were generated at Aberdeen and elsewhere in Scotland, and in the 1630s not in later 'presents' and not always as texts. In the end the paper or text debate was irrelevant as the argument could not, as outlined above, really exist. Many other texts here also cannot be read as literary works. Account books, which are used throughout this study, were attempts to record accurately, often under very difficult circumstances, the things communities as diverse as Dublin or Upton in Nottinghamshire, families like the Kenyons of the Isle of Man, or individuals like Alexander Fenes of Crathie, had lost because of the war.

Eric Hobsbawm recently pointed out that the postmodern approach appeals to excluded groups, those whose histories have yet to be written or incorporated into general historical understanding.[17] This is not surprising, it is understandable. If history can be fiction, or an untrue narrative, then exclusion is the misplaced result of a conspiracy, or a refusal to recognise the value of those excluded histories. Unfortunately in many ways this has a ring of truth; exclusion has been deliberate. Some histories have been written, if not by the victors alone, then by their beneficiaries – those in secure positions in peacetime, those living off the largesse of the successful state, who have lived, loved and absorbed the values of that state (in either a social or political sense). These tend in the main not to be men or women of the working classes, middle-class women, non-white or non-European people of either gender. It has been argued that we write about the groups from which we derive; we could add that we may also write about those groups to which we aspire as well. All of this then tends to exclude, but it does not make historical narrative a fiction. To believe that it does will not ease the problem of exclusion. For if 'traditional history' is a fiction, then so too would be any attempt to written inclusive, corrective or interest-group history. A collection of fictions would provide no basis for the development of an understanding of the contemporary world or optimism for the future. Instead exclusion makes historical narrative incomplete, partial, even ineffective if we take it to have the purposes of instruction, enlightenment and creation.

In a positive sense this exclusion gives historians a purpose, the eradication of as much of that exclusion as is possible. Here, the Aberdeen doctors are the excluded group, the defeated whose role has been often left out, ignored. For, rant and rave as some historians still do about the centrality of certain privileged groups, the Church, monarchies, oligarchies, political élites and of privileged ideologies, including religious ones, the days of such partial studies have really gone. True, there are muscle spasms which have influenced the national curriculum in England and Wales and there are those who have given a public voice to these outmoded questions and grist thereby to the postmodern mill.

The national curriculum has been attacked by some for containing too much social history and for trying to avoid centralising a few 'key personalities' at the expense of a broader approach to the nature of history and its relationship to the vast majority of people who read and learn it. This and the continued use of sources in school-taught history (i.e. the very stuff of history) is all part, commentator Melanie Phillips has argued somewhat bizarrely, of liberal self-disgust. In other words, to her and others the natural-born, important members of society have lost confidence in their role in the world. It is only because of this that there is a concern to explore the histories of other groups: women, losers, the working classes and non-Europeans.[18]

In the pointillism of history the newer studies may eventually dominate the perceptions of the observer. This is not to argue that we should not or will not study the dead political élites, the victors or any other dominating group – we shall and we must – but we must not privilege them as the sole theme of history, just as we should not privilege their living counterparts. History is about us all: we all, as Kate Grenville reminded us in *Joan Makes History*, make history, and history as a narrative should reflect as much of that as possible, even when distilled (but not adulterated) for ease of consumption for the as yet uninitiated. The distinction then between history and fiction is that history happened and historical narrative is based primarily on the demonstrable fact of that happening: fiction narrative as a whole did not happen, even if some parts of it are derived from history. The onlooker may use fictional descriptions to describe the real, but this is not the same as the fiction writer using the real to create the fictional. Unlike fiction, historical writing has to be meticulous in citing its origins. Whether primary or secondary in character it must demonstrate its relationship to the known, provable fact, or fall out of the category of historical writing. To argue that this is a fault, or simply a rhetorical device, because certain groups can construct false histories or propaganda and give them apparent credence by using historical referencing, is wrong-headed.[19] It would be as ludicrous as arguing that breathing is life-threatening because all things which breathe die.

Aberdeen exemplifies the lack of control that a historian has over history. Reasoned debate might be desirable and progressive, it may in the long term bring longer lasting results than war and revolution (although the end of the First World War and the Weimar Republic are useful reminders of limitations). The Aberdeen debate may have presaged the form of religious pluralism eventually to be found in Scotland. The plaque on the floor of St Giles commemorating Jenny Geddes' stool throwing certainly takes this view. At Aberdeen, the doctors' argument was entirely out of place: pluralism was not on the cards. The argument, which continued on paper after the Covenanters had proclaimed victory and left, had no historical impact beyond the continued misinterpretation of the doctors' position. The Covenanters could not listen to what the doctors said: the king did not. Covenanters knew that it must have no historical relevance; the king manipulated history to support his anti-Covenant stance and military action.

One thing which demonstrated the impetus which the Covenant debate had by the summer of 1638 was the embracing nature of the response to the Covenant. This issue is one of those things which gives the lie to the exclusivity of privileged groups. The power of the Covenanters and the powerlessness of a supposed privileged group – the doctors – had the same root, the support for the Covenant drawn from a wide social spectrum consisting for the most part of the supposedly excluded. Postmodernists claim to liberate these defeated or excluded groups from obscurity. This has been done by historians, such as E.P. Thompson, without the aid of postmodernism, although we could argue that his work exposed the liberated to the condescension of left-wing historians who then enchained them to a historical process, created, as postmodernists argue, in a present (the modern). The baxters, the husbandmen, the tenants, the alewives: men and women of Scotland were bonded for their salvation with God, this was their interpretation not ours. For this reason the Scottish rebellion cannot be written of in terms of one or two sections of society, and similarly the Civil Wars and rebellions which followed and touched the lives of all the people, and which were motivated in some way by their actions and aspirations, cannot be the preserve of one class. This work is an attempt to examine the wars and revolutions from across the social spectrum. This is not a new phenomenon in itself, many historians have attempted a form of social history which embraces the views and ideas of many people. There are passages in Herodotus' *Histories*, written in the fifth century BC, where the Greek historian wrote of the lives of ordinary people in the countries which he described, because he understood the way in which it was relevant to social, cultural and political development; for one example, see his detailed description of the way in which marsh dwellers of Egypt dealt with gnats. Herodotus also dealt with what we might call 'women's history' or gender history, a favourite discovery of the postmodernists, noticing distinct cultural differences when the Scythians encountered the Amazons.[20]

Some critics of broader views of history have tended to conflate social history with a history of a continuity privileged over conflict, as if social history tends to obscure the violent aspects of history or to marginalise them as something unusual, or against the grain of history's fabric.[21] This is entirely spurious. The effect has not been marginalisation but contextualisation. There is something of the counterblast of an old guard about this argument, as the corollary is that battles and therefore the political leaders which bring them about are somehow automatically central to every facet of life. They are not. War and conflict disrupt patterns of life as this book will show, but there are more important things to the lives of the disrupted than the interference. Life is and was full of interferences, and illness, crop failures through disease and infestation, war and the bloody deeds of kings and nobles were just others. One problem with this form of critique of social history (of 'history from below') is that it assumes that the study will be small scale, obsessed with antiquarian trivialities as well as rampantly subjective.[22] This is an illogical assumption given that there is far more below than above: the mass of history, as with an iceberg, remains below the surface. It is also a position which denies the notion of historical pointillism.

Postmodernists enter upon the debate too. There are those who have argued that the inclusion of history from below has been a postmodernist breakthrough. The refusal to privilege the narrative constructs of traditional history had resulted in the surfacing of the submerged groups. This is not true. The histories of submerged groups developed before the postmodern debate got under way and the suggestion that history as written is a fiction will just as surely see them submerged again as a non-history. Instead there is an element of truth to what was said by Peter Clarke when he argued that historians respond to their social position and intellectual bearings.[23]

The opening up of higher education in the 1960s and 1970s, and perhaps the mid-1990s; the continuance of WEA and other adult education (probably more so) have expanded the range of people involved in the study of history. As Richard Johnson and his colleagues have argued, developments in Higher Education allowed a broader examination of history and the development of oral and feminist history has taken that expansion further by leaving the academy behind.[24] So, if we all write about our own class, then the explanation predates the postmodern interpretation and relates to the sort of people studying history. We do not have to be postmodernists to study the excluded, and we do not do it because the postmodernists tell us to, because to do so would leave the histories of these former 'hidden' groups exposed to being irrelevant as history; they would have no history of their own, just a part in the history of their authors. What we do owe to the postmodernists is that they made us aware that there are many ways of examining this, through language and culture.[25] It remains questionable whether they were instrumental in this or simply reminded us of what others have said before in the pre-postmodern world.

This book premises that the Civil Wars happened and that they had major effects on the people who lived through them, not all of these effects long term, and not all what we might call bad. The events were not fictional; they do not depend upon my narrative for their existence. Moreover, I hope that I have written in a language accessible to the widest possible audience. Sometimes the language of the stars of the book will be difficult, and their spellings, where original, weird to us in the post-standardised language age, but the effort is worthwhile – it always helps to read their words out loud. Much of the postmodern debate is couched in a cliquish language deliberately obscure to appeal to an initiated group and to make outsiders aware that they are, well, outsiders looking in. That sort of history cannot be history at its best, because it is the dissemination of knowledge at its most restricted, exclusive and somewhat perversely, given their claim to rescue the excluded, élitist.

The moderate debate of the Aberdeen doctors and their tolerant stance may offer the imaginations of writers the scope for playing with the possibilities of history. But this would not be an historical discussion. The Aberdeen doctors won the argument, or at least the war of printed words that summer, but it was a phyrric victory. Really, they lost. They received praise from the king, who congratulated them for their work at the end of July. The Marquis of Hamilton wrote ten days later referring to the town's great zeal for his sacred majesty. The king pressed his thanks on the town again in September, and the following month the town subscribed to the alternative King's Covenant.[26] These were tainted and temporary rewards, and we can question if either the town or the doctors really wanted praise from someone whom they believed had acted mistakenly if not malevolently. The king's supporters held great expectations of the doctors that late summer in 1638, but these hopes were to come to nothing.

The Aberdeen doctors feared for their lives when they were expected to go to Glasgow for the General Assembly of the Kirk. There were demands in Aberdeen that the burgh's commissioners should refuse to participate in anything which went against the king's wishes, coupled with complaints against the expense.[27]

Their chosen delegates, John Forbes, Robert Baron and James Sibbald pled infirmity and did not go. Even the appearance of opposition was mitigated, for the university had sent another representative, a signatory of the Covenant, John Lundie. He had been sent to try and further the cause of one of the universities' factions, that which supported the New Foundation, before the Assembly. Instead, all of this was swept aside and Lundie instead became to the Assembly proof that Aberdeen University now supported the Covenant, and he was instructed to sit as a member. The assembly appointed a visitation of the university for the following spring.

Aberdeen maintained some element of defiance; in January 1639 the town would not participate in the county's war committee, choosing to maintain its own war effort. In March the town commenced the construction of earthworks, making the work compulsory; any freeman of the town refusing to participate was to be deprived of his standing.[28] When the visitors approached the city three of the doctors fled.

The vestige of the doctors' resistance remained, for the expectations of the king's supporters led to Aberdeen being targeted as the core of a Royalist rising led by the Earl of Huntly, which was put down by forces under the Earl of Montrose in mid-June that year. The town was devastated, looting took place in the wake of the rising and the local presbytery collapsed, so by August the town had to apologise to the General Assembly for not having sent a representative because of this. The town complained of its treatment to the king, making it clear had it had suffered because of its support for him. The king's reply came secondhand, and was non-committal; after restitution of looted goods, the king would 'take a course to give them satisffaction in such sort as they shall not repent their paines'.[29] That war followed was a clear development from the immovable positions developed at Aberdeen.

2

UNDER OCCUPATION: THE NORTH OF ENGLAND, 1640–8

After the failure of the Aberdeen doctors to widen the discussions on the National Covenant, the relations between Charles I and the majority of the Scottish nation declined. Attempts by the king to manipulate the General Assembly of the Scottish Kirk and the Estates (the Scottish Parliament) during the late summer of 1638 failed to influence the flow of events and Charles switched his policy to favour his military preparations. War broke out in summer 1639. The north of Britain was swept into the wars of Charles' reign quickly. Geography dictated that the far northern counties of England were the king's front line whilst the great expanse between them and the Trent was to be the marshalling yard for the armies of men, and for the convoys of food and weapons. The first 'Anglo-Scots' or 'Bishop's War' of 1639, because it was over in a few days in early June 1639, was very much a 'phoney war' as far as military action was concerned. In logistical terms there had been much action, much 'sound and fury' as the North mobilised its own resources and prepared to accept the resources of other regions. William Robinson of Falsgrave, Scarborough, was worried as the summer of 1640 approached. He was a skilled man, whose hands (and God's providence – he admitted) were his only means of earning a living for him and his wife; and now he was enlisted. He contacted his colonel who considered the case. William was probably hoping to be released from service, but the colonel's decision provided only a financial solution. William was given a suit of clothes by the constable, 40s by Ralph Pearson and 12d a week was to be paid to his wife during the period William was under arms. The town council did not want to go to the trouble of finding soldiers for the war more than once and was keen that soldiers dispatched to Sir Hugh Cholmeley remain under arms. Nevertheless, Sir Hugh decided that four of the town soldiers should not have been sent to him because of their family commitments and released them from service. The town wrote back, disputing the men's claims and asked Sir Hugh to recall them to the colours rather than burden the town with the effort of finding more men.[1]

That the king and the Scots were supposedly seeking a peaceful way out of the *impasse* which followed the Pacification of Berwick was a scenario optimistically adopted by many onlookers. If you lived near the beacon-crowned hilltops of Yorkshire, there may have been fewer grounds for optimism. These were not only being maintained, they were manned and in readiness as early as January 1640. By April, the Osgodcrosse Hundred Beacons cost £11 8s 1d to maintain, on top of which there was the cost of commandeering carriages, guarding the king's treasure at Ferrifriston and 'other employments', totalling £38 5s 11d to be collected by the high constable. A job that was onerous, especially if you were 'decripit' and the only help you had, a son, was in the army. This was the plight of gentleman Arthur Brigge who was discharged from the post of High Constable on 13 April 1640 at the Pontefract sessions.[2]

The cost of funding what was optimistically called the 'expedition to Scotland' began to cause other problems. In the East Riding villages around Hull the quartermasters were apparently practising extortion.[3] Civilian collectors were also breaking rules in the West Riding. In their rush to collect money some of those responsible were overturning tradition. At Barnborough the new assessments were levied on acreage, an unheard-of practice where lays were usually assessed on a mixture of both, at 4d per pasture beast, 6d per score of sheep, 2d an acre of meadow and 1d an acre on arable land. Assessments were made when the meadow was in use and that standard used throughout the year. Similar arguments interrupted collections at South Milford, Acton, Cudworth, Burghwallis, Smeaton, Carleton Hamlet, Sowerby and Wakefield, and all of the cases went before the sessions where the JPs always ordered that tradition be upheld.[4] Clearing up the financial tangles of the war took up a great deal of time in the October sessions, but they were dealing with attempts to maintain a sense of tradition or normality in a crisis. The political nation had been humiliated, but no one was going to prize levies from Yorkshire villages in a novel manner. What can we read into this behaviour? Those opposed to the collection of arbitrary taxation were not averse to using arguments based on malfeasance or mismanagement as a cover for political opposition. There was well-documented opposition to the war, from the ranks of the aristocracy to other sections of society. Clogging up the courts with disputes over taxation was not necessarily opposition to the war, but it was opposition to elements of arbitrary government at its lowest level.

There were problematic levy collections, unpaid dues and fraud to deal with. When William Pell of Walton had lent a wain for carrying the king's household from Ferrybridge to York during the war, he had to go himself to Ferrybridge with two oxen which he led to Bawtry. Two journeys, and over 80 miles of travel and none of it paid for by October. He had no other option but to appeal to the courts. The Justices of the Peace agreed something was amiss and ordered 30s to be levied on the hundred as a whole to recompense William. Skulduggery was involved further south. On the night of 28 June Constable Wright of Kirk Deighton, a village north of Wetherby, received a warrant directing him to levy a wagon team on the village. The team was needed to carry the king's household south from Wetherby to Doncaster. For some reason, perhaps because he could not persuade any of his neighbours to provide one, he crossed out Kirk Deighton and wrote Little Ribston in its place and sent the warrant on. About 2 miles up the road to Knaresborough, at Little Ribston, Henry Bigland provided the team, before suspecting that the warrant was not what it should be. It took until the Knaresborough sessions in October to get an order obliging Kirk Deighton to pay up.

At Newburn on 28 August 1640 the Scots received what Sir Thomas Hope called 'the woinderfull blissing of God in the victory off our armie in passing the Tyne': they defeated the king's army.[5] Although the English and Welsh forces had been defeated and then retreated south into Yorkshire after the fall of Newcastle at the end of August, a state of war continued until 2 October when the treaty discussions began at Ripon. There was little in the way of fighting except a few skirmishes between the two armies billeted as they were in close proximity. One of these fights gave rise to Martin Parker's ballad *Good Newes from the North*, in which the capture of 37 Scottish soldiers was turned into a victory which somehow 'paid them for their insolencies past'.[6] There were even less dramatic victories to provide crumbs of comfort. When a Scottish ship entered Scarborough Harbour in September it was seized for the king. The cargo of salt was to be looked after until the Lord High Admiral the Earl of Northumberland could send someone to take charge.[7]

The end of the fighting brought other problems too: at Brotherton, once the war was over the constable was left out of pocket because he had to lay out part of the war levy himself and the village refused to set a levy to pay him; the same was true at Greenhammerton.[8] Some of the soldiers returning home from the defeat found England not to be 'fit for heroes'. John Wilson had lived in Rastrick for 27 years, probably his whole life, before being sent into the army in the early summer of 1640. His brief experience of military service was the only time he had lived away from home, but it had dramatic results. On his return home after the war ended, he found his world changed. Perhaps it began with people on the roads into the village avoiding his gaze or pushing past him, apparently not recognising him. Whatever the case it was not long before he was made unwelcome: the village where he had spent his entire life refused to acknowledge that he had ever been a resident. Moreover, and here may have lain the root of the community's response, the Rastrick parish officials would not provide John Wilson with somewhere to live, now that he was a poor man. There are several possible reasons for such a reaction to a returning soldier. One is that John Wilson was already something of a problem, violent, light fingered or feckless; perhaps Rastrick had ensured his selection as a soldier in the hope that he would never return. Perhaps he had volunteered for the war against the grain of a community which opposed war with Scotland. It was clear that there was no mistake, the village was practising corporate deceit. The JPs ordered the Rastrick churchwardens and Overseers of the Poor to provide a house at low rent. John Browne returned to Harwood wounded and 'impotent' or incapable of working for a living with a pension of 40s. For some misdemeanour he lost the pension, but having no means of income the JPs had to provide him with temporary handouts into 1641. John Stringer of Woodlesford was also rendered incapable of earning a living and the Halifax magistrates gave him a noble.[9] The war may have been short and may have climaxed at Newburn, but for these men their lives had been changed, even wrecked. William and Mary Wright seemed to have left their home when he served in the king's army and it seems that she had accompanied him whilst he was on active service. The JPs at Knaresborough recognised them as genuinely homeless and allowed them to settle at Roecliffe. The churchwardens were ordered to provide them both with land and materials to build a house, and were even obliged to give them help building their new home.[10] Richard Eastbourne's wound, he informed Wetherby magistrates, had been received in the 'expedition to Scotland', but he'd been shot in the arm by accident, and was now described as lame; it had certainly affected his earning capacity. They gave him 10s there and then and instructed that at the next sessions he would be given a yearly pension.

At Fountains village, hard by the Abbey ruins and the beautiful butter-coloured hall built of the stone from the crumbling edifice, villagers were burdened with billeting as soon as the occupation began. English soldiers, close to the negotiations at Ripon, were in the hamlet: nine soldiers in four of the five houses listed by Constable Ewens. Four were in his own home.[11] Most of the Scottish regiments were stationed in Northumberland, close to Newcastle and the north of County Durham, although the Earl of Home's regiment was stationed on the Yorkshire–Durham border, some 25 miles from Fountains. Finding pay and victuals proved difficult. By the terms of an agreement negotiated at Ripon on 16 October, which were confirmed by the cessation concluded on 26 October, as soon as the authority of an English/Welsh Parliament could be obtained a nationwide levy would be established to provide £850 a day for the maintenance of the Army of the Covenant. Because the money was needed immediately the Scottish forces were given the authority to collect it from Westmorland, Durham and Newcastle, the areas occupied by the Scots: the Tees was recognised as the demarcation line. In extreme circumstances, money could be collected from Cumberland and Northumberland.[12] Levies would be collected in arrears from 23 October onwards and continue in the first instance to 16 March 1641. The levies would initially be backdated to 16 October, the date the arrangements were drawn up at Ripon. It would appear that the Scots attempted to employ the system used by their own war committees. Upon making an agreement with the Scots, landowners were to register their annual rents and hand over, as a cash loan, one quarter of their value, half immediately and half four weeks later. Additionally thereafter a weekly levy was due. Landowners were also obliged to sell supplies to the Scots at market rates and assist with military transport arrangements within a 12 mile radius of the their estates. In return the landlords and their tenants would be free from trouble and molestation.[13] The intention was that these loans would be repaid from the nationwide levy once it began to be collected: but the plan went awry. By

15 December none of the money, by now amounting to £30,000, had been received from the levy. Henry Blair pointed out that the money was supposed to be raised 'with all speed: that they sould not need to presse or in any sort to trouble these counties ... no violence hath been done and all possible forbearance of exaction hath been used'. This patience and forbearance could not last: the army was unpaid and short of food, and that sent from Scotland had been exhausted over the past five weeks. There was a real threat that soldiers would desert and that part of the army would shift westwards and billet itself on Westmoreland and Cumberland which were out of bounds. The situation improved somewhat but on the day that the first pay agreement ended Blair wrote again. By this time £80,000 should have reached the North, but only £18,000 had got there. Blair continued:

> The countrye people of the these counties have trusted the soldiers so long, as they have become wearie and are unable to furnish them: there Cattell & victuall being so farr exhausted and wasted, as is feared able to entertain themselves. The Markets are decayed because there is no money to buy the commodites & are become so deare that noe sort of victual is sould but at a double rate.

By this time some of the soldiers had shifted for themselves, as Blair put it: 'they must either starve or (some against their will) break their limited bonds'; they had gone into Westmoreland and Cumberland.[14] The effects of the Covenanter forces in Newcastle itself are difficult to determine, although the churches, assigned to the regiments for worship, must have been full. At nearby Gateshead the poor rates and so forth continued to be in surplus until 1642, so economic effects may well have been muted if indeed they were in any way deleterious.

The Covenanter Army left England in the third week of August 1641, after the Westminster Parliament had paid the last of the reparations. The English and Welsh Army disbanded shortly afterwards. No doubt this was a welcome event, but one which cost the people of the North more money. Commissioners for the disbanding of the army summoned constables and urban administrators to bring lists of inhabitants with the wherewithal to pay in early August 1641.[15] This was of course on top of the levies being made already to cover the subsidies ordered by Parliament. But the North only saw six or seven months without military preparations within its boundaries. The third period of militarisation since the signing of the Covenant began in March 1642 just about the time Richard Eastbourne should have been issued with his pension, when Charles I arrived at York and began scheming the capture of the massive arsenal which was still lodged at Hull seven months after disbandment. This time the threat of force being raised came from within, rather than from across the border.

The Civil War 1642–3

In York the king gathered around him armed supporters almost as soon as he settled at King's Manor, a complex of buildings which housed the headquarters of the Council of the North (which had recently been renovated by the late Earl of Stafford who was executed in May 1640 as part of the attack on the officials of Charles I's government). The king's military activities were closely watched by a commission sent by Parliament ostensibly to maintain means of communication with the king, but also to watch his military preparations closely. By the last week of April the king had enough forces to attempt to occupy Hull. The fairly simple plot centred on the king's naïve belief that his English subjects were more placid, if not actually more loyal than the Scots. Charles expected that the gates of Hull would be open to him because he was king. Instead the governor kept them firmly closed. Humiliated, the king had returned to York, but the stakes had now been raised in the political game and militarisation of the North began apace.

Parliament had already, in the Militia Ordinance, appointed a new lord lieutenant who should have begun to muster the trained bands in the county. Those in York were exercised for the king's benefit, something which by July 28 had begun to concern the city council and a petition was drawn up asking the king 'that none of the trained bands of this Cittie go forth upon anie occasion'.[16]

In Scarborough Lord Newport's regiment was recruiting and the town had to provide suitable clothes for 'his ma[jesties] service … '; at the same time the town was to ensure the maintenance of the soldier's families during their absence. A few days later Henry Belassyse's regiment was sent to Hull with the country providing all necessary carriages just as it had two years earlier for the expedition to Scotland. All arms in the town in private hands were to be seized for the king's use, it being alleged that they were 'embezilled' from the magazine or bought from the soldiers during the last war. This the town could not tolerate. The seas were dangerous because of the 'disquietness of the times as well as at sea as at land'. In other words, the collapse of government at home had left the sailors open to anarchy. This was a well-aimed swipe at those who now sought to strip the vulnerable of a means of defence and who might well be blamed for the disquiet.[17] It is no coincidence that when Sir Hugh Cholmeley occupied the town for Parliament in October he offered to pay for any weapons sent to him.[18]

Money of course was a major consideration, but Charles had the advantage of geography. One of the last instances of co-operation between king and Parliament in 1642 had been action over the war in Ireland. On 15 February an Impressment Act gave JPs the power to conscript men for an army to serve in Ireland. Another act had parcelled up a quarter of a million acres of land supposedly belonging to Irish 'traitors' for purchase by investors willing to lay out a million pounds to fund the war. A third plan involved the raising of £400,000 in taxes across England and Wales from a wide social range, well beyond the normal bounds of taxation levies. Collection of this levy began quickly, but it was soon misappropriated. No money from any northern county was received at Westminster. It is certain that Charles redirected the collections in Wales to his own coffers during 1642, and it is possible that he was doing the same in the North whilst he was based in York. This does not mean that he was collecting vast sums of money, as the list that details the lack of payments from the North also shows that there was precious little coming in from even the home counties.

Collection of the levies was slow despite the fact that fears of an invasion by Irish rebels were very real even as far inland as the West Riding of Yorkshire.[19] Partly these fears were generated by the streams of refugees coming into England. Very soon after the rebellion English settlers began to flee Ireland and they may have spread fear inland. Irish Sea coasts had soon felt worried by the proximity of the Catholic rebels, but as the refugees spread inland from Welsh ports, and both east and west coast ports in England, they achieved two effects. First they enhanced general fears with their tales of the 'massacres'. Second, they often travelled in large groups, probably a reverse reflection of their more hopeful outward journey. This resulted in an atmosphere of terror. An autumn fast sermon in Pudsey was interrupted at 3 pm by the sudden news that the Irish rebels were at Rochdale. A man called John Sugden had mistaken a group of Protestant refugees from Ireland for an Irish rebel army. Fearful of their lives, for they suspected that 'Incarnate Devils and Death would be there before us' the congregation returned to their homes in Bradford. It was evening before the truth was discovered. The presence of troops in Yorkshire similarly brought fear to the 'godly community' of Puritans. Whilst these were probably the remains of the army assembled for the wars with Scotland, to some observers they were associated with Charles I's dubious designs for Church and state. Joseph Lister later wrote that:

> Mothers and Children expecting daily when they should be dashed in peices one against another; everyone now began to shift for themselves, but they had no way of escape left them in the world, that they knew of; some indeed, in time, got into New-England, but they were but few, and that too with a great deal of difficulty; some made their escape into Lancashire, hoping to pass thence, but always shut up, few could make their escape.[20]

This was a heavy influence on the people of the region. For in the West Riding the parliamentarian Fairfaxes found a rich recruiting ground for soldiers. Samuel Priestley, a local man, declared that he could not stay aloof from the fighting when there was a danger that the massacres he believed were happening in Ireland might be enacted in England.[21]

A real army and real fighting broke out when the king made his second attempt to gain access to Hull's arsenal. This time the king moved the court to Beverley and armed forced ringed the port. Offensive and defensive works were dug and Holderness echoed to gunfire from 10 July onwards. The garrison mounted a series of sorties from the town and destroyed Royalist earthworks, and by 27 July after large-scale attacks from the Hull forces, the Royalist siege ended.[22]

Across the Pennines Lord Strange's recruits were also embroiled in fighting. He seized the Liverpool arsenal and then on 15 July, whilst the siege of Hull was in progress, entered Manchester where fighting broke out. War in the North had broken out less than two years after the Second Bishop's War. However, the king's early failures brought a temporary pause. The king decided to launch a campaign to seize the magazines further south in the Midlands and August saw him spending time in Lincolnshire, Nottinghamshire and Warwickshire. Northern recruitment campaigns, led by the Earl of Newcastle in the four northernmost counties and Lord Strange in Lancashire continued alongside the Earl of Cumberland's far more desultory campaign in Yorkshire.

War returned to the region in the final months of the year, once the field armies had demonstrated at Edgehill that the war was not to be decided by one major battle. The northern earls were having mixed successes. In the north-east the Earl of Newcastle had much of the argument go his own way. There were few opponents powerful enough to challenge him, and apart from trouble with the Trained Bands in Durham, Newcastle met little opposition to his creation of an army. In Lancashire, Lord Strange, raised by the death of his father to the earldom of Derby, continued his campaign to dominate affairs in Cheshire and Lancashire, a county with prominent pockets of Puritanism. He again attacked Manchester which was now garrisoned for Parliament. A ten-week blockade on the town and a week's close siege ended in failure, but the town remained somewhat isolated. Derby's forces were able to dominate the rest of the county with impunity. At the very end of the year Derby, based at Wigan, planned the control of Lancashire with garrisons established at Leigh, Warrington, Wigan, Preston and Brindle. The most heavily garrisoned were to be Wigan and Warrington with 300 foot soldiers in each, and Wigan also had a troop of horse and 100 dragoons. Derby was aware that recruitment might not have produced companies of the appropriate size. The three companies at Wigan, under Captains Charnock, Chisnell and Barrowe were to recruit the required number to complete the 300.

At Warrington, two of the four companies were Welsh, but all four were suspected of being under-armed. Instructions were issued to governor Edward Norres to take arms from inhabitants 'such as doe not appeare to doe service'. Some of the garrisons were tiny. That at Leigh consisted of 20 men, who were victualled for a week and had £12 in cash. Two dragoons were sent there, probably for scouting and communications.[23]

That Lancashire was to be put on a war footing is not in doubt. The Royalist garrisons were a spine up the centre of the county linking Chester with the Earl of Newcastle's north-west counties. The small Leigh garrison were in the proximity of the two hotbeds of Puritanism, Manchester and that little Geneva, Bolton. Moreover, the resources of the county were to be controlled. Derby set prices for produce bought by the quartermaster general Henry Ogle; butter at 3d a pound, cheese at 2d a pound and bread at 16lb for a shilling. Hay was to be bought at 2d a stone and only oats were to be bought at market prices. The consequences of this would be important. Lancashire producers would either lose out directly, by being paid these usually undercut rates by the constables charged with their collection, or indirectly. Evidence from other constables' accounts shows that the producers were sometimes paid the difference between the 'official price' and the market price from community funds. In such a case the whole community, including the producer paid the cost of the official plunder. Unofficial plunder was prohibited by Derby.

In Yorkshire, it was parliament's garrison at Hull which proved the most aggressive. Troops from there encroached upon the king's former headquarters, placing themselves in Cawood, the archbishop's palace south-west of York. It was this turn of events which led the frustrated Royalists of York to request the assistance of the Earl of Newcastle, who in response brought his army south-wards and began a campaign to dominate the county which would culminate on the Leeds to Bradford road at the end of June 1643.

It took some time for the earl to establish control of the West Riding where the Fairfaxes, father and son, led the parliamentarians and in the East Riding where powerful gentry families like the Legards of Anlaby and the Constables, assisted by the Hothams at Hull, successfully maintained an important presence, buttressed by Sir Hugh Cholmeley at Scarborough. The North Riding, adjacent to the earl's northern command, was soon under Royalist sway. As battles were fought south of York at Tadcaster and Wakefield innholders took advantage and began to overcharge customers for food and horse fodder in York pubs. Reasonable rates were ordered and the prices publicised at Bootham Bar.[24] York and the North Riding communities provided funds. Officially Royalist taxation has passed down through history as the contribution. We have not listened closely enough to the people of Yorkshire who knew it as the Great Sesse. The second levy was being collected in York as early as 23 February 1643.[25] Close to York the villages on the roads north were being visited regularly by collectors. Wigginton and Haxby were two linear villages along a road stretching between the York–Sheriff Hutton road and the River Fosse. Both villages were of a similar size at about 2,000 acres each and both were to some extent arable communities, although pasturing, which in later centuries took up over a third of Haxby's lands was important as it was between there and York where the land-scape was marked by abandoned field strips. Both communities had moor land bordering their northern limits. Wigginton was owned by one of the king's chief opponents, Lord Howard of Escrick, a signatory to the twelve peers' petition, Haxby's descent is 'impossible to trace'.[26] In early 1643 both villages appear to have begun to pay levies to the army. In the space of three months up until 22 April Haxby had to find £113 11s 0d and Wigginton £117 15s 1d for levies. By October that year at the very latest both villages were billeted upon by soldiers led by Captain Duncomb or Duncan. Smaller and poorer communities in the same Bulmer Wapentake, were also taxed: Earswick, a small part of Huntington parish, was charged at a rate of £7 7s 11d a month.[27]

At Fountains, where taxation problems beset collections during the Bishops wars, levies were still a problem, forcing the Royalist commissioners based at Ripon to consider the case carefully at the end of 1643. At first the committee seems to have decided that Fountains was associated with nearby Markington and ordered that for every levy of £30,000 Fountains should pay 40s of Markington's levy. However, even this order contained the admission that it might not hold, and it did not. On 23 November the committee again made a declaration. Now it had been proved that Fountains had never been a part of Markington and so it was to be taxed separately as part of the Claro hundred levy. It was a bittersweet victory, for this time the levy was raised to 6s 8d assessed on Richard Evens for the park and 40s for the tenants of Mrs Ann Martin.[28]

Further north on the fringes of the North York Moors nestled the dispersed communities comprising Whorlton. Five townships, Faceby, Swainby, Potto, Goulton and Whorlton took up some 8,200 acres of mainly pasture on the slopes of the Cleveland Hills. Only about 25 per cent of the parish was cultivated, the majority was uncultivated moorland to the south of the towns. Nearby, to the north and downhill were the parishes of Rudby, East Rounton, Seamer and Hutton Juxta Rudby.[29] All were ranged close to the main road which went from York via Thirsk to Whitby. They were also close to the Yorkshire Durham border watched by the Earl of Home's regiment during the recent occupation. The villagers in these communities were keen to reclaim their war-time losses at the end of the Civil War and left meticulous accounts enabling the reconstruction of the defeat of the Royalists in 1644. The villagers of Rudby were clear that the Royalist levies began as early as Martinmass 1642, although most dated their accounts to 14 November, three days after the festival. Martinmass the grim reminder of winter's privations that year brought with it the first levies of an unremitting burden of heavy direct taxation which was to last until the 1660s.[30] Just as people of the North Riding would have begun the business of slaughtering livestock for salting to see them through the winter, the Earl of Newcastle began to impose order on the fragile Royalist administration in Yorkshire. Part of this 'order' was the first imposition of contribution, known locally as Newcastle's Great Sesse, which was set quarterly, the second one being set in February 1643 and so on until Martinmass 1643 when a new constable kept the records and so on until the arrival of the Scots in the Spring of 1644.

Thomas Sayre's accounts clearly delineate the quarterly sesses. He grouped his payments for the two years of Royalist rule. Therefore there are four recorded sums for 1642–3, although he only made two distinct entries for 1643–4; the first would have been at Martinmass, and the second in February 1644; thereafter there is a great pause in his accounts. John Sayre's accounts are similar, recording the four quarterly levies of the Great Sesse in 1642–3 and then six payments made monthly from October 1643 and ending on 6 March 1644. Over at Whorlton, Thomas Peacocke's records do not show any such break.

From 28 October 1643 to 18 October 1644 his records at first glance show an unbroken list of four-weekly payments. However, the appearance is deceptive. After 4 March the sequence goes awry, catching the writer unawares, for Peacocke may have given his evidence verbally. Either the writer thought Peacocke had said as he had to every entry, 'to a bill' or if he was copying from another list had simply got into the habit of writing the same formula. The bill would have been the constable's authority for the levy. But Peacocke had actually said 'paid in provision' and the writer crossed out the first entry and duly inserted the correct form for the 5 April. Thereafter bills were presented as normal but their collection was less regular, two payments totalling 18s, the usual monthly amount, were collected in May on the 12th and 16th. There was no further collection until 28 July, but this was only £1. In September 3s were collected, but in October 30s had to be found. Even without the benefit of hindsight we could detect that something was amiss. What was amiss was that the Royalist authorities, guarantors of order in the accounts, had been driven from the region.[31]

The second occupation, 1644–7

On 18 January 1644, for the second time in four years, a Scottish Army had crossed the border into her southern neighbour's lands. During the previous year, whilst Charles neglected to ease their fears, the Scottish commissioners to England had been courted by John Pym and his middle group in Parliament. In Edinburgh, Charles' apparent ambivalence towards the Catholic Confederation in Ireland appeared to be dangerous; surely he must take their Catholicism as a threat to his three Protestant kingdoms? That he did not, and that there were rumours of him coming to some form of agreement with them were compounded by the threat of attempts on the Scottish mainland to effect a Royalist rising in the north-east and the Earl of Antrim's correspondence which hinted that the rebellion could spread across the North Channel to the Western Isles and Argyll. In this background of rumour and fear the Estates sent their information to Westminster where it was greeted with almost equal horror. From July 1643 onwards negotiations opened with the aim of establishing an alliance to oppose the Royalists. On vague promises of establishing a form of Presbyterian worship in England and Wales, and in return for pay, the Estates assembled the army which entered England the following year. In the North of England the Earl of Newcastle was able to meet them with some portion of his large army and a string of strengthened garrisons, designed to interrupt the Scots' lines of communications if they failed to put a brake on their southward movement. Throughout a harsh winter, the earl tried to manœuvre the Earl of Leven into a battle. At Durham it appears that the earl was ready to do so. Then the fragile military structure failed. About 70 miles to the south at Selby on 11 April the army, which the marquis had left behind to keep the Fairfaxes from going on the offensive, was defeated and the remains driven into York. Newcastle had to run for York and the Scots followed, as the Royalist war effort imploded and the Great Sesse brought to an end, the Scots arrived on the fringes of the North York Moors.

The period of confusion which leaves blanks in Thomas Sayre's accounts and an irregular set of payments in Thomas Peacocke's represent the period when Yorkshire was a battleground. Defeat at Marston Moor on 2 July 1644 cost the Royalists their hold on the entire North, except for the scattered garrisons, once the guarantors of regular taxation, now islands the occupiers of which depended upon arbitrary collections to survive. Regular taxation resumed in the villages of North Yorkshire, but it was the Scots who collected it. The sesses resumed with vigour from Martinmass collected by the new constable at Rudby, George Hunter. The Great Sesse had been paid weekly, this new sesse was officially the Weekly Assessment. Thomas Sayre may have been paying arrears. For eighteen weeks, up until 2 March 1645 he paid in total £10 12s 0d, or an average of just over 11s 8d a week, the equivalent of seventeen days wages for a field worker or between fourteen and twenty days wages for a foot soldier. He had paid only an average of around 5s 6d a week in the Great Sesse. If this increase was to cover arrears for the summer of 1644, then they were considered cleared by May 1645 when Sayre's tax fell to between 5s and 6s a week, collected by Mr Ogle. At Whorlton, Thomas Peacocke registered less of an interruption, continuing to pay levies throughout the summer, which by October were acknowledged to be collected by and on behalf of the Scots Army.[32]

On the east coast there had been a considerably more involved series of changes to every day life. When the Earl of Newcastle battled for control of central Yorkshire, the coast had been left to Parliament, dominated by the great port at Hull and the smaller port at Scarborough. The little ports of Bridlington and Whitby were also occupied by the parliamentarians. Scarborough had welcomed Sir Hugh Chomeley, perhaps because he offered to pay for the weapons of 'privaite men' – the ordinary rank and file soldiers – out of his own pocket. The town did have to pay for its own defence. A nightly watch of eighteen men was established, with every householder serving a turn or sending a substitute (or paying a fine of 12d). This probably meant that every male householder was expected to serve, whereas women householders would provide substitutes, probably men from their extended family. The town council levied £50 for repairing town gates, clearing ditches of rubbish, weeds and more likely trees and shrubs which would provide an enemy with cover or a means of crossing the ditch. New walls were also built in certain places. The town gaol was turned into a guard room or court of guards to defend the Newborough gate. A company of dragoons was also raised at the charge of the council members during November 1642.[33] There also seems to have been a complex system of rental for the horses used in Captain John Legard's troop which came into effect if they were used outside the town. The owners were paid ½d for each mile travelled by the horse, paid out of a levy laid upon the whole town. On 21 February the council ordered that the guards be increased to 60 men a night 'duringe this present time of danger'. Two days later, the queen landed at Bridlington on the day that an oath of allegiance was recorded as applied to six captains, a lieutenant, and ensign and John Bowmham. Sir Hugh Cholmeley changed sides, having met the queen on her journey inland towards York, he took his garrison and the town over to the Royalists. Of this momentous change there is little record in the official papers of the town; repairs to the fabric of the town's defences still continued, levies were still made, brewsters were still licensed, illegal brewers were still hauled before the court. There was something, a reward for the town from the Royalist command at York and the king. The customs duties traditionally levied at Hull were switched to Scarborough. This would have given the town an important income from the amount allowed to it, but it also points to the importance of the town for the Royalist cause in the North; it was a major source of income and a crucial trading route with fruit, cider and sack being bought in alongside Norwegian deal planks and Scandinavian iron. Iron was sent on to Royalist garrisons in the North: some 10cwt 16lbs (28 ends) was sent to Sir William Saville at Sheffield at the end of 1643. Although considerable amounts of iron moved eastwards too from York to Sir Hugh for the use of the garrison.[34] Scarborough ships were also involved in international trade out of Royalist east coast ports other than Scarborough itself. Vessels from the port were involved in the dangerous trade of exporting coal from Sunderland to the United Provinces and Flanders. In the quarter from October to December 1643 the customs totalled £513 5s 0d, although £200 0s 9d was owing. The merchants using the port clearly show that this was the height of Royalist control. Not only were they based at York, but also at former parliamentarian towns of Whitby and Leeds. The town was also important for the importation of weapons. In November 1643 the ship *Mary* from Amsterdam delivered 1,390 muskets, 100 pairs of pistols with their holsters, 100 carbines, 100 barrels of gunpowder and 50 bundles of match.[35]

But what of the Scarburians: what had the war meant for them? Many seem to have resented the town's interference in their business, many refused to have their weights and measures checked, Peeter Horhan refused to do so until the town's own standard weights were up to scratch.[36] Robert Burge of Thornton was caught using false measures and abused the juror John Newton who found him out with 'evill lengutges'. William Newton similarly heaped abuse on the ale 'finers'.[37] There was of course concern to maintain some elements of normality and the courts prosecuted anyone who defied usual regulations just as they did in normal times. It is difficult to know if these little acts of rebellion bore any relation to the presence of a war-time administration. The fishing trade was carried out on many different scales within the town, from the larger boats down to smaller cobles. This north-coast boat was a keel-less clinker-built vessel used for a millennium on the northern coasts. Because of its shallow draft and lack of a keel the boats could be dragged easily up the beach. In Scarborough it was forbidden to buy fish direct from the boat owner and then sell it on again. It was a form of forestalling; the act of buying goods cheap and then selling them on at the market for profit. There was a concerted effort by a group of Scarborough women to make a profit from fish sales. At one point they were described as fish-wives, and the town seems to have resented their participation in the market. Clearly they were ready at the sands as the boats were beached. A group of Scarborough women made several appearances in the courts during the war. At the general sessions on 6 October 1645 Elizabeth Lambe was indicted for 'bying fish as it comes in the cobells and sellinge the same again contrary to the statute'. She was not alone, charged alongside her were Jayn Morre, Cattoran (Catherine) Fleck, Ann Honnam, Elizabeth Meggisson and the wife of John Hill. Six months later Jayn Morre, Elizabeth Meggisson and Hill were at it again, along with goodwives Honnam and Hall and widows Elizabeth Clarke and Margery Wolfe. A year later some of them were again in court, this time in the company of Goodwives Stone and Thompson. In this case the relationship to the war is clear. By selling the fish on the sea front they avoided excise taxation.[38] In other parts of the country, notably in Derby, women led the fight against the excise. In Derby in May 1645 and again in July, women had led riots in the town as part of a protracted dispute over excise taxes in the market. They had disrupted county committee meetings by holding rallies to the accompaniment of drums outside the mayor's window and enchained a soldier who escorted the taxmen.[39] Women's roles as producers and consumers of the goods affected by the increased prices caused by taxation inspired their actions in persistently opposing the levies, by stealth as at Scarborough or by direct action as at Derby.

The siege of Scarborough cost Scarburians dear. A catalogue of the disaster is included in the town records. The town estimated that £3,000 of ships belonging to the 'well affected' were lost through their being abandoned on the sands or disabled by the Royalists. Others were stripped of sails, anchors and cables perhaps for the use of Royalist ships. The town's fields were stripped bare by horses of both sides quartered on them. St Mary's church near the castle was ruined, having been used as a gun emplacement for the attacking forces and thus the target of fire from the castle, except for the walls and some part of the roof which was formerly in good repair. Moreover all four of the town's mills had been destroyed. The expense that the town had laid out for the construction of the defences was laid to waste as they were destroyed and the richest men of the town were now 'found delinquents & their estate sequestered to the publique use'. The public use was not, it is being made clear, Scarborough's use.[40] The money did not come from Parliament and Scarborough had to make its own way. The swinefold was rebuilt, and the site of a demolished house used as a new site for common fold. Some of the king's rent held by the coroners was set to make temporary repair of the church. Full repairs never came and the old nave is still a ruin.

Immediately following the capture of the town by Parliament's Northern Association army the town requested that the pier be repaired, as money normally levied for its upkeep at Newcastle and Sunderland had been used by the town for military purposes. Almost as quickly the town's parliamentary representation was addressed, Hotham was now dead and Sir Hugh Cholmeley was barred from the house. Whilst the town was told to choose a burgess for the good of the county of York which 'hath suffered for the want of able men' and was exhorted to choose omen of 'good integrity', Lord Fairfax instructed the council to choose his candidate, James Challoner of Guisborough.[41] This was contested by Luke Robinson of Seamer who wrote to the council on 7 October requesting that they carefully consider their choice because of 'how much your towne and the kingdom suffered by your last choice' and eleven days later sent them a copy of a 1641 House of Commons order which instructed boroughs to ignore the wishes of the peers who wrote to them and to send such letters to Parliament. Robinson denied that he had intended to impugn the nature of Fairfax's (his 'honourable and noble friend') intentions. The town council elected a series of new burgesses too, reflecting the change of power. The new members of the council included the High Sheriff, Sir Matthew Boynton, the parliamentarian governor, Matthew Boynton esq., three of the garrisons officers and Luke Robinson. It was this same Robinson, who with the High Sheriff, was elected in the recruiter elections. Boynton had to step down as Sheriff before he could accept his election.[42]

Scarborough's history was bound up very much with nearby Bridlington. Bridlington was a twin settlement from the foundation of the Augustinian Priory to the mid-nineteenth century. A mile inland was the town, clustered around the priory ruins and the makeshift parish church formed from the nave of the Priory church building. Government of the town was centred on the old gatehouse, the Bayle where the Lords feoffees who owned the manor met and where the papers of the officials, the overseers, the four constables and the churchwardens were kept in a locked chest bought for the purpose sometime before the war and which is still used for the purpose. The Lords feoffees had 181 tenants in 1637, farming either town land or desmesne lands. By the sea, at the mouth of the Gypsey Race was Bridlington Quay which was generally involved in coastal trade, usually exporting malt, grain and pulses to Newcastle. In 1654–5 of 21 sailings from the harbour, 17 were northbound and only four southbound. The towns' imports included coal and salt. The power of nominating the rector of St Mary's was held by Sir Matthew Boynton.[43] Parliamentarian forces did not occupy the town on a long-term basis at the outset of the war although the Boynton interest was protected. On 23 February 1643 the queen landed at the Quay, precipitating Sir Hugh Cholmeley's change of heart. From then on the town was garrisoned by Royalists and taxes paid to Sir Hugh at Scarborough or at Burton Agnes Hall, 5 miles inland on the Driffield road. On 1 December 1644 £95 was sent there covering the Great Sesse.[44]

At the beginning of the following year Bridlington was involved in the Fairfaxes' attempt to seize the Yorkshire coast. On 14 February Sir William Constable attacked the Royalist forces quartered in the Wolds and captured Bridlington before seizing Whitby and defeating the local Royalists at Driffield.[45] Unfortunately for the Bridlington constables, this was not the signal for a complete change of fortunes. Cholmeley was still able to exercise some authority and constable Richard Thompson was arrested presumably for paying a levy of £24 15s 4d to Constable's Lieutenant Colonel Needham. For five weeks he languished in Scarborough and later at Kilham near Burton Agnes. In May, after the north of the county had fallen to the occupying Scottish forces and Rudby and Whorlton were paying irregular taxes, Constable Thompson resumed paying levies to the Royalists at Scarborough.

It was November 1644 before the words 'for the Scots assessment' appeared in the accounts. In 1645 there were some 154 people eligible to pay a levy for the Northern Association forces. The monthly levy for 1646 was set at 4d for the dwelling place, 4d for a cow on the pasture and 4d each for an oxgang of demesne land or townland, and 8d per score of sheep. The general run of goods sent as part of the assessments match those generally exported from the Quay, malt, peas and grain. Mutton, reflecting the grazing sector of Bridlington's economy, is also evident in several assessments. Pork and beef were supplied to a quartermaster Foster in late 1644, but they were comparatively rare.

The collapse of the county's Royalist war effort did not end the effects of the Royalist cause on Bridlington or Scarborough. Instead the ports which had once housed Royalist ships and dealt in Royalist trade were now exposed to the attacks of Royalist shipping. In February 1645 the 'Quayamen' and their townie colleagues joined the inhabitants of Whitby and Scarborough in petitioning the House of Commons. Some five or six Royalist ships sailed the coast, attacking ships from Whitby, Scarborough and Bridlington, two boats had been taken from one of the petitioners and the others were frightened to set out to sea. The petitioners also knew that Great Yarmouth boats had been attacked. Luke Robinson from his position as MP for Scarborough added his weight to the call for ships to defend the local shipping and received assurances that five ships were to be sent.[46] It is possible that this did not really solve the problem, for a later letter referred the continued presence of two or three Royalist pirates which kept 20 laden ships penned up in Scarborough harbour. Nine ships had been captured off the coast, three of them between Scarborough and Bridlington off Filey Brigg and Flamborough Head.[47] The problem continued into the last days of the first Civil War. On 19 April John Harrison and Thomas Gill informed the burgesses that a Royalist frigate of 22 guns had only the day before captured three ships within sight of Scarborough. The captain of the frigate had told the men he released that he was sinking and burning small fishing boats between Yarmouth and the north east, despite the presence of parliamentarian ships. In response the admiralty agreed to investigate the apparent negligence of its fleet. In all, ten English and four Scottish ships should have been on duty: nine on escort duty and five in pursuit of Royalists.[48]

Further down the coast, Hull suffered occupation by larger numbers of soldiers, and had been effectively militarised since 1639 when the town had been restricted to using three gates and the Manor House had become an armoury. The town had undergone a series of defensive measures within and without.

Defensive works had been dug outside the town and suburbs had been destroyed to prevent their use as cover by attacking forces. Inside the walls flammable roofs were removed and replaced with tiles after the siege of summer 1642 was over.[49] The governors of the town, John Hotham and, after his disgrace and arrest, Lord Fairfax, were resented by the town government (known as the Bench) as a threat to its independence, and the expensive property alterations inside and outside the walls must have rankled. However, they were necessary, for a year after the first siege ended, on 9 September 1643, the Earl of Newcastle and the great Northern Army arrived to complete his summer success over the Fairfaxes and the town was plunged into a seven week siege.

Supported by reinforcements shipped into Hull and by the presence of a parliamentarian fleet, the town withstood the new siege. It was, however, a case of utilising the help of everyone in the town. John Jekyll, a Presbyterian merchant from St Stephen Wallbrook parish in London, who had only a couple of months earlier had been caught in Bristol when the Royalists captured that port, was in Hull during the siege. His wife Elizabeth Jekyll, who was keeping a record of God's mercies to her and her loved ones, recounted how as he was filling gabions (baskets filled with earth and stones for use as protection), 'their [sic] came a bullet from the Enemie and fell down at his feet and did him No hurt'. This was more than just luck:

> This was the mighty work of God in preserving him blessed be his name for Ever and Ever. Thus the Lord made good his promises that when he was Even in the fire God delivered him as he promised to his people that when they pass through the fire they shall have no power on them. [50]

The siege ended on 12 October, the day after a large-scale attack lasting seven hours was launched on the leaguer. It was a day of celebration which bound together the town community in commemorative events until the Restoration. Hull continued to provide a base for the Yorkshire parliamentarians until the spring offensives in 1644 and the summer successes following the Battle of Marston Moor. Ships from the town served in the siege of Scarborough, one, the *Covenant* under Captain John Lawson, was responsible for capturing ten guns from vessels off the Scarborough coast, and the *Hector*, belonging to William Peck and William Railes, served Parliament throughout the war. Hull was of course concerned by the post-war piracy and naturally joined in the clamour for naval protection.[51]

The West Riding of Yorkshire experienced similar mixed fortunes during the period of the first Civil War. There was some stability in the far north where the Royalist garrison at Skipton was able to dominate the region. The Great Sesse first appeared to make itself felt here in April 1643 when High Constable Matthew Ward recorded that he was first asked to collect the money by the garrison at Skipton. Ward was responsible for part of Claro Wapentake, the area around Harrogate, during the war and sometime after 1649 he was asked to account for his work. The first Great Sesse amounted to £2,950 in Claro although it declined to £2,000 a year later. This sum included all the provender taken from the communities by the quartermasters, and later was to include the horse taken from them as well. Goods and horse were receipted and the amounts deducted from the cash levies. The system was clearly too expensive, for when Captain Robert Benson collected the receipts 'he had power to disalow a great pte of the them'. When the levy instructions went out the following year, the taxpayers were initially told that assessments of goods and so forth were on top of the cash levies. This was later rescinded and a third of the costs of the additional charges was allowed out of the cash levy. The charge on 28 villages in Ward's division for 1643 was £983 6s 8d, of which the £169 arrears were finally paid to Sir William Carneby on 29 February 1649.[52]

The South however was a battleground from the moment that the Earl of Newcastle began to challenge the Fairfaxes' control. Some communities were paying the Great Sesse early in 1643. There survives an assessment for Tankersley which shows the two constables William Vix and Ferdinando Richardson collecting £28 1s 4d from thirty-three men and two women in May.

Whilst Tankersley near Whortley was held in the thrall of Sheffield's garrison under Sir William Saville, the areas around the parliamentarian garrisons at Bradford and Leeds were less secure during this early period. The fall of the garrisons in the wake of the Battle of Adwalton left the areas open to Royalist exploitation. This was felt to be a great moment, and a divine judgement on the Fairfaxes. The Earl of Newcastle's daughter Jane Cavendish thanked God 'who gave thy bounty large' for the victory in her poem *On the 30th of June to God*:

> So let them now thy works plaine see
> Sayeing my little flock shall Conquerers bee
> And it was true ffairfax was then more great
> But yet Newcastle made him sure retreat
> Therefore I'll keepe this thy victoryes day
> If not in publique by some private way
> In spite of rebells, who thy Lawes deface
> And blott the footesteps of thy sonns blood trace

Others felt abandoned by God and in fear of their lives or their freedom. The towns of East Lancashire began to fill with refugees, including John Lister's master Joseph Sharpe. The opening of the siege of Bradford had a deep affect on Lister's mind: 'our troubles began again, fresh storms arise and clouds of sorrow gather blackness over our heads threatening us with greater distress, if possible than hereforeto … '.

Defeat fulfilled this promise. As Sharpe fled:

> Every countenance overpowered with sorrow, every house overwhelmed with grief; husbands lamenting over their families; women wringing their hands in despair; children shrieking, crying and clinging to their parents; death in all his dreadful forms and frightening aspects, stalking in every street and corner.

The war brought its allies, death and plague, to Bradford, causing the number of burials in the year of the siege to number 493, a peak even for the war years representing a five or six fold increase. No wonder it preyed on Lister's mind in the way it did.[53] Samuel Priestly, a man who had earlier declared that he could not sit on the fence whilst war was fought around him was already dead. His belief in humanity had overcome his conviction that if his cause be good then its enemies were bad. In October 1643 Samuel was caught up in a skirmish. One of the Royalists was pitched into the river trying to escape and Priestly leapt in to save him. That night he served his turn on guard duty still in his wet uniform. Exposure to the cold of an October night brought about an illness that within three weeks left him dead.[54]

The exiled Joseph Sharpe was reportedly more pragmatic than the doom-laden soul of Lister, sending instruction back to his wife, left behind in the West Riding,

> go home ... buy a cow to give you some milk, and get the grass mowed, and help to get the hay; and perhaps the enemy will be called away shortly.[55]

Indeed they were, but although two cows which Mrs Sharpe bought were stolen by the Royalists, their departure after their defeats in spring of 1644 was followed by the arrival of new armies. Some of the refugees never returned to their Jerusalem. The parish registers of Rochdale, Bury, Colne and Burnley carry entries for the Yorkshire men and women refugees who did not live to see their towns rescued. At Bury, a former Halifax minister, William Alte, buried some of his former parishioners including Mary Barraclough and Phebe Clay who had until their escape been residents at Alte's former vicarage. On 21 January 1644 Alte recorded the death of 'Robert Broadly, a very Godly man, exiled from Halifax ... '.[56] Even so some of the survivors determined to win back the West Riding. By the end of the year they formed companies of foot soldiers in Lancashire and the Craven region of the West Riding to do so.[57]

On 2 July 1644 the Battle of Marston Moor was fought. A combined army of Scots, the Fairfaxes' forces and the Eastern Association Army defeated both the Marquis of Newcastle's army and Prince Rupert's forces which had been sent to rescue the marquis who had been trapped in York for eleven weeks. After the battle part of the Army of the Solemn League and Covenant marched to Leeds. The Scots were in South and West Yorkshire during early August, but many regiments then returned northwards to the siege of Newcastle before the end of the month. But during August the cramped conditions in Halifax saw Lister's spectre of death on the streets. Plague broke out, killing 84 in August, 153 in September and 216 in October, before subsiding from November onwards. At Sowerby Bridge the constables slung a chain across the street and kept watch to prevent infected refugees from coming down the Halifax to Rochdale road.[58]

The arrival of the Scots in 1644 brought no relief for any area of the north. The village of Hulam, 3 or 4 miles inland from the Durham coast, was charged £60 3s 0d for the Great Sesse of 1642–3. The last six months of Royalist control saw a dramatic increase to £49 0s 5d between Martinmass 1643 and April 1644. It would appear that the Marquis of Newcastle's attempts to stop the advance of the Scots and even broader strategic moves caused some of these additional costs to the community. As well as regular levies, the constables recorded payments to Sir Charles Lucas for leading a brigade of horse north, toward the Scottish border. Payments were also made to Sir Richard Clavering, charged with helping the Earl of Montrose to assemble an army to go north into Scotland.[59] The year following from April cost £90 9s 1d in payments of parliamentarian taxes, including the 'British Army' in Ireland, levies for the Scottish army and for Colonel Richard Lilburne's regiment based in the county.

Some 50 miles to the north-west of Whorlton, the neighbouring villages of Croxdale and Sunderland Bridge in the palatinate county of Durham, came under the ministrations of a series of Scottish regiments. The first news of this appears to have come fairly casually. In February 1645 a rather tardy soldier and his horse turned up with an order for billeting directed to Mrs Salvin by Captain Edward Scurfield, a local captain of the Trained Band. But this fairly informal beginning quickly led to the family being swept up into a thorough and unremitting system of tax collection. It is also possible that the family were supplying materials to several regiments including Middleton's and the infamous regiment, Jonas van Druschkes' horse, but fortunately, their principal dealings were with the Mearns and Aberdeen Foot regiment of Earl Marischal. The regiment returned to County Durham after the Hereford campaign, but some of it then served at Newark before again returning to the Croxdale area after the end of the siege. For much of the period starting in late 1645, through until 25 January 1647, the family dealt with one man, Major Andrew Leslie, the regiment's effective commander during the Newark campaign. Leslie must have cut something of a comic figure, for on the back of a receipt for £2 6s 4d dated 4 July 1646 is a drawing of an outlandish figure in tartan trousers and a large wide-brimmed hat, probably a portrait of Leslie himself.[60]

Delinquents and Catholics were also placed under sequestration. The Salvins were no exception. At the end of 1645 Gerald Salvin explained his service with the Royalists: his family kept him in Croxdale. He had 'a great charge of Children which he could not remove out of the county'. It got worse: 'yor petitioner was forced by the power of the earle of Newcastles Army and with a Troope of Horse [presumably billeted at Croxdale] compelled to sit and act as a committeeman for the Earl of Newcastle in the said countrye'. Gerald attempted to claim that he was 'never forward to advance that service'. He was not believed. That he had come into compound was not really much of a saving grace when he really had no choice.[61] By the end of the year Salvin was engaged to pay £800 composition over the following eighteen months. Moreover, Salvin had to sign the Covenant; this and the payment of an initial £200 freed him from immediate sequestration, but not, of course, from the billeting.[62] The payments were not made according to schedule, perhaps because of the continued presence of the Scots forces. By the end of the second Civil War Gerald Salvin was paying money to Sir Arthur Hesilrige, commander of the garrison at Newcastle and this was claimed as part of his composition, of which there appeared to be £400 outstanding.[63]

At Murton on the Moor in the parish of Dalton in the Dale, 7 miles north of Hulam, Isabell Hixon was sequestered on grounds of her Catholicism; by November 1644 her entire estate had been passed to the former shepherd of Easington, Thomas Ellison, who had carried messages between the Scots and the Fairfaxes earlier in the year. For Mrs Hixon this was a disaster. Ellison refused to pay her the third profits due from the estate and he began to ruthlessly exploit her two farms, ploughing up meadows and felling timber for quick profits.[64] The effects on Mrs Hixon and her daughters, Margaret and Jane was dramatic. Reduced to living on a fee of only £6 a year from Ellison, the girls had to be sent to live with friends. Ellison argued that he was not exploiting the estate, but instead was improving it, bringing wasteland under cultivation. As for the timber, he had had to sell that to fund the building of a new ox-house and for necessary repairs to the estate's buildings and fences.[65] It took Isabell until 1649 to recoup the arrears due to her and the one-third of the estate that sequestration legislation allowed her. Being a Catholic, Gerard Salvin esquire was also sequestrated and he had to enter bonds for payment of over £600 in £20 six-monthly instalments starting in December 1645. The general collections of taxation from the Salvin lands only came to an end when the Scots surrendered Charles I to the Westminster parliament. The last recorded payment was for £3 2s 0d made on 28 January 1647.

The rest of Croxdale too had to pay for its liberation from what was termed the 'popish' army of the Earl of Newcastle. Collections of taxes were made to pay the wages of the regiment garrisoned at Easington, which was possibly that of the Earl Marischal and that at Durham, the maintenance of Raby Castle as well as Scurfield and the county militia. However, it is clear that a large number of other regiments were passing through the area, The Earl of Buccleurch's, Lord Home's, Sir James Ramsay's horse and the artillery train. These charges cost the community £33 3s 8d between 1 May 1645 and the following 11 November.[66] Not all of the payments were for the soldiers nearby, there were the British forces in Ireland to pay for, the upkeep of the gaol at Durham and the 'infected people' to whom some £2 10s 9d of the money went. Durham was gripped by plague during the period covered by these Croxdale accounts.

Nicholas Sheiffield, parish clerk of St Oswald's after 1645, recorded the names of those who died of the 'great Visitation' in a separate section in the register.[67] St Oswald's parish lay on the southern side of the river Wear, covering the old barony of Elvet and the Old Borough, partly in view of the Cathedral across the river. Sheffield began his list with June 1645, when 43 people died, including his predecessor, Richard Atkinson. In July the death toll rose to 56, before falling to 41 in August, 18 in September, 10 in October and 6 in November. It is clear that the plague did not infect the soldiers, only two are recorded in the lists for June. After this the army probably moved to a safe distance, but the people who lived there could not. Women and children were hit particularly hard, 33 per cent of the victims were women and 43 per cent of the total were children. Death struck across social boundaries, 5 per cent were accorded gentry status by Sheiffield and occasionally he recorded extra details about them: Mrs Jane Dawson died aged 22, and the burial date of Dorothy Hillyard, 28 July, is noted in the margin. Other representatives of the city's administration died too; an alderman and a bailiff succumbed as well as Sheffield's predecessor. Weavers, labourers, potters and joiners died along side two children of Watte the Scot. The details of the other deaths are no less poignant. Henry Farrow and his five children died early in the outbreak, two unnamed maid servants died, their only record being that of their masters, Joseph Weaver and Mr Sedgewick, cheated by war of that most basic right, the most common form of history's recognition, a properly recorded burial.

The county as a whole had debts to cover too. The collapse into the hands of the Scots had been rapid, indeed progress towards Durham had been quite slow but when Newcastle turned back to York, the county was theirs. Like many taxes, the collection of money for Ireland was not collected between the arrival of the Scots in the wake of the Earl of Newcastle's rush back to York. Collection seems to have begun formally in November 1644 when the county was charged £541 13s 4d a year.[68]

In some areas of the north the Army of the Solemn League and Covenant was more than just and encumbrance. Weldon's horse exacted revenge on the villagers of Haltwhistle, Knarsdale and Kirkhaugh for their constables' reluctance to pay cess. The villages are on the extreme edge of Northumberland and were due to pay some £60 in levies for the support of Thirwall Castle. On 14 October 1645 three troops of horse appeared in the area, they attacked the home of High Constable Blankensopp and took away £1,168 10s worth of his property. They took another £2,782 5s worth of goods, animals and free quarter. Furthermore the troopers attacked the villagers, killing one man and wounding several others.[69] One regiment in particular had a dreadful reputation in the north and as far south as Derbyshire and the Nottinghamshire and Lincolnshire border. Van Druske's regiment of horse was notorious for its behaviour. During the siege of Newark parts of the regiment simultaneously imprisoned constables from the Lincolnshire villages of Epworth and Axholme and plundered the West Riding Osgodcross Hundred villages of Rawcliffe and

Snaith. After the siege of Newark was over, the North Riding felt the effects of the regiment. They roamed the countryside, attacking people on their way to market, and imposing heavy levies on the villages that they camped in. The regiment moved quickly from village to village. Where they stopped they levied food and cash as well as a peck of oats a day for each horse. In nearby villages, quartermasters appeared charging inhabitants as much as £240 in a day.[70] One of the reasons that the regiment was so vicious in its proceedings was its composition. The field officers were a Dutch man and a German and the soldiers were chosen on grounds which left a lot for the Scottish Army committee to desire. Many of them were former Royalist soldiers, some even drawn from Newark after the siege. The regiment used the Book of Common Prayer, insulted Parliament and was, by the end of the war in England, composed of men clearly seeking to use the dysfunctional situation to their own advantage. Because of its behaviour steps were taken to disband the regiment, not an easy task given its nomadic existence. It took until the end of December 1646 to disband it.

The Church Lawton constables appear to have come into office at or around Lady Day, the old style New Year, thus when the constables stated 1642 as their year of office, they referred to a period we would understand as being 25 March 1642 to 24 March 1643. This is true of many constables around the county, allowing them to take an oath of office before the JPs at the Easter Quarter sessions. Two constables served in Church Lawton each year. The details submitted to the exchequer are audited sub-totals. They do not list the day-to-day accounts of the constable, nor do they list the tax payments as they happened, they are listed in the totals for the year. Sometimes there are further subdivisions when totals are grouped together according to whom they were paid. The accounts also detail the name of the treasurer to whom payments were made. The period covered by these extracts covers the first Civil War in England and Wales from around the end of September. The accounts refer to paying six-months pay for the village's soldiers in the county Trained Bands in late 1642–1643. Constables' Rowley and Shaw also detail the wages, equipment money paid out for the trained band as the war began in 1642 and for the support of Sir William Brereton's forces at Nantwich, horses and then 8 measure of oats.

By 1643 both sides had developed financial systems to fund their war-efforts. In one sense Parliament treated Cheshire differently from other counties and in a manner different to the Royalists. Both sides grouped their counties into associations. Cheshire was placed into an association embracing the marcher counties and North Wales, under Lord Capel. Parliament left Cheshire to stand alone, technically, although John Morrill shows that conversely the county's parliamentarians worked well with neighbouring areas, largely due to Brereton's willingness to help parliamentarians in other regions in the early months of war.[71] Cheshire also differed in that no central county committee was established. In most places the deputy lieutenants originally assembled to support the Militia Ordinance appointed lieutenant, became a committee, and in a way this happened in Cheshire too, but without the deputies adopting the title of county committee. There were thirteen deputies at any one time and several supernumeraries who assisted in business but never initiated it. The people of Church Lawton though, had most of their contact with smaller committees established in prominent towns to administer the financial arrangements in each of the seven hundreds. Some of the accounts of these committees can be found in the Harleian Mss in London.[72] The Church Lawton constables refer to the treasurers that they dealt with as Mr Ralph Judson the county treasurer for levies and Mr Ralphe Poole collector for sequestration. Judson, based at Tarven was responsible, it seems, for areas in Nantwich and Broxton hundreds, although the Tarven committee was supposed to be responsible for only Broxton and Wirral Hundred.

At Church Lawton the constables for 1643–4, Nicholas Hobson and Richard Purcell, detailed expenditure of £59 2s 4d, all but £3 11s 8d of which went directly on military resources, Trained Band wages, saddlery, tack and horses. Most money and produce went to local forces and to support campaigns within Cheshire. However, six horses, worth £19 10s, went to Yorkshire regiments under Sir Thomas Fairfax, presumably during or just after the Nantwich campaign in January 1644, and 18s was committed to the siege of Oswestry in Shropshire.

In 1644–5 constables recorded 42 payments to parliamentarian forces in the county and 13 to the Scots at Bechton and Sandbach amounting to £48 18s 9d. The village provisions included beef, butter, cheese and bacon, all of which was sent to the (Edisbury) hundredal committee at Tarvin, which seems to have had some authority over Northwich hundred and to Nantwich. Remember that just as is the case with Lord Derby's instructions regarding provision prices, these will have been 'official' artificially low prices. On top of this, £22 17s 9d was paid for the Trained Band costs. There was a further £6 2s 6d to 'ye Yorkshire Army at Congleton and Ashebury'. Taxes in 1645 came to £46 11s 10d and Trained Bands money to £24 5s 4d, but in 1646 only £3 15s 0d was paid in tax money before the constables drafted their report.

The second part of the report consists of the accounts of thirteen male ratepayers in Church Lawton. Their accounts detail payments for trained bands men, quartering charges and losses through plundering. For example let us consider William Lawton's accounts. Lawton constructed his accounts in three main sections which follow a single entry for the 'first position money' which accounted for the money raised for Parliamentarian forces in 1642. His subsequent heading dealt with: quartering, plundering, and 'for his man forth on service'. The quartering charges are high, costing Lawton no less than £26 11s 6d. The soldiers he quartered were from various regiments, although most of them were from local regiments including Colonel John Bromhall's, Colonel John Boyer's, Thomas Mytton's and Colonel George Booth's. However, there was also reference to a Warwickshire regiment of horse and of three Scottish soldiers. The financial costs were not the only consideration: for no less than 147 days and nights during the first Civil War, Lawton had soldiers staying with him, sometimes one or two at a time at others four, sometimes foot soldiers, sometimes troopers with their horses. The longest single period was one of 25 days when three troopers and their horses stayed. Taking the war as beginning on 1 October 1642 and ending on 6 May 1646 (a conservative estimate), it lasted three years, eight months and five days (or 1,313 days); William Lawton provided accommodation for over 11 per cent of the time, roughly one night in every nine.

Lawton also financed a soldier serving in the county Trained Band forces. He financed the soldier whilst on active service. Lawton's soldier served not only in the county, but also in Lancashire and the north Wales campaign of late 1643, when the soldier was on service for three weeks. Later in the war, Lawton's soldier was on permanent service under captain Handcock, costing Lawton £4 4s.

William Lawton's accounts sum up much of the experience of war for people right across the British Isles. Under the heading of plundering Lawton referred to theft or unpaid commandeering of a horse by forces at Crewe Hall and by Colonel Rigely. Rigley was certainly a parliamentarian, and other plundering Lawton recorded was by parliament's allies the Scots. Whilst the Army of the Solemn League and Covenant was based at Sandbach, it relieved Lawton of five measures of oats. Some Scottish soldiers also 'violently brake his glasse windows wch cost him in makinge up againe} 0 4. 0'. Indeed much of the recorded plunder seems to have been taken from the village by the parliamentarians and the Scots. The Scots army passed through Cheshire on its way south into Herefordshire during the summer of 1645. The Church Lawton accounts have a close resemblance to those from Hartpury in Worcestershire which demonstrate the capacity for the Scottish army for plunder in its march down into the south Midlands.[73]

There is no recorded instance in the accounts of Royalist plunder: this may mean that at Church Lawton, the constables had no confidence that anything recorded as taken by the Royalists would interest the parliamentarian exchequer. Other accounts returned to London do contain lists of things, sometimes taxes, taken by Royalists. The things that were taken from Church Lawton inhabitants were mainly immediately useful items, like food and horses. These things were normally taken on promise of payment and rather than really being plunder, they could have been simply forgotten about by the takers, like the 'marre, packe saddle, wounty and gurthe taken by the Scotts Army' from John Poole. Many things were not taken under any form of licence and sometimes services or labour was not paid for: Hugh Halle was not paid for the work he did shoeing the horses of Scots soldiers. Also taken were a few things of less obvious value to the military. John Chantler lost a mixed collection of items, some of which were clearly for military use, others not so, to Sir William Fairfax's men: two flax shirts, 5 yards of wool cloth, two silk garters, a hat band, two knee-breech bands and a pair of stockings as well as six 'handcarchaffes'. Will Waram lost a 'good new testament' worth 4s and Thomas Shawe also lost a New Testament, as well as some pewter. John Booth was angered by the loss of a 'hat off his hed'.

By 1645 in Lancashire, as the war settled down after the end of the Royalist renaissance of summer 1644, Thomas Blomeley in Lancashire had a good idea. He created a 'very necessary and profitable [table] for all gentlemen of account within the county ... '.[74] Blomeley devised a table which divided the county firstly on page one into its six hundreds, and allocated between them the portions of levies set upon the county. He divided his theoretical county levies into £1000, £500, £200, £100, £50, £20, £10, £5, £2, and £1, by which any real levy could be worked out by adding the theoretical sums together as required. He then tabulated the proportions to be paid to each of these theoretical sums, thus towards a levy of £1,000 Derby Hundred would pay £240, Salford £140. Each hundred's portion could be established by the same means. On the subsequent pages he took each hundred in turn and listed, community by community each town and village which comprised it. These too had their portions set out according to theoretical sums set on the hundred as a whole, beginning with £100 and ending with 10s. To a levy of £100 set on Derby Hundred, Warrington would pay £1 11s 3d, to a levy of 10s it would contribute 7½d. The table was recognised as so useful that in 1666, to deal with Charles II's levies, the table was copied out by hand.

In December 1646 protracted negotiations about the arrears due to the Army of the Solemn League and Covenant ended and the Scottish commissioners at Newcastle handed over the king to the English. On 30 January 1647 the Covenanter army marched out and an English army marched in. All over the north of England Covenanter regiments marched from their billets. The plague on the house of Salvin, Andrew Leslie, collected a last payment of £3 2s on January 28 and marched off. Within a month, the Mearns and Aberdeen regiment of foot had ceased to exist, disbanded soon after its return home.[75] To the south the Scots had left East Rounton three days earlier. The last date of payment to them was 25 January. It must have been a relief to see them go. George Humphrey the constable recorded the amount paid to them since 11 May 1646, which roughly equated with the surrender of the king to the Scots and Newark to the English army, as £676 2s 2d, until the date of their departure.[76]

Of course taxes did not suddenly disappear; paying the Scots had been in lieu of paying the monthly tax. The supplementary levies for the British Army in Ireland had been collected alongside the larger levies, and these were now joined by the monthly payments direct to the Committee at York. In county Durham efforts were being made to catch up with missing payments. The county was charged at with £544 0s 8d to cover the money due for Ireland for the nine months from June to March 1647–8, a rise of around 25 per cent on the sum collected in 1644–5.[77] Nor did the northward march of the Scots end the presence of the military. Several places, like Bridlington and Scarborough were still garrisoned into 1648.

Between August 1640 and August 1648 the north of England had been graced with the presence of Scottish armies for a total of 50 months out of 96. Those armies had cost money, eaten into the resources of the country, destroyed ships, coal stocks and mines. They had besieged towns and castles, collected taxes from communities and individuals and occasionally murdered people. The effects of being occupied were unlike any of those experienced by any other region of the country. There were far more foreigners on English soil in the north than anywhere else. True there were Welsh men and women in Oxfordshire with the king's army. So-called Irish forces landed in Bristol and north Wales from the end of 1643 onwards, but these were largely Englishmen returning from service abroad. Only in the north was there a concerted number of foreigners constituting one distinct force: an army of occupation.

3

EXPERIENCING REBELLION IN IRELAND, 1641–9

Under the united monarchy of England, Wales and Scotland there had been state-approved Scottish settlement in Ulster. This reversed the English government's discouragement of Scots settlement. The influx into Ulster of Presbyterian ministers seeking to avoid censure at home early in the seventeenth century was less approved of, but this did not become a major problem until the reign of Charles I. During the later 1630s Lord Deputy Thomas Wentworth's administration made them less than welcome. Wentworth and Bishop John Bramhall attempted to ensure liturgical conformity upon the Church of Ireland, aiming to eradicate the very laxity which had allowed the Prebyterian to find livings in Ulster parishes. The clashes between Charles I and the Scottish people exacerbated the difficulty as Wentworth struggled to prevent the development of close links between the Scots in Ulster and the Presbyterians in western Scotland. There were strong ties between Scotland and Ulster for many reasons. The apparent laxity of the Church of Ireland had allowed some Presbyterian ministers uncomfortable in the Jacobean Kirk as well as displaced English or Welsh ministers to take up parishes. In some cases the connections were caused by the two-way migrations which had continued despite attempts in the sixteenth century to discourage Scottish settlement. The chiefs of the MacDonalds for instance had once, as Lords of the Isles, ruled a scattered fiefdom which spanned the North Channel. Successive Stewart monarchs eroded their titles and power, and some of the centre of the MacDonald chiefs' power shifted westward. Somhairle Buidhe (Sorely Boy) and his heir Ranald consolidated a hold on the north-east of Ireland, where their names became recognised as MacDonnell. By the reign of Charles I the clan was in royal favour and its head ennobled as the Earl of Antrim. Something of a divorce between the principle sections the MacDonalds had been effected by Somhairle Buidhe's seizure of his brother' lands, and title divided between the MacDonnells in Ireland and the MacDonalds in the Highlands: even so the cultural links remained strong. These links were to prove important when the Highland and Island MacDonalds fell to in-fighting, which left them open to the crown's wrath and James VI's employment of the Clan Campbell to destroy the power of the MacDonalds and bring peace to the region. This struggle also developed religious overtones and many of the MacDonalds, or MacDonnells as they were known in Ireland, had remained Roman Catholic. By 1639 there were now two reprobate groups with links across the channel, the Catholic MacDonalds and their client clans and the Covenanting Presbyterian Scots.

The Earl of Antrim, whose political interests spanned the religious and geographical divide was not slow to appreciate this divide. He would use the religious antipathies of his clan and of the king to the Presbyterians to overturn the political exclusion of the MacDonalds. Accordingly he offered military assistance to the lord deputy. Whether or not Wentworth was able to discern Antrim's true aims or simply identified him as a feckless adventurer, the effect was the same, the king should not, he advised, call on MacDonald assistance. Despite this advice, back in England it was believed that Wentworth was prepared to use Catholic forces against the Covenanters and the issue resurfaced when Wentworth was brought to trial in 1641.

The Protestant English, Welsh and Scottish settlers in Ireland comprised that most elusive of peoples, the British. Only outside their own countries were these outsiders grouped together by the officials of royal governance of Ireland under this still nebulous term. Outside their own land they were regarded as a homogenous group of incomers, connected neither to the Old English (or New Irish) Catholic families nor the newer Tudor settlers. In documents generated by the rebellion of 1641 colonial officials in Ireland named all settler victims of the rebellion 'British Protestants'.

Perhaps more than any other collection of sources for the history of the seventeenth century, the '1641 Depositions' have remained controversial since the time they were first compiled and therefore something needs to be said before use is made of this collection during this chapter. At the worst, they have been a weapon in a religious war. From 1641 onwards, Protestant commentators and militants used them to tar the Catholic Irish with blood guilt. This misuse, for even at first they were intended as a legal record of loss and criminal activity, rather than a weapon, accounts largely for their haphazard collation. As they now exist the depositions are assembled into 31 volumes, and grouped into counties, some like Kilkenny occupying part of a volume, others like Cork requiring several volumes. There are no entries for County Down and the imbalances are explained by the numbers of Protestant settlers in the counties, the proximity of the counties to Dublin and the ease of exit from Ireland through ports in English hands. Furthermore, the accounts are assembled according to the needs of several later editors and their chronology is fragmented.[1] The name of the collection is the first major inaccuracy, for although the first evidence was collected in the old calendar year 1641, the depositions continued to be taken throughout 1642, into the year following and on into 1644–5. Some were even collected in 1647. Again in 1652–3 commissions were set up to investigate some of the accusations made in the original depositions. All of this material is bound together, sometimes the earlier evidence is put with later material dealing with the same events and so on. To ease the original editors' use of this material, some of it is indexed and complete with references and extracts.[2]

The use of these depositions as weapons in a sectarian war has at times led the despairing to dismiss the information as useless, or in the words of Professor Perceval-Maxwell, the 'very attempt to use the depositions can be interpreted as the actions of a partisan'.[3] Is it true, as some critics have observed, the accounts are replete with lies, hearsay and speculation, and also contain conveniently rounded sums of money representing financial losses and irretrievable loans. However, they also contain much of what was true, and they demonstrate what many witnesses believed to be the truth.[4] More recently they have been seen as an important source of information on the Rebellion and they have also been seen as a major source for the social history of the plantation and colonial history in a provocative essay by Nicholas Canny.[5]

One thing that has united approaches to use of the Depositions has been the tendency to see them as unique. In some senses they are unique. They were taken from the survivors of a particular set of circumstances, but even here we may be being impressed by scale. The Depositions in some ways resemble the evidence taken by commissioners for oyer and terminer, the panels of judges set up to hear and determine important incidents such as the English midland riots of 1607. In some cases, particularly with regard to the 1652–3 examinations, the depositions read like any other court case examinations. In another respect the depositions fit a formula familiar to those working on the Civil War's financial exactions. One purpose was to assess the cost of the rebellion to each of the deponents and so each one listed what he or she had lost through theft or through having had to flee their homes. Material losses, losses of income and debts rendered desperate by the rebellion were all accounted for. In this the depositions look much like the accounts returned to the Westminster exchequer and to the Edinburgh Committee of Accounts and Monies. Even these latter sources, whilst ostensibly concerned with losses contained details of violence and murder.

Rebellion in Ulster

The depositions tell us much about the spread of the rebellion into west Ulster and into the other three provinces. North of the seat of the rising, in County Derry the effects were felt quickly, Anne Smyth of Moneymore said that on the Saturday afternoon 23 October, brothers Cormack and Owen O'Hagan with forty others got hold of the keys to Castle Drago. Charles Anthoney of Bellaghy knew by Saturday morning that the rebellion had begun and gathered his neighbours together for safety at Henry Conway's Castle. The citizens of Magherfelt also made their way there. Yet even in the heart of the rebellion attacks on Protestant estates could be patchy. James Smith of Moneymore, who was in Dublin at the time heard that his estates were attacked only on 4 November and Christopher Moore of Ballynamean confirmed that date when he said that the rebellion began around 6 November.[6] To the south in Tyrone, on the Saturday

Henry Boyne was at the home of his friend Andrew Stewart when a Scottish man came to tell them that Mountjoy Castle had fallen, English colonists at Donaghmore were being attacked by members of the Quin sept, and ministers like Boyne were being attacked. Around the same time an Irishwoman went the 6 miles to Boyne's house from Donaghmore to warn his wife that their lives might be in danger as Reverend Madder, Minister of Donaghmore was already dead, murdered by some of the Donollys. Although Boyne's house had been rifled before he had returned, the Quins were coming back for him.[7]

In Donegal the rebellion was underway within the week, with Christopher Parmenter of Killmire suggesting that he was robbed, and forcibly despoiled of goods worth £480 18s 0d sterling at the 'beginning of the rebellion 23 October 1641'. His precision is a little disturbing and perhaps the more vague Mullroney Carroll of Castle Doe is nearer the mark with his dating: 'about the last of October'.[8] Certainly in County Monaghan people were swept into the rebellion immediately. William Grave, a yeoman living in Drumbote, was attacked by the son of Art Oge Neale and 100 of his tenants. Grave's house was robbed and rifled before the rebels moved on to his father's house and thence to Sir Henry Spottiswoode's place. Richard Grove, William's brother was told of the intentions of the rebels by Patrick Mc Cardow:

> this was but the beginning: But before they had done they would not leave one alive neither rich nor poore who went to church ... by the next night Dublin would be too hott for any of the English Dogges to live in.[9]

Reports of attacks in Monaghan confirm the early start of the rebellion, although most early attacks began on Saturday 23 October rather than on the Friday. Katherine Allen's husband Michael was dragged from their Grangeboy home that Saturday and taken before Rory MacMahon in whose presence he was murdered. By the end of that Saturday Edmund Keating had lost £450 of goods, chattels and so forth.[10] In County Louth settlers were being attacked as early as the beginning of the following week, some like William Sellis on the Sunday and others like Amy Briscoe on Tuesday 26 October.[11]

Amongst the reasons for taking the depositions was the desire to get the necessary evidence for securing the recovery of British Protestant property after the rebellion had been quashed. This entailed two things, compiling an estimate of losses and their nature, real estate, moveable estate, loans and cash, and second to gain the names of the Irish men and women responsible. The latter were needed first as a source of redress for the named losses, second, as culprits in the theft and murder perpetrated during the rebellion and third, after March 1642, these persons were to be dispossessed of their own estates and property. The Westminster Parliament, with the agreement of the king, had initiated a plan whereby investors could 'adventure' money to support the war against the rebellion, in return for a share of 2,500,000 acres of Irish land to be confiscated when the rebellion was put down. The names in the depositions would provide a kernel of those whose estates would be forfeit. Except, not all of those named had estates to lose. Many were propertyless Irish men and women.

The depositions are probably not wholly reliable when they deal with the losses sustained. Many of the deponents expressed their losses in a series of formulaic statements, corresponding to the framing of the questions put to them. In Leinster for example, they were 'robbed and forcibly despoiled', in Galway 'deprived, robbed and dispossessed'. The deponents' losses were similarly expressed, as household goods, animals and crops. In many cases these were listed in convenient amounts, thus Mullraney Carroll of Castle Doe, Donegal recorded his total losses as being a neatly rounded £1,500 even though they embraced diverse things such as cattle, hogs and fishing boats.

Extensive evidence of credit networks which crossed the ethnic boundaries appears; clearly there was an expectation of, if not a reality of, most people loaning money to others in great and small amounts, ranging in County Londonderry from Anne Smith's £13 to James Smith's £720. Both of them, like the others, recording loans to both settlers and Irish. Only irredeemable loans were recorded, but specific loan amounts are not always referred to, with only the totals given. Because most of the deponents lent to both fellow colonists and to Irish people, almost invariably in their depositions, recorded loans were divided between those lent to despoiled English folk or to rebellious Irish; in both cases lost or desperate. James Smith of Moneymore, County Londonderry recorded his debts as those due 'from rebels' and those due from those the 'rebels beggared'.[12]

Rumours about the nature and aims of the rebellion abounded in the period just after it commenced. Naturally many rumours centred upon the brutalities; murders can be found reported in all counties, mass murders such as that at Sligo are referred to in the depositions from neighbouring counties Roscommon and Galway, that at Portadown (Blackwater) in neighbouring Ulster counties including Londonderry. As the deponent was further and further removed from the scene of an incident the vaguer or sometimes wilder the descriptions become; there is a greater tendency also for the deponent to resort to stereotypical descriptions of horror and massacre owing something to descriptions of the St Bartholomew's Day massacre, images of the war in Europe or the work of the Inquisition. Some deponents could supply few details. Christopher Parmenter of Killmore, County Donegal confessed at one point that he had seen no outrages, but added quickly 'though he [I] am psuaded & have heard there was many'. He did also remember having seen a smith 'that made and headed pikes for English' who had been disfigured and had had his hands cut off by rebels.[13] Others of course had direct evidence of murders. On 30 October forty-eight settlers in Monaghan town had been confined in the tiny gaol for fifteen days. The pews from the church had been pulled out and piled up on the gaol's trap door to keep it closed. The conditions were so cramped that the prisoners had to lie on top of one another. As well as the cramped conditions there was the psychological terror to cope with: whilst in the gaol, Brigitte Lee was later to allege, she had heard friar Richard O'Connolly threaten to set the pews on the door ablaze to burn the prisoners to death.[14] Others had witnessed cruel murders directly, several people, including Anne Bull aged just 6 years, had seen Thomas Parker of Ballyrath wounded in a fight with rebels and then stoned half to death. Parker's still living body was then thrown into a ditch and covered with earth.[15] It is this type of murder, isolated and of one or two persons in a spontaneous act of violence, which dominate the Depositions. Systematic mass murder is rare and cases referred to, that in Sligo and Portadown and in the mines of Tipperary are repeated in garbled fashion in many accounts. It is probable that the true numbers of Protestants killed in the rebellion was under 5,000 including those who died as a result of being cast out of shelter in the autumn and winter months of 1641–2.

Within the depositions is some evidence of the expectations of the Irish men and women in rebellion. The deponents were asked if they had heard any traitorous words, in other words whether they had heard any discussions about why the rebellion had taken place, who led it and what their motives were. Several things appear from the answers, some degree of confusion about the nature of the rebellion, but more than this there are two distinct strands. The rebellion had the highest authority at one level, but moreover their rebellion was morally, socially and legally justified. In Donegal Mulraney Carroll heard the rebellion tied to St Columcille's prophesy that the Irish would reconquer Ireland for themselves in the future.

The inquiry was very interested in the origins of the rebellion and many witnesses were found who had 'evidence' of there being a long-term plot within Ireland, or on the part of the king or the queen; it was also a short-term reaction to the deposing by the English of the king, or the murder of the queen's priest. The rebellion was also said to have the aim of crowning a new king or offering the throne to a foreign monarch. In Tyrone, Archdeacon Wright of Dromore heard Friar Malow, whom he met at Skerry, say that he had worked fourteen years to bring the rebellion 'to pass'.[16] In Londonderry Charles Anthoney, fleeing from his Bellaghy home, heard that the rebels claimed to be acting for the queen. And as for the immediate intentions, in Monaghan, on the very first day of the rebellion, Richard Gore was told that:

> This was but the beginnings. But before they had done they would not leave alone neither rich not poor who went to [the established] church … by the next night Dublin would be too hott for any of the English Dogges to live in.

It was declared by one priest to Charles Campbell of Sanmullagh in the same county, that it was 'no sin to kill protestants as they were damned already'.[17]

The injunction to kill Protestants had some limitation at least in the early days of the rebellion. In County Carlow Constance Crawley heard through a friend,

Margaret Comberford, that the queen's priest (presumably in England) had been hanged 'and that they (meaning the Irish) would be revenged'. The rebellion's most notorious forgery (if it ever existed at all), King Charles' supposed commission to Phelim O'Neill authorising the rebellion, was mentioned by several deponents, especially those from across Ulster. In Monaghan Anne Howten was told by one of those who robbed her that they had 'the king's broad seale to … do what they did'.[18] Luce Skell, trapped at Skerries when the boat she was travelling on was forced to dock there because of a storm, heard a version of this idea. Whilst being held prisoner she overheard a discussion to the effect that the Prince of Wales would be installed as viceroy and tutored as a Catholic. The king would move to Scotland and in a pan-Celtic alliance the Scots and Irish would attack the English with help from a Spanish army and all puritans and protestants would be put to the sword.[19] The notion that the Scots and the Irish would be natural allies was further substantiated by other witnesses. According to Mr Wright the archdeacon of Dromore, Phelim O'Neill claimed that he had one commission from the king and the English nobility and another from the Marquis of Argyle, leader by that time of the Scottish Covenanters. No doubt this latter claim was bound up with O'Neill's attempt to divide the English colonists from the Scots. The Scots themselves in the early days of the rebellion were not popular with the fleeing English colonists who saw them as dubious allies. Charles Anthony of Bellaghy said that in Coleraine the Scots forces plundered the town, something more commonly associated with Irish accounts of the behaviour of Scottish forces. There was considerable suspicion of the Scots in the early stages of the rebellion. Some English settlers found them to be of little help. Christopher Parmenter commented upon the suggestion that the rebellion was not against the Scots, claiming that some Scots actually sided with the Irish against the English. This he saw as part of a complex plan: 'after the Rebells had overcoman & weakened the English, then they fell upon and robbed the Scotts'.[20]

This phase did not last long in any case and references in the depositions to murders embraced Scots and English under the name 'British' making it difficult to ascertain just how much of a distinction was made in practice. Some assertions were made that the rebellion plan had been hatched in England. Garrard Colley was told by Collogh McBryan and Patrick McLaughlin McMahaurne:

> That the present business (meaning the present rebellion) was first conceived in England & that with him & and the rest of the Northern rebells, most of the Nobelitie & great ones joyned & and their handes could be produced to that purpose.[21]

In Dungannon, County Tyrone, the question of the aim of the rebellion was answered by the suggestion that Phelim O'Neill would be made king. This was made by some of the Irishmen guarding English inhabitants in the session's house after the town had been taken by O'Neill. In Carlow they were less specific; Margary Bellingham was told by rebels that one in their army would be king and that a crown had been brought out of Spain before Christmas 1641. In neighbouring Kilkenny Edmund Purcell was told by Elizabeth Gilbert that rebels had told her that a foreign king was being brought in.

There were alternatives too; not all of the rebels were monarchists. Whilst William Fritton esq. of Anye in county Limerick was being robbed of £800 he asked Robert Freeman what the Irish were aiming to do. Freman replied: ' … it was the Irish intencons to have a free state of themselves as they had in Holland, and not to be tyde unto any King or Prince whatever'.[22]

Freeman was unusual, most rebels the deponents recorded believed that some form of monarchy would be in place. Few believed that they personally were to reign, but Nicholas Shewgill of Monaghan and his followers did think that Nicholas was to be king. When they had heard that Charles I was dead and a new king required, Shewgill 'accordingly took it upon him to be soe' Brigitt Lee told her examiners.[23]

Whatever the legitimacy of the rebellion, there was a uniform expectation of the outcome. The Irish expected, after years of oppression, a restitution of what was theirs. Charles Coote's burning of Clontarf on 12 December 1641 drove many Catholics from their homes. Gear Devenish and his wife reacted to this in different ways whilst taking refuge at Ballinruddery. During the course of a conversation heard by the captive Luce Skell, Mrs Devenish was angry and bewildered: 'what have the English brought [us] to? The curse of God be upon them'. To which her husband replied 'Be contented wiffe for when these two or three dayse Dublin will be taken and then we shall be paid double for what we have lost.'[24]

The Depositions' main fault is that for the most part they tell the Protestant side of the story only. Naturally this has had consequences for the way that they have been used over the centuries. There are mentions of kind deeds by individuals and the *bête noire* of the English, Sir Phelim O'Neill is usually written of with respect and sometimes gratitude by Protestants who came in contact with him, the same is true of Nicholas Plunkett, and of Friar Malow, referred to by Mr Wright. The Earl of Clanricarde was allowed to live in peace in England during the Protectorate for his protection of refugees in Galway. Other Irish people are mentioned for acts of kindness; Mary Hammond was, on her horrendous journey from Tuam to Galway, twice rescued by two of the Joyces and later housed by an Irish family in the village of Claregalway.[25] John Bellew, a prominent Louth rebel, was remembered with gratitude by Cecily Jones who offered evidence at the enquiry in 1656 of his role in the war.

> at the beginning of the rebellion, john eden, richard Lason and myselfe came accidently to Mr Bellew of Willestone in the county of Louth, house wher our lives were preserved by him, and ourselves civily enter-tained and safely conveyed by him to Tredath and i do further certify

that I did then observe that the said Mr Bellew and all his family were as much for the preservation of the English as any could be.[26]

The devastation of the war in Ireland is shown through the accounts of observers. Owen Roe was shocked at the state of parts of Ulster he saw and Friar O' Mellan commented on Tyrone in November 1644:

> The land was a virtual wilderness – farms, estates, whole tracts – from the Bannfoot in the north to the gates of Dundalk, and from Canmore of Sleive Beagh to Tory in the north only eight people were left in the Lough Laoghaire and wight on Loughinisholin ... [27]

The vast number of mentions of Irish people are usually related to acts of cruelty and so on, the atrocities of the Scots forces are rarely mentioned, although there are accounts in Friar O'Mellan's Journal.[28] That these had effects upon the Irish is not doubted, and they had formed the background to Gear Devenish's conversation with his wife overheard by Lucy Skell. Most of the accounts of Protestant destruction come from 1642 after the arrival of the Scottish army in May 1642 which 'came ashore in Trian Conghail and burnt and plundered the Irish till they reached Newry'. Trian Conghail Clairingnigh was the Irish name for an area covering most of Antrim and Down. O'Mellan described the capture of Newry and the hanging of a monk and a priest, after which some of the army was 'ordered back to ravage Trian Conghail'. O'Mellan recorded incidences of murder of priests by the Scots. For instance in May 1643 he recorded the deaths of Father Henry MacIlmurray at his parish of Dromragh on 7 May and Father Eoghan Mordatha O'Crilly less than a fortnight later.[29] English forces, after failing to capture Charlemont, took revenge on the local people:

> they killed old men, women and children, took away the herds of Hugh Bui, son of Colbach. They arrested the good priest and skilful preacher and chorist, Seamus O Fallagan, and Hugh O Quin. Their lives would have been spared had they renounced their religion. Instead they were hanged and gibbeted.[30]

The Depositions do contain information about atrocities committed upon the Irish as well as those alleged to have been committed by them. There was a massacre of significant proportions on Island Magee in Belfast Lough but there was also a series of killings around Lough itself. Katherine Gilmore believed that ten families on the Ballydavy townland in Castlereagh barony in County Antrim suffered between them 73 deaths. Katherine herself survived the massacre because she was able to hide in a ditch overnight, although her husband, her sister-in-law and two male relatives were attacked and killed. James Gourdon also survived to corroborate the story. The massacre was well planned and at first the killers had been welcomed into the settlement by the inhabitants. The murderers were settlers from Bangor, Ballydavy and Holliwood some of them tenants of Andrew Hamilton. These people killed neighbours with whom they worked and traded, and many of them could be named by the survivors.[31] This was a seemingly unprovoked attack on Irish people uninvolved in the rebellion. The case was investigated in the 1650s and one important feature is that the massacre took place around Christmas 1641, long before the Scots army arrived to exact revenge.

Amongst the depositions there are some extraordinary personal narratives which round out and add colour and depth to our perceptions of the experience of the rebellion. Anthoney Stephens presents one such case in Ulster. Stephens was from Abbey Boyle in County Roscommon, where at the beginning of the rebellion he lost his lands and goods to the value of £150. He joined the Protestant armed forces and appears to have seen action across Ulster; he claimed to have been at the battle of Turvagh. He also described seeing lands deserted by the 'British' in Londonderry and Antrim and also the bodies of 'many' Protestants in heaps fed upon by dogs. He and many refugees ended up at Coleraine and other towns, creating atrocious health hazards there:

> a most lamentable mortality fell amongst them at Coleraine aforesaid. Insomuch as this deponent hath scene one hundred and forty of them buried at one tyme in Coleraine in one deep hole or pitt & laid so thick & close together as he may very well compare it to the making or packing upp of herrings

Stephens' account is one of those which betrays the enormity of what people were experiencing, he manages to convey his grasping for something to bring a sense of familiarity to a terrifying scene, hence the image of herrings to describe the dead at Coleraine. This experience also demonstrates the impossibility of encompassing all of the enormity without descending to cliché or generalised stock phrases. Immediately after his own personal description of what he saw, Stephens comments that 'those who survived were scarce able to bury the dead' – a cliché at least a thousand years old before Stephens repeated it to the clerk taking down his deposition.[32]

By the summer of 1641 in the face of the intervention of the Scottish and English forces in Ulster and the strong defence of the pockets of territory around Dublin and Cork, the rebels began to create a national basis for the continuing war. As early as April 1642 clergy from Ulster met at Kells and began to draw up plans for financing the war in the Province. In May a synod of the Catholic Church met and verified these aims and asserted that the rebellions across the country were all part of the same whole. In June meetings of clergy from the other three provinces created an Oath of Association. Through the reinvigorated parochial structures which the Catholic Church had established in Ireland this oath was sent, like the National Covenant in Scotland, throughout Ireland. The oath bound the swearer to adhere to the aims of the national rebellion and the Catholic religion. From this unified scheme grew the government established at Kilkenny in October 1642. The Catholic Confederation created a central government consisting of an executive body, the Supreme Council and a legislative body, the General Assembly. Each province was to have a council composed of representatives from county councils. Generals were appointed to command the armies in each province and the regular collection of taxation, customs, excise and the General Applotment established to fund government and the armies.

A major part of Confederation strategy was to remain the defeat the Scots in Ulster, a feat which was never achieved. The Old English component of the government never trusted the Ulster commander Owen Roe O'Neill. His zeal for complete restoration of the Catholic faith and consequently his alliance with the Papal Nuncio appointed in 1645, Giovanni Battista Rinuccini, contrasted with their moderate desire for limited toleration and a restitution of the power they had lost steadily since the previous century. This resulted in the underfunding of the Ulster campaigns and in O'Neill being subordinated to the command of the Earl of Castlehaven during the 1644 campaign. The early stages of the rebellion and war in Ulster is perhaps best known for the myths of the Protestant massacres and stories similar to those recounted to the Chief Justices were told across the Irish Sea in England, Wales and Scotland. These stories created the panic in the Halifax region that Lister wrote of. There were other myths which grew out of the war in Ulster, sometimes on a smaller scale. One of the legendary figures amongst the Confederate forces was Maolmordha M'Brian O'Reilly of Kilnacrott. Known to some by his Anglified name Myles, O'Reilly became a Captain of Horse in the Confederate forces, gaining the reputation and nickname of 'the Slasher'. In the campaign of 1644 when the Confederation forces were preparing for an attack on Ulster, the Earl of Castlehaven's forces were based in County Longford, and in early July he heard that Monro's army was marching through Cavan towards him. He sent Colonel John Butler, Lord Mountgarret's brother, with a detachment of horse including Captain O'Reilly to hold the bridge over the river Inny at Finea near Lough Sheelin, whilst the army encamped at Grannard. Castlehaven's main force retired to join Owen Roe O'Neill at Portlester. The Scots advanced on the bridge and in the fighting Maolmorhda O'Reilly was killed. Butler's forces and reinforcements from O'Neill were defeated, allowing Monro to advance into Longford where he burned Carlonstown, before retreating, having heard that O'Neill and Castlehaven had joined forces.[33] O'Reilly gained a enhanced reputation as a second Horatio and the following day when his body was found it was taken back to the family vault in Cavan monastery. Maolmordha became the subject of a lament, *Myles the Slasher*, penned during the mid-twentieth century which located Moalmordha amongst the defenders of Eire against the

> Ruthless pressure, born of pressure, germinated in the East
> When savage evil-Genii call their carrion-flock to feast

he was clearly one of the heroes
Such a One fell by these waters, and upon this ancient sward,
'MYLES THE SLASHER', Myles O'Reilly, of the keen two-edged sword
Desperate odds and desperate slaughter 'ere the gallant band was sped
And the Chieftain and his kinsman numbered 'midst the mighty dead
Peace and Honour, Maolmordha! Honour to your Cavan grave!
On the land we loved so dearly, happiness! Salute the Brave![34]

There is more than one problem with this salutation. Later genealogists of the O'Reillys of Cavan challenged the date of Maolmordha's death. It appeared that Maolmordha, son of Brian O'Reilly, died in 1675, aged only 53, and that his daughter had confirmed this to an eighteenth-century family genealogist. The lament had been written on the basis of the original 1786 genealogy. The tombstone of the dead 'Slasher' was destroyed along with Cavan Monastery earlier in the century.

According to Father O'Mellan, O'Reilly was not the leader of the Butler's horse at the bridge. Instead it was Brian Rua O'Neill, son of Conn Rua, son of Art, son of Fieardorcha and nephew of Owen Roe, who commanded the detachment, although there were three troops of horse which could have been under O'Reilly. Mellan mistakenly thought that Brian O'Neill had been killed when the Scots captured the Bridge. Finea was clearly a place of mythical death.[35]

The war in Ulster failed to dislodge the Scots completely. The Cessation negotiated with Ormond in September 1643 ended much of the fighting with the English until 1647 except for Munster, when the forces there sided with Parliament from 1644. The Cessation did not embrace the Scottish forces and war in Ulster continued unabated. Attempts to draw the Scots out of the province by sending a small army to Scotland drew only a portion of the Scottish forces home. Only in 1646 with the assistance of new weapons and financial support brought to Ireland by Rinuccini was O'Neill able to defeat Robert Monro's army. Even then the victory was not thoroughly pursued and the Scots remained ensconsed in Down and Antrim. It was not to be the Confederation which destroyed their resolve, but instead developments in Scotland and England broke up the unity of the Scots and finally shattered their alliance with the English.

Rebellion throughout Ireland

The Irish rebellion spread quickly throughout Ireland and impinged quickly upon the rest of the British Isles. Ports in Wales and in the south-west of England would be used soon to supply the English administration's forces in Ireland, but the proximity of rebellion also induced fear of invasion in both countries. These fears were never realised, but the rebellion had the major consequence of leading to the outbreak of war in England and Wales during 1642.

The rebellion was able to disrupt the rule of the English partly because the fabric of government was flawed. Hitherto compliant Catholic Irish or Old English members of government sided with the rebellion during the weeks following the attempt on Dublin Castle. In Louth at least one-third of the recently appointed subsidy collectors joined the rebellion.[36] Prominent amongst them was John Bellew of Willestone, the county sheriff. Bellew took some time to throw his hand in with the rebels. He seems to have undertaken to Lord Moore, besieged at Drogheda, that he would negotiate with the rebels for an exchange of papers. Moore exhibited a cautious attitude towards Bellew's offers of help and expressed his concerns in a letter to Christopher Barnewell, another county gentleman involved in local government. Unfortunately for Moore he also turned out to be a rebel. William Moore of Bartmeath in Louth suggested that Bellew joined the rebels after returning from the brief sessions of Parliament on 16–17 November, almost simultaneous with the beginning of the siege of Drogheda, and before Bellew was employed by Moore to treat with the rebels.[37] Bellew was accused of encouraging others, 'by his example and by his labour' to join the rebellion, in fact just as Alderman John Stanley told Moore, the county gentry were siding with the rebellion, and Bellew began to raise soldiers for the county forces.[38]

In County Dublin some of the gentry were trying to remain aloof. At Malahide John Talbot succeeded his father to the estate in 1640 and he may have wished to keep a low profile despite being related to the Plunket family through his marriage to the Earl of Finglas' daughter. When the Louth Old English gentry, including Finglas, met with the rebel leaders at the hill of Crofty near Tara, Talbot probably did not go, but neither did he go to Dublin when summoned by the Lords Justices. For this he found himself outlawed and Malahide sequestered.

By March 1642 his castle was occupied by Ormond's forces as a bulwark against the rebellion. In the wake of this Talbot gained custody of his own estates in return for paying rent to the Lord Justices. Ormond had realised that the earlier policy of destroying crops, estates and fishing villages was starving the Dublin forces and Talbot benefited from this. His productive estates were to supply first the Royalists and then the Parliamentarian and later the Commonwealth forces throughout the 1640s and early 1650s.[39]

For some of the Catholics the choice of which side to adopt was made with alacrity, rather than having, as John Bellew in Louth did, the decision forced upon him. William Esmond of Johnstowne, County Wexford, made no attempt to go to the safety of his uncle, Lord Esmond's, garrison at Duncannon, as many of the local English settlers from the barony of Forth did, despite ample opportunity. Johnstown had almost immediately upon the rebellion reaching south Wexford, been in rebel hands, but many off the prominent men of the barony had gone to Duncannon with Lord Esmond. Indeed, one witness at the 1653 enquiry alleged that William Esmond had actually accompanied his uncle there in November 1641. Nevertheless, Esmond eschewed the chance to join the

Protestants gathering in the fort. On 21 December 1641 he was in the town hall at Wexford when a meeting voted to raise 800 townsmen as part of the proposed 2,000–2,300 strong county force.[40] From then onwards his role and that of his sons John and Peter became more public. In 1642 William took the oath of association and became a county councillor in February or March that year. John served in the county troop of horse led by Captain John Roche, and Peter too served in the local forces. Whilst the clerk of the council, William Stafford, who gave evidence about Esmond to the commissioners in 1653, could stress that Esmond had not taken goods belonging to Protestants for private gain, he was able to detail some of the seizures made by Esmond in the council's name. He cited the one-third of Nicholas Codd's goods seized in 1642 by troops acting under Esmond's orders. Codd was one of Esmond's former neighbours. This action was confirmed by Nicholas Stafford, who added that Esmond had also taken goods belonging to Adam Waller. Peter Esmond was also accused of similar activities by witness Nicholas Stafford: of seizing Sir Arthur Loftus' cattle and sheep whilst serving at the siege of Duncannon.

In County Carlow in south Leinster, although some deponents such as Thomas Poole of Cranisake claimed to have been attacked as early as 28 October, many others suggest that mid-November was the point at which the rebellion hit Hacketstown. Thomas John was attacked and robbed on 10 November, Mr Gibson's lands were ransacked on the 14th, Anne Lister and William Baillie on 17–18th and George Allebone on 22 November.[41] In neighbouring Kilkenny details about early incidents are few; there are references to Michaelmas and to 'a little before Christmas' and 'about the latter end of 1641'. John Moore, cleric of Arghouse, said in his deposition that it was about the middle of December last that 'the rebells began to act their robery and rebellion against the protestants of the sd county', although he later clarifies this to mean somewhere around the end of the first week, which was when the rebellion began in the rural areas. It was to be another ten days, on 17 or 18 December that it spread to Kilkenny city. Whilst Moore is supported in his claims about the city, Jeanne Springs of Killnaburke claimed she was robbed and forcibly despoiled on 30 November.[42]

In Munster, the rebellion broke out in a more patchy manner. In county Clare trouble seems to have begun around late November and early December, although there was a clutch of attacks around Christmas time, and again in January and February 1642 – a pattern repeated in County Limerick.[43] In County Kerry, according to John Bastable of Tralee, the rebellion began around 20 October. However, he seems to have backdated his collected losses to a time when, several months on, he knew the rebellion to have started. Most Kerry deponents seem to suggest that their problems began in late January 1641. William Haynes of Castlemaine, Daniel Spratt, a clothier of Tralee, Josiah White of Ballymcarty, Nicholas Roberts of Ballymkilly and others all reported attacks occurring at the end of January, and into the middle of February.[44] In Connaght, depositions from Galway suggest there was much less of a delay between the rebellion breaking out in the east and the effects being recorded there. Mrs Julian Johnson, re-married widow of William Johnson offered 'around November' for the date when she and her husband were robbed and had to flee to the Island of Inch for safety. Maltster William Lincolne suggested 1 November for his losses of £295 in Galway itself.[45] In neighbouring Roscommon, Nicholas Mostyn suggested the rebellion began on St Andrew's Day (30 November), but Anthoney Stephens at Abbey Boyle set the beginning of the rebellion at 1 November, only a week after the initial rising, and this was confirmed by Ann Hawksmore, remarried widow of Edward Newsham.[46] The spread of the rebellion was therefore very quick. Within a week counties across north Ireland, in Ulster and Connacht were affected; within three weeks it was in south Leinster and spreading through Kilkenny in the days after that. As far away from Ulster as County Kerry, the rebellion was affecting the colonists no more than ten weeks after the initial seizure of Dungannon and Charlemont.

Enquiries in Dublin

A principal objective of the Irish rebellion on 22 October had been the capture of Dublin. This important part of the enterprise failed and Dublin remained in English hands throughout the wars which followed. As soon as the English administration in Dublin realised that it had had a lucky escape, investigations began. Strangers in the city, generally Irish men or women, were hauled in for questioning and asked to explain their presence in the city. As it was a major market town there were a lot of people with good reason to be there and most investigations ended with witnesses validating suspects' explanations. Irish soldiers awaiting shipping to Spain under Colonel Barry were questioned because some people had claimed to overhear a number of them whispering about wishing to go north to join the rebellion.[47] As October drifted into November investigations continued, but the scope had changed, people were coming forward with stories of conspiracy. Edward Escott from County Cork said that he had heard seditious discussions in Tallough, County Waterford. A silver-haired 60-year-old Colonel Barrie was heard discussing the 'young blades' at Youghall who would deal with the Scots.[48]

Alderman Edward Lake and his wife Elizabeth brought a very vague story to the fore. They had been in London in the previous July. One night they were at dinner at Thomas Hickes' house on Fleet Street in company with a Dr Moore who was either a doctor of physic or an apothecary – the couple disagreed over his profession. Moore had asked why the couple wished to return to Ireland, when they were not Irish themselves. He wondered why they did not stay in England where they were 'well-beloved'. The couple replied that their meagre fortunes were in Ireland. Moore replied, 'if the papists [in Ireland] were as hardly dealt withall as they weare in England it is likely there would bee cutting of throats or some troubles ere it were long'.[49] In normal circumstances the story would have been of very little significance as Moore was making only a vague prognostication.

Because these were not normal times, misunderstandings could have dramatic consequences. In one case a misheard conversation involved the justices taking a series of depositions from people involved in a drunken chase in the St John's area of the city. One morning in early November 1641 Bartholomew Lenman went to William Cox's house, probably on New Row at the end of Cook Street, for an early morning drink. Lenman was a tailor of St John's Lane where he is listed amongst the contributors to the parson's cess in 1640. When he arrived at Cox's a party of drinkers was already assembled. William Savage and his servant Edmund Casey of Castle Street, carpenter Phillip Maxwell of Wood Key, Elizabeth Moore and her servant Ellen Birne were enjoying Cox's company. Holding forth was George Hackett of Ballynahuichy, County Wicklow. Hackett was married into the Byrnes of Wicklow, and was regaling the company with his assertions that not only was he 'chief amongst them', but also that he had come into Dublin to offer his services as a captain of 200 Byrnes to fight the rebels in the north. At least this was the gist of what most of the drinkers claimed to have heard. Bartholomew Lenman on the other hand was sure that he heard Hackett blame the king for the rebellion. Only one other witness, William Cox, interpreted Hackett's boasts in this way although his testimony and therefore perhaps his memory of the morning was quite vague. Lenman was so certain of what he heard that he left the house very quickly. Out in the street he found a constable to arrest Hackett. On returning to Cox's house Lenman found Hackett had gone. Lenman and the constable set out to find Hackett and he was soon seen in Fishamble Street and the pair gave chase, eventually cornering Hackett in a house. It took a fortnight to get around to clearing the matter up. Although we are left guessing what the outcome was, Lenman's almost complete isolation from the testimony of the other witnesses suggests that Hackett was released and the justices' time was wasted because of the misunderstanding.[50]

Although the rebels had failed to capture Dublin rebellion lapped around the city. On the north coast of the bay lay the fishing village of Clontarf. On 11 December a Liverpool ship ran aground on the shore. Rebels, led by one Fitzsimons, from Raheny, a village north of Clontarf, turned up and robbed the boat, and according to David Powell murdered a miller who tried to stop them and compelled another man to save his life by converting to Catholicism. On 12 December Sir Charles Coote struck out of the city and burned Clontarf, reserving particular violence for the castle, home of George King who had been at the rebels' meeting at Swords. This did not deter the Clontarf and Raheny rebels, for a couple of days after Coote's raid Clontarf fishermen turned up and looted the ships' ropes and the coal and salt remaining on the boat. The Clontarf rebels also tried to incite the captains of ships' riding at anchor in the bay. Theodore Schons told an enquiry that rebels on the shore had called out to him offering him and another captain £40 to cut the anchor ropes of the other ships in the bay.[51]

Robbing beached vessels was not an unusual occurrence in coastal areas, but that the incidents at Clontarf were part of the process of rebellion is shown by the particular features of the robbery: the extreme violence and the enforced conversion of one of the men trying to stop the robbery. The attempt to disrupt the trade of Dublin by interfering with the ships in the bay again illustrates the broad-ranging aspects to the events around Dublin.

The 'aims' of the rebellion

The depositions from around Ireland also demonstrate, as did those from Ulster, the expectations and reasons behind the rebellion. One rebel told Elizabeth Beucanon of Killaly, County Mayo, exactly why he was in rebellion: 'Because they [the English] had gotten all from them by their Courts and Assizes.'

Encapsulated in one sentence was the main theme of the peoples' rebellion in Ireland. Complete dispossession and the concomitant imposition of foreign authorities: Quarter Sessions courts and the assizes had alienated the people of Ireland.[52] Perhaps more worrying for the Justices was the alleged leadership of the rebellion: there were plenty of rebels throughout the province who told their captives or victims that Charles I had authorised it. John Bradish of Limerick was told that the king had turned to the mass. Roger Sedley was told that the rebels had the king's warrant.[53] In Waterford too the king's broad seal was the authority cited to John Anderson of Aghauhery and John Bucknor of Dromow.[54] More specifically, in Connacht counties the king's broad seal was the authority for taking Englishmen's goods.[55] Dame Elizabeth Dowdall, defender of Kilfenny, was told by Lieutenant General Patrick Purcell that the rebellion was to defend the king's prerogative, first in Ireland and then in London itself.[56] Archibald Campbell of Cashel in Tipperary was told that the rebellion was under the great seal, but by the queen's command and the king tolerated it.[57]

Others, including Nicholas O'Helahen, a JP, thought the queen and the pope were responsible; together they had given orders 'to robb the English & to strip them naked'.[58] The soldiers who attacked Mary Powell and killed her husband at Cronrow, County Wicklow at Allhallowtide (1 November) 1641 said that they were the queen's soldiers and these were the queen's wars, and that the queen would send the rebels military aid.[59] In Limerick Ann Etone was told by Nicholas O Lelahen, a JP, that he had 'order from the pope & the Queen of England to robb English and to strip them naked but if she would go to mass she would enjoy all [her property].[60]

Events supposed to have taken place over the Irish Sea were also cited as impetus to rebellion. In County Leitrim, Connacht, there were rumours of rebellion in England: George Gonne was told that the rebels were rising because in England there was a plot to 'cutt off the king and his posterity'. John Browne heard that 'they had rebelled in England & crowned a new knig [sic] & intended to take the [real] king prisoner'.[61] Down in Waterford Judith Phillips was informed that the Protestants would receive no help from England because 'they being up there one agst another the king having left his crown'. John Anderson was told that the Protestants in England and Ireland were rebellious rogues who deserved to be hanged.[62] Such notions of the universality of the wars in the two countries were not confined to Ireland. Over the Irish Sea, from his residence in London, the Venetian ambassador, Giovannie Guistinian, had heard that the rebels in Ireland were intent on invading England to support the king, 'Thus England' he wrote, 'is menaced from every quarter with the fire of long and ruinous Civil War.'[63]

There was optimism amongst the rebels too. Mary Powell was informed by the 'queen's soldiers', who assaulted her so seriously that she suffered two broken ribs and various cuts to her arms, that they would surprise Dublin, 'and they would leave never a mother's son alive', further:

> Some would have St Patrick's Church and some Christchurch wherin they said all the English treasure was which treasure they would share amongst themselves ... [and] their wives would have clothes of ladies and gentlewomen of Dublin.[64]

One rebel, Roger Freeman in Limerick, saw beyond a rebellion in the name of the king telling William Frytton 'it was the Irish intencons to have a free state of themselves as they had in Holland, and not to be tyde unto any King or Prince whatever'.[65]

As for the immediate intentions, most deponents were informed that the king or the queen's warrants were to permit the stealing of English goods, prior to driving them from the country. English people at Waterford and Limerick were protected from the worst ravages of the mayor and corporations of the cities, and were eventually transported out of the port on hired ships. The mayor of Limerick Pierce Creagh allegedly refused to allow any massacre in the town when the lord of Castleconnell asked him to send the English colonists to Kings Island 'that his followers might butcher them & putt them to the sword'. Pierce replied: 'during his time of mayoralty there should be none of them suffer'.[66] Daniel O'Donovan esquire of castle Donovan, County Cork had a similar attitude. Neighbouring English colonists reported twenty years after the event, that he was affectionate to the English and preserved them and their goods from the 'rapine and pilladge of the rude multitude'.[67]

It was not an easy time, however. At Waterford, Benedicke Claybrook left a detailed description of life there before the evacuation. In the hinterland of the port Protestant goods were not safe. He lost his cattle by 1 November to John Poore of Ballykeyenny, who later claimed that he had only taken one under the king's warrant. However, Poore's wife Frances was described by Claybrook as being a 'notable and prime robber and taker of the goods of the English'. In the city things were safer. Mayor Francis Briver defended the Protestants from the common people 'in all wch time there was not one dropp of Protestant blood there spild'. Protestants from the county were let into the town, and those at Passage 5 miles away were relieved by the mayor. Even when county gentlemen commissioners representing Waterford, Kilkenny, Tipperary and Wexford arrived in January 1642, demanding entry and access to English goods, the mayor kept them out. When one or two commissioners were let into the city for negotiations they were guarded by the town militia, including Protestants like Claybrook. The mayor's plan to evacuate the Protestants in mid-March had to be brought forward. In February County Waterford commissioner Sir Nicholas Walsh got into the city and incited the Irish to hold the English prisoner. He suggested that if left free the English would join the Lord President of Munster's resistance to the rebellion as he claimed had happened at Youghal and Cork. With the aid of boats from Youghal and Waterford itself, the mayor got many of the English away. All lost their goods but all of them left with £5 in cash.[68]

Not all of the English left at that time, and conditions for those that remained deteriorated. Judith Phillips recalled that around Shrovetide the remaining Protestants – men, women and children – were assembled by the constables. After two days imprisonment they were all expelled towards Passage, guarded by Captain Strange, with only a farthing worth of bread each. En route about 48 people died and were left on the beach, Judith herself was beaten badly as she tried to protect her child from being clubbed with a musket for attempting to get extra food. The beating caused Judith to miscarry. At Whitsuntide, according to a Waterford glover, Lawrence Hoog, the Irish began to dig up Protestant graves in the town. There were two reasons: first the Irish claimed not to want even the Protestant dead to remain with them. In accordance, Protestants who died from then on were buried outside the town by the wayside. The second reason related to the desperate shortage of gunpowder. Far from an ideological impetus, the graves were being emptied so that the soil from around the decomposed bodied could be boiled down to extract saltpetre.[69]

Naturally the war impinged on normal life, but because of this the depositions show up certain features both of the Irish and colonial culture. Fostering may be one of those areas where, as Nicholas Canny has instructed us, there was a cultural interchange with the colonists absorbing Gaelic practice. Fostering was still a part of the Irish manner of childcare. One fosterer, Gullopatrick O'Durane of County Limerick, was arrested in March 1642 by John Lacy and taken to Castleconnell. O'Durane was fostering the child of John Arthur, a yeoman. Arthur's payment for the fostering was as usual, in the form of loaned cattle, from which O'Durane would derive benefit during the term of the fostering. O'Durane was arrested on a charge of treason to the 'Irish government' and his herd was confiscated. Arthur presumably had a close relationship with the fosterer of his child and made efforts to secure his release. He went to Limerick to get permission to take a letter of commendation to the lord of Castleconnell. However, by the time he got there, O'Durane had been hanged. The issue now turned to one of financial necessity, and Arthur tried to secure the release of his cattle. John Lacy appeared sympathetic and suggested that if Arthur could prove the cattle were part of the fostering arrangement he could have them back. But as Lacy and Arthur both knew the fostering bond was one of trust and not of written legality; Arthur could not prove ownership with any form of document and the cattle were lost to him. As a result he could not recreate any other fostering arrangement. He seems to have whined to Lacy about this to receive only the response 'provide for the child otherwise'.[70] There is other evidence that the colonists were fostering children with Irish families. Across in Wicklow, Luke Toole's men who attacked Ashram proclaimed, alongside the threat to hang, draw and quarter any Englishman or women who did not leave Ireland in 24 hours, that: 'the Irish homes that kept any of the English children should be burned'.[71] In County Leitrim the rebels who arrived in one village entered the house of Hugh McArran and asked who the child in the house was. She was Isabell Stevenson, the daughter of Archibald Stevenson, a Scots settler. On hearing this one of the kernes 'took the child by the heeles and ran to the door and bett out the braines of it against a tree'. It was a barbarous act and the soldier's fellows 'seemed to be ashamed'. The murderer was arrested by Con [McDonnell] O'Rourke, and there was a suggestion that he be sent to the English garrison at Jamestown for punishment, although because of English suspicion this seems not to have happened.[72]

As with the case of the Ulster deponents, the claims for recompense were all apparently rounded upwards and listed in convenient amounts, thus Robert Dedson of Hacketstown County Carlow recorded that he had been robbed of corn at £30, hay at 40s, salted hides at £27, tanned leather and shoes worth £38, cattle worth £40 and household stuff and provision to the value of £13.[73] Thomas Poole's losses included the £30 worth of household stuff and £20 worth of cattle. John Davies lost £10 worth of fruit, four swine at 20s and calves worth £10 at Killingford. He further lost £9 worth of cattle at Bullingford in County Wexford and £9 10s worth of clothing, apparel and dairy produce at Hacketstown. Richard Gibson esquire, JP of Williamstown, recorded his losses as being his whole estate consisting of townlands in Williamstown and Lisnavaghe where for 26 years he had built up a castle and estate only to see it taken from him by the Byrnes. His losses he recorded as the estate at £500 at least, 1,000 acres and £1,200, with £640 worth of goods taken from him later. Many of those attacked in the county lay the blame upon the Byrnes of County Wicklow, including Turlough Byrne of Killrathe Coole, Cahir Byrne (a 'notorious rogue') and Jason Byrne of Rahen.

The name of a former high sheriff of County Carlow, Walter Bagnall, crops up several times within the depositions from Carlow and he is also associated with one of the alleged murders in the county. A party of the county's Protestants had been gathered at Castle Leighton to be transported to (New) Ross just over the border in Wexford. On the way Richard Lake of Leighton was hanged by the rebels. Bagnall as governor of the county and of Leighton was believed responsible, although several witnesses recall eleven years later that they had no proof that it was by his order, although James Kirwan when called to give evidence remembered that the soldiers who killed Lake were from Bagnall's company under Sergeant James Feeney. Feeney himself when questioned blamed the constable of the fort at Killcranth, Charles Dempsie.

Bagnall's name also occurs extensively in the depositions from the neighbouring County Kilkenny, where he appears accused of rebellion and robbery. He also appears on the sidelines of one of the murders, at Inniskirk, of settlers from Grange being escorted to (New) Ross. One of the accused, Gibbon Forestall, in 1652 suggested that the murders were carried out on Bagnall's orders. Amongst the murdered men was Walter Shirley, a carver who made pistol butts and carbine stocks for Bagnall. This work earned him a letter of protection from Colonel Edmund Butler. His wife Francis took the letter back to her husband's captors, but when 'they saw her coming with a paper hanged him forthwith so as he was hanged dead and cutt downe before she could come to him though making haste towards him'.

Others murdered there included according to one, 'a piper', two women and a child, and John Stone and his wife. Another man widely reported killed was William Stone a boatman whose crime, according to his murderers, was to have built a boat for Sir Charles Coote. Elizabeth fferal of Grange who says she was certain of the event because her master Henry Bennett tried to save his life by pleading with Gibbon and Garrett Forestall.[74]

Losing the possibility of regaining money loaned is a feature to be found in depositions from throughout the provinces of Ireland. In County Kerry, Henry Escham listed five men by name and implied that there were other Englishmen to whom he had loaned money and now these same men had been robbed by the rebels. He had also lent money to seven named Irishmen and others unnamed who were now in rebellion; in all over £200 was lost. In addition he had lost £128 on debt due on bonds to other Irishmen. John Bastable of Tralee similarly lost £150 in loans to distressed Protestants and Irish in actual rebellion. These latter included a shoemaker and five gentlemen.[75] Ann Etone of Limerick was relatively rare in listing the names of three of her creditors. John Commin, gent., Joane Roberts and An Bloomer of Limerick were now in rebellion, according to Ann, and this was perhaps one of the principle reasons for naming them.[76]

Daniel Spratt of Tralee, a clothier described by the clerk writing down his deposition, recounted his rebellion experiences in detail and named those he felt had been in league with the rebels. The rebellion in Kerry for him began at the end of January 1642. He was 'robbed and forcibly despoiled' of his goods and deprived of hope regarding his debts, totalling £157. His goods were taken from his estate by Captain John Fitz Garret and other forces taking part in the siege of Tralee castle. He himself was one of the wardens of the castle during the siege and he described how he and the other warden were approached by Mr Edward Roukley the elder, gent. of Tralee. Roukley had sided with the rebels having got his wife out of the castle, 'instead' as Spratt put it, 'of joining her'. The castle surrendered after six months and the defenders were, Elizabeth Harris claimed, drinking 'puddles & corrupted water', something she believed had contributed to her husband Sir Thomas Harris' death. In the surrender conditions the garrison got security for their lives only, although Spratt's suspect Mr Roukley got his goods back. Spratt also accused Captain John Crosby of Bullingay Island of having 'discourse freely with the rebells yt came … and brought forth drink and drunk freely with them Morrish McElligot of Bally McElligot gent. Captain Walter Hussey … Desmond O'Dingle of BallyMcCarty gents'. McElligot was one of the principle commanders in the county, described as bearing arms and commanding a company of men. He was also described as the man who took Tralee. Walter Hussey was also described as assisting McElligot and 'marching with a party of the Irish in the same year 1642'.[77]

In the province of Connaght, the rebellion broke out in a fragmentary fashion. Galway's rebellion broke out slowly. The fort built early in the century around the Augustinian Monastery 200 yards outside the city walls was one reason that this was so. The fort, newly repaired in 1636, was held by Sir Francis Willoughby. The Earl of Clanricarde was also responsible for the slowness of the town to become embroiled in the Confederation. After initial harmony between the town and the fort, the deputy governor, Captain Willoughby, antagonised the people. Clanricarde tried to calm the waters. On 19 March 1642, led by Dominick Kirwan, a group of merchants siezed a ship in the bay, taking the goods and weapons involved. The mayor tried to excuse the action by saying that Catholic population were frightened by tales reaching them about the oppression of Catholics in Cork, Youghal and Dublin. With these weapons some attempts were made to capture the fort. Clanricarde besieged the rebellious town and recaptured it on 10 May. Willoughby's continued atrocities further alienated the town and Lord Forbes' arrival with his seaborne adventurers drove in the final wedge. Forbes' men attacked the homes of hitherto loyal Catholics. Forbes tried to force a garrison of his own on the town, obliging Clanricarde to intervene to try and get Forbes to leave. Instead Galway was attacked by the adventurers who destroyed St Mary's. This all opened the way for Galway to welcome the visit of John Burke, general of the province's Confederate forces. By April Burke had returned with armed forces and attacked the fort and town. By June Galway was in Confederate hands and the fort demolished.[78]

Throughout Connacht those not fortunate to have made it into the protection of the Earl of Clanricarde suffered cruelties at the hands of the rebels. Edward Pierson of Roscommon was robbed, expelled and deprived of goods to the value of £408 and he, his wife and children were stripped and exposed to the cold by Oliver Boy Fitzgerald esquire of Ballyliege, County Longford, whom Pierson had heard had hanged sixteen English there. Pierson was also certain that a number of Protestants in his own county had been murdered, but could offer no details. He did, however, go into some detail about the Shrewle massacre, including that he thought about sixty had been killed, information he claimed came from those that escaped. He also said that he believed that all Protestant English and Scots found in Sligo and Mayo had been murdered. Here he let his imagination or that of his informants run untrammelled, reporting that sometimes the rebels forced wives to kill husbands, sons to kill fathers, daughters to kill brothers. This is clearly Pierson's attempt to bring to the attention of his hearers and recorders the enormity of the rebellion. The acts of murder here recounted represent the overturning of the state, with subordinates in law and custom killing their superiors. He did give some examples which may suggest that there was a sort of foundation for his belief, but he was unclear about his sources and he certainly was not a witness.[79] Elizabeth Holiwell too believed that cruelties had happened just out of her ken. When the Protestants of Roscommon town were held prisoner in the town, she said that some were let out only to be murdered. A pregnant woman was slit open and the foetus killed. This story at once provided horror and hope, for Holiwell related that the woman smiled at her murderers, assuring them that she would be with God that night.[80]

Little comfort, and little in the way of embellishment can be found in the very personal narrative of Mary Hammond, wife of William Hammond clerk of Tuam. Her Spring 1642 journey from Tuam to join her husband at the Galway fort was full of incident: she was attacked twice and on both occasions rescued by members of the Joyce family. However, for much of the journey she was refused help, refused lodgings and when she was finally given a bed to lie in was subjected to horrendous treatment whilst she endured labour. Help was only given grudgingly and the child was born dead.[81]

The experiences of the Gonne family of Drumcrane, County Leitrim exemplify the hazardous experiences of Protestant settlers swept up in the rebellion. On the night of 25–26 October the Gonne house was attacked. The rebels claimed to be acting to defeat an English plot to kill the king. Their methods seemed a little obtuse. They seized George Gonne's wife and threw her around the room before sending her out to take refuge in a sheephouse where she gave birth. George Gonne had already left the house because he had been told that his life was in danger. He met up with the rest of his family in neighbouring County Longford as they made their way to his mother. The Gonnes took refuge at Longford Castle from where George set out alone. Whilst he was away, the castle was surrendered and the Protestants expelled. Mrs Gonne and the children set out for Dublin, and George told his examiners that he had heard that they had reached Mullingar in County Westmeath, but after that he had heard nothing. He feared that they were dead or at best enduring a 'most miserable liffe'.[82] Anne Read of Camcarrick in Drumlighe parish was driven from her home on 28 October. At the time she had a daughter fostered out with Ellen O'Reilly. Ellen's husband Donnell was a noted rebel. According to Anne Reade, Ellen stripped the foster baby of its clothes and took it home, where it died, possibly of exposure. Anne's six-year-old son Steven was also fostered out and lived with James Graid of Cavan. Steven was attacked in the street by six children who 'burst and break out his brains put out his eyes and bruised his body extremely … So that he by theis wicked youge impes (who were non of them as she is persuaded above eight years of age) not long after died & had been killed outright in the place had not an English woman commen thither … ' Steven's rescuer asked his assailants why they had attacked him, only to be threatened herself. Anne Read named her own assailants as members of the O'Reilly family including Edmund O'Reilly, the high sheriff's son. One of the family, Phillip McMulmore O'Reilly, had been 'formerly very kynd to the robbed and spoiled English and releaved them very much'. He was not a rebel in arms but 'out of fear', Anne believed. The rebellion cost Anne her husband, Hebekiah, and two children. She and three children survived to present her statement in July 1643.[83]

For women as for men the rebellion tested them in many roles: victims, survivors, protectors and rebels amongst them. Women participated in the rebellions, taking leading front line roles, or as Mistress Martha Cullen reported in Monaghan, they would 'follow after the Irish rebel souldiers & put them foward in crueltie with these and such like words, spare neither man woman nor child God so pitty ye soules as you pity them'.[84] Women also made depositions in their own right or on behalf of dead men, usually husbands. Wicklow depositions, for example, enumerated sixty-seven deponents. Five or seven per cent were women. Together these deponents claimed losses of £9,625 1s 2d. Three men claimed no financial loss. Women therefore were 8.5 per cent of those claiming losses and between them recorded £247 in goods, cattle and so forth taken from them, just 2 per cent of the total claimed.[85]

In Monaghan there were more women proportionately in the list at the beginning of the volume. Of thirty-three names, no less that eleven (33 per cent) were women. Two men and two women listed made no financial claim, the thirty people who did together listed losses (chiefly rounded to whole pounds) of £16,742 13s 4d. Women claimed £2,047 6s 8d, or around 12 per cent.[86] Women were always the smaller group of deponents, in Tyrone just under 25 per cent of those giving evidence in 1641–3, in Londonderry, 33 per cent 1641–6; Donegal, 20 per cent; Louth, 11 per cent; Kilkenny, 39 per cent; Carlow, 18 per cent; Limerick, 15.5 per cent; Kerry, 5 per cent; Clare, 17.8 per cent; Roscommon, 24 per cent; and Galway, 11 per cent. Central Ulster shires, Kilkenny and Roscommon, areas which witnessed the most violence, returned higher proportions of women deponents, perhaps because of a higher male mortality in those counties.

The depositions largely cover the outbreak of the rebellion and concentrate upon the sufferings of the victims. Details about the organisation of the rebellion were incidental, although the Chief Justices were keen to find out who was involved in organisation. They intended that such evidence would be used against the rebels after the rebellion was crushed. To ensure that the rebellion was crushed resources were urgently required by the Dublin government. Ordinary as well as extraordinary measures were used to ensure this. The traditional trading routes between Ireland and Britain were used to try and supply the English forces fighting in Ireland. The account submitted to the Lord Justices by Thomas Lawton in September 1642 show how these routes were employed.[87] In July 1642 Lawton was commissioned to import 20,000 pairs of shoes from England for the army.[88] An agent of the Lord Justices in Chester, Charles Whalley, was ordered to help and Lawton carried instructions with him when he crossed the Irish Sea. Hopes that the shoes would already waiting at Chester were unfulfilled so Whalley had to procure £500 for buying shoes elsewhere. Lawton's bill for £14 10s 02d in wages and his claim for expenses shows where and how he went about purchasing the materials. Lawton crossed from Dublin to Anglesey, which cost 3s 6d. He then rode to Manchester, hiring horses at Beaumaris and changing mounts at Chester and Kirkam at a cost of 14s in total. One hundred and eleven drifats or barrels were bought or hired at a cost of 6s. Three shillings were spent on having them packed, whilst a cooper charged 2s 6d to hoop and head the barrels. The nails for this cost 6d, but the barrels may not have been nailed down until they reached the port of exit. A cart was hired to get the shoes to the inland water craft known as a gaberds and porters were paid to load them on to carts and then later onto the gaberd itself which was possibly at Chester. All of this cost 5s 6d. Then the plans were changed and the shoes put back onto carts and carried by land to Caldy on the Dee estuary to be put on a barque there. The shipping charges for the shoes, 2 drifats of caps and 6 trusses of shirts (in total 10 tons) came to £4. These were sailed across the Irish Sea to Dublin's outer port at Ringsend. There they were transhipped onto 8 gaberds and sailed up the Liffey to the crane near the Custom House in St John's parish. It took no less than fifty-two valuable days to complete the importation of the urgently needed shoes.[89]

The advantages gained by Ormond's forces in Spring 1642 and the success of the Scottish forces in Ulster could not be exploited fully during the summer. The collapse of government in England and Wales and the war which broke out in the late summer paralysed the funding arrangement which had supported the war against the rebels. Most of the money raised in England and Wales was used to fund the armies raised there instead. As a result the rebels seized the initiative. The Scots were confined largely to eastern Ulster and the government forces were penned in around Cork and Youghal in the south-west and around Dublin. Quickly the Irish situation became embroiled in the complex web of Charles I's attempts to defeat his enemies in England. Whilst the reports of the Chief Justices were made to Parliament and not to the king once he had left London in January 1642, Ormond was loyal to the king. During the peace negotiations with Parliament in spring 1643 Charles ordered the Chief Justices to open negotiations with the rebels. The lord deputy, the Earl of Leicester, who had replaced Strafford, had been forbidden to take up his post and was detained in Oxford. It was Ormond who led the discussions with the rebels. However, by the time this shift in policy occurred, the Irish had formed their own government based at Kilkenny. A supreme council formed the executive, with a general assembly as the legislative: each county had a council of its own and these were in turn represented in provincial councils. Each province had a president and a commander in chief of its own forces. The Confederation of Kilkenny remained loyal to the king whilst in rebellion against the Westminster parliament. It was this loyalty which the king hoped to tap into and urged by Lord Taffe, an Old English lord serving at Oxford, Charles considered seeking access to the resources of the Confederation. In the short term, however, because this was such a high-risk strategy, the king sought to use a peace treaty to facilitate the return to England of the troops sent out in 1641 to tackle the rebellion. Negotiations continued throughout 1643.

In September 1643 the English government at Dublin negotiated a truce, known as the Cessation, with the Confederation at Kilkenny. Most of the fighting in Munster and Leinster came to a halt, although on the fringes of the rival territories skirmishes continued. In Ulster the Scottish forces did not acknowledge the truce and campaigns continued with Owen Roe O'Neill attempting to drive the Scots from the province. The issues of financing the war were complex. The ties became entangled further after the Cessation when the financial and credit resources of both the English and the Confederation had to be used for mutual causes. The attempt to send MacColla to Scotland would have come to nothing had it not been for the efforts of Patrick Archer, an old English Catholic merchant of Kilkenny and Waterford. Archer was from the Kilkenny Archer family; he had married into the Shee family of the town. By 1644 he had extensive trading connections with Flanders and this commercial interest was more important than his signing of the remonstrance of the Catholics back in 1641. The attempt to divert the Scots in Ulster under Robert Monro from their opposition to the Cessation was crucial. Troops would be sent to Scotland to raise a rebellion there in the king's name in the hope that it would force the Covenanters to draw troops home from Ulster, England or both. The men were raised by MacColla and Antrim, the ships were a different matter. Ormond confessed later to Charles II 'I knew not how to perform the service.'[90] Two Flemish ships *The Christopher* and the *Angel Gabriel* were available at a price but together they were insufficient. It was Patrick Archer who came to the rescue. He offered the security for the vessels that the Flemish merchants required and provided a ship, the *Jacob*, which he part-owned with another Waterford merchant. Unfortunately for the two Irishmen, the *Jacob* was lost at sea, possibly in a fight off Mingary on 20 July 1644, or by being captured on 10 August.[91] Archer's losses were estimated at £2,600 in shipping, freight and victuals.[92]

The Cessation produced other crises. For Murrough O'Brien, Lord Inchiquin, it was to be one of the things which drove him to join with Parliament. Inchiquin was a Protestant Gaelic leader with ambitions to be the king's President of Munster and his change of heart was in part due to great feelings of being personally slighted. The combination of the Royalist defeat at Marston Moor in June 1644 and Charles' failure to confer the presidency upon him convinced Inchiquin that his future did not lay with the Royalist cause. He returned to Ireland and led the Munster enclave into the parliamentarian camp. For others the Cessation provided a breathing space to regroup. That was how Lord Esmond in Duncannon fort saw it. When he was later confronted by Inchiquin's insistance that he too side with the Westminster Parliament and its Scottish allies, he averred. Parliament was insisting that its supporters sign the Solemn League and Covenant and it was this to which Esmond raised particular objection. He was by this time in a difficult situation: his fort had been cut off from supply by land since the war had begun, and sea-carried supplies had declined since Bristol had fallen to the Royalists. Then in March 1645 a ship, the *Jeremy*, brought a printed copy of the Covenant to Duncannon. If the garrison did not sign, then the ship would not land supplies. At least one company of Esmond's own regiment of foot, Captain Capron's, signed the Covenant. Eventually even Esmond's chaplain, Richard Underwood, signed too in the hope of keeping peace in what seemed to be becoming a rebellious garrison. Esmond began writing to both General Preston and Ormond trying to secure help. Ormond seems to have offered no help, Preston encouraged surrender and eventually Esmond, having tried to get Protestant officers placed in charge of the fort, handed over the fort to the Confederation.[93]

The Dublin experience

In Dublin, despite periodic sieges, some elements of a recognisable life continued. The Parson's cess [levy] in St Johns' central parish continued.[94] St John's consisted of some of the oldest inhabited areas of the city, including Wood Quay and Winetavern Street, scene of extensive Viking settlement and now the governmental heart of Dublin. The street names remain the same, but no evidence of the 1640s buildings remain above the ground. The parish consisted of only one other major thoroughfare, Fishamble Street, which had two alleys, Copper Alley and Stable Alley incorporated in it. There were two small adjacent streets incorporated in the three main roads, Rosemary Lane and St John's Lane. St John's Lane was a paved street which ran between Fishamble Street and Winetavern Street at the apex of the unequal triangle formed by the three principal streets between the church and Christchurch cathedral. Rosemary Lane, with its handful of taxpayers, was at the very end of Winetavern Street where it joined Wood Quay. This area may have still been empty of houses, or fronted by new buildings on the site of the great Wood Quay explosion of 1596 when gunpowder being unloaded at the custom house crane exploded.[95] In some recordings of the levy either or both of the two small streets are missed off the list, their inhabitants ascribed to Fishamble or Winetavern Street. Tax collectors in the parish usually set about their business by the church at the top of Fishamble Street, walked downhill, then at the opposite end of the road, facing the River Liffey, turned left into bustling Wood Quay, where Lawton's cargo of shoes would have been unloaded inn 1642, walked along with the river on their right, and then turned left again onto Winetavern Street for the final uphill stage. The pattern was regular and the collectors of the Parson's cess must have been able to do it in their sleep. The collectors of the military levies were probably the same men, no doubt they would have taken the advice of the traditional collectors; certainly their pattern of work was very similar.[96] It was an industrial hub with well placed service industries. Unsurprisingly, Winetavern Street was the scene of many of these, the Golden

Dragon, The King's Head and the White Horse are listed in one parsons' cess for 1646, and there had also been the Spread Eagle which was registered as empty in 1643, as had been the King's Head. There were other inns still open, as six men were registered to malt and to sell ale in the parish, and three of them lived in Fishamble Street. There were many other trades: merchants lived on Wood Key alongside chandlers, sailors and garbardmen, rubbing shoulders with John Browne and Joseph Pailyn, described as Hotwatermen. There were shoemakers, including Widow White, bakers, tailors, millers, surgeons, attorneys, glaziers, bricklayers, water bailiffs, gentlemen, esquires and knights, and two aldermen, William Smith of Wood Quay, mayor in 1646, and Nicholas Hutchinson of Wine Tavern Street in the parish. During the 1630s and as late as 1641, Wood Quay was the home of Sir Faithful Fortesque, who in 1642, having gone home to his native England and enlisted for Parliament, changed sides dramatically, with his troop of horse, on the field of Edgehill. The complexion of the parish's population was soon showing unmistakable signs of the war: there were an increasing number of officers resident in the parish as the 1640s wore on.[97]

We are unable to explore the effects of war in the parish for much of the period of the rebellion. Certainly the parish would be busy, and it was here that Lawton's consignment of shoes would have been finally unloaded amongst all the other cargos destined for the government's war-effort. However, the effects of war are difficult to discern until the period when the city was taken over by the forces of the Westminster Parliament. The Cessation of 1643 had allowed Ormond to send English and Welsh troops back from Ireland, but a final treaty with the Confederation proved elusive. Ormond was unwilling to allow the Catholic Irish open freedom of worship, hoping to persuade the Old English in the Confederation to accept this position. The Catholic Irish were not, however, to be brought around to this position. Supported by first papal legate, Pier Francesco Scarampi, and then the nuncio, Giovanni Battista Rinuccini, the Irish wanted open acknowledgement of the Catholic religion and for this reinvigorated church to hold onto the reclaimed church property now in its hands. King Charles attempted subversion of Ormond, whose position on Catholicism was a deeply held personal one as much as a political conviction. He sent the Earl of Glamorgan to negotiate secretly with the Confederation in 1645. Glamorgan, himself a Catholic, conceded to the Irish demands, but his insistence on the treaty's secrecy prompted Rinuccini's mistrust and the negotiations stalled. In any case the king repudiated the treaty once a copy of it fell into Parliament's hands and Ormond angered by Glamorgan's apparent betrayal of the king's official position arrested the earl. After the defeat of the king's forces in England and Wales and his imprisonment by the Scots, Ormond's position in Dublin soon became largely redundant. He attempted to negotiate a new treaty with the Confederates and persuaded the Old English faction in particular that an open treaty was a better option than Glamorgan's secret and politically explosive terms. Moreover, Ormond convinced them that a secure future lay with a restored king, not with the victorious Parliament. Rescuing Charles with the military might of the confederation was therefore sold to the Confederation as the certain way to their own success. However, the dramatic victory at Benburb in County Armagh on 5 June 1646 changed the situation. The battle was won by Owen Roe O'Neill, General of Ulster, and saw the defeat of Robert Munro's Scots forces. O'Neill was a supporter of Rinuccini's hard-line position on the future state of the Catholic Church. Benburb, won with weapons supplied by papal funding, and strengthened the nuncio's hand against the more liberal sections of the Confederation which would have been content with tacit and covert toleration. This coupled with the knowledge of the king's desperate straits as a virtual prisoner of the Scots at Newcastle, convinced Rinuccini that he could prize better terms from the king. Ormond's treaty, optimistically proclaimed in Dublin on 30 July was repudiated by a synod of the clergy at Waterford and annulled by Rinuccini's faction; Catholics who supported it would be excommunicated. In despair Ormond, now virtually redundant at Dublin, began to believe that the security of the Protestants in Ireland lay not with a perfidious king but instead with Westminster, and he began discussions with Parliament. Having fought off Confederate attempts to capture the city, Ormond agreed to hand Dublin to Parliament in the summer of 1647

Ormond's successor as commander of the English forces was Michael Jones, son of an Irish bishop. His arrival in Ireland imposed burdens on Dublin immediately. From the accounts generated by his administration we can begin to see something of the effects of war on the people of St John's parish. On 20 October 1647 he demanded £300. The city, impoverished by war and siege, raised £244 16s. Nine days later he asked for another £300, this time he got £116 5s. Twelve days after that he moderated his demands requesting only £150, he got the full sum. At Epithany he set a weekly rate of £433, but just a month later Jones raised this to £463. The council pleaded with him to reduce the rate. Jones agreed that any income from the customs, which was increasing because of the improving communications with England and Wales, would be given to the town to pay back the 'loan', and he also suggested that customs money from Drogheda, Dundalk and Wicklow could also be used for similar payments. But of course not one penny could be got from these places, as they were not in the hands of the English Parliament. He did agree to forget £63 a week for the time being. For the immediate future this seemed to have secured reasonable payments.[98] There were shortfalls, the council had to make up the money by £21 11s in March, by £47 9s in April and by £56 7s in May, but income was relatively high.

During 1648 there was something of a crisis in tax collection. In St Nicholas Without parish 16 people paid no tax in March, 12 paid only one of the four levies, 7 missed two payments and 11 missed one. Forty-six people out of 84 (55 per cent) did not pay some or all of their taxes. In St Nicholas Within of 74 taxable people, 58 (78 per cent) paid less than the full amount, 35 (47 per cent) of them nothing at all.[99]

Both the men and the women householders in Dublin paid the levy. In St

Nicholas Without women generally paid between just under 5 per cent and just under 9 per cent of the levy in 1648. In 1649 their contributions hovered around 10 per cent and in May during the payments crisis, they contributed around 13 per cent. In St Brides women paid a higher proportion, in 1648 during April and May levies hovered around 15 per cent, although a year later they had fallen to under 4 per cent. At St Nicholas Within, the proportion was much smaller at less than 3 per cent of the total in February 1647. At St Warburgh's the proportion was around 11 per cent, but only two women actually paid, a Mrs Hill £5 and Mrs Bassett 8s of a £48 6s levy. By August 1649 there were four women paying levies in the parish constituting just over 8 per cent of the payers. In St John's parish too, women's proportion of the levy fell between 1648 and 1649; in March 1648 they had paid, either alone or jointly with a man, 2.25 per cent; in April, 6 per cent; and in May, 5.5 per cent. In the same quarter the following year, the rates fell to under 1.5 per cent in March and 1 per cent in April, rose to 2.5 per cent in May but hovered around 1–1.5 per cent in June and July. This shows a pattern with the Parson's cess contribution from the same parish. By 1647 women's contribution to the levy, which had in 1643 risen to 12.46 per cent of the levy had fallen to 8.46 per cent. The general cess suggests that the proportion had continued to fall. There was a shifting population in Dublin during the 1640s. The rebellion and war had changed the gender proportions in the city, as men were drawn out to fight in Leinster campaigns. This was then followed by an exodus of both sexes to England and Wales, but an influx of refugees from the rest of Ireland, and the encampment in the town of, first, Ormond's garrison and later Jones' army. Also during the war residents with relatives in the Confederation territory were expelled and this probably had a disproportionate effect on women householders, as it would seem in St John's, where the proportion fluctuated. Before the war the Parson's cess had fallen on a group of taxpayers of which women comprised 10 per cent, and this rose in the early stages of the war to around 13 per cent, before falling back to pre-war levels by 1646.[100] The cess collections show that this proportion remained constant in 1648, but that it fell again dramatically to under 5 per cent in 1649. There is a suggestion that St John's was different to other Dublin parishes, for neither St Nicholas Without nor St Brides parishes showed such consistent decline in the proportion of women householders in 1648 and 1649. At St Nicholas Within, where women comprised 7 per cent of payers in 1648, by August 1649 in a less widespread levy for fire and candlelight (coal and candles), women amounted to 14 per cent paying 27 per cent of the levy. At St Audons for the same levy women comprised 14 per cent of the payers and paid 14 per cent of the levy.[101]

There were minor fluctuations, people disappeared off the lists of payers for a few weeks at a time, or failed to pay their portion of the levy. One of the tailors in St John's parish was Robert Landers. He and his wife probably lived at the south end of Winetavern Street near the White Horse tavern. In 1645 Patrick was elected sidesman of the church along with Nicholas Eddis and two other men. Whilst Eddis went on to be an auditor of the accounts and later an applotter, Landers disappeared from the list of church and parish officials, although he continued to contribute 10s to the parish cess as late as the 1646 collection. By the time Michael Jones' levies were imposed on the town, Patrick was dead, although his burial is not recorded in the Parson's Cess book. In February 1648 Widow Landers was the householder, contributing 10s to the 5 February cess. Her payments continued throughout the military Cess book entries, dropping to 3s 6d a week by May 1648. Widow Landers was still on the street paying taxes in March 1649 but then disappeared from the records for three months, returning in June and paying levies through the summer months. Other Dubliners ceased paying their levies at various times during the period covered by the cess books, taking the opportunity to leave the city for other parts of Ireland or Britain, leaving the city underpopulated by the 1650s.

Incomers who the collectors did not know were referred to by trades, such as the 'cooper' in the cess lists. Some were buried anonymously, as were the three dead 'poor' found in the street in the winter of 1644–5, the 'widow' in 1646 or the 'yonge man from Howthe' in 1647.[102] Those who did not die could be listed as being from some other town, or ascribed a name based on a characteristic, like 'Toole the sneezing man' from somewhere near the East Mill in the parish of St Nicholas Without in February to March 1648. Not until April was Patrick Toole recorded by his own complete name.

4

THE SCOTTISH EXPERIENCE
OF THE WARS IN THE FOUR
NATIONS, 1638–48

The Bishop's Wars

The objections of the Aberdeen doctors did not really slow the onward sweep of the Covenanters into political power at the centre. There were areas of Scotland where no central directive was necessary. An area Robert Baillie, minister of Kilwinning, was very familiar with, the south-west of Scotland, had 'developed a distinctive cast to its religious life'.[1] Throughout the 1620s and 1630s the area had undergone a form of revivalism centred upon the lectures given in market places on market days. The ministers of this revival saw themselves as conservatives, defending the Church against the Episcopal innovations of the Stewarts. Their desire to defend a past religious approach or reconstruct something that had actually never been rendered complete was perhaps really a radical desire to complete the reformation of the Kirk and ensure its separation from the state. In the south-west a number of aristocratic women, the Countess of Eglington whose husband controlled the incumbancies of Kiliwinning and nearby Irvine, and Lady Boyd, provided funding for ministers unable to find livings or those ejected from Ulster parishes across the North Channel for their religious views. By doing so they ensured the continuance of a radical-conservative tradition in the region. This created an effective network which could ease the passage of the Covenant when it had been sent out for signatures, and for organising the broad-based opposition to the innovations of Charles I. The networks formed first between members of the aristocracy and then within the laird class and middling sort of Scottish society, forming the basis for religious and political allegiances which transcended the years of peace and allowed for the passage of the Covenant and the later formation of the radical organisations which emerged at the end of the 1640s.

Leading Covenanter lawyer Archibald Johnston of Wariston asked God directly for advice in difficult times. In March 1638 he was attempting to write an answer to the king's proclamation against the Supplication, but he found 'myselth dull'. To get him out of the predicament he begged God to inspire him with a 'neu influence of his Sprit'. Within days, God had responded and thoughts came to Archibald whilst in bed. There were additional practical benefits: God also protected him from being hit by a piece of lime plaster blown from the roof which crashed to the ground near him. If God provided for his safety and gave him inspiration, then there were more earthly guides too; Archibald was reading history and he consulted Henri Lancelot Voison de la Popliniere's *Histoire des troubles et guerres civiles en France pour la fait de la Religion, 1555–1581.* We might be tempted to believe that Archibald's thoughts were framed by the act of making his imprecation, and that his appreciation of the range of possible consequences was also being formed by his study of recent history rather than by any message from God. Archibald Johnston himself would not think this way and so he admonished himself for not taking more note of God's blessing in directing the fall of the lime. In any case he soon believed that he had been called to account for being so remiss because three days later his son James was dead 'qhuilk neues dasched me and confounded my wyfe'.[2] It was a reminder that the Kirk's defenders were not working in their interest but God's and his providence worked not for them but often, as Johnston realised, 'against our wils'.

Whether or not it was against their wills, by April 1638, Robert Baillie was fairly confident that the Aberdeen doctors' arguments would receive no support in Edinburgh, but as for Glasgow he was less sure. His real concern was that even the airing of the controversy would open up older divisions within Scotland which had been masked by the outrage that had greeted the imposition of the Prayer Book. The Highlands, he suspected, were about to descend into anarchy: 'Our country is at the point of breaking loose, our land this twelvemonth has been silent; divers misregards their creditors, our Highlands are making ready their arms, and some begun to murder their neighbours. ... '[3] By July he was confident that clans Campbell, the Fforbes, Frasers, Grants, McKenzies, McKays, Mclaines, MacIntoshes, MacDonalds, Irwines and Innices 'are zealous subscibers' to the Covenant.

In July 1638 it was Archibald Johnston of Wariston's responsibility to ensure that the leaders of Glasgow University signed the Covenant. Like the Aberdeen doctors the Glasgow provost was concerned about the implications for the king's prerogative and the consequences for the episcopacy of the Covenant. Johnston's task was particularly important because the General Assembly was to be held in the city later that year. Johnston overcame all argument that the Covenant was an infringement on the king's rights and referred to the Negative Oath approved of by James VI. The Glasgow doctors had offered to sign, if they were allowed to issue a declaration setting forth the limitations of their apprehensions. This was not acceptable to the Covenanters – a wedge must not be made which the king could then hammer home, signature had to be 'without expression of any reservation quhatsomever'. The Covenanters were successful, the ministers apologised from the pulpits, the Glasgow doctors signed unconditionally and the negotiating team were made burgesses of the city. God was thanked and Archibald went off to discourse with the Countess of Loudoun until two in the morning. Because of her devotion, she was recommended by him to God in prayer.[4]

Baillie continued to implore God's help as the Assembly's appointed date grew closer. He was not alone, as Lord Advocate Sir Thomas Hope, once associated with the king's rigorous attack on his enemies, was also earnest in his desire to explore God's will regarding the forthcoming Assembly. He was no longer convinced that the king was in the right. On 31 October 1638 Hope, after a conference with the Marquis of Hamilton, then the king's commissioner in Scotland, fell to his knees 'thairto cravit the Lord' help and assistance'. That same month Baillie took it as a sign of providence that his second son narrowly escaped being killed when he had made a grab for a pot of 'seething wort'. That the pot had fallen straight down rather than tipping onto the lad had not simply been a lucky accident, but 'a demonstration of god's love ... bot now I and all that loves me, are obliged to rejoyce in god's gracious providence'. It was evidence not just of God's favour to the child, but to Baillie and to Baillie's cause.[5]

At the General Assembly, the king's commissioner, Hamilton, was unable to influence proceedings. Once Sir Thomas Hope judged that episcopacy contravened the law an the 1581 Negative Confession, the entire episcopal framework was swept away. Charles had already considered taking military action against his Scottish subjects and by the following spring war between England and Scotland became almost inevitable. An anxious Sir Thomas Hope began to implore God to help Scotland, and was surprised by an apparent reply:

> I fell in ane ernest incalling of the lord that his Majestie wald pittie his peopill, and vindicat them from the power and rage of their adversaries, and wald establische the glorie of his blisset treth in the land. Amd quhills I wes praying, thir wordis wer spokin, but wither by mee or some other I dar not say, but the wordis wer, 'I will preserve and saiff my peopill.' Quhairupon I awakit out of my drusines; for I wes not sleipin, but as it wer oppressit with grieff and tieres, till theis words were spokin and certanlie hard be me. Blissit be the Lord, quho hes a cair of his awin. And askit my wyff if scho hard any speaking quho hard not; and I told her quhat I had hard.

God had not entirely answered Hope's request, there was no mention of 'His Majestie' in God's promise, but again on 18 May God made the same promise to Hope.[6] Again on 29 May and 8 June God appeared to have spoken to Hope, first answering Hope's request that he arise and help Scotland, and secondly admonishing Hope for doubting him. On June 14 God confirmed that His cause would be successful.[7]

The first military conflict, that of summer 1639, was brief. Elaborate plans had been drafted by the king for invading Scotland at the eastern and western borders and for an amphibious landing at Aberdeen to support a rising by the Earl of Huntly. The Marquis of Antrim had suggested that the MacDonalds invade Kintyre under his leadership. In the end these plans were scaled down and one large English and Welsh army was encamped on the Eastern border near Berwick upon Tweed. On 4 June a detachment of English forces under the Earl of Holland marched into Scotland. Near Kelso this force ran into a major part of the Army of the Covenant and fled after a bit of shooting. This unlikely action ended the war in the south, although it was only a few days before the Earl of Montrose defeated Huntly. Peace negotiations began almost immediately at Berwick. The Countess of Mar's letter to her daughter-in-law, Lady Bandeth, probably dates from these days. The Countess commiserated with her over the absence of her husband and passing on the news that

> there is good apirences that all will goe right and that there shall be pace presently, we hard word hir yesternight that itt was concluded be the King and the comisioners bott I dar not belive till I heare itt confermed againe. I preye god itt be trewe ... [8]

However, the peace negotiated at Berwick was not seen as final by either side; the king hoped that a new General Assembly and the Estates called for August would somehow be packed by his supporters, or be sufficiently alarmed by the act of going to war to overturn the work of the previous year. If not there would a renewed war. By the end of the year Charles and his lord deputy in Ireland had devised a plan which involved Parliaments at Dublin and Westminster voting the money necessary for a massive military campaign.

True, invoking God's help was one way of testing the righteousness of this momentous decision to enter into war with a lawful king, but there were more earthly measures for ensuring success. The Venetian ambassador, Giovannie Giustinian, wrote that he understood that 'both men and women are engaged' on building defences on the Scottish border during May 1639.[9] Two days after Hope had heard the second imprecation, those who trusted in God and their own participation in this particular salvation called on Hope. Edinburgh women had established a fund to supplement the war effort, they prised 5 rosenobles out of him.[10] This was of course an additional levy. The Scots had taken a series of highly effective measures for raising the funds necessary to fight the war.[11] A series of county committees were established around the country charged with levying taxes and other measures such as a compulsory levy of plate. The committees were composed of people of local standing loyal to the Covenant. These people were generally those who held responsibility for running county government anyway.

The Caithness committee is a case in point. Caithness is the most extreme of the northern counties of Scotland. It was also a county undergoing changes during the seventeenth century. The east of the county spoke Scots rather than Gaelic, and the Presbyterian discipline seems according to one historian to have been effective in controlling society, at least in terms of illegitimacy.[12] The county was also undergoing the strains of changes in land tenure, and feudal dues were giving way to modern rents – the basis of the new taxation.[13] As with the county society generally, the county war committee was dominated by the Sinclairs. Out of a total of 33 men appointed to the 1640 committee of war, 12 were Sinclairs. The majority of the committeemen themselves lived around the coastal strip of the county whilst their tenants farmed inland.

For the renewed conflict in 1640, the arrangements were even more firmly in place. On 6 July 1640 the Committee at Kirkudright drafted a list of its most financially able people within the eight towns in its division. It found 31 men and one woman. A week later it listed those most able to loan money, a further 22 names. The lands of anti-Covenanters, Lady Kenmuire and Lady Elizabeth Herries, were also to be used to further the cause.[14] By September silverware was being collected in. Marion MacClellane and Grissell Gordoun were both made to hand over silver which belonged to their bairns and Lady Cardyness deposited 15 ounces and 15 drops, which was more than was required and a small amount was returned. The stricture with anti-Covenanters could have resulted in destitution for their dependants, but allowance out of their confiscated estates, called a competence, was made. This was set at one third of the value of land worth less than 1,000 merkis a year; property worth more was handed over to the government and the Estates would arrange maintenance payments. Agnes Gordoun was given a competence of her anti-Covenanter minister husband's income, which amounted to the kirklands of Dunrod which she had to till and farm.[15] Some women did not take confiscation lightly. Margaret Dunbar refused to accept the commandeering of her husband Gilbert Browne's lands which had evidently been in the second category. Instead of watching his corn harvested and taken away for the use of the state, she intrometed it, in other words Margaret went to the lands in Nuntone and cut the corn herself and took it away. For this she was arrested and put into 'suir ward' until she found 'caution to abstein'. This of course did not solve the problem that had been one of the causes of Margaret's action. She and her children had no means allowed to them upon which to live. But because the land was valued at over 1,000 merkis she had nothing until the Estates sorted out a competence. The committee at Kirkudbright was powerless in the matter, Margaret was advised to go to the estates herself and 'use her best diligence' to encourage action in her case. This could not happen before 1 January 1641. Faced with the impossibility of Margaret's present situation, nine days after her arrest the committee had to order the Commissioner Deputy William Glendonyg to give her three 'bolls was of meil' (meal). On 1 January as Margaret should have made her way to Edinburgh, the committee again received a petition from her and in response allowed her three bolls of meil, again to last her family three weeks. This time would be the last until the Estates issued the necessary instructions.[16] Margaret Dunbar was not alone. Mary Murray and Bessie Geddes described themselves and their children as reduced to 'extreme miserie and hardness', when they petitioned the committee for competence [an allowance] from their husbands' estates. Margaret Vans said she and her four children would be rendered destitute through the intrometing (seizing) of her husband's lands by the Estates.[17] The Committee of War was given a complex set of instructions regarding the allotment of Margaret Vans' husband's estates in her favour, coming to a total of 800 merkis a year.

Way to the south in London, the Venetian ambassador was very perceptive when it came to analysing what was the second war since he had arrived back in August 1638. He had picked up on, or been fed, the notes of discontent. He had remarked in 1639 that the king's religious policy in England was 'estranging people from their prince, whose love was a treasure only recognised in extreme necessity'. For the wars with Scotland the king was attempting to draw upon that treasure. Giustinian had noted on the eve of the first war in May 1639, on the arrest of Lord Saye and Sele and Lord Brooke for refusing to take the oath of loyalty devised by the king, that everyone was 'freely saying that the severity will only hasten greater troubles in England'. He had also noted when reporting fenland riots in south Yorkshire, that the king's officials were being attacked. From this he could draw the conclusions 'Thus the king had few friends in England, less in Ireland and none in Scotland, and if he does not change the nature of his rule, one foresees some irredeemable disaster.'[18] Whether or not the events of summer 1640 constituted that disaster as far as the ambassador was concerned, we cannot be certain, but he did not doubt the outcome of the war. The king's army in the North assembled slowly over the summer months of 1640, and in late August as the Scots invaded the North stood ready to defend the line of the River Tyne, with their right flank resting on the garrisoned town of Newcastle. On 28 August, General Leslie crossed the Tyne at Newburn, defeated the king's army and went on to occupy the north-east. Giustinian wrote of the battle:

> Everyone here expresses gladness at the news, and although it is forbidden under severe penalties to speak favour of the rebels, and many persons have been arrested for the offense, such devises are quite inadequate to restrain this free spoken people within bounds, so powerful is the sentiment of liberty and the question of religion, under which the Scots cleverly cloak their ambitious greed.

In the North he commented the 'country folk' readily supplied commodities to the invaders.[19]

Although the war was over very quickly, in Scotland as in Yorkshire, there were years of legal and administrative wrangles ahead. Petitions to the Estates' committees poured in. Whole communities put in claims for compensation. The people of Musselburgh petitioned for relief because of entertaining or billeting what they seemed to have referred to as the 'south regiment'. They were awarded £12,000. The bailies, provost and council of Perth was repaid £2,539 18s 1d for the donation of silverware. Baillie James Law of Kirkalsoe received £5,000 as part payment of £11,514 18s of victuals loaned for the public use.

Dundee was repaid only 3,014 merkis of the 14,000 merkis loaned and was paid £6,333 3s 3d for the silverware donated during the war, but only in March 1642.[20] Individuals claimed too: Robert Buchan's estates were being intrometed despite his sufferings and loss in the late troubles. Florence Gardiner's meadows at Cortophine had been eaten up and destroyed, she received 560 merkis compensation, Baxter James Gib had given over 100 bolls of wheat and bread to the army. It took until March 1642 to receive 1,000 merkis compensation. A widow, Isabel Attane, too received 1,000 merkis compensation for her losses.[21]

Some compensation claims took a good deal of examination. Four commissioners were appointed to examine claims that a bark from Berwick had been stopped at sea and robbed of their cargo of biere (barley). The four survivors out of the five witnesses were called, Thomas Forves, John Kennedy, Alester Lidney and John Sidney, to give evidence. However, the order issued on 8 November 1642 acknowledged that the hearing would take some time as the men were all sailors and at sea for much of the time.[22] The maimed soldiers had to be attended to and this could also take some time. Davis Edmestin had been 'schott' and wounded at Edinburgh Castle, but his case was not dealt with until December 1641 when the committee ordered Archibald Sydserff to pay compensation for the future 'And yt for all bygones precedit this dait'.[23]

At the beginning of the 1640s Irvine in Ayrshire was a growing market town and port on the River Irvine developing a sense of its own identity. In the wake of the Bishop's wars the burgh had secured the recognition of its corporate rights by the Committee of Estates.[24] The burgh had had to pay heavily for the war. On 20 January 1641 the town was presented with the bill for its contribution for repayment of a loan advanced by merchants in far off Campvere (Veere).[25] Veere in the Netherlands was the staple port through which Scottish merchants traded with the United Provinces and there was a sizeable Scots community there. The merchants were governed by a conservator and factors. A battle developed within this administrative group in 1637. The office of conservator was a royal appointment and the holder Sir Patrick Drummond remained loyal to the king. The factors, including Thomas Cuningham, with whom Drummond was already at odds, took the side of the Covenant. Sidestepping Drummond the factors and the other merchants collected arms and supplied ships for the Covenanters.[26] They also sent 150 guilders as a loan. This had to be paid back at a rate of 8 per cent interest, and Irvine had to pay its share. The money was required by 13 May and the Estates felt the obligation was a heavy one. The burghs were ordered to collect their contributions straight away and then deduct it themselves from future taxation levies.

In the wake of the second Bishop's War the defeated king himself had to confirm all of the political and religious changes forced upon him. In August 1641 Charles travelled to Scotland to ratify the constitutional changes and the Treaty of London which officially ending the war. The presence of the king during 1641 was a problem for the Covenanters. In England the king's opponents were finding it difficult to keep up the momentum for further reform.

Strafford was dead and Laud was imprisoned and the war with Scotland over, and the king seemed less of a menace. For the Covenanters too it was increasingly hard to present the apparently impotent Charles as an enemy of Scotland, even though they were rightly suspicious of his intentions. The king had hoped to foment trouble by creating a 'Royalist' party. A planned *coup d'état* , in which Charles was heavily implicated, was exposed in October. To prevent any threat from people openly expressing support for Charles, the Covenanters wanted to have soldiers on duty in high-risk areas. But they needed pretexts, so for instance forces raised in the south were to guard against 'moss-troopers' who were allegedly at work on the borders. With these units they maintained a threatening force going 'to and fro through the country, to terrify disaffected people'.[27] The exposed *coup*, known as the Incident, was soon swept aside as news of the Irish Rebellion reached Edinburgh and negotiations for a joint military response opened between Edinburgh and London. These negotiations were soon subsumed into wider discussions on the king's role in these planned military operations. In England this issue quickly became part of a wider argument between king and Parliament which saw the development of two armed camps by late spring and open war by the autumn.

The Civil Wars, 1643–7

In 1642 the first reaction of the Scots was to remain aloof from the growing estrangement between Charles I and the English Parliament, the second reaction was to offer mediation once war had broken out. The king treated these moves coolly and distanced himself from the Scots commissioners sent to meet with him at his war-time capital Oxford during 1643. He preferred to work with the Marquis of Hamilton who suggested that a moderate faction in the government could hold Scotland out of the war. He was also considering a plan for armed intervention in Scottish affairs. Rumours of this and hints that Ormond was negotiating with the Irish rebels convinced many in Scotland that there was a danger of invasion from Ireland and negotiations were opened with the Westminster Parliament. Before the news of the Cessation arranged in Ireland reached Scotland the Estates had joined with the Parliament in a Solemn League and Covenant. A Scottish army would be sent into England in January 1644.

The rumours picked up in Edinburgh had foundation, for plans were drawn up to send a small Irish force into the west of Scotland to try and draw the Scottish forces out of east Ulster. These ideas were given concrete form once it was clear that the Scottish forces in Ireland were determined to continue fighting after the Cessation. Alasdair MacColla's first campaign in the Western Isles placed an immediate burden on the Scottish Burghs. MacColla had been sent with Ranald MacColla on a 'prolonged raid' through the Western Isles in November 1643 with about 300 men. This was one shadow of the Earl of Antrim's plan to link together the still fairly distinct conflicts on either side of the Irish Sea through an alliance between the king and the Confederation of

Kilkenny. The plans were not fully realised in 1643, because widespread acceptance of a deal between the king and the Irish Catholics would be impossible to obtain; the king's Protestant friends as well as his Protestant enemies would be appalled and alienated. Besides which, the Earl of Ormond was determined to act as a bulwark against any close relationship with the confederates whilst open freedom for their faith remained a crucial part of the their terms. This limited the appeal of such an alliance for the confederates, only the Old English faction showed great enthusiasm for Ormond's terms. The MacColla raid was almost the only manifestation of the Antrim plans, and it could be seen to relate most directly to Antrim's clan ambitions rather than any grand strategy, as it was focused on 'lost' MacDonald lands in the Western Isles and Kintyre.[28] By the end of November the news of MacColla's expedition had reached Edinburgh and the Estates quickly dispatched the Earl of Argyll to the west. On 6 December, just a fortnight after Argyll had been given his commission as king's lieutenant to deal with what was described as a 'foreign' invasion, Argyll contacted Irvine. He asked for 1,000 lb of locally produced powder for his forces 'that are going out in the expedition against Alaster McDonald and his complices'. The town excelled itself, for a fortnight later 10 barrels from the newly constructed powderhouse on the Golffields had been sent to Argyll.[29] At the end of June, Argyll reported that the rebels were defeated, although at great cost to himself. The main thrust of MacColla's raid was over and the leaders driven to the far-flung isles.[30] It was costly for the burghs in the area, such as Irvine, for despite Argyll's boasting, ammunition was still needed. Ayr and Irvine had to supply another 2000 lb 'to the effect it may be haisted to me with all expeditioune possible ffor I stand in neid of it' wrote Argyll from Ardnamurchane on 9 August.[31]

Argyll's boasts were shallow ones; the following year, MacColla was back in the west with his Irish and Highland forces. Moreover, in July 1644 he was joined by the Earl of Montrose with a commission from the king. This renewed campaign saw the extraordinary success of the small Royalist-Irish-Highland army right across the country. Montrose and MacColla defeated all the armies sent into the Highlands after them during 1644 and 1645. After the king's standard was raised on 28 August Montrose advanced on Perth and defeated a Covenanter force at Tippemuir on 1 September and entered Aberdeen after a fight at the Justice Mills on 13 September. Over the winter, attempts were made to trap the Royalists in the Highlands but on 2 February 1645 Montrose defeated the Earl of Argyle at Inverlochy. A new army was sent to trap Montrose as he advanced on the lowlands in April, but this army was in turn defeated at Auldearn on 9 May.

Two months of campaigning in the Cairngorms ended on 2 July at the Bridge of Alford when Montrose defeated William Baillie's forces. This battle was in turn followed by an advance into lowland Scotland. By now news of Charles I's defeat at Naseby in England had reached the north and Montrose planned to lend support to the king. The remains of two defeated armies followed

Montrose's march towards Glasgow. Baillie wanted to turn the Royalists before they reached the second city, but Argyll wanted to crush his enemies. Montrose turned to meet his pursuers at Kilsyth on 15 August and defeated them. The last of the Covenanter home armies was destroyed and Scotland seemed to lie at Montrose's feet.

It was not until after this spectacular campaign had reached its climax that Irvine had to undergo its greatest trial. Even with Kilsyth won, Montrose could not advance on Edinburgh because of plague there. Instead he had to summon a meeting of the Estates at Glasgow, something David Stevenson has argued lessened the credibility of his victory.[32] Even so, people began to court him and Montrose received the submission of the timorous Royalists and Covenanters at Bothwell castle. MacColla, on the other hand, turned to the west to prevent the re-establishment of Campbell or Covenanter fortunes and to try and raise recruits. Diehard Covenanters, the Earls of Eglinton and Cassillis were known to be in Ayrshire raising forces. When MacColla approached the earls disappeared, but they left behind everyone else and the landowners and tenants were forced into buying MacColla off. Eglington's tenants met and offered MacColla 4000 merks, 600 of them immediately, the rest at the end of September.[33] The army then marched down the road to Irvine. What happened there was described a couple of years later by John Dunlop, a former baillie of the town, when he tried to claim compensation for his own losses. Many people were claiming compensation, but Dunlop tried to emphasise his particular worthiness by contrasting it with the behaviour of other members of the town's governing class. Dunlop had been a baillie when MacColla arrived.

> I may say the most considerable persones and most powerfull within this burghe and ane great many mae who could win away and our Ministeris heir having fled and transportit thameselvis thair wyffes bairnes servands familie guids and geir yea even as we say bag and baggage so much they were habile to get transportit to Yrland or uthir partes beyond sey …

Needless to say this was because of the fear of MacColla's approach, but it also did nothing to calm things, 'thair being universallie upon all ranks but exceptioun a universall panik'. The magistrates of the town (and Dunlop implies that he was one of them) sent away their wives and goods and prepared to leave too. The 'crafts and commonalitie' who could not run then turned up and demanded that the baillies stay. Dunlop and the others were told in no uncertain terms that if they left and did not represent the town then the fear was that 'it was the hei way to mak tham sack rase and distroy the whole toun … that thair sould not be a memorie hearefter of a toun'. Dunlop and the others were then told that if they betrayed the town in this way 'we sould gett many a curse'. So they stayed and negotiated 'tollerabile quarters' from MacColla. MacColla confirmed that fleeing would have resulted in the town being assaulted and suffering 'more scaith and hairscheip than he could speak of'. Their 'selfless' action, Dunlop reported, thereby saved the people who stayed. Perhaps with undue smugness he added that those who returned from their exile 'had aither house or hold undestroyit to returne unto'.

Dunlop's particular gripe was that having saved the town he was then after the war fined by the zealous committees investigating the actions of suspects during the war. Dunlop was fined 80 merkis for 'comlyence'. With some justification he was calling for the town to compensate him for the fine.[34]

The Royalist campaign was to suffer a major defeat when the main army lost the Battle of Philliphaugh on 13 September 1645, but scattered groups continued to fight on in the Highlands. Attempts to defeat those under MacColla in the days after Philliphaugh cost Irvine more powder in February 1646. Argyll had written to the provost, James Blair, of a 'want of ammunitione for the Expeditioune I intend and because it cannot be brought in time from such place quher it may bee', Irvine was thus asked for two barrels 'and lykeday matche proportionabll'. The war itself still cost money: bills totalled on 19 January 1647 for Irvine showed that the burgh had paid £1,863 for nine months maintenance by that date.[35] At the same time there was widespread plague and coping with this required yet more money. The bubonic plague, which had stopped Montrose reaching Edinburgh, had been affecting southern Scotland for two years and the burghs were expected to help the victims; Irvine sent £90.[36] In the wake of the war there were the military casualties to care for. The Irvine baillie, William Wishart, was in charge of distributing the allowance for the families of soldiers wounded or slain in Ayrshire. Between 1 February and 14 March 1648 he paid out over 4,340 merkis to thirteen parishes.[37]

War and private concerns

Of course, Civil War could be used as a cloak for revenge. In 1644 Aberdeen merchant Alexander Jaffray, the thirty-year-old son of a three-times provost, was a graduate of Marischal College and had been married to Jean Dun for twelve years. He had been a baillie of Aberdeen in 1643 and now he was a stentor or tax assessor charged with raising the town's contribution of 18,400 merkis, for the 'Ingland expedition'.[38] Jaffray's father had been provost in 1638 and had been one of the first in the town to sign the Covenant and Alexander himself had taken the Covenant in 1638 when the Commissioners came to Aberdeen to debate with the doctors. During the early months of 1644 Jean Dun was seriously ill. At seven o'clock in the morning of 19 March Sir John Gordon, Laird of Haddo, with a handful of other lairds and about sixty armed men came to the Jaffray household to seize Alexander, his brother John and two colleagues. The prisoners were victims of the Marquis of Huntley's north-eastern rebellion and had been seized as Covenanters and enemies of the king. The quarrel between Jaffray and Haddo was now closely related to the ongoing war and some elements of the affair had its origins in 1638 when Haddo tried to have

Alexander's father indicted for treason. There were more recent manifestations of the quarrel with no real political content. In 1643 Jaffray as part of his duties as a baillie of Aberdeen arrested a servant of Haddo's for assault. Haddo reacted violently, attacking Alexander and his brother John with pistols (which fortunately misfired) and with swords, wounding them both. In turn they prosecuted the laird before the Committee of Estates, and won substantial damages, although Haddo had effectively gone to ground, only re-appearing when the Royalist rising began. Now in 1644 Haddo had concocted a story about Jaffray and the others having passed information to the government about Huntly. Once again Haddo was very violent during the seizure of Jaffray and his colleagues; he had fired his pistols at Jaffray as he chased him through the study of Jaffray's father's house. Haddo also took the opportunity to steal Jean's rings and chains as well as 'silver work' and papers. Three days after their arrest, Jean died. Not being with her when she died was one of the great regrets of Jaffray's life for which only his belief that God was with her brought relief. The prisoners were held for about seven weeks. The last five weeks were spent at Auchendown Castle until Huntly expelled them as the Marquis of Argyll's forces began marching northward. The released men then went on to join Argyll's siege of Haddo's house at Kelly, where, ironically, Haddo was based. After the house was surrendered, Jaffray went to the now imprisoned Haddo to get back the stolen property and to try and get the laird to confess his wrongdoing, and perhaps to acknowledge speeding Jean's death. When he gave back the jewels, Haddo also told Alexander stories about how his trusted pistols had only ever misfired when pointed at Jaffray. God, Jaffray concluded later, had marked him out.[39]

He could only draw the same conclusion when looking back at the storming of Aberdeen by MacColla and Montrose on 13 September 1644. Jaffray, again a baillie of the town and member of the Estates for the town, fought at the Battle of Justice Mills and luckily escaped with his life when, fighting with the town's armed levies, he had 'staid too long in the field, after our men began to run'. A fellow baillie, Matthew Lumsdenen, was killed at the fight and two more burgh officers were killed when the town was stormed.

> for the enimye entring the toune immediatlie, did kill all old and young, whom they fond on the streittes, amongst whome wer two of our touns officiares, called Breck and Patrick Ker. They brak up the prison hous doore, set all warderis and prisoneris to libertie, enterit in verie manny houssis and plunderit thame killing sic men as they fand within[40]

Jaffray's father's house was one of those destroyed by the occupying forces and Jaffray himself fled with Lord Burleigh and took refuge with the earl marischal at Dunottar Castle.[41] In their wake Aberdeen was occupied for several days by the Irish and Highland forces:

Thus, Thir Irishis contynewit Fryday, Setterday, Sonday, Mononday. Sum Women thay pressit to deflor, and uther sum thay took perforce to serve thame in the camp. It is lamentabill to heir how thir Irishis who had gottin the spoyll of the toune did abuse the samen. The men that thay killit thay wold not suffer to be bueit, bot tirrit thame of thair clot-this, syne left thair nakit bodeis lying above the ground. The wyf durst not cry nor weip at her husbandis slauchter befoir hir eyes, nor the mother for the sone, nor dochter for the father; whiche, if thay war hard, then thay war presentlie slayne also.[42]

Although appointed to Estates committees and to the Committee of War for Aberdeenshire in the summer of 1644 and a target for arrest during the Royalists' campaign in Scotland, Jaffray managed to keep out of the Royalists' way for most of that catastrophic year. After the battle of Kilsyth he was taken prisoner. Jaffray was now locked into a cycle of revenge. He was blamed for Haddo's execution following his capture of Kelly in July 1644. One of the treason charges levelled at him was Jaffray's earlier imprisonment.[43] His new arrest was accompanied by violent language, but in response to what Alexander believed was God's wonderful providence towards him,

all the time of our being prisoners, which was for the space of either five or seven weeks, though they were a company of as vile, profligate men as any I did ever see; yet there was so much restraint laid on them, as they carried themselves very before us. And somtimes some of them were content to be present at our privaye exercise of God's worship, morning and evening, which was constantly performed by that gracious and worthy man Mr. Andrew Cant ... Yet they did go on, in the frequent practice of their drunkeness and abominable vices ...

These vices seem to have driven the prisoners into a desperate plan to free themselves. They seized control of the house where they were kept and held it until rescued by Middleton's forces. By this time the Battle of Philliphaugh had been fought and the Royalist cause was in decline.[44]

In one sense the cycle of revenge continued. In February 1646 Jaffray was appointed to the committee of Estates for proceeding against Malignants and Delinquents which was to deal with the defeated Royalists. Jaffray was involved in the committee work at Dundee. In later life he looked back at what he did there with regret: 'We sat at Dundee for the space of three months, and proceeded too rigorously in these things committed to us; and sometimes since, I have had some desires to repent for that unwarranted zeal.'[45]

That same year, God again preserved Jaffray against harm saving him from infection during the five or six months that plague was raging in Aberdeen. Jaffray as a magistrate was involved in the attempts to contain the infection and the provisions for dealing with the sick and dying and as he said 'I was every day among the sick people.' The reasons for Jaffray's survival would only become clear to him at a later date; at the time he probably took little time to consider the reasons. His life was busy, he remarried, this time to the godly Sarah Cant, daughter of his friend the minister. Together they had eight children of whom only three survived; only one of ten of his children with Jean survived until Jaffray wrote his memoirs.[46]

Perspectives on divisions within Scotland

Charles I surrendered to the Scottish forces besieging Newark in England on 6 May 1646. This was not so much an attempt to end the war, but the beginning of an attempt to continue it by other means. By surrendering to the Scots he hoped to drive a wedge between them and the factions which opposed both the continuance of the Scots in the war south of the border and the establishment of a Presbyterian church in England and Wales. This policy would bear fruit at the end of 1647, but it would be a more complicated outcome than Charles probably expected for it would break apart Scottish unity. In Scotland there were critics of the 1643 alliance who were happy to join sides with the king in 1647, but many for whom such an alliance was abhorrent.

The alliance with England known as the Solemn League and Covenant dragged Scotland into the war with the king in England and Wales. Not all of the Covenanters were convinced of the Westminster Parliament's war aims, or its plans for the Church. Henry Guthrie signed the Covenant in 1637 and accepted that his title of Bishop of Stirling was a vain and unnecessary title. Since 1638 he had sat in the General Assembly of the Kirk. This past and his fears for the future were revealed when the state of the Church of England was being debated. Scotland was to send representatives to the Westminster council of Divines. This was to be an 'all party' discussion on the Church and was open to all shades of protestant opinion, although many conforming or Laudian members of the English Church refused to attend. Guthrie was clearly aware of the discussions in the Westminster Parliament during 1640 and 1641. He knew that the London petition which became known as the Root and Branch petition, because of a phrase calling for the abolition of the hierarchy of the Church 'root and branch', had failed to win sufficient backing. This he seemed to believe was a mark of how undecided the English were on the issue of Church reform. He echoed the London petition when in his diary he recorded his own declaration to the General Assembly upon its receipt of letters from London to the effect that 'they purposed to extirpate Episcopacy root and branch'

> he observed the assembly of divines in their lette, and the parliament, in their declaration, were both clear and particular concerning the privative part, viz. that they would extirpate Episcopacy root and branch; but to the positive part, what they meant to bring in, they huddled it up in many

ambiguos general terms: So that whether it would be Presbytery, or Independency, or anything else, God only knew ...

This clearly meant to Guthrie that Scotland, with its special Covenant with God, and a Church which was constructed to the unadulterated law of God, could not join with the Westminster Parliament. For this reaction, Guthrie was cried down and presented as a malignant seeking to confute the work of the Church.[47] It is clear from the concerns expressed here how a convinced Covenanter like Guthrie could apparently drift from the position of 1638 to one in which he later sided with the king against the Westminster Parliament. Guthrie had always sought the defence of the Kirk against foreign intrusion. In 1637 this had been Anglicanism. In 1640–41 the king had been brought to (apparently) agree with this stance. In 1643 there was a new threat, from the congregationalists who did not want a state or monolithic Church. By 1647, when Guthrie believed that Scotland sold out the king, Charles was the only political body promising to defend, or at least not expose, the Kirk to independency. It was a path he was not travelling alone.

Others of course did not concur immediately. Robert Baillie went southwards on the signing of the treaty and sent public reports home from London where he was based as a representative to the Council of Divines. On 14 May as the Army of the Solemn League and Covenant achieved control of northern England, he reported firstly upon the attempts to attack Oxford, the king's headquarters, and then turned to the north. There was he wrote:

> small hope of relieving Yorke, or saving any part of the North, from the hand of the Scotts. Their hopes in force are near an end; they have therefore returned to their old wayes of treacherous plotting.

But Baillie was really worried about something else. There were unfounded rumours that the king was preparing to come to London and throw in his lot with Parliament. This would endanger the position of the Kirk, for Baillie feared that this meant he was going to side with the anti-Presbyterians: 'This is now our greatest feare.' His brief report on the council business was exceedingly vague in this letter. In it he mentioned a fast and seemed hopeful of progress, but no details of the work were given. In a private letter three days later to Mr Spragg, he elaborated on his fear of the Independents, something which was bringing him closer to Henry Guthrie's position on the dangers expected from England.[48]

The war in Scotland which developed from the small campaign of Alaistair MaColla in the summer of 1644, soon dominated correspondence between Baillie and others. This was a puzzling time, for God was clearly angry with the Scots. Already by April 1645 when a worried correspondent communicated with Baillie, the Marquis of Argyll had been defeated, Aberdeen stormed and the Argyll region plundered. Only the Lord could be responsible, for 'The world believed, that Argyll could have been maintained against the greatest armie as a countrie inaccessible; but we see there is no strength or refuge on earth against the Lord.' And this defeat was inflicted by 'Some fifteen hundred naked Scots Irishes'.

Perhaps some of the blame lay with Parliament which 'had triffled much time in neddles debates' or on the people upon whom 'a careles stupid lethargie had sesed upon'. This did not only affect Scotland, for it threatened the Four Nations, but if Parliament and the people had to return to their old rock, God, and put aside 'jealousies and divisions', then

> Scotland shall be in peace, and send back the sojours now it makes use of, with such increase, that Lesley, with ane better army than yet he has commanded, shall march across the Trent, and Monro to Connacht and Munster.

England could not be relied upon, for the New Model Army consisted of inexperienced, 'raw sojours'. Few of the officers were thought to be deserving of their position, and worse still, 'many of them are sectaries'. In the House of Commons Baillie saw about him Erastian 'lyke to create us much more woe than all the sectaries of England'.[49]

When the war was nearly over Baillie was no less uncertain, writing:

> The leaders of the people seem inclyned to have no shadow of a King; to have libertie for all religion; to have bot a lame Erastian Presbyterie; to be so injurious to us, as to chase us home with the sword.[50]

On May 15 he reported that the Scots commissioners' letters were being opened by command of the Westminster Parliament, prompted no doubt by the surrender of the king to the Scots a week earlier, by which he had intended to drive wedges between the allies. Baillies' hopes for Presbyterianism were now resting in the king.[51] They did not remain there long. In August Baillie had become convinced that the king's refusal to accept the proposals put to him at Newcastle would end his reign and take the monarchy with it. 'We have small hopes of doeing any more with him and many thousands more of his best subjects.' This would lead to the triumph also of the Independents, or as Baillie called them 'the schismatics'.[52]

The experience of war

The wars had had enormous effect on people's estates and the lives of those who survived, as Jaffray's family history proved. When he petitioned the Committee of Accounts and Monies, John Linsey of Wilmerston in Fife noted that he had been personally involved in the wars since the first expedition against Aberdeen and the Marquis of Huntley, and he had barely escaped at Kilsyth. During the Civil War he had been raided by Lord Gordon's horse which had taken 'horse meile and uther movable to a considerable sume'. Not only that but he had been taken prisoner northwards

> where they deteinit me for the space of one yeir and ane quater in great misere quhill I was necessitat to pay for my freedome the soume of 4500 merkes for the which I have recevit no satisfaction thus with the common burdens ... I can hardlie maintain my old father and family ... [53]

Lady Helen Elphinston claimed that in 1644 she and her tenants had lost over £3,147, due to plundering and quartering. Alexander Campbell had lost £3,835 on his Isle of Bute lands because of the 'public enemy'.[54]

Sir John Murray, 'an aged man' of Philliphaugh, lost more than that. For many people the battles of the Civil War in Scotland produced additional personal burdens. Whilst many could view them with some detachment others could not. Detachment did not mean that they could be viewed lightly, for those who believed that God was directing the actions of the Covenanters, Inverlochy, the Bridge of Alford, Auldearn and Kilsyth must have imposed great mental burdens, inspiring soul searching to find the cause of these grievous defeats, but for others the defeats were more personal. Of the effect of the war, Sir James claimed 'I am uterlie ruined ... tenantis was spoyed plundered and taken away ... '. But more than that, he continued:

> [I remain] ... a faithful and honest as becomes a firm Covenanter and good patriot. And I find that it is noted how I lossed a hopefull gentleman that was my son at the battle of Auldairne who was the staff of my old age. In the north against the said rebell James Graham qhuch many of your number can certifie and that my quality and condicion before my sad loss was in honest way of living with my wyffe and numerous childrin and family.[55]

Catherine Findlay was reduced to petitioning the committee of Accounts and Monies for her husband Lieutenant John Shyne's arrears; he had been killed at Kilsyth.[56]

On the Highland fringes the shifting alliances of 1644–5 had allowed for traditional clan rivalries to be continued under the cover of war. The Frazers carried the war to their rivals the MacIntoshes and the Inverness Committee of War on the first two days of August 1645. The committee ordered the Frazers to recompense the MacIntoshes for the losses, some of which had been extensive. John MacIntosh had lost 12 oxen, a calf, a bull, 2 'twa year olds', 32 ewes, 8 weders, 3 lambs and a goat amongst other things. Janet Myne lost 4 oxen. The raid seems to have been little more than a cattle raid, for although some 'stookis' [stooks] of corn along with a few bolls were taken most of the losses were live-stock, kine, goats and sheep.[57] It would seem that the case for recompense dragged on until at least 1648.

Although the war in England and Wales had ended in 1646, there was a great backlog of claims for compensation and demands for repayment of loaned money. The problem of dysfunction in some elements of national and local government led to the bitterness of late 1647–8 and the renewed war, yet at least for a time there was no fighting. In Scotland there was not the luxury to regard the war as a past issue. Continuing warfare in the Highlands meant that, unlike England and Wales, Scotland did not have a period of even relative stability. Claims for financial compensation, restitution or freedom from future levies were therefore up against the demands for continued high levels of government expenditure and were often dealt with only slowly. By 1647 Captain John MacNab was claiming destitution for his 'affection to this cause', as he put it in his claim for Scots £15,000 to the Committee of Accounts and Monies. Most of the MacNabs appear to have been embroiled in Montrose's campaigns under the leadership of the clan chief Smooth John MacNab.[58] If Captain MacNab had gone against this trend it cost him dearly. His estates were clearly used by Royalist forces, for he declared that his 'ground was altogether wasted and nothing left to his familyee to live upon'. MacNab was awarded Scots £3,000 for his present needs on 1 August 1647, and the Commissar's deputies ordered to despatch a hundred bolls of meal straight away. Nothing happened. For twenty-three months, MacNab paced Edinburgh corridors, seeking out Sir James Stewart daily, writing and presenting petitions. Not until 24 July 1649 was the man rewarded for his loyalty, not with the £15,000, but with the overdue bolls and £3,000.[59]

At Crathie in the inland Aberdeenshire Highlands, this long continuation of the war is clearly seen.[60] Most of the twenty-four people who registered their losses with the Committee of Accounts and Monies referred to three occasions when the village was descended upon by armed forces: by Lord Gordon's section of the Royalist forces in 1645, by Lieutenant-General Middleton's portion of the Army of the Solemn League and Covenant in 1647 and by David Leslie's Covenanter force in 1649. Seven people mention other visits in the summer of 1647, again by Middleton's men, and a further visit in November that year, where again the implication is that these are Middleton's men.[61] For most people the visit of Middleton's men was the most dramatic. Indeed of the Scots £3,851 19s 4d of livestock, plaid and victuals taken in all of the recorded raids, almost Scots£2,500 worth was taken, 65 per cent of the total, in 1647. This figure needs explanation. Certainly there are some factors which skew the sum. The minister, Alexander Fenes claimed losses of £951 16s 8d, all of which (apart from two pistols at £16) was lost in 1647. Yet even with Fenes removed from the equation, 1647 still accounted for 53 per cent of the losses. Certainly too these recorded sums owe something to the imagination. When they do embrace a fraction of a pound rather than a whole sum, the amount is usually 6s 8d or 13s 4d, in other words a noble or a merk. There are other factors to consider. The money handed to Lord Gordon, the enemy of the government, may well have been considered lost money, useful as a background to Crathie's claim to be allowed lenient collections in future levies, whereas the money paid to the state, that is to Middleton and Leslie, might be reclaimed in part. Therefore the ratio may have been weighted towards the reclaimable money. In any case, clearly the people of Crathie were manipulating history in order to try and exercise control over their future. By steering their past losses towards the reclaimable section they were manipulating their collective memory or experience in the hope that they would receive either compensation for past losses or a reduction in their future payments to the public purse.

However, this may be taking caution with the Crathie figures too much to the extreme. The people of Crathie may have suffered more at the hands of Middleton, and to a lesser extent Leslie, because they were Highlanders and because they were in Gordon territory. The regiments are only named in the minister's account; there is a reference to the laird of Boyne, possibly Sir Walter Ogilvy of the Banffshire Committee of War; the troops with him would have been his retinue, veterans of the north-eastern campaigns against Montrose. The other regiment was Colonel Henry Barclay's newly formed regiment of horse, part of the Scottish New Model Army, assigned to Middleton's forces in 1647, campaigning against the Gordons. Middleton's expensive visits may have been punitive raids and the ratio of expense a reflection of this.[62] At John McKenzie's, Middleton's men did not simply take things, they destroyed them: four bolls of victual worth £26 13s 4d. The sheep farmers lost heavily, James Allmarche had thirty sheep killed, Marjorie Mitchell and Alex Ogoe twelve sheep and three lambs apiece. Many other farmers lost ewes and lambs that April and three people, including a poor cottar, watched as their spinning wheels were smashed.

5

EXPERIENCING WAR IN WALES AND ENGLAND

Wales

The Venetian ambassador's view of Wales was that it remained loyal to the king. In May 1642 he reported that the Welsh people had offered the king refuge. Certainly, Guistinian considered that Welsh loyalty could offset the lukewarm reception the king appeared to be receiving in Yorkshire. He also reported that Welsh representatives had been sent to Parliament to declare opposition to further payments of tax and to the Militia Ordinance. Levies would not be paid until the Trained Bands were in the hands of men appointed by the king. Within a month the ambassador had heard that the thirteen counties had between them offered the king 10,000 men immediately and a further 20,000 if the situation got worse. The Welsh, he believed, would devote their lives and fortunes to the king.[1] Indeed for much of the war the secretary's view would seem to be valid. Apart from Pembrokeshire, most of the country was in Royalist hands. Parliamentarian incursions eastwards along the south coast from Pembroke or the incursions into southern Wales in Spring 1643 tended at first to have temporary effects. From late 1644 onwards, however, concerted attacks into north and central Wales by troops based in the Marcher counties began to destroy the solidarity of the Royalist hold on Wales.

There were of course Welshmen and women for whom the Royalists' early hegemony was nothing short of a military occupation and even a disaster. The outbreak of hostilities in England were of great concern to Samuel Woodds, the steward of the MP Sir John Trevor's estates at Trevallyn, Denbighshire, but Wales's presumed loyalty to the crown was not top of the agenda. The letters Woodds sent to Trevor between 1637 and 1649 provide an immense amount of detail about the management of an estate in the mid-seventeenth century.[2] The vast majority of the one hundred or so letters concerns matters such as the planting of crops and lime trees and the building of walls. We are fortunate that Trevor was in London, first at the Inns of Court and then at the Westminster Parliament where he was MP for Grampound in Cornwall, for without his long absences we would not have been presented with Woodds's detailed three-paged letters.

Woodds was lucky in having a contact at the centre of things who could pass information on to him from Westminster. The descent of the two nations into war left him perplexed and worried. Events outside Woodds's locale were more worrying because they were unexplained. On 4 June 1642 he wrote to Trevor, 'no letters have come to me from you this fortnight (which makes me fear the state of things)'; by July he was referring to 'these busy and troublesome times'. On 6 August it was he who was passing news; he informed Trevor about the disruption of the market at Shrewsbury when Captain Ottley and 'his company' offered to rout what Woodds referred to as the committee – probably the deputy lieutenants in charge of enacting the Militia Ordinance. Woods portrayed the confusion: Ottley's militancy was in contrast to the other commissioners of array who 'did carry themselves fairly to the committee there' in order not to provoke hostilities. The trained band itself was divided in its loyalties and this reflected in Woodds' letter the state of the country. He asserted that the 'north parts' 'violently bad [bayed] for warre', whilst Chester and Cheshire were more for the Militia ordinance, Lancashire was carried by the Commissions [of array]. The quiet which he suggested was experienced in Flint and Denbighshire could not last long. He had heard that 'many of the gentry that had been hard at York & (as they are out) have pressed the king to draw down great forces of horse and foot from Wales … '.

'Every man' he concluded was 'favourably bent for war and bloodshed.'[3] The attempted neutralism of nearby counties, Staffordshire and Cheshire, were felt in Denbigh and Flint; on 24 November four days after the Staffordshire declaration of neutrality, Woodds reported the activities of the deputy lieutenants who drew up a list of the gentry and freeholders and issued instructions for them to be ready within fourteen days to march to anywhere in the county to deal with any disturbers of the peace. It was similar to the 'third force' established in Staffordshire and had just as little effect. By the following Spring the county was militarised and occupied by Royalists. Woodds reported that the county was quiet and the way to Chester was open but there were guards on the Dee bridges. Nevertheless, 'all men are fearful for the most pt' Woodds added.[4] A month later the general condition of the times was affecting Woodds's work. With regard to setting the pear and lime trees: 'but we have forborne both this year of troubles and I think the trees will better'.[5] At this point the letters cease; the Royalist occupation must have begun to close down the routes to London and Sir John. Only one more letter for the period of the First Civil War remains, on 23 October 1643 Woodds seems to have felt confident enough to send a long letter to Westminster; Trevor's mother had died, and the question of her inventory was problematic given the war and the commissioners of array's search for money. Woodds reported that he had been asked to rent a house to Royalist Thomas Eyton, a countyman of 'fiare condicon' who had lived many months on the county near Ruabon. Trevor's mother's house seemed appropriate and business was business.[6]

The Cessation of 1643 had great consequences for the Welsh, for the north coast was a prime site for landing forces brought back from Ireland as a result of the truce. The king wrote to Welsh sheriffs to reassure them that the soldiers landing on their coast were 'English Protestants'. He added that 'Rebellious subjects were the promoters of the rebellion in Ireland, and now they untruly charge the King ... with bringing over the Irish rebels.' Of course this was not simply to ease the minds, it was to smooth the way for the sheriff of Merioneth to collect shoes, stockings, cloaks and other apparel for 500 of the soldiers and food for 4,000 more, as 'Merioneth having been freed of many burdens which other counties have sustained in the paying and free billetting of soldiers.'[7]

The sudden appearance of soldiers could have strange consequences: Parish registers could be abandoned by fleeing ministers or simply not filled in. In the Mold in registers for 1645 is the note: 'The forces came from Worall on good Friday the 4th of April and departed not until May the 18 following being Sunday during which time no register except Mr Ellis have it.'[8]

At Panteg in Monmouthshire the carelessness of the curate and rector, absent for much of the war, was blamed for disappearance of the register, along with the behaviour of the soldiers who damaged and stole the church fabric and contents including the church chest.[9] The parish registers which did not disappear show the other effects of the war on local communities. Chepstow was garrisoned throughout the war and its baptismal records demonstrate something of the effects of war in the presence of soldiers in the town. There was a marked decline in the number of recorded baptisms during the Civil War period, something which is reflected elsewhere, such as Odiham in Hampshire where the clerk felt it necessary to comment on the irregularity of the records. In 1637, for instance, there were 29 baptisms, 27 the year following and so on; the annual average number 1637–42 was 26.5 baptisms; 1643 and 1644 were similar, but the numbers had fallen. In 1645, following a year which had seen a great deal of military action in the county, there were 39 baptisms. But by 1646 this had fallen to 11. 1647–9 saw only 20 baptisms in total. 1650–2 saw only three recorded baptisms. The numbers picked up in 1653 to eight but fell to four and three respectively for the next two years. The dissolution of the omnipotent church was having marked effects on the habits of the people of Chepstow. Burials increased dramatically as might be expected during the war, peaking at 42 in 1644 from an annual average of 25 in 1637–42. A minority of these deaths were soldiers, and the general downturn in health conditions in the town seems to have been affecting the health of everyone. Some of the soldiers died anonymously; one was 'of the trine band his name unknown killed with the fall of a wall' on 22 January 1645. A month later 'A souldier dying at the George his name unknown' was buried too. Where possible the soldiers were not left anonymous, efforts were made to record where they lived, who their commander was and at least where they had died. 1646 saw only ten burials recorded, and 1647 just two, coinciding with the dramatic downturn in the baptismal record. Just as people had not stopped being born, people in Chepstow had not discovered longevity; rather they had stopped recording their rites of passage with the

Church. There may have been a personal element to this loss and the question of replacement, for the minister Abraham Drew died in October 1646. Unfortunately the burial records are lost for the 1650s and the baptisms too are irregular after 1655.

The illegitimacy rate is worth considering as a demonstration of the disruptions caused by war to people and communities. Normally in Chepstow there seem to have been very few recorded illegitimate children baptised; there were none in most years before the war. Four appeared at the font in 1640 and the war years saw one in 1642, three in 1644 and four in 1645, thereafter none appeared. All of the illegitimate baptisms in 1645 took place in February, and all had been fathered by soldiers. Joane was the daughter of 'a soldier his name unknowne but quartered in Edward Phillipiss house in Backe Lane'. Elizabeth was the daughter of 'a soldier his name unknowne but quatered in the Courthouse'. William was the son of a 'stranger' and Anne the daughter of 'a soldier his fathers name unknown who was quartered in the widow Levis house in the Welshe street'.[10] Chepstow was held by Royalists for much of the war, but during the period when the four children were likely to have been conceived, the area of the country had been subject to Laugherne's advance from Pembrokeshire.

Trade links between South Wales and Ireland provided existing channels for the passage of war traffic. Before the war Ireland had been major market for the export of Welsh trade in coal, slate, fish and cloth and corn, although imports from Ireland were unwelcome in Wales. From the south coast Welsh traders exported a variety of raw materials and finished goods.[11] The ports in Cardiganshire and Pembrokeshire were again used in the war. Milford Haven boats plied with Cork. Even in early 1646 as trouble brewed in South Wales the ports of the country were providing a life-line to the isolated pockets of parliamentarian forces in Ireland. In February 84 barrels of malt and 180 half barrels of oats (in Bristol measures) were sent by Rowland Laugherne to the parliamentarian garrison at Cork under Inchiquin.[12]

Within Royalist-held Wales parliamentarians faced great difficulties. In Flint Evan Edwards, who may well have even served in one of the administrative posts under Royalist direction, was one such case. He had been one of the barons of the exchequer in Chester and therefore may well have been chosen for some minor role in the financial administration in the area. After the war when General Mitton and Lieutenant Colonel Gilbert Gerard sought to protect Evans from the enquiries of the County Committee, the latter referred obliquely to a possible role when he wrote he never 'used any violence or extremity to the country in forcing contribution to the Commission of Array when they were in action there'. Both Mitton and Gerard testified that Edwards had supplied parliamentarian forces himself from 1645 and had encouraged others to do so. It is clear also that Edwards had sought to flee the county during the war. His friend William Griffeth at Gareglwyd sent a long letter to Evans offering accommodation for him if he could flee. It does not appear that Evans took up the offer, because Griffeth could not find accommodation for the Evans family as he already had his brother living with him as a refugee.[13]

Little evidence survives in writing for the sufferings of Welsh men and women in their home towns and villages.[14] Generally the system of tax collection was the same as that imposed in England. With the Royalist domination of mid-Wales there seems something of a prolonged period of anarchy. The Royalist garrison at Abbey Cwm Hir began to take horses from Radnorshire communities on an arbitrary basis. Several Nantmel villagers tried to impress upon Parliament in 1646–7 the problems which were still caused by this dislocation. Edward ap Rees claimed a red mare as well as £4 of goods and chattels lost. Edward ap Stephen Meredudd lost a 50s white horse. Gruffydd ap Stephen lost his means of gaining a living. As a 'poor badger' he and his family were dependent upon the two horses, one red, one black, to carry grain from market to market. The theft of the horses and 21 bushells of grain was a disaster for him, his wife and their six children. It was an unresolved problem three years later. Families like Gruffydd ap Stephen's could not draw upon other resources to compensate: there were no other estates, rents or sources of income available to them. There was also the fear of anarchy and violence. Stephen Powell recorded: 'they in the nighttime threw open the doores of his house and tooke from him divers goods and some wearing apparell and in money three pounds or thereabouts, one bay horse worth 3li 10'.[15]

By comparison the steady collection of tax must have paled even when it was continuous and heavy. By autumn 1645 Parliament was collecting taxes regularly at Lanstantffraid in Elfael and backdating them to May that year. Three months money every two months, ensuring that by June 1646 payments were being made in advance. On top of the taxes was quartering and in some cases scrupulous records were kept as at Bettus Disswerth. At Nantmel however, the costs could not be verified.

In Lantillio Crosseny, Walter Powell kept a diary of which a major part was back-dated. He filled in details of his early life when he began to keep the diary proper as a record of passing events. It is not entirely clear when he began to keep the record daily, it may have been at the end of the war. It does appear clear that he either kept notes at the time or collected material from the newspapers to enable accurate dating later. Much of Walter's diary records the life of Lantillio Crosseny; he records deaths and births, the illnesses of his friends, and the visits of his family and their journeys on business to 'Bristow'. In 1640 he gives an insight in to the problems suffered by his Catholic neighbours. He records their burials at night. One, William Hughes, he recorded as dying on 13 February. On the night of 14 February, two butchers buried Hughes 'unlawfully' at night.[16] In April 1639 Powell's diary began to record the national affairs with which it was to become briefly obsessed. Under April that year he recorded 'Ye soldiers pressed to go for Scotland', but it was in 1643 that Walter's diary became absorbed by the war. By then Powell was working for the Royalist administration and his papers included details of the taxation in Skenfrith

Hundred and for the tax collected in his own village.[17] He still kept details of the life and death of the parish, but national and local Civil War events intruded extensively. He was clearly writing the fair copy of the diary – that which has survived amongst his papers – at a later undisclosed date, probably after the war, possibly in the early 1650s. It is possible that he put it together on an annual basis. That there is a later compilation date is shown by his entries which record battles on the date they occurred, not on a later date when the news reached him. Brentford on 12 November 1642 for example is recorded precisely.[18] The campaign of Spring 1643, when Sir William Waller attempted to drive a wedge between the Royalist forces in Wales and those in England, is recorded in great detail especially when Waller entered Monmouthshire and captured Monmouth on 3 April. Waller moved to Chepstow on 5 April and to Usk a day later. The Royalist commander, Sir Richard Cave, arrived in Lantillio on 11 April and county forces joined him there on 14 April. The gathering of Royalist forces continued until the last week of the month when with Orlando Bridgeman's assistance, Monmouth and Chepstow were retaken. Parochial matters dominate the few entries for the summer of 1643, but the siege of Gloucester was recorded by Powell as soon as the Royalist forces began to arrive there in mid-August. On 28 August Powell's interest became personal. 'My son Richard went towards Gloucester siege and was abroad till 1646.' There was no discussion of Richard's role at Gloucester, the diary entries are for the most part one line entries of factual information with little expansion. The raising of the siege by the Earl of Essex was recorded by Powell but there appears to be no mention of the subsequent battle at Newbury.[19] Powell's diary entries betray concern with the military campaigns of south Wales and the adjacent parts of England. In 1644 he recorded Prince Rupert's brief stay at Monmouth on 24 August and the capture of the castle by Edward Massey's Western Army a month later.[20] The concerted effort to re-establish Royalist control of the region the following spring took a toll on Powell's own resources. On 11 January Sir William Blakiston was 'at my home'. This was the time when the Northern Horse was stationed in the county. On 3 March Walter recorded: 'little nagg taken away'. The collapse of the Royalist cause created many entries recording the fall of Cardiff although there is no specific mention of the Welsh rejection of the king which precipitated the crisis.[21] By the end of summer 1645 constant demands for cash and soldiers had provoked a clubman rising in Glamorgan where the 'Peace' or 'Peaceable Army' was formed. The aims of the movement were similar to those of the English club movements, but here the demand for local officers meant Welshmen rather than foreign Englishmen. In August 1645 Charles I was temporarily powerless to refuse the demands that the county set its own taxes and create an army led by countymen. However, after making initial concessions, Charles returned to the region in September and forced the disbandment of the Peaceable Army, moreover, co-opting 1,000 men into his own forces. It was too late when the leadership of the July revolt switched allegiance to Parliament and on 17 September forced the surrender of Cardiff.[22]

The collapsing fortunes continued in 1646. Powell may have ceased working for the Royalist administration at some time in the winter. He certainly fell foul of the local Royalists. On 25 May he 'was committed prisoner at Raglan by the marshall of the garrison where I remained close till 8 June'. Whilst he was there on 29 May 'My house was plundered by parliament [forces].' Raglan was besieged by these same forces from 3 June onwards. On 8 June, probably to preserve resources, Powell was sent out towards the leaguer. He continued to record details of the siege, including Fairfax's arrival on 6 August and the eventual surrender on 19 August.[23] Powell did not keep many details of national events thereafter, indeed his diary is almost completely free of them and he returned to brief records of the local deaths, marriages and business transactions. The renewed popular revolts in South Wales in February 1646 and June 1647 are not detailed. In both of these cases they sprang from similar complaints against the county administration which had caused the collapse of the Royalist cause in 1645. The larger revolt in 1648 is also almost unrecorded. It may have been that as a former enemy of the state, Powell, decided not to keep records which may have betrayed a dangerous interest in these reactions to parliamentarian rule. The only entry made related to the capture of Chepstow from the rebels on 25 May.[24]

Letters from Trevalyn begin again in August 1646, and for the most part deal only with estate business, although the effects of the end of the war and Parliament's victory crop up. In August Woodds told Trevor that General Thomas Myton was seeking to put an army chaplain into the incumbency at Trevalyn. Woodds was doing his best to resist this with the help of Sir Thomas Myddleton. Trevor's own son, John, was being proposed for one of the vacant Commons' seats and two colonels were campaigning in the north of the shire for his cause, suggesting that there was no opposition to him there.[25] The end of the war brought administrative difficulty for the county. In November 1646 the county tried resurrecting the quarter sessions. There had been a single session held in September 1645, but none since. A major stumbling block was the absence of a gaol. Traditionally the county gaol had been a tower at the castle. The use of Holt castle as a garrison had stopped this, all the prisoners had been released by the Royalists probably at the outset of the siege to preserve food stocks. As for the new garrison 'those that hold that garrison now do hold in their power a tower in that castle of Holt which ought to be the only prison' and they showed no interest in letting it be used again, and the sheriff could find no alternative site.[26]

There was also the question of who was going to sit on the bench. Many commissioners of the peace had been Royalists, and Trevor fished for names to put forward to Parliament as suitable men. Woodds was one supplier of names, but he could not be very helpful; only six names in two letters were forthcoming, and they were not really impressive – none were listed as esquire, one was referred to as a relative of a knight 'but not a familiar of his', with the second recommendation 'he was once the coroner'. Only one, Robert Southey, could he say was of good estate and 'forward for the county'. One person he did name became Sir John's agent in the county and his correspondent in the 1650s, Mr John Peck.[27]

The war had resulted in damages to houses on the estate and the latter stages of the siege of Holt caused problems for tenants in the town. Some of their houses around the castle were burned or pulled down, probably by the defenders; naturally they could not pay rent.[28] Woodds heard in January 1647 that the castle itself was to be demolished and he wanted to get the timber from it to rebuild the lost town houses: 'others whose houses have been burnt and spoiled by the warre for without houses the lands will be worth little but if this and the building of the two other houses I will godwilling rectify'.

The question of the cost of the war imposed upon the estate as a whole was to concern much of the correspondence between Woodds and Trevor for the rest of the letters. That the estate had been under the rigorous control of the Commissions of Array is made clear in a letter of 15 January 1647 from Woodds to Lady Tirringham. The income of the almshouses maintained by Sir John had been seized as part of the estate's sequestration. The almshouses were managed by the four newly elected almoners for the duration, who had even repaired the houses during the war. Woodds was concerned to explain that the Royalists had misused the appropriated tithes of the nearby chapel, in the belief that they were traditionally used as almshouse funds. It was now a question of re-establishing some sense of normality in the running and funding of the houses.[29]

The tenants of the estate were further angered by continued billeting on them during 1647. Trevor sought the names of the officers complained about and Woodds supplied them, although he added that with regard to the quartering and associated levies:

> but they were not so much at fault as the neighbours & constables who out of duty or ill will were earnest in pressing them to it. But they are all gone ... there charge was but a night for some & another night for some other householders ... I hope we shall hear of it no more for the constables dare not come out ... since.

Disturbances in the area broke out in May, and prevented any disbanding of troops in the county. Woodds' details of the disturbances are vague, but he laid the blame for the 'outragious tumults' on 'cavaliers and women', hoping that the costs of the necessary quartering could be borne throughout north Wales and not just Denbigh. In October Woodds was tied up by the work of getting the county committee to remove sequestration from some of Sir John's land in Shropshire which had been leased to a Royalist, but to no avail, 'I lost my labour because they wanted a full number.' By the latter end of the year, Woodds was a little happier about the taxation situation, the area had as he'd hoped back in May 'supprest and quietly settled'. The numbers of troops in the county had been reduced and the county was to be charged £300 monthly maintenance.

The county, Woodds reckoned was now to be 'less chargeable than quarters or compounding for quarterering'.[30]

The war in Ireland continued to be a drain on Welsh resources. The proximity of Wales had always meant that when recruits were required for war in Ireland, Wales was looked to sooner than England, sending 1,000 men a year.[31] Before Parliament and the New Model Army became locked into their argument about the arrangements for the conquest of Ireland, Wales was sending soldiers over the sea. After trouble at the beginning of the year, the Glamorgan county committee, with the backing of Rowland Laugharne, began levying soldiers from across the county. Laugharne, the successful parliamentarian commander from Pembroke, had been appointed commander in chief in the county following the Sir Edward Carne's revolt of February 1646. The rebellion had been directed at the parliamentarian garrison installed in Cardiff following the defeat of the Royalist cause by the Peaceable Army. Following the defeat of Carne's rising Laugharne was able to levy men throughout the county. The gentry of the hundred of Neath were charged with raising money and horses to be sent to Swansea for service in Ireland. Gentlemen were grouped together and charged together £10 or a horse.[32]

The south-west of England

For much of the war large swathes of the south-west of England escaped military campaigns. The area had been a battle ground from the end of 1642 as the Royalists and parliamentarians fought for control of Cornwall and Devon. The Royalist leader, Sir Ralph Hopton, had initially struggled to gain control of the region. The Royalists' early stronghold in the region, Portsmouth, had been surrendered in September 1642 and then Lord Hertford's force had been driven into south Wales. Hopton had stayed on with the horse, raising foot regiments in Cornwall before being able to challenge the parliamentarian leader, the Earl of Stamford. At the Battle of Stratton on 16 May 1643 Stamford's army was destroyed. Sir William Waller was forced to abandon his attempt to destroy the Royalist hold on the Marcher counties and he marched southwards to block any Royalist advance on Bristol. He defeated Hopton at Lansdown on 4 July and pursued him into Devizes. Hopton was rescued by a flying army under Prince Maurice, which made a lightening march from Oxford and destroyed Waller's force on Roundway Down outside Devizes on 13 July.

From then onwards, much of the region remained in Royalist hands and with the capture of Bristol at the end of the month the king gained an important port facing Ireland and potential recruits amongst the government forces and the confederation.

Gloucester remained an important parliamentarian garrison and a barrier to easy communications between Oxford and southern Wales and the ports of Plymouth and Portsmouth remained important parliamentarian bastions which defied Royalist attempts to capture them. In the summer of 1644 the Earl of

Essex marched westwards to be pursued by the king and the Oxford Field Army. This campaign ended in Essex's defeat at Lostwithiel in Cornwall, but an enhanced parliamentarian presence was established in the region. Some thought that there was a good deal of support for Parliament in the region. Exeter, claimed the queen when she arrived in 1644 fleeing Essex and Waller's encirclement of Oxford, was no less rebellious than London, at least according to the Venetian secretary in London, Geralmo Agostini. This purported perception would certainly have confirmed his earlier optimism about the unpopularity of the Royalist cause in the west: he heard early in 1643 that Exeter had refused to pay Royalist taxes.[33] However, such optimism had resulted in Essex launching his ill-fated western campaign in the first place. In truth Exeter paid levies like anywhere else, and spent £4,374 11s 3½d on defence works between November 1642 and August 1643. This included materials such as tiles and timber, the collecting of turf to face earthworks, felling of trees for planks for walkways and buildings. The gates and bridges of the town were fortified, batteries were built and protected by specially made woolsacks. Eight houses were demolished and they impinged on the security of the walls. Wells in the castle were cleaned and repaired. Women were employed on the building work, being paid for 'carriage of stones to the Citty walls'.[34]

Urban life was generally disrupted by the war, often in unexpected ways. The borough-subsidised choir at Worcester cathedral lost its income in 1645–6 'in regard of the said warres and the kinges enemies prevalency in the same time'.[35] The outskirts of Worcester had not only seen the first pitched battle of the war when Prince Rupert defeated a detachment of parliamentarian horse at Powick Bridge, but the city had quickly been occupied by parliamentarian forces. The burden on the city council required the augmentation of the number of constables as early as 11 October 1642. More worrying was the interference in the town government by the Earl of Essex. He had at least three councillors expelled. The change of administration when the parliamentarian abandoned the town did not end interference. The new Royalist governor, Sir Martin Sandys, was admitted as a freeman and as usual in such cases entry fees were waived. The three expelled men were officially welcomed back, but Sandys wanted to know who had left the city since the Royalists arrived, presumably they were suspected of parliamentarianism. Royalist gentry were incorporated as freemen 'out of loyalty' and because of their desire 'to assist'. The council apparently bridled under the interference and sought clarification of the taxes Sandys wanted raised. In March the town balked at paying the £180 per month whilst the county was charged £3,000 a month, and suggested that the council would decide what was to be paid. They failed to move the Royalist authorities and the levy came into effect on 1 March 1643 to be assessed as a levy of a fifteenth. Only the soldiers were recorded as exempt and this caused a shortfall as some of the garrison soldiers were townsmen who normally contributed to the levies. Clearly some of these men who had employed a substitute or sent a servant in their stead were claiming exemption. An act of 23 June 1643 restricted them to an abatement of just a third.[36] Later in the year when faced with making a loan of £4,000 the town again balked and firmly refused. A committee was created to see what could be raised and on 6 October £2,000 was promised. But the very effort of raising the money itself cost the town. By the same date the arrears of expenses due to the constables amounted to £118 15s 4d.[37]

In 1644 Prince Rupert demanded the reconstruction of the town's defences. As well as 300 workers paid daily every man was expected to work or send a man or a shilling a day. There were no exemptions: choristers, ministers, deans and prebends had to join in. Outsiders present in Worcester also had to work one day a week. Everyone had to bring a spade, shovel or pick; if they did not possess one they had to buy one. The city was divided into six parts and the men forming each part laboured one day a week in rotation.[38] Worcester found itself plunged into debt to prominent male and female citizens as it tried to balance a budget strained by the general tax levies, occasional loans, velvet purses and other gifts to the king and queen. The costs of government increased too. The already augmented number of constables was doubled again in March 1644.

With these burdens imposed upon urban and rural communities, the need for the county people to draft the Woodbury Declaration and the petitions to the king and Parliament on 6 December 1644 comes as no surprise. At Woodbury members of the county gentry assembled a mass meeting of freeholders and organised a declaration demanding order and stability be reintroduced into the county's military forces and administration. These demands were essentially conservative, accepting the Church of England and the framework of government as it had stood on the eve of the war. They were also neutral conditions addressed to both sides.[39] The councillors of Royalist-occupied Worcester considered joining in with the petitions, having discussed such matters three days earlier. The governor was informed and a delegation was chosen, but by 10 December the council had cold feet and pulled out of the county petition. Ten days later all of this seemed to have been subsumed into an official petition drawn up by the council and the military governor. The city became subsumed itself into the Marcher Association, just as surely as the local club initiative became bound up with the attempted reinvigoration of the Royalist war effort and presented the Association commander, Prince Maurice with £50.[40] Later that year Maurice's help was sought to arrest those who were refusing to pay tax levies. Shortage of money plagued the council for the rest of the war. The arrival of parliamentarian forces outside the town did not improve matters in early 1646. New levies were ordered to cover the expenses of the besieged town. Careful attempts were apparently made to sweeten the bitter pill of a £240 a week levy established on 23 May 1646. It was to stand for only a month and if the siege ended it was to be cancelled immediately. It was, fortunately for the town, the end of the war. The county committee which demanded surrender were told that the town could only be handed over with the king's express warrant. Charles had already sent orders for his soldiers to stop fighting at his surrender at Newark. Worcester requested permission to send a messenger to him for the required permission on 26 May. A month later it was over and the negotiations with Colonel Edmund Whalley began. Sadly this was not the end for the parliamentarians considered the Royalist levy of £180 to be a good one and it continued to be paid until November when it was reduced to £100 a month. Interference in the town government continued with expelled councillors re-admitted and prominent parliamentarians given freeman status at the request of the new governor.[41]

In rural areas the strains of supporting the warring sides which prompted the Woodbury declaration are quite easy to see from the experiences of people who recorded their losses after the war. The bishop's palace at Hartlebury was a Royalist garrison from the early days of the war. The Royalist county administrators, the commission of array, met there in 1644 and thus the villagers of the winding streets of Hartlebury had their lives bound up with the military and administrative needs of the Royalist war effort. Claims for recompence sent to the Exchequer after the first Civil War centred on the victualling of besieging forces, including the brief appearance of the Army of the Solemn League and Covenant in 1645, and the siege in the later stages of the war. There were other levies referred to: Rector Emanuel Smith had provided materials for the Earl of Essex's forces at the beginning of the war in 1642; he also quartered some of Essex's army. The Scots had taken £97 worth of goods from him during their stay, a sum not exceeded in the later siege when Parliamentarian taxes were back-dated. Overall the Scots proved expensive, taking large numbers of sheep from the community: 20 from Emanuel Ives, 60 from William Whorler and so on. Wholer lost more, as he wrote: 'at ye siege by ye soldiers my home was broken downe standing neere ye garrison which cost me to repair it ye value of £15'. Owen Powell was injured during one attack on the town. Soldiers took pewter worth £5: 'and also almost killed him ye chirugeon had of him 5li to heale his wounds besides he will be lame of them whilst he lives'.[42] How much strain on the community expenses could be escalated by war is shown by a brief statement taken from the papers of the village of Salwarpe in Worcestershire. A note of wartime levies for one year details an income of £39 10s 6d. This includes levies for a horse for Parliament, provisions for the siege of Worcester and general military charges. These totalled £34 9s 1d out of the total sum. For 'other ordinary charges' only £5 1s 5d was necessary.[43]

In Gloucestershire the Hartpury accounts were most scrupulous in showing exactly how the levies related to land-holding and how the holdings changed or were broken up or consolidated. There, men paid about 75 per cent of levy values, whilst women paid 25 per cent. The death of Mrs Dorothy Compton, who held lands worth £50, reduced the women's contribution during the later 1640s. Individuals in the county with large estates were charged substantial amounts by occupying forces. When Sir William Waller moved through the county in 1643 first Royalist soldiers and then 30 officers, 40 horses and 120 foot from Waller's army turned up and stayed for five days at John Chamberlayne's door at Maugerbury. It cost him £27 10s. This sum was large: it bears comparison with eleven months of contribution payments which cost him only £24 15s. In every case Chamberlayne's expenses for quartering heavily outweighed general taxation.[44]

In Cornwall the invasion of the Earl of Essex in the summer of 1644 caused problems for Jonathon Rashleigh MP of Menabilly. Rashleigh totted up the cost of 18 years involvement in the Civil Wars and Republic in a jumble of remembered entries. He lost to the parliamentarian army 550 sheep, 100 lambs, 8 oxen to the baggage train, 20 milk cows, one bull, 30 fatted and 60 store bullocks, 40 horses and 80 hogs. Old corn was taken away and used, growing crops were either eaten or trampled into the soil. Hay, grasses and orchards were spoiled, his house emptied of furniture. Wool was stolen and other goods from wagon wheels to jewellery disappeared. In all he estimated his losses in that short invasion to be £12,380. This was not the total of his losses, his house at Fowey, which he valued at £1,000 was lost to him. His participation at the parliaments held at Oxford cost £100 in expenses and £50 in loans to the king. He estimated that his attendance at the Oxford and the earlier Westminster sittings had cost him a further £400 and rather gruffly recorded that 'I have spent in perpetually riding about the counties for the King's service these two years at least £300.' The collapse of the king's cause exposed his estates to fines and he was driven out of the county, but his troubles were by no means over.[45]

Lady Anne Bassett reckoned that her husband spent £1,620 5s 8d on fortifying St Michael's Mount for the king. The garrison needed new batteries, new carriages and wheels for the guns that were there. Food had to be purchased and ammunition bought in. Most of the gun and muskets put into the fortress had been purchased for the king by Sir Francis himself. He also had to pay most of the wages of the soldiers manning the fort, even though the money was supposed to come from estates in the Scilly Isles. Like Rashleigh's expenses for 'perpetually riding about' Bassett's charges were not paid.[46] Sir Richard Vyvyan was a similar case. He paid out £6,015 to the king's cause in loans and arms and wages. He had also been responsible for contributing to the cost of fortifying Helford harbour and supplying the garrison there. Fourteen years later he had not received recompence and he still owed £2,055 to the soldiers from the Helford garrison which he had owed them at its surrender.[47]

In Devon the constables of Okehampton were forced into coping with garrisons from a different angle. From the beginning of the war, the town had to supply the Royalists. Walter Hall's year in office began with finding billets for soldiers and leading recruits to the 'lord general' at Plimton. Sir Ralph Hopton made his first appearance in the accounts within a month, sending warrants to the constable through a Mr Underdown, possibly the high constable. Hall's accounts showed the sort of demands which armed forced made on a small town. Prince Maurice wanted sack, 15 gallons of it, costing £6 6s. He also needed bedding for which Okehampton had to pay 8s towards its carriage to Tavistock. Thirty one pairs of shoes were required for soldiers as well as oats, barley and wheat. Individual men and women in the town were providing work too, Mary Smythe did three pounds worth of unspecified work for the artillery, Mr Drewe a merchant provided 36 yards of canvas as did other merchants.

William Hall's experience demonstrates that even at this level there was a high degree of travelling and staying away from home just as there was at the level of the upper gentry. He recorded in his accounts the trips he made during his year of office. He had to go to Modbury on three days, Tavistock and Exeter for two days each and to Plympton for five days. The distances travelled were not small, Tavistock was a 27 mile round trip, Exeter was a round trip of 36 miles and Plympton was 27 miles away: as the crow flies, Modbury is over 25 miles away across Dartmoor, the journey Hall would have had to take a round trip of around 60 miles, through Tavistock and perhaps Plympton. Most of the time Hall was able to send someone on his behalf to the army and the garrisons with warrants, horses, timber and provisions. All of this of course was passed on to Okehampton in the form of charges.[48]

Across the south and west of the British Isles the wars and rebellions of the 1640s had a variety of effects with varying degrees of horror or deprivation. No doubt there were those in Worcester who bemoaned the absence of the choir, or those in Chepstow who decried the moral turpitude of the women bearing illegitimate children. For others war brought homelessness and destitution and death. In some areas all of these facets of war would recur periodically as the campaign raged around the four nations. That the war had a four-nations aspect was not lost on the people who witnessed the events of the 1640s. in Warwickshire as well as Cheshire and the north-east the Scots made their presence felt. The people of the south-west and Wales were alert to the Irish aspects of the war as materials passed out of the ports and soldiers went to and returned from Ireland. In Ireland the deponents were constantly informed that their own king and queen had instigated their dispossession. The accounts and experiences of those who lived through the war demonstrate the multifaceted nature of the evolving wars.

East Anglia

For the duration of the first Civil War, fighting did not impinge upon huge swathes of East Anglia. Only in the fringe counties of the region did fighting take place. The region was firmly controlled and administered by Parliament through the Eastern Association.[49] But even here it was sometimes difficult for many people to have entirely lucid perceptions of the events around them during the 1640s. Perhaps Margaret Edwards, a fishwife in Barking, Essex, had more difficulty than others, but it is probable that she was not alone in her confusion. One day in 1645 whilst in Fisher Street in Barking she met Robert White, a local yeoman. Margaret was apparently loyal to her king and knew that White had parliamentarian sympathies. This made her angry and on this particular day she could not contain herself. She created such a great tumult that White feared for his safety. He told a court that 'he was constrained to take a marsh fork from a marshman to defend himself'. White was not the only man to suffer from Margaret's ire towards those she blamed for causing the war. Edmund Palmer was a draper by profession, but in 1645 it was his turn to serve as constable. As he tried to collect taxes from the Edwardses, Margaret reviled him with the bizarre claim that 'a company of you had brought a Popish priest to town, but … the King is a-coming now, and then we shall have a course taken with you'. Nicholas Cleere heard Margaret go on to accuse the newly installed preacher Peter Witham of being a 'Papist dog'. She threatened violence towards him too saying that if she had been at a funeral he had recently conducted she would have torn the minister 'in pieces like a Papist dog as he was'.[50] Margaret's confusion could have run deep. Certainly the propaganda put out by both sides had a tendency to minimise political differences, instead playing up moral issues which created bogey figures, which resulted in Margaret's lexical confusion of papist and puritan. Margaret would not be alone in her confusion: many Royalists would perhaps have seen little to distinguish the puritan from the papist. Both were potential enemies of the state.

As Clive Holmes' work on the region has shown, being divorced from the fighting did not mean that East Anglia was freed from the effects of war, and these afflicted the Essex parish of Waltham Cross. A good part of the churchwardens' accounts were generated by disbursements made to the poor of their parish whether in peace or war. They doled out money and, in cold weather, faggots to a collection of people including Ould Jolly and Widdow Birde and to those too ill to work. They also had a separate section accounting for money paid to 'Strangers'. Although this was also a perennial category of payment, it was in this section that the effects of war begin to appear when such money was paid. In this section they included money paid to Marie Lee, Marie Haines and Elizabeth Clarke whose husbands 'weare killed by the Irish Rebbels'. These and other refugees from Ireland passed through the town, generally on their way inland from London or going the opposite way towards the city. They were joined as well by the widows of soldiers killed in the war and by wounded soldiers. Also a recorded was a payment to a Devonshire couple who were plundered by Royalists.[51]

Norfolk accounts show that East Anglian villages had had plenty of time to become accustomed to the war and its causes.[52] The Scottish war brought home to the people of Carelton Rode the financial implications of Charles I's Scottish religious policy. The village is in the south of the county bordering the large parish of Wymondham. The two constables John Nixon and Thomas Nuby had a lot to organise for the war. Four soldiers, Will Hewinge, Richard Huby, Will Lewinge and Thomas Nuddes were each provided with knapsacks, and six days training at musters had to be paid for, their Coat and Conduct money, perhaps used for sending them northwards to the war, cost £5 1s 4d. Their bandoleers and muskets needed repairing, and powder and match had to be bought. Armourers were based at the neighbouring village of Old Buckenham at the expense of the villages round about.[53] The Civil Wars saw Norfolk grouped into the Eastern Association and Carelton Rode at first contributed four soldiers to the Association army just as it had to the king's 1639 army, but it appeared that new soldiers, possible augmenting the original numbers, were raised throughout 1643. It would appear that this continued throughout 1644. The religious wars of 1639–40 continued to influence the life of the village; Constable John Smyth had to collect a copy of the Solemn League and Covenant for the village. Carelton Rode saw increasing numbers of travellers. In 1643 twenty-two civilians and an unknown number of Irish refugees passed through the village. The following year 34 civilians and two groups of Irish refugees passed through, but the most important increase in numbers related to soldiers: 13 able-bodied men and at least 40 injured soldiers had to pass through.

The same sort of numbers were seen in the village of East Harling just to the south-west of Carelton Rode. In 1643 about 100 people, Irish refugees, injured men, some of them soldiers, groups of women and children moved through the town. The 'passengers' were moving southwards to Cambridge, north to York, east to Yarmouth and west to Ely.[54]

The Midlands

In recent years historians have offered various explanations for the risings of the neutralist clubmen in the south-west and the south and west Midlands during 1645.[55] The most recent of these goes farther and attempts to explain why there were no such risings in other areas by asserting that there was a series of circumstances which explain the absence of clubmen in the latter counties, involving the ability of the local garrisons to maintain regular collections of tax. This orderly conduct was less likely to inflame local resentment which could build into anger. This argument also stresses the ability of these same garrisons to maintain order amongst themselves and overawe the local rural and urban populations.[56] Much of the evidence for the realities of the Midlands situation comes from the accounts of local constables with whom the administrations worked. As with much local government, central policy stood or fell upon the effectiveness of the constables, churchwardens and Overseers of the Poor and the consensus reached between them and the local communities. From their papers, like those of Waltham Cross, we know a good deal about the methods of collecting war-time taxes. Not all the accounts survive; the constable of Rugeley in Staffordshire had watched his house burn down, taking with it the accounts for 1643–4.[57] Others were simply not preserved; the constable at Edwinstowe in Nottinghamshire wrote in 1647 in a space left in the accounts:

wheras ther wear manye maightye accompts in the years 1642, 1643 1644 betwixt the townsmen of Edwinstowe and Myles Ouldham the then constable of the same towne w[hi]ch by reason of time of the warr could not nether then nor this daye be p[er]fected.[58]

In Staffordshire the return of the local Royalists at the end of 1642 prompted local parliamentarians to defeat them, which ended the county's bid for neutrality. In November 1642 the special sessions of the peace had ordered the creation of a 'third force' to expel forces of both sides which might attempt to enter the county. Yet the constable's accounts clearly demonstrated that by the end of the year people across the county had been drawn into the funding networks. Petty constables had visited the 'commissioners' at Lichfield as early as 29 November 1642 within days of the Justices of the Peace's attempt to declare neutrality. They were again called to Stafford by Sheriff Comberford in February and by May a provisional levy of £2,000 pounds had been imposed on the county, and collectors appointed for each of the hundreds. Proportions of tax allotted to each division and parish it seems were related to the proportions used in the levies of ship money. Accounts from Mavesyn Ridware in Offloe Hundred reveal the process of allotment and collection.[59] Between 1643 and 1645 constables travelled fortnightly to Lichfield to pay contribution to cathedral chorister Jeffrey Glasier now serving in as a captain in Richard Bagot's foot and garrison treasurer. Evidence from elsewhere in the county supports this impression, Seisdon Hundred constables were expected to travel to their local garrison Dudley.[60] The costs to the communities of the Royalist tax known as Contribution were high and they escalated. Mavesyn Ridware accounts show the yearly contribution totals for 1642–3, 1643–4 and 1644–5. In the first year (which runs for the period October to October), the total paid was £30 13s 7d. By 1643–4 this had risen to £144 17s 4d, but in 1644–5 the total fell slightly to £128 13s 3d. Total village outlay could be even higher; from 1644 onwards there were periods when taxes were paid to parliamentarians at Stafford. In 1643–4 payments of Parliament's Weekly Assessment only amounted to £47 5s 0d but the following year rose to £87 7s 9d and Royalist levies fell. It is often difficult to compare these amounts with the pre-war levies, but a few such comparisons from Staffordshire can be drawn. Biddulph levies in 1640 amounted to £8 9s 7d whilst in 1645 they rose to £26 12s 6d, approximately a three-fold rise.[61] In Rugeley, accounts surviving a fire in Robert Burton's house show pre-war levies at around £17, whilst those for 1644–5 had reached £43 13s 4d, again approaching a three-fold increase. The income of garrisons too naturally increased; Lichfield levied £48 per month from Offloe Hundred in 1643 and about £100 per month in late 1645.[62]

Nottinghamshire's best accounts come from Upton near Newark.[63] Other county papers provide an important supporting role and all demonstrate the expensive burdens imposed on county villages quickly. In late August 1642 the trained bands had been summoned to Nottingham at short notice for the 'Raising of the Standard'. This required horses and at Upton three were hired at a cost of 3s 3d to mount the soldiers. Soldiers' wages cost 16s, and the constable had to accompany them which cost the village 6d in expenses and 2d in horse hire. Village armour was in a poor state, needing 2s 6d worth of repairs whilst another shilling was spent on gunpowder and matches. A month's pay, 10s 6d, handed to the high constable brought the total to £1 13s 11d. Nearby Coddington too had to find horses for its trained bandsman and a boy paid to help its constable to bring the horses back again with wages, powder and matches. The bill there came to 10s 6d.[64] Despite the hurried activity it is unlikely that the soldiers arrived on time, explaining the poor military turnout at Nottingham on 23 August.

The number of travellers along Upton's roads was already swollen by refugees from the rebellion in Ireland. In 1642 ninety-four men, women and children from Ireland passed through Upton; one woman colonist had been born in Southwell. Maimed soldiers from the king's army, wounded in the early battles, began to pass through in late October or early November. At Coddington 78 refugees passed through between March 1642 and the following January, including five soldiers maimed in the autumn fighting.

By February 1643 the Coddington constables were making trips to the commissioners at Newark.[65] Thorpe constables were also at the meetings, and copies of warrants were bought by Edward Milden at 4d each for his neighbours, the social equals who would share the village's administrative posts and duties with him.[66] These warrants represented the beginning of regular Royalist taxation which was set at £1 10s 0d a week for the next year. Taxation was being collected by the Royalists from most of the county, including places as near to the parliamentarian garrison at Nottingham as Arnold to the north-east and Clifton to the south. Villages to the south and west of Nottingham were exceptions where only parliamentarians could gather tax most of the time, because Royalist forces could not use Trent Bridge.[67] At Upton the total receipts of the 1645 levies brought in £133 0s 5d and the high level of taxes and the continuing ancillary costs resulted in the 1646 total disbursements remaining at £140 8s 0d.

The accounts from Upton also reveal how the demands of war reached deep into the workings of the rural community. We know who grew or made what only because the war effort was drawing them from the Nottinghamshire rural economy. The villagers with the larger houses were those chosen to billet soldiers allocated to Upton. Evidence from other accounts elsewhere demonstrates that the constables periodically drew up lists of the substantial householders for this purpose. At Upton innholders were selected for this duty. The Kirkes' Inn usually had soldiers lodging or convalescing there and Thomas Kitchen's household at Lane Head provided lodging for soldiers and stabling for horses, and more soldiers lodged with John Kitchen. In 1644 George Bilby and William Gill jointly quartered four gentlemen, possibly officers or people involved in the administration of the war. No precise figures for billeting costs are found in these particular accounts, but others suggest that they would be in the region of 4d per day for one man or one horse.[68]

Leicestershire resources were divided three ways for most of the war. In the immediate vicinity of Leicester, the parliamentarian county committee was able to collect assessments most of the time although at the end of 1643 they were having to be subsidised by money collected in Kent. The rest of the county was divided between the two Royalist garrisons at Belvoir Castle and Ashby de la Zouch; the lion's share went to the garrison and administrative centre at Ashby.

Principal accounts in Leicestershire include Branston, Stathern and Waltham on the Wolds, all in Framland and East Goscote hundreds which were assigned to Belvoir. One set, those of Belton, come from Ashby's territory, and demonstrate that the burden even in the early stages of the war involved a threefold increase in constables' levies.[69] Waltham Accounts show that even as late as 1645 regular taxes were being paid to Belvoir. Nearby Branston's 1645 accounts show the dilemma caused by divided territorial control: £50 paid to Belvoir and £90 to the parliamentarians at Leicester. Both Waltham on the Wolds and Branston accounts suggest that regular payments had been made to both sides for much of the war. Only during the period from Autumn 1643 to Summer 1645 were the Royalists in complete control.[70]

The Derbyshire commission of array structure was quite sophisticated devolved government, with part of the commission based at Ashbourne to deal with High Peak. Most the commissioners probably remained at Tutbury, but there was also a contingent in the Chesterfield area. There are no surviving constables' accounts which cover the early part of the war and so the taxation details remain largely a mystery, even though the division of the county between the garrisons can be worked out. It would seem that county borders did not dictate divisions between garrison territory whereas hundredal ones did. For instance, tax was collected in Derbyshire by the Tutbury garrison in Staffordshire. In this case the taxes were probably being levied in the Honour of Tutbury, the areas in both counties charged with the upkeep of the castle. However, no such traditional arrangement would present a precedent for the allocation of Repton and Gresley Hundred to the Leicestershire garrison at Ashby de la Zouch.

In Rutland the taxation process only becomes clear after the county was in the hands of the parliamentarians from 1644. The village of Preston paid tax to the county committee at Burleigh House for much of the time, but on some occasions had to make payments to the committee of neighbouring Leicestershire.[71] At Hambleton, about 3 miles away, it was the Burleigh and Rockingham garrisons which drew upon the resources of Abel Barker's estates. Between 16 December 1644 and late June 1645, Barker despatched £19 0s 9d worth of peas, oats, straw, beer and 'provision' to 'Burley' at weekly intervals. He also provided five horses, which he valued at £40 to Rockingham.[72] In 1645 the Monthly Tax levied on the county's five hundreds amounted to £510 10s 0d, with the village of Hambleton paying some £16 10s 0d a month, and only Wissondine, Ashwell and Burleigh paying more.[73]

The weight of evidence for the period before late summer 1644 points to the type of stability which would obviate the financial impetus for clubmen risings. Taxation was regular well into 1644 in many of the villages in the region. Even in this period there were areas where such stability did not exist, parts of Staffordshire adjacent to the garrisons of Lapley in the south-west and Eccleshall in the north changed hands with the vicissitudes of war. The former changed hands twice in quick succession and the latter once in the second half of 1643. The situation in Derbyshire in the same period was far more confused than that in other counties because of the rapid establishment of Royalist garrisons. Moreover all the villages in the immediate vicinity of all the county towns were faced with Royalist incursions throughout the war.

In Lincolnshire Royalist confidence at the beginning of 1644 resulted in demands for back-taxes in Lincolnshire. The Grantham Common Hall was faced with such a bill for arrears at their meeting on 2 February. The Lincolnshire commissioners of array ensconced in Belvoir Castle demanded £125 for new taxes and all monies still due from previous levies to be paid by 6 February. The town was unable to meet the payments, two comburgesses and the chief constable were sent to Belvoir to plead the town's case with Sir Robert Thorold with a letter, possibly penned by the alderman during the meeting, promising to pay something immediately.[74]

If the first part of the war was generally stable, the campaign in the Newark area in March 1644 heralded a sea-change. At the beginning of the month Sir John Meldrum and an army of 7,000 placed the Royalist garrison at Newark under close siege. The resources of the area around the town were stretched during the next three weeks. Meldrum's defeat by Prince Rupert and Lord Loughborough was followed by billeting of Royalist regiments from Loughborough's North Midland Army which took peas and oats to feed their horses and tried to take new mounts from Upton.[75] The Upton Accounts clearly show a new phase in the war when resources were used more. Within ten days of the siege, the village was contributing labourers to the rebuilding and expansion of Newark's defences. Thorpe village accounts show that the villages were charged with the construction of certain amount of earthworks, assessed in ten-yard stretches.[76] We can get some idea of the costs involved from the Upton accounts: labourers were escorted to the bulwarks by the constable and they did a day's work for 8d each, which compares with 8d for a day's work mowing hay in Lincolnshire in 1621, or between 6d and 10d a day as a foot soldier.[77]

Grantham was soon reoccupied by parliamentarians as they took over the county, but of course this only added to costs and the constables put in a bill for £26 1s 9d for billeting charges in July. The problems of being in authority were hammered home to Alderman Edward Christian in 1644, for the reoccupation of town required the payment of back-taxes to parliamentarian coffers amounting to £300. Sir Thomas Fairfax was not patient when the town experienced difficulty in paying. Christian was apparently held as a sort of hostage by the army for 20 weeks.[78]

It was events further north which were to have a major effect on the north

Midland counties. On 11 April the Yorkshire Royalists, defending the Marquis of Newcastle's rear whilst he tried to halt the advance of the Scots army, were defeated at Selby leaving the North under threat and York itself in peril. Newcastle retreated to York and sent his horse south to camp in Nottinghamshire. This drained the stocks of fodder in the Midlands, according to the Upton accounts where the entries from the end of April to late May are dominated by the demands of horse regiments for peas, hay and oats as well as by new billeting arrangements.[79] In Derbyshire Colonel John Freschville wrote to Lord Loughborough in May 1644 complaining that Lord Goring, commander of the Northern Horse, was expecting a 'greater quantity' from the county than 'the place can possibly afford'.[80]

Meldrum's three-week siege of Newark had started the payment of taxes to Nottingham by the Upton villagers, and despite the Royalists renewed hegemony in the region, parliamentarian taxation was to be an intermittent feature of life at the very least. By September chaos had increased on the Derbyshire and Staffordshire borders, with Sir Andrew Kniveton, governor of Tutbury writing:

> our contribution being much lessened by reason of the country's poverty and the enemy appearing daily in our quarters, and having no better a means of supply than by sending to particular men for some small sums such as they are well able to bear ... [81]

In other areas the Royalist war effort was becoming internally riven. In north-east Leicestershire the governor of Belvoir Castle ceased to recognise the authority of his commander Lord Loughborough. Since the summer of 1644 and the flight of the Marquis of Newcastle, Gervase Lucas argued that Loughborough's commission was null and void, as he had been at one stage Newcastle's appointee. Lucas stopped attending councils of war, refused to help Loughborough's attempt to rescue the garrison at Wingfield, and challenged his commander's right to allot taxation areas. Lucas' men were collecting money from all of Framland hundred, which was shared between the two garrisons, and from East Goscote and Gartree which had been assigned to Ashby alone. Moreover, Loughborough also accused Lucas of badly treating Royalist supporters, persecuting a Mr Yates whose two sons had been killed in the king's service. Such actions could not win hearts and minds and belie some degree of panic. The recipients of Kniveton's loan letters may too have felt betrayed by those supposedly protecting them from arbitrary demands. Lucas' action was not solely inspired by rivalry with Lord Loughborough, nor was it entirely as Loughborough asserted, corruption. Belvoir's financial situation was becoming desperate. Lincolnshire, from where a good deal of Lucas' taxation had come was now in the hands of the Eastern Association forces and administration.[82]

Disputes also beset Staffordshire where Thomas Leveson governor of Dudley accused the Lichfield garrison of forcibly interfering in Dudley's tax collection.

The dispute dragged on into the following year when Leveson went on to allege that the county's commissioners of array were not authorising the collection of monies due to his garrison.[83] These quarrels were not helped by the confusion of commands at the level immediately above Lord Loughborough. Four of his five counties had been under the command of the Marquis of Newcastle, which had itself dissolved when the marquis left the country; the fifth, Staffordshire, had been grouped under Rupert's command since Spring 1644. This not only allowed Lucas to claim that Loughborough lacked authority, but also allowed Leveson to appeal over his head to Prince Rupert in 1644 and in 1645 to Prince Maurice.

Whilst not seeing any mass protest, the East Midlands did see the use of petitions by local inhabitants. In March 1643 people living in the Vale of Belvoir, which stretches through Leicestershire and Nottinghamshire, tried to protect their property. They petitioned the Nottinghamshire parliamentarians about the commandeering of horses. Soldiers had been plundering the vale, probably during Major General Thomas Ballard's brief siege of Newark at the end of February, and the people of the vale felt the garrison at Nottingham was responsible for this and for attacking people who were not in arms against them. The Nottinghamshire committee replied that the soldiers doing the plundering were not actually their troops but other parliamentarians assigned to work with them. Every effort was made to prevent the plundering, but they proved to be beyond control. The petitioners claimed that the Newark Royalists were behaving differently, although the parliamentarians challenged this assumption, suggesting the Newarkers treated anyone who was not a Royalist as an enemy regardless of neutrality. Moreover, the committeemen reminded the petitioners, some of the people in the vale who had complained were actually Royalists in arms at one of the garrisons and some others had offered horses to the Royalists, but not to parliamentarians. In short, argued the committee, they did protect the vale, by only taking things from those who supported Royalists, and even then they would only take things in equal numbers to those that had been supplied to the Royalists. The Newark Royalists replied in a similar vein to the petition presented to them. The parliamentarians could not be trusted as they had seized a man from his home and had plundered homes in the vale of women's and children's clothes. The parliamentarians' reply was a tissue of falsehoods which the Newark commissioners would expose. Also, the Royalists claimed that they had tried to get the parliamentarians to arrange a meeting to make a bilateral engagement on the issue of commandeering goods, but they had refused.[84]

By 1644 a second petition revealed that the decline in Royalist effectiveness was not yet clear to all observers. A petition sent to Parliament from Leicestershire in late 1644 protested the ineffectiveness of the county committee in dealing with the Royalists. It claimed that:

the enemy's [sic] are so much strengthened and increased, that the well-affected are daily exposed to the loss of liberty, their goods to plunder, and their rents sequestered and seized on by the adverse party, that till of late had never the boldnes or power to attempt it.

This claim that the people of Leicestershire were now subject to the 'now unbounded enemy' does not sit well with either our understanding of the situation in late 1643 when the Royalists were ascendant, or late 1644 when they plainly were not.[85]

This petition's claims on this point only really make sense if we put them into a context of collapsing war-effort when sporadic tax collection had replaced effective systems. It was a period in which Abel Barker, a member of the Rutland County Committee, could question the value of the cause when it could not protect him or his property, and a fellow countyman Francis Wayte claimed that the parliamentarian cause did not preserve his house from plunder or stop 'myself [being] carried away as most of our gentry already are'.[86]

There is other evidence that the breakdown in the Royalist control of the region was having widespread effects. At Upton just after 3 July 1645, William Robinson was murdered by soldiers from Newark. Constable William Cullen arrested the soldiers and led them to Newark. On 10 July, he, Robinson's wife and other witnesses went to give evidence before the Council of War. By that time there were parliamentarian soldiers in the area, some based at nearby Norwell.[87] Taxes were being paid to both Newark and Nottingham but the collections were less regular. Parliamentarian journals even suggested that the Newark forces were threatening to burn down empty houses, on the basis that their owners had fled rather than pay taxes, whilst they were collecting arrears. Whilst there is no corroboration for this claim, there is no doubt that Royalist systems were breaking down and new parliamentarian ones were not yet established to take over from them.[88] Evidence from the extensive estates of the Mellish family, covering several villages in the north-east of Nottinghamshire, indicate that the dysfunction engendered by the breakdown of control was also affecting rent collection. On the eve of war total rents collected ranged between £628 and £690 per year. For 1642–3 they remained high at £650 14s 1d, and the following year they were still at £652 8s 1d; they remained the same into 1644–5 but by 1645–6 they had fallen to £410 4s 9d (a 37 per cent fall).[89] This in part must be because the Mellish estates were on the fringes of territory which the Newark based Royalists could control by 1645. The cumulative effects of the levies upon the tenants' ability to pay their rents would also be a factor.

It is possible that for many places such disorderly behaviour was a brief occurrence with limited effects. Elsewhere in the region, where control passed swiftly into the hands of the parliamentarian forces and administration, the changeover could be marked not by instability, but by a sense of *déjà vu* as parliamentarian levies were set at almost exactly the same rates as Royalist ones. The Mavesyn Ridware accounts show that in some areas where there was a prolonged period of dual assessment, both sides made an effort to reduce the possible problems by lowering their levies by approximately one third. As part of the surrender terms at Welbeck in autumn 1645, the parliamentarians, under Thomas Gell, agreed to collect Royalist contributions representing the back pay of the besieged garrison.

For the people of the area surrounding Newark the cost of the war escalated at the end of 1645 when the town was again besieged by Lord Leven's Covenanter army and Sydenham Pointz' Northern Association Army. This siege lasted some six months but even when it ended in May 1646 the departure of first the Scots, then the Royalists and finally the northern parliamentarians did not significantly reduce the costs of war. One mark of how little was to change is the way that 6 May, the day the siege ended, was passed by the constable of Upton in collecting parliamentarian taxes in Morton. Whilst the Scots' levy may have ended that very day, he now had to hand over all the money to the parliamentarian county committee in Nottingham and two weeks' money, representing the period since the siege, was paid over on 26 May. Newark was now afflicted by plague and occupied by John Hutchinson's regiment from Nottingham. His wife recorded this as the 'greatest danger of all' he underwent and recounted with relief, that 'it so pleased God that neither he nor any of these fresh men caught the infection, which was so raging there that it almost desolated the place'.[90]

This would seem to suggest that the infection was closely related to the unhygienic living and diet of the straitened garrison and that the soldiers with fresh food and supplies were able to avoid infection at this stage. On Monday 11 May workers from the nearby villages were set to work to destroy the earthworks established by both sides. The labourers from Upton were given the task of demolishing the king's Sconce on the Spittle which they themselves had constructed two years earlier. Many of the earthworks were levelled or at least rendered unserviceable within days. Work was quickly halted by the plague in Newark and the villages sealed themselves off from the outside world as much as possible. On 26 May, Constable Richard Gibson at Upton gave 10d worth of bread, cheese and beer to 'six people of Newark which the watchman kept out of the towne the[y] desiringe relief, returned to the wood'.[91] The payments to support the people in the plague, which visited towns all around the country, continue to appear in the Upton accounts throughout much of the rest of 1646.

Mass movement of people across the country had really begun in 1641 with the migration of refugees from Ireland, but now a great throng of people was moving along England's roads. The year from 6 May 1646, the first after the war ended in the vicinity of Upton, saw at least 58 Irish men, women and children pass through, along with three disabled people, nine soldiers returning home, at least nine children, six women and eleven men of various qualities, in all at least 96 people. Initially they may have used Upton's roads to avoid plague-ridden Newark and many people would have been turned away from the town by watchmen there. Yet it is clear that the plague was only one reason for people passing through Upton and the surrounding villages as it cannot account for the continuing traffic of the displaced which continued for several years. Three years later, in 1649, the numbers on the road were even greater. This time 16 Irish women, 1 Irish child and 1 Irish man passed through Upton. In addition there were 16 women, 7 men, 17 disabled people, 8 children, 24 discharged soldiers, 11 maimed soldiers, 15 people of unspecified gender as well as a further 6 'companies' of poor people and 16 Irish 'companies' of unspecified numbers passing through. Whilst the sight of so many travellers may have been unusual in Upton they added little to the financial demands on the town. Payments to these travellers cost the community over £2, or only about 3 per cent of total expenditure for that year or about 5 per cent of the village payments other than those for the monthly tax and billeting charges. Despite Professor Wood's assertion that 'the normal trade of the countryside soon began to flow into the market place', Newark's role as a major communications route was seriously disrupted.[92] People now used other roads. Upton was passed through by people generally moving north to south or vice versa; York, London and Parliament were common destinations. It is interesting that there was so much traffic through Upton as the village was neither on the main roads north and south, nor on the direct route between Nottingham and Newark. For much of the war period and after it seems likely that people following the Great North Road were having to skirt around Newark to avoid the normal routes as bridges and roads had been damaged by siegeworks and fortifications, perhaps by way of Long Bennington, Cottam, East Stoke, Fiskerton Ferry, Upton Norwell and Tuxford.[93]

The end of war did not end the problems of billeting because there was no immediate demobilisation of Parliament's forces. The facilities of towns offered advantages for army units. Towns had public buildings which could be used for courts martial and lock-ups useful for detaining prisoners. This seems to have been true at Grantham where a court martial was held in October 1647. Of course this cost the town money and £10 was levied for the payment of the guards and the provision of candles and firewood for them. Collectors were appointed and refusers were to be dealt with in the normal way of distraint.[94]

In spite of the very great depredations and the overall uncertainty caused by the collapse of the Royalist war effort, no club risings took place in the north Midlands and this poses interesting questions. It is possible that the establishment of order in these regions is important: in areas with the most effective military control, and the most regular system of taxation, order and stability were preserved, leaving little reason for widescale popular outrage. Garrisons in these areas were effective at minimising minor military incursions from outside. Tax collection probably entailed almost constant patrols. Colonel Staunton's regimental accounts show that collection entailed long journeys, often to distant communities.[95] This constant presence would have had an intimidatory effect or may have had the effect of enhancing a sense of security. In the north Midlands there are two problems this argument. First, it fails to explain why the disorderly effect of marching armies passing through regions which was a problem in

Worcestershire was not such a problem in the north Midlands. There had been many occasions when Royalist and parliamentarian armies marched through and lingered in the region. In 1643 and 1644 the Royalists armies of Newcastle, Prince Rupert and Lord Goring travelled through or even stayed for a considerable amount of time causing considerable hardship.[96] In 1645 the king's own army was in the region three times between May and November. Several parliamentarian armies, under Thomas Ballard, Cromwell, Grey and Meldrum had been in the region in 1643. Meldrum was in the region again in Spring 1644, the Earl of Denbigh in the south during June, Manchester in August and in 1645 the New Model and the Scottish Army had all disrupted any sense of normality. The Upton accounts show that the burdens imposed by outside forces were erratic and potentially destructive. Second, the period which saw the clubmen activity at its most intense in the south Midlands, the Marches and the south-west coincided with the most destabilised period in the north Midlands. The defeat of the North Midlands Army at Denton in October 1644 had relegated it to being a garrison-based force providing temporary detachments to other armies. Even so the North Midlands Army presence was still large enough to allow Royalists to dominate significant areas ensuring that Parliament's forces could not hold the territory in the same thrall as Lord Loughborough's men had in the period autumn 1643 to spring 1644.

The region was not entirely quiet, but disturbances in the area were an urban rather than a rural feature. As in Royalist Chester the previous year, parliamentarian Derby was beset by anti-tax riots.[97] In May 1645, two unnamed women,

> went up and down the town beating drums and making proclamations
> … that such of the town as were not willing to pay excise should join
> with them and they would beat the [excise] commissioners out of town.

Attempts by the county committee to negotiate with them failed and as the committee sat at the mayor's house, one of the women stood banging her drum outside the window drowning out the debate. This tactic worked and the excise was not collected again until July. When it was again levied a soldier was seized by the townspeople and fastened to the bull ring in the market whilst 'the women did beat the drums as before'. It still proved impossible to collect the money, despite orders from London. When the excise commissioners could do their work again the tax was this time used primarily within the county and not sent to London. Sir John Gell the governor of Derby, partly for his own ends, probably persuaded Parliament that this was more acceptable to the rioters.[98] If indeed this had been an aim of the rioters, as well as that of Gell, it fits in with some of the demands of the club movement, and the gentry petitions which a few months earlier pressured the king to keep locally collected taxes within the area for regional use. Royalist excise was collected in the region, and there is some limited evidence for its organisation and implementation. However, as it came into force just as the Royalist cause went into decline in the north Midlands, its effects seem not to have been prolonged enough to have provoked complaint.

We need other explanations for the absence of clubmen risings. Absence does seem to support Professor Hutton's assertion that the club phenomena were individualist in their composition, demands and behaviour.[99] That there were no risings in the Midlands at a time when there were so many of the prerequisites found in areas marked by club risings, would suggest that there were particular circumstances and general conditions which did not occur within the Midlands. The answer may lie between the two extremes of class conscious risings and individual self-expression. Risings elsewhere undoubtedly had several things in common. The clubmen and women in all cases were defending themselves and their communities against damaging outside forces. They were relating their own personal circumstances and those shared by their neighbours to the general instability within the state represented by a breakdown in government. Risings were organised and led by those involved in the lower, community levels of local government, high and petty constables such as High Constable Thomas Careless of Broxash, prominent in the Herefordshire club movement. They were also the people charged with administering the war efforts at community level. This suggests that the club risings are an example of a clash caused by there being even in war-time two concepts of order. The order of the constables and local communities being at variance with that of the central representatives of order – in this case Royalist and parliamentarian authorities rather than traditional functionaries of government. In this circumstance the clubman constables and their neighbours represented order and the soldiers, commissioners and committeemen disorder. In the north Midlands, whilst the centre tottered and changed its face, it certainly never fully collapsed or embraced unacceptable practices as it did elsewhere.

Absence of prominent Roman Catholic figures removed one other area of contention. The Worcestershire clubmen exhibited 'extraordinary venom' in their attacks on Catholics. Hutton identifies the prominence of the Earl of Shrewsbury, in the Marcher Association, as a major cause of the clubmen activity there: powerful Roman Catholics were an unacceptable part of government. Although Henry Hastings, Lord Loughborough, had been accused of favouring Catholics in his forces, the accusations did not stick and whilst there were two Roman Catholic colonels in his army, the overall proportion in his officer corps remained low at as little as 15 per cent. There were no Catholics in the administration. The one exception was Thomas Leveson at Dudley who was widely described as a 'rob-carrier', and who managed to persuade the king to make him high sheriff in 1645, but who was generally kept isolated by the Commission of Array, effectively localising opposition to his presence in the area.[100] In fact, Leveson was perhaps the nearest thing the region got to the other spark for club activity, the militant swordsman who like Barnabas Scudamore at Hereford provoked armed local opposition to his heavy-handed policies. Leveson's isolation and the actions taken by the king and Princes Rupert and Maurice to bring him into line prevented any escalated action against him.

This all seems to suggest that a combination of general factors and specific factors were necessary to prompt people into taking up arms against the protagonists. Whilst the general causes of the Civil War – deprivation, uncertainty and heavy burdens combined with a decline in stability and confused control – were to be found in the north Midlands, particularly after summer 1644, other more specific grievances were absent. In the north Midlands circumstances surrounding the Royalist defeat and determination by both sides to ameliorate the worst effects of the war mitigated these problems. For a significant amount of time the consensus between centre and locality obtained: Roman Catholics were rare, no colonel or governor was too arbitrary in his actions, and the needs of Lord Goring's forces were incorporated into an effective logistical framework and thus he did not engage in the kind of arbitrary taxation which was, later in the war, to provoke the people of the south-west into rising.

For the people of Warwickshire the effects of the Bishop's Wars probably caused financial problems from the very earliest days for some people, in ways which went beyond the obvious. In 1639 Richard Goodall and his daughter Susanna obtained a licence to sell ale. They may have needed the money, for Susanna's husband James was a Trained Band soldier serving in the North. The problem was that the three of them had been banned from holding a licence the previous Easter.[101] Thomas Taylor of Solihull returned from the Bishop's Wars to find himself in debt, for which he was thrown into prison. When Thomas was sent to the war by the village, he was told that his rent would be paid for him by the village: it was not. He was arrested for 30s of debt. His legal charges and the cost of imprisonment added another 22s. The court agreed that he had been badly treated and ordered that Solihull pay.[102]

During the first Civil War, Warwickshire was a frontier county. From the summer of 1642 rival forces attempted to stake their claim. Parliament's county committee sat generally at Coventry and had garrisons around the county. Royalists also had garrisons at Tamworth in the north and Compton in the south of the county, although both of these had fallen into parliamentarian hands by 1644.[103] There were, of course, refugees in the county. Mary Prorsor returned to the town of her birth, Ullenhall, with three of her six children. She had migrated to Ireland with her husband, but at the rebellion had fled, leaving her husband in the army and herself penniless. Mary informed the court that she was willing to get a job, but that at the moment she had nothing. The JPs paid her an allowance from the maimed soldiers' money to tide her over, whilst Ullenhall sorted out a house and poor rate money.

The arrival in the West Midlands of the Scots brought additional problems to the region; Ann Hughes suggests that the Scots caused some of the greatest problems for the people of the county and the county committee's estimate of £120 a day for 14 days paled in insignificance besides the amounts collected by the Scots themselves.[104] Lord Leven, along with other officers, were unhappy at the treatment meted out to his army. He had been promised a friendly and 'plentiful country' but instead he 'found nothing by the way but solitude – plentiful places indeed for grass and trees but no other refreshment'.[105] As a result the Scots took what they could. At Studley they stayed three days and four nights, in July 1645, costing innkeeper William Toupley £15 10s in food and grass and free quarter, and he was not alone in finding Scotsmen billeted upon him. The Scots returned later in the month to the Studley and Alcester area, before moving west to besiege Hereford. They returned once more to Warwickshire after the siege had ended and so early in September the Scots were again drawing upon the resources of west Warwickshire, taking sheep, hay, barley, wood, blankets and even two hives of bees from John Tew of Charlecote.[106] Mr Rogers of Sherbourne remarked that the Scots took things from him violently. Thomas Walker claimed that he was cut and abused and had to flee his home to escape.[107]

There were petty arguments too. In April 1644 Balsall and Barston, adjacent villages south-west of Solihull, a levy of £3 was made to cover the cost of a horse bought by Constable William Essex from Thomas Palmer for the Earl of Denbigh's forces. The arrangement was fairly simple: the villages would share the cost with Balsall paying £2 and Barston £1. However, Barston did not pay its portion and two years later William Essex was being held responsible by Palmer. The solution the court decided was simple, the constable should immediately levy Balsall.[108] Whether this worked or not, Essex's troubles were not over, nine months later he was back in court trying to get the outstanding portion, £10 16s 8d, owed to him by the Balsall inhabitants. It would appear that Essex had also been the constable during the previous year, something not clear to the JPs when they ordered the collection of Palmer's money in the earlier case. The village's assessors had managed to delay payments by setting some of it on the desmesne lands of Balsall Temple, which were liable for Balsall taxation. The court decided that the village reassess the levy on property that was eligible, in other words, on themselves.[109] These were minor arguments, but they were no less annoying to the minor public servants trying to balance their communities against the demands of war.

More crucially, by this time the physical effects of the war were beginning to impinge upon the county treasury and maimed parliamentarian soldiers were returning home. Diverse wounds and missing limbs prevented the men from earning a living. These survivors seem to have been given a lump sum of £2 for immediate needs whilst the regular pension, often 40s a year, was calculated.[110] Widowed women also began presenting petitions to the court to try and get financial support. Like many of the maimed soldiers they had to present relevant war records. Thus Margery Brown of Over Pillerton just east of Edgehill, recounted her husband's service under Colonel Castle, and his death at the siege of Banbury. She had two children and now no income to support them. In her case the village was ordered to pay maintenance from the poor rate, whilst the lump sum of 40s was paid to her from the 'maimed soldiers' and mariners' money'.[111] Hester White of Stratford-upon-Avon also lost her husband during fighting at Banbury in 1644 and in her plea for support at the end of the war she recounted how she had nursed two parliamentarian soldiers after Edgehill for three months. It had been a difficult job: the soldiers were in great distress because of their wounds and Hester had to spend many nights sitting up with them.[112]

At county level committeemen and commissioners made use of traditional arrangements to make their job easier. Just as in Lancashire where they used the table drawn up by Thomas Blomeley, in Bedfordshire they used a traditional calculation which allotted the tax between the hundreds of the county. It was a fairly complex system which still left the issue of allotting the smaller amounts between the villages within the hundreds. First, Bedford was allocated a thirtieth of the total. The remaining sum was divided by twenty-one parts. Ten parts of this were allocated to the three hundreds of Manshead, Flitt and Redbourne Stoke. This sum was subdivided into seven parts, three of which were allocated to Manshead, and two each to Flix and Redbourne Stoke. The other eleven parts of the original sum were allocated to the six remaining smaller hundreds, and in turn was divided into 21 again. Ten parts were allocated to Wixhamtree, Clifton and Biggleswade and the remaining eleven to Willey, Stodden and Barford. In practice this meant that the Propositions levy of 16 May 1642 saw £2,022 15s 0d levied on Manshead, Flitt and Redbourne Stoke, and on the remaining six hundreds was imposed £2,224 15s 0d. Bedford paid £124 16s 0d.[113] The system was not universally approved of and in August 1644 the whole system was enquired into by Sir Beauchamp St John and Sir William Bryars.[114] The burden on the county was probably the main inspiration for the inquiry rather than its antiquity. It may be that the hope was that Bedford might have taken a larger share. That the burden was difficult to collect is not in doubt. Much of the money went to finance the garrison at Newport Pagnell. These payments appear to have been largely theoretical by 1644 when Sir Samuel Luke wrote from the garrison on 13 August. By then, he reminded the county committee, the county was five months behind with its monthly levies and owed £1,000 in other levies. At the time the garrison was trying to improve its defences, which of course cost money. It was proving to be a hand to mouth experience because the work force would only work if it was certain of being paid every night at the end of work. Luke told the committee if they did not send some money that on the following Saturday work would come to an end. To try and put moral pressure on the committee, Luke told them that he had also written to the Cambridge committee, even though Cambridge was only two months behind with tax and it had sent £2,000 for the works: he snapped 'and you none at all'.[115] The issue of free quarter was also a problem. In 1645 the county MPs at Westminster were being urged to try and alleviate the billeting problem in Redbourne Stoke, Flitt and Manshead where 300 households were coping with 200 men. Some of the soldiers which the committee had raised never reached their billets. In March 1645 the committee drew up a list of 80 men who ran away after being enlisted, clothed and armed.[116] By this time the new monthly levy was in place and the system of division remained in place for that and for the levy for the Army of the Solemn League and Covenant. However, even these levies were soon in arrears. By 1651 the arrears would build to £13,184 13s 1½d.[117] Money was not the only concern for the hard pressed committee and the people of the county. During the 1646 siege of Oxford, Sir Thomas Fairfax drew further upon the Bedfordshire people. The hundred of Willey was charged with providing 103 mattocks, spades, shovels and hatchets 'of which one third to be mattocks at least'.[118]

Of course the duties of war-time administration had personal effects as well as economic ones. Enforced absence from home was common for the parliamentarian county officials in the same way as it was for Royalists like Rashleigh in Cornwall. Hellen Boteler wrote to her father, the chairman of the Bedfordshire county committee that

> our greatest want is your company which wee extremely long to see but wee must wait with pations lett it please God that we shall be so happy in the meene time my ernest prayer s to God for the preserve you in this dismill time ... [119]

This dismal time was to impinge yet further on the relationship, for on the back of Hellen's letter her father wrote a series of calculations for taxes paid for the Scots.

Almost an isolated bastion of Royalists in the parliamentarian-dominated south, the garrison of Basing House in Hampshire wrought havoc upon its neighbours because of its location in what was really enemy territory. One of these neighbours, Sir Thomas Jervoise, recorded the effects of the problem. At the end of the first Civil War, Jervoise compiled a list of his losses during the 'late unnaturall warr'. His property at Herriad was subjected to demands for corn and cattle. His manors there and nearby Southrope and Lea Farm were furthermore occupied by the 'enimie of ye Sd Garrison' for three and a half years (he meant the Royalists from the garrison at Basing) and they cut down timber and dismantled buildings, taking dressed wood from the manor house, the barns and outhouses which were dismantled. The rents of the manors of Birtford and Northfield were taken in for three years and the tenants were so impoverished that they were still not able to pay their rents when Sir Thomas compiled his list. Sir Thomas was beset by bad luck, for he had a house in Worcester too, and this had been occupied by the enemy for three years also. Sir Thomas was vague about his losses when it came to estimating them. Figures in his list are neatly rounded, the rents of Birtford appeared to have been £2,500 exactly and those at Northfield £3,000. His losses in cattle and corn over three years came to a surprisingly exact £4,000 'at least' He also added that there were 'many other great losses he have suteined wch he omitts to mention'. Even so, despite this kindness, he put in a bill for £13,448 for his loyal sufferings. His plea met with success. On 14 September 1649 Jervoise had been allowed substantial income from the estates of the Marquis of Winchester, fitting recompense as it was the garrison at Winchester's mansion which had inflicted the losses on Jervoise's tenants. Jervoise had received the income of over 20 manors across Dorset, Hampshire Wiltshire and Kent for two and a half years. Many of the manors were close to the estates ruined by Winchester's garrison. Part of the allotment was the rectory of Herriard which had been in the marquis's hands. However, this income had already been allocated by the Committee for Plundered Ministers to a dispossessed minister, John Garth; this caused problems which were to drag on for several years. Weston Patrick, with rents yielding £41 11s 4d a year was nearby, other towns were scattered throughout the east of the county.[120] Most of these lands rested in the hands of Jervoise and the Treason Trustees briefly. Jervoise appears to have bought only one property, Englefield Manor in Berkshire, in 1652, which he had been allocated at the end of the term.[121]

In Surrey accounts from the village of Elstead show the collection of levies from 1644 until 1651.[122] Levies were in the first instance paid to the parliamentarian garrison at Farnham Castle. The parish of Elstead was in Farnham Hundred, one of the principle allocations of territory for the castle. On 1 May 1644 a levy covering four months' pay was collected costing (at £3 17s 1d a week) £61 12s 4d between then and 1 October when a levy for three months was charged on the town. From 25 April 1645 the town was paying money for the New Model Army and still paying for the garrison at Farnham Castle. There were other levies too: in June a levy to cover six months' contribution towards maintaining the British Army in Ireland cost the town £7 10s. On the same day a further £7 was levied for the 'Supinumyary Company at ffarnham'.[123] By now the usual levy for Farnham had decreased to £3 a month whilst the money for the New Model was set at £20 a quarter, which seems to imply that the outgoings of the village had fallen from £185 a year to around £138 a year in 1645. This was probably the result of a complaint made to the committee which was recalled in the accounts in 1648.

A Nu Reat mead for the 3 months Assotiation in the pesh of of Elsted wch was due the first of October :1644 but the hundred greed together and went too the hed comeety at Kingston and mead ther complaint of ther great charg of quartering of Sir William Wallers whole Army for A great space the whole Comeety took it into Consideration and did abate the hundred of Farnham for this great tax wch was £15 8s 4d the mounth and there was pynted too collect itt the whole

Edward Wheller ffrancis Denyers
William Billingham & Richard Payne } Collectors [124]

Of course there were some additional levies still remained such as £2 5s for the garrison at Newbury and the £11 for the Army of the Solemn League and

Covenant. Levies continued after the war, the Scots were still being paid for until September 1646 and the levy for Ireland continued into 1648. In 1647 payments had changed, Collections were still made for the New Model Army at £20 a quarter and the British army was still £15 a year, but there was now a county force and troop, the equivalent of the Trained Bands which had replaced the Farnham garrison. In 1648 the levy for the New Model Army was reassessed. Now it was set at the equivalent of £56 a year: 'this was granted: 9 mounths wherof: 3: of them was taken of for the quartering the fyrst year so: 6: remained for the souldiers to pay for ther quartering from the 15 January 1647 [1648]'. [125]

The second Civil War cut into this reduction. On 3 August £5 16s was collected 'for the raising of the hundred horse for this county', and the Irish levy increased to £9 6s 8d for six months.

The second Civil War continued to burden the communities of England. The collectors of tax in Midhurst in Sussex, Gilbert Hanam and William Fewer, recorded their collections from John Waterford, Ann Duckett, Ralph Croucher and Nicholas Suckett, who all rented houses which had belonged to the late Henry Haukes. George Rowe and Thomas Redman, agent of Lord Montague, also paid levies on land they rented from Haukes. The levy on Haukes' houses and land was set at 6d in the pound a levy of a fortieth (or 2.5 per cent). Each house was rated at £3 per year and the land was valued at £6 for Rowe and £10 for Montague. The householders all paid 1s 7d each for the three months' levy on 10 September 1648, Rowe paid 3s 3d and Montague 5s 5d.

In neighbouring Surrey, three letters from Lady Elizabeth More give hints of the conditions in a county which saw very little in the way of fighting. The first letter, to Anne More, her sister-in-law at Godalming, begins with a discussion of her own eye ailment, and then with her young son's growing teeth. She then added that there was an atmosphere of fear in the area. Rumours were spreading that the Royalists were at Bedford and there was news that there had been incursions into Hertfordshire. The Surrey Trained Bands were in arms. Elizabeth was worried that her planned trip to her sisters might have to be cancelled because of the worries. There is acknowledgement in her letter that her own difficulties were not that great. News had reached her from Lincolnshire where her uncle was 'undone by the caveleires thay have taken all his writings and bonds'. Elizabeth was not beyond using the sad times as a excuse for not keeping in touch with her relatives. A note sent to her 'sweet sister' on 5 February in 1645, possibly Anne again, blames the time entirely for her neglect in being a more frequent letter writer.

In Oxford the presence of the king's court and his field army was to cause great difficulties during the first Civil War. The accounts of the Bodleian Library demonstrate a few of these problems. At first, as the armies were assembled in 1642, the town and the university fell under the sway of Parliament, and levies were paid from the library's properties at Cookham and the two tenements owned on Distaff Lane, totalling £1 19s 10d – both amounts were paid by the tenants themselves, but deducted from their rent to the university.[126] The occupation of the town and its being turned into a garrison involved library staff. Thomas Roche, a porter at the library, was nominated to work at the bulwarks one day a week, but he was allowed to hire a substitute or more probably contribute the wages of a replacement, initially, it appears at his own cost. For 31 weeks the substitute laboured at the works once a week. At some time during the year Roche died, possibly of a plague or infection rife in the town, and his widow was reimbursed the 12d a day wages, a total by then of £1 11s.[127] Amongst the books purchased by the library during the war was a collection bought in 1645 from the study of the late Richard Branthwayt. This demonstrated the Library's intention to maintain a stock of material on current affairs ('the occurances of the times') and may have included papers published in London and brought into the town by Oxford booksellers with their strong London contacts.[128]

It is difficult to assess the generality of opinion during the Civil Wars; most people left no record and therefore the records that do exist tend to reflect the unusually motivated or the unguarded blurtings of a few. This is true of those who volubly expressed an opinion about the state of affairs and found themselves hauled before one of courts which still sat. Middlesex was one of the counties which operated its courts throughout the war and there were people who expressed their discontent. During the wars with Scotland, the king's religious policy was attacked by Joan Worrall, a spinster of St Martin in the Fields, who said that the king had a crucifix in his chamber and he 'did bowe to it'.[129] On 13 April 1642 William Turner of St Clements Danes had declared in public that 'The Booke of Common Prayer is lyes and that they were fooles and knaves that will maynteine itt' whilst his fellow yeoman Richard Bailye agreed with him 'the Booke of Common Prayer was all lyes'.[130] But the king's opponents were not the only ones dragged to court, for on 25 July another yeoman, William Spencer, declared at St James, Clerkenwell, that Parliament had imprisoned the lord mayor for 'nothing else but because he was an honest man and did the King's service'. He also said that the Earl of Holland 'was raised from a beggar by the Kinge and that now he did what he could to cutt the king's throate'. And when Elizabeth Humphries said 'The devill take Parliament' at Whitechapel she was fined 40 nobles.[131] Even during the war challenging the pretence that the Parliament was fighting for the king was punishable, as Bodicemaker Robert Hands of Whitecross Street found out when on 11 March 1643 he said 'The King [is] a traitour and his Crowne was the whore of Babilon.' True, spring 1643 was a sensitive time as the king and Parliament were again engaged in negotiating the Oxford Treaty. A week later Joseph Brandon, a gentleman, declared that he 'wished the Parliament Howse to fall on' Lord Saye and Sele, John Pym, because they were traitors. He also demanded that the lord mayor be 'hanged and drawne' because he was a traitor too. Unfortunately, if he had actually said this, he had done so in front of Alice Jackson. Alice was no friend of his nor of the king and it seems that when she was herself arrested she accused Brandon of being a Royalist. She had declared that when she

sawe two sheeps heades in a poll shee wished the Kinges and Prince
Rupertes heades were there instead of them, and then the Kingdome
would be settled, and the Queene had not a foote of land in England
and the Kinge was an evill and unlawfull Kinge, and better to be
without a Kinge than to have him Kinge.[132]

This may have been an uncoordinated verbal blast but it was radicalism of a sort
which remained illegal for some time. In January 1644 Mary Giles, wife to a
lawyer Edward Giles, was charged with treason for saying 'I will kill the King of
England.' Moreover the religious freedom which many claimed had not yet
penetrated the heart of Presbyterian London, for John Platt yeoman and Susan
his wife of Cripplegate were dragged before the court for jointly claiming that to
'baptize an infant was noe more effect then to baptize a catt or a dogge'.
Certainly Susan Platt was being maligned, for in October Katherine Foy was
bound to appear for claiming that Susan had baptised a cat herself as well as
having spoken out against the ritual.[133]

The Venetian ambassador's view of London was fairly pessimistic. In the
spring of 1643 he reported that commerce was in decline, shops in the city were
closed, some because troops were attacking those which had not paid levies and
other because their owners were leaving town. He returned to this theme in
October when writing from The Hague. He commented that artisans and
wealthy people were moving to the United Provinces. This, he alleged, made the
Dutch reluctant to see the war end because they were benefiting from the wealth
brought into the country. In London conditions had declined further. He
complained in August 1643 that food shortages were causing major problems,
largely because, as he believed, peasants supplying London were being seized by
Royalists.

When a man was hanged in December 1643 for bringing secret messages to
the lord mayor, Agostini wrote that Londoners were angry at the use of martial
law.[134] Other executions of course raised less rancour; priests seized in London
were being executed at Tyburn during the early 1640s and others who
harboured them were brought before the courts, and like Mary Powell could be
themselves hanged as well. Other religious issues also appeared in the court
records, and the court records show the delicate path that Parliament and local
government had to tread when at war against the king and his religious practices. To malign the Book of Common Prayer, although it was soon to be
discarded, was still a criminal act in 1643. In April yeomen William Turner and
Richard Bailye both declared that the book was 'all lyes'. John Sprint, minister of
Hampstead, was no such fool, but he was tried for not adhering to the Book of
Common Prayer as late as October 1643: the jury found him not guilty. Rachel
Pollester was in no doubt 'The Kinge is a papist and a ranke papist and
cromoled.' Joan Sherrard was accused of wanting another Felton to deal with
the 'stuttering fool' of a king, for which Mary Giles had offered her services.
There were Londoners who did not approve of Parliament's actions and it was

defamed. Such actions cost Elizabeth Humphries 40 nobles (£13 6s 8d) when she suggested that 'The devill take the Parliament' and Sarah Dennis was fined £40 for attacking verbally Parliament and Lord Saye and Sele. But when John Draycott was tried for berating Parliament for being composed of 'roagues' in 1644 he was found not guilty.[135]

More specific cases could appear as well. In the aftermath of the Battle of Naseby not all were convinced by the revelations of the king's cabinet of letters. Thomas Sampson had allegedly said 'that the letters were not of the Kinges owne hand-writinge, but that the State did counterfeit his hand'.[136]

In October 1642 London had become the refuge of Lady Anne Clifford, Countess of Pembroke and Dowager Countess of Dorset 'when the Civill Warres between the King & Parliament began to grow hotter and hotter in England'. Her husband the Earl of Pembroke needed to be near to Parliament. Anne stayed there for six years and nine months, the longest single residence of her life to date, at Barnards Castle in London: 'it was a place of refuge for mee to hide myself in till these trouble were over-passed'. The war brought unexpected outcomes for many, for Anne it brought her heart's desire. Anne was the only heir to her father, an Elizabethan admiral. When she was 15 her father died and left everything to his brother, her uncle. She campaigned for the next 36 years, trying to overturn the will. However, her uncle died at the beginning of 1641 and his son and heir, for a while Royalist commander of Yorkshire, died at York in 1644, and she became heir to all of the Clifford estates and high sheriff of Westmorland. Unfortunately, all the estates were in the North, the principle house, Skipton Castle was a Royalist garrison, but all the properties were inaccessible whilst the war raged.[137]

Across the east and south-east of England the experiences of war were varied. There are few general rules to be drawn about the experience of war here and little that distinguishes these regions. The general patterns witnessed elsewhere, the unremitting burdens, the interference of war-time administration and the escalating economic costs were no different here than they were in the north or the south-west. The appearance of armies from outside the regions imposed additional burdens on top of the usual demands with which communities and individuals already struggled to cope. Soldiers with strange accents or an unfamiliar language had been a slightly more frightening spectre initially, but their demands and needs would be familiar if unwanted. The major distinction within these regions would be the presence of fighting. Major parts of the east and south saw no prolonged fighting, but otherwise the progress of the displaced, the return of the wounded and the absence of the dead unified even these areas with the regions fought over by the roving armies.

6

THE REVOLUTIONARY PERIOD, 1648–53

This chapter covers the period that began with renewed war in England and Wales and concluded with the culmination of wars of conquest which saw Ireland and Scotland subsumed into a Republic of the British Isles. It is the period in which the monarchy was slued off in the wake of a revolution that in itself grew from the anger generated by the second Civil War and the king's failure to conclude a peace. In perhaps the most thoughtful and thought-provoking book on this revolution, Brian Manning has looked at the way that it affected the various social groups and classes as well as different generations and genders.[1] In that work will be found discussions of the activists who comprised the various stages and elements of the revolution. This chapter by contrast contains the experiences of many who were observers or participants at the fringes of the English Revolution, such as John Clopton and Walter Powell who kept diaries of the period which avoided direct references to their 'interesting times', or poets in Wales who celebrated the times but bemoaned Wales' distance from the heart of the revolution. There are Scotsmen, once the centre of religious and political affairs, who became aware that they were being sidelined and losing control of what was once their cause. The revolution forced introspection on many people; for the most part this forced a concentration on their own affairs at the expense of their involvement in the massive changes wrought around them: what John Morrill recently called the victims but not the heroes of the 'English Civil Wars'.[2] The major or most dramatic actors of these years often appear then, not centre stage as we are used to seeing them, but as characters who are sometimes off the set like Shakespeare's characters from *Hamlet*, in Tom Stoppard's *Rosencrantz and Guildenstern are Dead*.

In 1648 within England and Wales a new Civil War sprang from a series of rebellions in England and Wales which embraced localist rebellion, Royalist risings and an invasion of England by a Scottish army raised to support Charles I. Scottish commissioners negotiating with the king were panicked by the Independents' domination of political and military affairs in England and by prospects of Charles I doing a deal which negated a Presbyterian Church settlement in England and Wales. The king had been presented with a set of terms, the Four Bills, which relegated the Church establishment to the rank of a second-rate issue to be discussed only after the initial Four Bills on military, political and civil affairs had been agreed. Frantically, the Scots worked on the king to try and secure a treaty which safeguarded their religious interests at home and in England and Wales. Charles played the increasingly desperate Scots off against the Westminster representatives, carrying the Four Bills. Around Christmas they persuaded Charles to sign an Engagement with them. To get this far they had to sacrifice many of their aims: neither Charles nor his English and Welsh subjects would be compelled to sign the Solemn League and Covenant, although this bond with God would be confirmed through a Westminster Parliament. In return for these fairly weak concessions the Scots would send an army into England to restore Charles to his dignity and authority. Not surprisingly these lax terms divided the Scottish government and the Engagement was truly supported by a political faction, comprised of conservatives and Royalists. Nevertheless, under the terms of the Engagement the commissioners and their supporters at home had committed their countrymen and women to supporting an invasion of England to restore Charles I to his political power. However, the military fruits of this agreement came somewhat tardily, for rebellion broke out in Wales and England before the Engager Army was created.

Rebellion in Wales began when Presbyterian military commanders' resentment at the drift towards Independency broke into open revolt. John Poyer, the governor of Pembroke Castle, refused to hand over to a New Model Army officer in February 1648 and sparked revolt across southern Wales. This was defeated in the field during May at the Battle of St Fagins, but it took Cromwell and part of the New Model Army until 11 July to capture Pembroke and end the rebellion. In England rebellions broke out in May in both Kent and Essex, but these were only the most violent and sustained of the attacks on parliamentarian rule. Many counties experienced troop mutinies and spreading lawlessness which seemed to cause the echoes of instability at the heart of national government to reverberate. Appeals and demands were made to Parliament for a quick peace settlement and in many places, such as Norwich, Bury St Edmunds, and London at Christmas, were exploited by Royalists. Although these outbursts were brief, the attempts by local government to open legal proceedings against the perpetrators provided a second flashpoint, and in Kent particularly a Royalist leadership was waiting and ready. Even so these armed rebellions were crushed quickly before they were able to spread out of the south-east. The rest of the second Civil War in the region became a pursuit and clearing-up operation. Fleeing rebels from Kent and Essex united north of the Thames and made it into Colchester hotly pursued by Fairfax and his section of the New Model Army. After a siege lasting until late August the Royalist rebels were obliged to surrender.

It was only on 8 July that the Engager army under the Duke of Hamilton crossed the border to try and restore Charles to power under the terms of the Engagement. Cromwell, once freed by the capture of Pembroke, dashed northwards to join John Lambert's forces in Yorkshire, crossed the Pennines and defeated Hamilton at Preston on 17 August. Apart from rounding up the soldiers of the shattered Engager Army and sieges at Scarborough and Pontefract the war was over by the end of August.

Anger amongst the army rank and file at the king's continued refusal to treat with the victors brought with it a demand that Charles be brought to trial, which spilled over into the army leadership. Failure in last minute talks instigated by the Presbyterians in Parliament left some men, like Henry Ireton, with apparently little room for manœuvre and the death of a king now identified as a 'man of blood', bearing responsibility for all the blood shed in the wars, seemed to become the only clear answer to the political impasse. Against objections from Presbyterians who were excluded from Parliament, the House of Lords which was closed down and Lord Fairfax himself, a trial was arranged. The Levellers, who had suggested that the monarchy should be abolished, objected on the grounds that one tyranny should not be replaced by another. They believed that the army was clearly overturning law and precedent in a way which at least rivalled the worst of the king's mis-government.

The Scottish government was now dominated by hardline Covenanters known as the Kirk Party which had driven the Engager faction from power after the defeat at Preston. Regicide was not, however, part of this group's plans and they made strenuous attempts to ward off the trial. Objections were to no avail and the king was tried, found guilty and, on 30 January 1649 executed. This chapter begins by looking at the experiences of some of the observers of those days before looking at the establishment of the Republic in England and Wales. This Republic sought to end the continuing conflict in Ireland and this became a priority in 1649. However, the execution of the king had driven a new wedge between Scotland and its neighbours and war broke out in 1650 which transformed into another war of conquest for the Republic.

Wales and the revolution

The Just Judge sent us blessed news by Peter, Paul and John
That winter shall not always last: now pleasant spring come on.

So wrote Morgan Llwyd in his poem *1648*. Much of the poem lamented Wales' distance from the heat of reformation, declaring that in the 'British climate' of Wales 'souls froze to death'. For Llwyd the work of reforming the Church had failed and this made kings, queen and princes rejoice.

Our Reformation mangled was, our blossomed truths were ripped
as errors and heresies, our Christian freedom clipped.

In another poem, *Charles the Last King of Britain*, Llwyd celebrated the defeat of the king and his execution. He instructed his readers to find the reason for the king's fall not in the works of the king, probably a reference to *Eikon Basilikon*, but in his deeds:

> Not in his fair words, but all his swords
> enraged by his command,
> that sheathe themselves in Christians' hearts
> should make you understand

Eikon Basilikon was becoming a potent enemy, for the moderate tones of the author, whether it was Charles I himself who in whole or part was the author, could potentially isolate the readers from the victors. Llywd clearly believed that the war had long-term origins. The poem exhorted the readers to reconsider the history of the Stuart monarchy which culminated in Charles' fall. The poem served as a warning to all monarchs but also to Parliament:

> Make not, O kings, your curbs too sharp,
> but truth and justice seek!
> O land, avoid king's evil now;
> O Parliament, be meek.

This suggestion that Parliament might inherit the earth is followed through in another of Lloydd's poems, *Awake, O Lord, Awake Thy Saints*, in which Wales and England are exhorted to go to war against Holland and use the opportunity of France's internal distractions to become a major force in Europe.[3] Not every poet in Wales agreed with these sentiments; Llwyd's contemporary, Rowland Watkins regarded the people as a many headed hydra. In *The Common People* he suggested allowing or encouraging their participation in public affairs was a mistake:

> Constant in nothing but inconstancy:
> When these together swarm, the kingdom fears;
> They are as fierce as tigers, rude as bears.

Watkins did not like the war. To him the passive tolerance of Charles' reign was preferable. In *Peace and War* he wrote

> … I do prefer by far
> An unjust peace before the justest war.

Whether complacent or not such a sentiment must have been echoed by many who had suffered ten years of wars and political instability and for whom the purgative of war and revolution had been worse than the illness of Charles I's reign.[4]

Other Welsh people were careful to hide their feelings about the execution of the king. Walter Powell's diary went into a deep silence on national affairs after his period as a prisoner at Raglan at the end of the first Civil War. On

30 January 1649 in an entry which again betrays the later compilation of the diary, Powell wrote simply 'King Charles beheaded after he hath had raigned 23 years and 10 months missing 2 dayes' and that was it.[5] The wider ranging consequences of the political revolution went unrecorded and the diarist was primarily self-obsessed. By the end of 1649 Walter had fallen ill: 'December[:] my right eye began to faile & I fell sicke shortly afterwards & was like to dye at Christmas. January I was still ill all the while February very sicke. March still ill.'

At this point the structural coherence of the surviving diary was lost as entries for 1652 appear.[6] A little later the entries return to an ordered state, but the national scene is still largely absent. The exception is in 1651 when again war in England drew close to the Welsh border. On 25 August Powell recorded the raising of county Trained Bands and their muster at Monmouth as Charles' Scottish army neared Worcester. Under September's entries Powell recorded 'the fight at Worcester' but continued immediately 'I bought 11 sheep of Black John for £2 2s 6d.' Powell began to enter fewer and less detailed accounts.[7] What is clear from the entries for the 1650s is that the traditional means of government in Monmouth continued to function and were regarded by people like Powell in the same way as before the war. Baronial Courts, Great Sessions and Oxford Circuit Assizes still met and Powell may well have gathered with the other gentry at Monmouth to attend them but his diary does not make this clear. Whether or not he was taking any interest in politics by 1652 is unclear, for after recording his cataract problems his entries read: 'June: Nothing; July: Nothing, I had the cateract; August: nothing; September: I was sicke; December: I was very sicke.' At the end of the diary in a nineteenth-century hand it is recorded that Walter Powell spent his last years, which the author dated to the end of the Civil Wars, collecting receipts or remedies for the plague and this may have taken precedence over the diary keeping.[8]

The costs of the war in Ireland were to continue to affect life in south Wales for years, as Powell no doubt knew through having to pay continued taxes even though he did not record it or any other fiscal details in his diary. Whilst the second Civil War rebellion continued in Pembrokeshire, the business of trying to conquer Ireland preoccupied Parliament and preparations had been made to raise £50,000 to fight the war. In February 1649 the effects of this decision were to reach Glamorgan. The money was to be raised by leasing out Welsh land confiscated from Royalists. The trustees leased out to Colonel Phillip Jones the manor of Wrinston, Michaelston, West Orchard and Lancarvan, formerly property of the Earl of Worcester, for £90 a year for three years.[9] This was one of the earliest aquisitions of the man later described as 'the most notorious of all the traffickers in Welsh sequestration'. He was a member of the sequestrations committee at Goldsmiths Hall, London but was obviously able to extend his influence to Weavers Hall where the trustees for Ireland were based. His main efforts at raising a dynasty in South Wales were confined to his home county of Glamorgan, but he was able to extend his influence throughout the south, becoming, during the 1650s, a close adherent of the Protectorate.[10] On the other hand, for other inhabitants of the county the war in Ireland provided trouble and a further drain on their resources. Ports along the coast were home to soldiers waiting to be shipped across the Irish Sea. In December 1649, for example, as the war in Ireland became bogged down in the winter along the south coast, 67 soldiers were quartered in Swansea at a cost of £11 3s 4d to the inhabitants with large enough houses.[11]

There remained a need for soldiers in Ireland for years afterwards. On 15 May 1651 soldiers for Ireland were being mustered at Haverfordwest. Thomas David, a mustermaster, was paid £35 to get men from Carmarthen to the port. The east of the county also had to provide soldiers: 50 men, a number consistent with the county's trained band contingents sent to the Bishop's wars 12 years earlier, were sent from Brecknockshire, again at the expense of £50, paid to a mustermaster.[12] Counties in north Wales sent their troops to Ireland via Beaumaris. This was a continued heavy burden, for in addition to these forces Wales still had its own county-based militia on duty to pay for. So the counties were also faced with paying for wages, saddles, trumpets for the militia and even in Cardiganshire 'a gratuity and incouragement to the said troop for their forwardness in the public servive', given to Lieutenant Richard Evans' troop of horse on 14 September 1651.[13]

Haverfordwest was not a town overjoyed by its role in the reconquest of Ireland and the rescue of 'our brothers' there. Town MPs were reminded how much the town had suffered and the borough drafted petitions setting out the problems in November 1649. A later petition in August 1650 referred to the free quarter of Cromwell's army for Ireland assembled during the summer of 1649 and the subsequent levies which had passed through the town. The petitions both referred to the demolition of the castle by Cromwell's order at the town's expense and the continuance of the general taxes. These costs were consequently driving people out of the town which would, argued the authors, in the long term prove the ruin of Haverfordwest. Further petitions also rehearsed the damage caused by Charles Gerrard's siege during the first Civil War and the costs of the defences built during the siege. Later still the total rateable value of the town was demonstrated to be unequal to the demands placed upon it.[14]

A further petition, probably dating from 1652, referred to the levy of £45 per month then being imposed on the town which, it was averred, Haverfordwest was ill-equipped to pay. The town was said to have no trade by sea or land, its principle business had been the manufacture of winter coats known as friezes worn throughout Wales. By 1652 this fashion had declined and the town had not yet established a replacement industry. Moreover, the town buildings needed attention. Three churches needed constant care and repair, as did two aquaducts, two bridges, two quays, two almshouses and there was little income from borough rents with which to do it. By February 1652 plague was in town, although the council gave thanks for it being such a mild case. However, there still was not the money to cover the required emergency measures if the situation deteriorated. Although orders were sent to neighbouring villages warning then to prevent people travelling from or to Haverfordwest, the borough council was concerned that the scale of the plague was being exaggerated in the countryside. It was not long before the town had to consider closing the markets and asked the county committee to raise a county-wide levy to provide financial aid for the inhabitants of the town if the markets had to close.[15]

Throughout the spring of 1652 the borough council prepared the grounds for another appeal on the levies raised in the town. They carefully enumerated the taxes raised to cover quartering wounded soldiers from the second Civil War up until 1651. They prepared the grounds for using two prominent sons of the town, Colonel Thomas Pride and Colonel William Gough, to represent the town in London. Cromwell, whom they had once impressed with their plight back in 1649 whilst he waited to embark for Ireland, was also contacted, and so was William Lenthal, Speaker of the Commons. Nevertheless, it proved difficult to get Parliament to listen to the problems of the town. On 18 May 1652 a concerted effort was made, but pressure of Irish business forced Haverfordwest off the Commons' agenda. It was to be some weeks before the town was relieved of its burden.[16]

The surviving correspondence of Sir John Trevor, which provided an insight into the first Civil War in North Wales, continues into the 1650s. His main correspondent in these revolutionary years is Mr John Peck, who is one of the men recommended to Trevor as a possible JP in 1647.[17] Woodds, the steward who was Trevor's main correspondent for the 1630s and 1640s, had disappeared from the scene, and Peck is attending to Trevor's business, both estate and state. Early problems with the tenants are exacerbated by Woodds not having made all the estate details available to Peck, so arrears of rent are a great problem. Since many of the tenants were pleading poverty Peck felt unable to collect the rent until he checked past details.[18]

Neither Peck nor Trevor were without enemies in north-east Wales. The Wrexham party which included a Captain (Thomas) Ball and Captain Ellis, seem to have been particular enemies, succeeding in 1650 in getting a new commission of the peace for the county which included Captain Ball, but initially excluded Peck, 'the first justice that took oath for the parlement and did the business of the whole county along time myself alone'.

He wrote with a deep sense of being wounded to Trevor on 17 August 1650. These men also attempted to interfere with the estate, claiming the right to hunt deer at various times from out of Harding Park, and Ball was also behind attempts to increase the levy of horses on Trevor from one to two in September 1652.[19]

Scotland

At Irvine on the south-west coast, the military costs of the war continued to accumulate, some continuing to dog the burgh for years. From back in December 1645, six months before the first war ended in England, to 1 March

1648 on the eve of the second Civil War, Irvine had contributed to the costs of the locally raised regiment of horse under Colonel Viscount Hugh Montgomery. Levies were collected even after the regiment was disbanded on 10 February 1647, and so perhaps they were to cover back pay. No sooner was this obligation discharged than the burgh was paying money to Lieutenant-Colonel Sir William Livingstone from the Earl of Callandar's regiment of foot, part of the Engager Army. Cash was evidently needed so quickly that it could not await ingathering and had to be borrowed from James Blair, a former provost. It remained unrepaid until 1659, the debt lasting much longer than the regiment.[20] The defeat of the Engager forces meant that Callandar's regiment had a short life. It was left at Carlisle when Hamilton invaded England and abandoned in the town in the wake of the duke's defeat at the Battle of Preston on 17 August 1648. In this impossible situation, the regiment disbanded itself shortly afterwards.

The collapse of the Engager government brought a new regiment to the region: Argyll reappeared and Irvine had to finance those of his troops that survived their defeat at Stirling during the Wiggamore Raid. Radicalised Covenanters in Ayrshire, Galloway and Clydesdale took the defeat at Preston as a signal to bring about the end of the Engager government. Armed forces marched from the south-west on Edinburgh, led by Argyle, Lord Leven and David Leslie. Although the Engager government panicked and fled the city, troops loyal to it defeated Argyle at Linlithgow, driving them back to their homelands. These forces had made their way to the Irvine region where they quartered from December to February, by which time the billeting bill had reached £540. They stayed on during March and April at the cost of another £360, but in May the regiment was recalled to Edinburgh by the established Kirk Party government.[21]

The wars between Scotland and the English–Welsh Republic drew deeply upon the resources of the town. During 1650 and 1651 Irvine had to find £12,000 worth of oats and oat meal, a total of 1,200 bolls at £10 a boll to feed the Scottish armies raised to support Charles Stuart's claim to the thrones of the British Isles. Also 793 stands of arms had to be paid for at 20 merkis a stand: a bill of around £10,600. Because of the 'troubles of the kingdome' no more than £200 had been paid at the time, and arrears dragged on throughout the next decade.[22]

In the far north-east the Engager war had drawn upon Caithness' resources. Sir John Sinclair's receipts for the war survive. He was taxed by the county at £440 for five months, August to December 1648, compared to an earlier year when he was charged only £297 15s for ten months. He also had to pay a further £15 5d for the army still fighting in Ireland and he had to contribute 205 merkis to horse levies in the county on 15 August, and it would seem £70 14s for the garrison at Inverness.[23] Sir John Sinclair of Dunbeath was similarly charged heavily for a range of levies, including excise taxes by the war committee.

Robert Baillie was possessed throughout these confused years by concerns over divisions not between Scotland and England but those within Kirk and country. Threats to internal unity and to the unity of the nations of Scotland and England had the same source: English Sectaries. The impetus for Church reform along Presbyterian lines in England had faded during the mid-1640s. The army in particular had contained a number of men who rejected the over-weening nature of Presbyterianism. Furthermore, the willingness of the parliamentary Presbyterian faction's desire to pursue a settlement with the king despite his obvious duplicity led to their expulsion from Parliament in December 1649. This left the political and religious impetus to the Independents, or Sectaries as their enemies disparagingly referred to them, and now these divisive men threatened Scotland. Baillie had accepted the Engagement hoping that it signalled the safety of the Church rather than of the king, but the Kirk's alliance with Charles had brought into Scotland some of the king's supporters, who Baillie could not refrain, even in the middle of the 1648 crisis, from calling 'malignants'. To his mind it was these very men who had thrown the great enter-prise of 1648 into danger by seizing Carlisle and Berwick during April, a move which would have provoked the invasion of Scotland by the 'army of sectaries' – the New Model Army. The greatest threat to the Covenant had been placing the Engager Army in the hands of the Duke of Hamilton, the Earl of Callandar and other Royalist or conservative Covenanters. When these two took command of the army themselves, Baillie despaired, 'From that day we lost the Army.' For Baillie the Engagement was quickly becoming a disaster, the government was being manipulated by Royalists: 'Lauderdale with grief, the Treasurer with many tears, told me, how sore against their heart they went they way now they were in.' Worse, the army had dithered and failed to take advantage of Cromwell being in Wales and Fairfax's preoccupation with the risings in the south-east of England.

Even in Glasgow Baillie found much to despair over. Members of the town council had been imprisoned in the Tolbooth for failing to muster the militia and impose the new financial levies to support the Engagement. In their place excluded councillors previously barred from sitting because of their Royalist leanings were recalled to form a new council. At around the same time, horse and foot were billeted on the town in the houses of

> the most religious people of our town, hudge burdens did fall; on some ten, on some twenty, on some thirty sojours, and more did quarter; who, beside their meat and drink, wine and good cheer, and whatever they called for, did exact cruelie their daylie pay, and much more. In ten days the cost a few honest but mean people, above forty thousand pounds [Scotish money], besides plundering of these whom necessity forced to flee from their houses. Our losse and danger was not so great by James Grahame[24]

For some the response to this was to discuss resisting the Engagers and eventually led to the Wiggamore rising. Rumours of discussions at Irvine between Argyll,

Cassillis and Eglington were tied into this. Armed men and deserting soldiers met at Loudon Hill and proposed 'resistance in the west'. Baillie opposed this direct action and suggested only passive submission to the government instead. But some of the determined resisters made a stand at Mauchline Moor were they were attacked and defeated by John Middleton, now an Engager general. The western rising had to await the Battle of Preston for its moment.

Some protests were on a smaller scale. One Edinburgh baker became irate. He did not approve of the Engagement and took this out on the Marquis of Hamilton. Hamilton could well be blamed for the Engagement, although perhaps the panic-stricken commissioners on the Isle of Wight might have been more directly responsible. Without their hurried action, Hamilton would have had difficulty in swinging the estates into such an alliance with the king. These subtleties, if they occurred to Alexander Denholme (there is no reason why they should not have done) did not bother him one June night. At 11 o'clock Alexander found himself in the same street as the marquis. It was too good an opportunity to miss. He was armed and angry, nevertheless he was only accused of assaulting the marquis with rash words.[25]

Baillie reported the opening stages of the brief second Civil War after Mauchline Moor to William Strang, who was in Danzig, in a letter on 23 August 1648. He was at once amazed at the size of the army, 'twenty-two thousand foot, and eight thousand horse, which common report made them' which he described as 'the greatest that came from Scotland since the beginning of these troubles' and then horrified at the cost at an estimated £100 for each foot soldier and 300 merkis for each horse soldier and mount. He was also appalled at the 'unlimited plunder of many good and pious people'. And for what? Baillie gave vent to some wishful thinking, based on a situation where Prince Charles blocked the trade of London, and forced the collapse of the New Model Army through lack of funds: 'the cursed army of Sectaries should evanish in smoke'. Counter-factual or virtual history perhaps, but no more than a desperate man's fantasy. Baillie himself recognised that even if the king was somehow restored the result might be liberal religious toleration, which we in a secular age might approve of, but to him it was a disaster: 'the most that shall be obtained be but ane Erastian weak Presbyterie, with a tolleration of Poperie and Episcopacie at Court and of diverse sects elsewhere'. Worse was more likely. Baillie felt powerless: 'We, who might have been the cheefe instruments to have stopped this evill, are for the time so farr at odds with our State, Army, and King, that the despite which I feare all thre hes at us, is lyke to further much that evill in England, and draw it ere long on Scotland also.' On top of these fears, the plague in Aberdeen, Glasgow and Edinburgh bothered him and the heavy rains damaging the crops during the harvest month added to the gloom.[26]

In the Scottish countryside as a whole the effects of the continued wars would be physical as well as mental. The surviving papers of the Court at Cortaquay, held by the Earl of Arlie's baillie show how local manor courts, where they survived, acted as the intermediary between the county committees of war, and the individual sessions in 1648 and 1649 demonstrate this. The baillie, John Ogilvy of Caley, convened the court as usual but part of the business was a response to a levy for three foot soldiers imposed in November 1648 amongst the general run of business. In the following February, as the news of Charles I's death sped northwards, Margaret Moyle and her husband Thomas Gorden had more important business. They were in court accused of molesting and 'trubling' Margaret's sister Isabelle. The court ordered them to keep apart thereafter, Margaret and Thomas were ordered to leave the parish immediately. If they did not they would be fined £40. The same session also had military business, deciding upon the levy to be paid by the tenants. The estate as a whole was levied at £27 a month, but the tenants only paid £1 6s 8d of the levy as ordered by the court.[27] To support the wars against England a more extensive levy, this time of 12 men was made within the court's jurisdiction. As usual the basis for the assessment was the amount of ploughlands, one man levied for each plough. Within a short space of time a second levy of six more men was ordered and divided up by the court.

The last recorded military interference at Crathie in Aberdeenshire was made during 1649. David Lesley's forces arrived in April. They killed David Brebner's plough ox on Lesley's first visit and returned in May to take away crops and lambs from Brebner and others including widow Agnes Andro who lost four goats. Edward MacHardie lost two oxen, the most expensive of the animals, he rated them at £52 13s, whereas Brebner had priced his at £20, and Alex Ogoe priced the one plough ox he lost at £26 13s 4d. The loss of goats at Crathie, where there had been years of deprivation, would have affected the ability to make a living from marginal land. The loss of the oxen which would have worked the available arable land was also likely to have been expensive if not devastating.[28]

War between the Republic and Scotland

The execution of the king resulted in the long descent into war against the Republic of England and Wales. The Scots willingness to embrace Charles Stuart changed the relationship between the English and Welsh and their former allies and brothers. Two cousins, John and Adam Baines were serving in the North of England in 1650 when the prince travelled to Scotland. John Baines wrote to Adam on 11 July 1650 from Newcastle. He believed that the Scots had crowned the prince, but hoped that Cromwell's declaration to the people in Scotland, which was being drafted, would stop the Scots from siding wholeheartedly with his cause. In 1650 war between England and Scotland broke out and the New Model Army was mobilised in the north of England ready to invade Scotland. On 22 July Cromwell, Lord General after Fairfax had resigned the post, crossed the border. An early attack on Edinburgh failed and the English forces retreated to Dunbar. Supplies were slow to reach the New Model Army and disease weakened the army considerably. A second attack on Edinburgh again failed and the English returned in late August to Dunbar. This time the Scots followed closely, but Leven expected Cromwell to retreat further, thinking his army to be disease-ridden. Instead it was Cromwell who attacked and on 3 September defeated the Scots. Defeat prompted a reshuffle in the political picture at Edinburgh and the hard-line approach of the Kirk Party had to be ameliorated to rebuild an army with a broader political base. A decision was made to allow Engagers and Royalists to join the armed forces.

For some Scots the execution of the king had been so horrific that explanations had to be sought. Some saw the origins in Scottish dealings with England in late 1646. Henry Guthrie, one time Bishop of Stirling, and former member of the General Assembly, saw the money sent to Scotland by the Westminster Parliament to pay of a portion of the arrears due to the Army of the Solemn League and Covenant as blood-money, because the Scots then handed over the king to the English. This guilt was not to be laid upon the whole nation.

> The guilt an stain due to the act should not, with reason be imputed to the generality of the Scots nation, in regard, First concerning the nobility, that whosoever shall be at pains to compare the list of Scots noblemen, with the sederunt of Parliament [the list of those in attendance], will find that the third part of the nobility was not present, very many having been secluded for their known affection to the king, and others who would have been admitted, did, upon their own accord withdraw, being on the omne part, resolved not to comply, and on the other hand, loath by their dissent to offend the prevailing faction, lest they should encroach upon their fortunes. And for the gentry, burghs and commonality throughout the land, Fife and the western shires betwixt Hamilton and Galloway, being excepted, there were an hundred for one, all the kingdom over that abhorred it, and would have never instriucted their commissioners that way: So they alone have to answer to God for that deportment.

The disease, Guthry implied later, was very much an English one and was introduced by them into Scotland back in 1647. He noted that when the English commissioners arrived in Edinburgh that year with the money, one of them, a minister named Mr Herle, did not offer prayers for the king when he preached at St Giles.[29] Guthrie had sided with the Engagement, for which he was deprived of his place in the Assembly, and thereafter his was amongst the dissenting voices. Moreover, Guthrie believed that the execution of the king, whom he referred to as 'the best of princes, being cut off in his prime of his age by the barbarous hands of his unnatural subjects' was a long established plan. Guthrie believed that when Cromwell was in Edinburgh back in September 1648 he had discussed 'his design in reference to the king' with Argyll, Loudoun, the Earl of Lothian and others and gained their consent. This design encompassed the death of the king.[30]

Despite the gloom after the king's death, Baillie was able on 7 February 1649 to appear optimistic when he wrote to Sprang. He joyfully announced the proclamation of Charles II and added his hope that the new monarch would sign the Covenant bringing the religious security Scotland sought after.[31] Alexander Jaffrey was not so optimistic. By now he was again a borough representative for Aberdeen in the Estates and still on the Aberdeenshire Committee of War and Provost of Aberdeen. He was sent as one of the commissioners to Holland in 1649 to discuss terms with the prince. He seems to have been glad that the initial discussions came to very little. However, the following year, whilst a member of the Committee of Estates, the 'snare and entanglement' God had preserved him from the previous year could not be avoided. He held himself to blame:

> we did sinfully both entangle and engage the nation and ourselves, and that poor young prince to whom we were sent; making him sign and swear a Covenant, which we knew, from clear and demonstrable reasons, that he hated in his heart

The Scots were not solely responsible for this dilemma.

> Yet, he finding that upon these terms only, he could be admitted to rule over us, (all other means having then failed him,) *he* sinfully complied with what *we* most sinfully pressed upon him:– where, I must confess, to my apprehension, *our* sin was more than *his*.

When looking back on it as he composed his memoirs, Jaffrey, having tried to explain how he was impressed by the arguments of his superiors and how, despite their sinfulness, they had never intended what later transpired, wrote: 'I think the Lord hath justly reproved us, and the whole nation – especially the leading men of church and state – for so much prevarication; in pretending his glory.'

Jaffray knew that many Presbyterians in Scotland were frightened by the prospect of what was becoming apparent in England. Instead of the Presbyterian Church hoped for in England there was instead 'a lawless liberty, and toleration of all religions'. This was the reason why the Scots negotiated with Prince Charles and brought him to Scotland. But this was also Jaffray's own journey and he tied up God's work with his own personal realisation that the preservation of the all-embracing Kirk was not truly God's will, but mens'.[32] Further manifestations of this were seen when again Jaffray emerged from danger unscathed. He had been appointed to greet the prince on his arrival in Scotland and served on Estates committees charged with war preparations. On 3 September 1650, he was wounded four times at the Battle of Dunbar and captured. He was one of the prisoners quickly exchanged that year. These incidents forced on him a new 'take [tack] of my life' (in English, a new lease of life).

He reassessed himself, convinced that God had given him a clear sign. The incidents of the past six years became part of that message. Furthermore, in 1651 after first meeting with Monck, perhaps to allay the levying of high taxes on Aberdeen where he was now provost after its capture on 7 September, he had also begun to meet with Cromwell and Charles Fleetwood and the divine Dr John Owen. These meetings confirmed his doubts on the issue of the alliance with Prince Charles and on the nature of the Covenant and the Solemn League and Covenant, both of which he now began to see as erroneous. Naturally this affected his relationships with his friends. Andrew Cant, his one-time fellow prisoner and since 1647 his father-in-law, refused at first to even read Jaffray's meditations on the Covenant. Still Jaffray continued to pursue his path of questioning the actions of the past thirteen years, and after meeting the members of the General Assembly in October 1651 who set aside time to debate his questions, Jaffray came to a conclusion. Whilst the founders of the reformed Kirk had set out with great intentions a century earlier, their successors had turned from necessary continued reform instead to defence of what had been achieved. The defence of the Kirk in its perceived perfect form ('the *only* way of Jesus Christ') from 'being brought back to Popery', became an end in itself distracting the nation and its divines from the true path of understanding God's intentions. Dunbar was the deciding factor prompting this enquiry and its decision. 'The dreadful appearance of God against us at Dunbar, after so many public appeals to him' was how Jaffray, attacked by former friends and others for having being beguiled by men (probably Englishmen at that), justified his actions some six years later. The mistaken purpose was the root of the divisions between the Presbyterians themselves into Resolutioners and Protestors. It also explained the clashes between Arminians, Anabaptists and others who had once been united against popery. Jaffray's tone was markedly liberal, believing that all groups were composed of truly godly men.[33]

The new war embroiled Edinburgh in long continuing costs; in 1649 the city was charged £90,000 and people refusing to pay had soldiers billeted upon them. In July 1650 the town fencibles, men of service age, were gathered together to defend the town because of the 'approache of Cromwell and that sectarian partie'. The city's physical defences were improved by the removal of houses on Lieth Wynd and in St Mary's Ward. Somewhat less directly related, the council decided that the moral defences of the city were threatened by the presence of women taverners and the 'fearful sinns committed by them'. All vintners were ordered on 6 March 1650 to sack their women staff and employ boys in their stead.[34]

Across the country, Glasgow responded to the emergency by tightening its financial belt. The poor were ordered to search out strangers who were claiming relief and inform on them. If they failed to do so their own pensions were in danger of termination. There was a problem with those who should have paid too, many were refusing and they were threatened with billeting. The city was also providing soldiers, on top of a levy of 50 men in July 1650 another 100 were demanded as the New Model Army approached Scotland. The city had to raise 9,000 merkis at short notice to support them, and by November those who refused to pay were threatened with the Western Army. There were also the losers to cater for. Widows and orphans had to be provided for.[35]

The presence of the English in the west from the summer of 1650 had immense consequences. By the end of the year the town's magistrates were in a moral dilemma. They had been ordered to billet these 'Inglishes' which they could not bear 'as being a thing accessorie to their oppressing of the people'. The compromise seems to have been trying to get several Glaswegians to voluntarily offer accommodation at a meeting. But five days later on 16 December they had to be more practical and appoint a committee to assess the burgh for English taxes.[36] When the New Model Army moved from the city Glasgow was able to send £100 sterling to Charles II, and to compensate Janet Tilloche for the 6 gallons and 3 pints of ale she had provided to the English during their stay. During the dash southwards by the king's army, Glasgow supplied the fortresses of the defensive lines across the waist of Scotland, raising excise taxes and sending bedding to Stirling and Dunbarton.[37]

When, after Dunbar, the government decided to allow former Engagers and Royalists to join the army, Archibald Johnston was incensed; they were allowing the 'tagg and rag of Ingagers' as a remedy for the shortcomings of the cause. In his diary he fulminated against not having punished them more severely in the first place. He saw any use of the 'malignants', the former Royalists, as a 'sin indangering the cause' and he feared that plans to compromise on the issue were putting the king's cause before God's.[38] The compromise when it did come left Archibald in some despair. On 19 April 1651 he wrote:

> I earnestly intreated the Lord to reclayme any of His awen that had gon on in the present cause throw oppression maiking wyse men madde and to spaire them tho mingled in the day of battel. Thy awen, tho they be humbled, but to execut Thy anger agaynst Thy incorrigible enemyes on both sydes ...

When in June 1651 he heard that the Estates had rescinded the Act of Classes passed to categorise the level of guilt of those who had fought against the government in 1643–7, he was even more despondent. He felt that giving liberty to those previously imprisoned who were now released and the employment of others was like expelling God and calling in the devil: 'al jeues, Turks, al Rome but not Protestants' he groaned.[39]

Baines had accompanied the invading New Model Army into Scotland and remained there after the Battle of Dunbar. In April 1651, by which time the Scots had crowned Charles II, he reported the discussions with the ministers of western Scotland, including Patrick Gillespie, where Lieutenant General Lambert had failed to come to any real agreement with him. This area might well be the least enamoured with the compromise with the Royalists and

Engagers at Edinburgh, but this certainly did not make them friends of the impious Independents, even if Lambert promised to aim for a better understanding between them.[40]

Baines' April letter had been written during a lull in the campaign largely caused by Cromwell's illness. It was a lull taken advantage of by Francis Lambert, wife of the lieutenant general. She wrote to Adam Baines of 'sume dayes I Happly enjoy my dearest frend' before Lambert went into the field again in July. Mrs Lambert had travelled into Scotland with Captain Robert Baynes, Adam's brother who was in Lambert's own troop, and it is clear that she thought well of him. The relationship between the Lamberts and the Baynes family was close and would continue over the next decade.[41] Mrs Lambert's letters to Adam Baynes contained both news of her husband's victory over the Scots in the wake of Charles Stuart's rapid march into England, and domestic matters. There was an air of diplomacy and humour to some of her affairs, she was particularly concerned to get a yard of French lawne sent up to her, 'for I have nothing to wear about my neck, and I dare not go bare, for feare of giving offense to tender saintes'.[42]

For others the bare neck of Mrs Lambert was not a concern. Rumours of the behaviour of the English soldiers related to more than moral matters. John Nicholl in his diary recorded a story told to him in the beginning of the 1650 campaign:

> They ... tuik sum of the Scottis men prissoneris; amongst quhom ane simple sodger, quhois eyes they holkit out of his heid, becaus upone his back thair wes drawn with quhyte calk thir wordis I AM FOR KING CHARLES, stryped him naked of his cloathes, and sent him bak.[43]

There is no verification for this story; Nichol himself had earlier gleefully recorded the arrival of Charles Stuart into Scotland and his bias may well have led to credulity. The editor of his diary points out, however, that Nichol bent as the willow and tried to walk a tightrope to produce a diary which would not incriminate him with anyone. Indeed it was not a safe time to proclaim bad tidings too loudly. Nicoll recorded the attempt to keep rumours and treasonous words in check as the wisdom of taking arms in Charles Stuart's name was being debated at large.

> Much falset and sheitting at this tyme wes daylie detectit by the Lordis of Sessioun; for the quhilk their was daylie hanging, skurking, nailling of luggis, and binding of pepill to the Trone, and booring of tounges; so that it was ane fatall yeir for fals notaris and witnessis, as daylie experience did witnes

Two years later Nicoll recorded the destruction of the symbols of monarchy at St Giles in February 1652. By now the English were not a fearsome crowd miles away. 'The same day the lyke was done at the entrie of the Parliament Hous and Nather Bow, quhair the Kinges airmes or portrat wes fund … The lyke, also in the Castlell of Edinburgh, and the Palice of Halyrudhous.' Moreover the 'Enfglisches' had control of the political world too. When 'ane gallant Englische gentillman' drank a toast to Charles Stuart his ear was nailed to the gallows and them cut off completely. Two other 'Englisches' who followed his example were tied to the gallows at Edinburgh and whipped. Then their ears were nailed to the posts. One of the men had his ear 'cuttit from the ruitt with a resour' the other had his mouth 'skobit' – wedged open with crossed sticks whilst his tongue was pulled between the sticks to its full extent and then tied in place with thread for about an hour.[44]

Archibald Johnston met Cromwell when Edinburgh fell to the English army in 1651. On 5 May he and Cromwell discussed the English invasion. Cromwell saw the Scots as erring brothers, but fundamentally good.[45] He was determined to find common ground through discussion. With Johnston he was trying to justify the Republic's invasion of Scotland by arguing that it paralleled the Scottish invasion of England in 1640, as both were designed to defeat a wrongful monarch. Despite his personal doubts about the alliance with Charles II, Johnston could not agree. He told Cromwell that the Scots had only invaded England in self-defence,

> because Ingland had refused our offer of treatyes, imprisoned our commissioners, declared us rebels and traitors, raysed an airmy against us and wes marching towards our Border, and the Deputy of Ireland coming in upon the West-land; then out of meir necessity, besett by sea and land, we wes forced to goe for our defence [46]

By 8 September news of the Cromwell's defeat of Charles Stuart, at the Battle of Worcester five days before, arrived in Scotland. Archibald's renewed pleas to God had brought the usual response. He was working his mysterious way, revealing little of his motive for interpretation. Archibald was particularly struck by the coincidence of it happening on the anniversary of Dunbar.

The consequences were potentially devastating: Johnston suspected that Scotland would be colonised in the same way as had been proposed for Ireland when he heard that English officers had been allocated parcels of Scottish land. His fears had some justification, but it has been argued that they were not fully realised as the terms of the union of Scotland and the Republic was more of a negotiation between equals than that imposed on Ireland, and the numbers of dispossessed major landholders remained low.[47]

After the battle of Dunbar, Baillie did not go as far as Jaffray in his assessment of the catastrophe, but the battle did force him into reconsidering his position and he returned to his belief that the Scots themselves had somehow thrown away God's victory, because of their own divisions. His apprehensions were no doubt deepened when the Remonstrants appeared in late 1650. The

Remonstrants were drawn chiefly from the west where the opponents of the Engagement had derived. They objected, through a remonstrance, to the inclusion of former Engagers and Royalists in the newly reconstructed army formed in the wake of the defeat at Dunbar. Baillie could not agree with the Remonstrance itself, nor was he happy with the drawing up of objections at this time and he was very disappointed that many of his friends and colleagues had become associated with it. He told David Dickson, 'you consent to put upon our church the foullest blot that ever it yet got', and Robert Douglas was told that 'you will contribute to give our Kirk and State a wound which in haste will not be gotten remedied'.[48]

One of the men Baillie began to suspect of fomenting the debates and divisions in the Scottish nation was Patrick Gillespie a man seen to be forward in raising troops to defend Scotland from the English. Baillie suspected him in 1650 of raising forces in the west which would refuse the deal with Charles II whilst ostensibly raised for the king's defence. But as soon as the regiments were given legal status and money raised in Clydesdale for their support, one of the leaders, Colonel Strachan, declared that not only would his forces not serve with David Leslie, but that these western troops would fight independently. Strachan, Baillie recalled, had been an associate of the Sectaries in London and had fought with Cromwell at Preston in 1648. Gillespie appeared keen to delay any deal with Charles until his commitment to the Covenant was proved. For Baillie unity was central to winning God's favour and a victory. When that victory failed to materialise and the English and Welsh forces occupied Glasgow, Patrick Gillespie appeared again as an enemy to that unity, responsible for an attack on the government of the town, which resulted in a scuffle which had to be broken up by English troops.

For many, the cost of having a monarch was not an issue of conscience, but one of finance. In the wake of the Battle of Dunbar and the compromise with Charles and his Engagers and Royalists the Estates issued instructions for levies. The Stirling Committee of War met with Lord Erskine to discuss the Estates' instructions. A levy was set at one horse per every 1,000 merkis of rent but there was some evidence that there may have been some local opposition to the levy, and by extension, the alliance of the Kirk with the newly installed king.[49]

Just as in England the problems caused by the wars of 1642–6 had not been cleared up. In was not until March 1650 that John Drummond of Lenoch (Lennox, north-east of Glasgow) had his case resolved by the Second Triennial Parliament. It was recognised that he and his 'boundis people' had suffered because of 'James Grahame and his adherentis' when the marquis' Royalist forces had been in Scotland. His appeal to the Committee of Accounts and Monies was really based on his inability to pay current taxes for the coming war against England. The Parliament ordered his exemption.[50]

England

The letters sent by representatives of the Venetian State were compiled from information sent from England in Paris and forwarded to Venice from the summer of 1645 until 1652. The information conveyed illuminating if conflicting views of England. When the captive king was brought southwards after the Scots had left him to the English, the report contained the description: 'Everywhere on the road the people flocked to see him in great numbers, but they were not allowed to bring the keys and the sword with other marks of sovereign power.'

At first this sits uneasily with the later report that the publication of *The Case of the Army Truly Stated*, which set out the grievances of unpaid and unsatisfied rank and file of the New Model Army, caused great excitement, borne of enthusiasm, and fears that it was causing disorder, led to searches for its author. However, the reference to the flocking of the people may only refer to the official gatherings of borough officials who were obliged by their charters to present the reigning monarchs with the symbols of their town's government, swords and keys coupled with local curiosity.[51] There was greater apathy than either of the quotations could relay, despite the real anger behind the representations made to the government which lay behind the risings of May 1648. Much of that anger was stirred up by Royalists making use of discontent and trying to force a national rebellion against the government.[52]

On 8 July 1648, the Marquis of Hamilton led the Engager Army into England, crossing the border this time near Carlisle. It had only been seventeen months since the Army of the Solemn League and Covenant left the North. For six days he lingered there before moving further south. The army was joined by Sir Marmaduke Langdale and reinforcements at Penrith. The only element of surprise in all of this was the use of the western route into the country. On both previous occasions the Scots invasion forces had entered Northumberland. This time there was the expectation that some of the Ulster Scots forces, which had agreed to the Engagement would cross the North Channel and join them. The progress of the Engager army was slow. Harassment of Hamilton had begun as early as mid-July and by the time Oliver Cromwell joined General Lambert on 27 July, he had only reached Hornby in Lancashire. The effects of this military appearance were slight by comparison with the occupation by Scots forces in earlier years. Although the army was of comparable size with both those that arrived in 1640 and 1644, it was only there for a couple of months rather than years.

At Hutton Rudby on the edge of the North Yorkshire moors the second Civil War continued the drain on the village resources. The fight against the Scots entailed the calling out of the Trained Bands as well as the use of the New Model Army, and William Armstrong recorded the payments made from the tithes. Captain Best of the Trained Bands was the recipient of extra levies on the village, set at 8d per oxgang on 20 June from the village tithes, 3d per oxgang on

3 July, and 10d on 8 July, before claims were made on the tithes for coats for the soldiers, a party of light horse. Before the campaign against Hamilton was over Armstrong had paid out £5 17s 6d, on the Trained Bands and on Cromwell's section of the New Model Army as it marched through the county.[53] The light horse Armstrong recorded were charged on the area, for the Bramsburton lands of the Royalist Sir Arthur Ingram were charged £12 by collector Anthony Shaw on 28 August. The siege of Scarborough where the second governor in five years had changed his allegiance affected many Yorkshire communities. Hutton Rudby too had to pay for it.

Billeting and other costs in central Lancashire where the invading army was defeated proved a problem during the second Civil War and its aftermath. During the invasion, for example, three regiments of Scots had been stationed around Dunkenhelm for three days and they took all of the hay in the area. After the Battle of Preston the New Model Army arrived along with Lancashire-trained bands. The accounts amongst the Petre of Dunkenhelm papers of a probable head constable in Blackburn Hundred record the billeting imposed on one woman inn-holder. They came:

> by iiii, vi, 9, 10 or xv att a tyme, some all night and some but meale and drinke and away both horse and foote, but moste foote and all vict-ualled by Margaret and nothinge sett downe for itt: but for that charge and muche more shee is allowed vl for her victuals in vii yeares and this time [?] she said all her prvision gone both meale, maulte and hosre bread, drinke and many other things[54]

The cumulative effects of the war were beginning to have an effect on individuals, and the militarisation of the area was not over yet.

Even when the Scots had been defeated at Preston, Wigan and Warrington, not all of the local soldiers were allowed home. According to the accounts remaining in the Petre of Dunkenhelm papers, 15 September in the Dunkenhelm area of Lancashire, looked promising for James Whitehead, Robert Eastwoode and their 13 colleagues. They were all paid the first instalment of 16 weeks back pay. They had been assembled in the last week of May. The war might have appeared over, but they were not disbanded, and the accounts show that these soldiers were kept in pay right into the winter. Moreover, the communities around Billington in central north Lancashire also had to cater for Colonel Aston's soldiers. In some areas this caused difficulty. The levies for quartering were made by 'way of assent' – getting the community to decide which houses should provide lodgings, but as early as August 1648 the villagers of Conliffe near Billington were unable to accommodate the soldiers and other communities had to take up the burden. Billeting continued at least until March 1649 and usually the householder was paid. In February 1648 the levy of John Hayhurst of Conliffe house, Billington, came to £3 10s for one and half men and horses for three weeks, or around 15s 6d a week for a man and a horse.[55]

In Scarborough's council minutes the first recorded intimation of castle governor Matthew Boynton's change of heart came at the end of July, when the governor ordered a stronger guard in the town and summoned householders 'of what degree soever' to a meeting. On 1 August the governor asked that a company of 80 soldiers be raised at the town's charge until he could repay them; £20 a week was charged on the common hall. A loan of £80 was requested of the council, but because of 'the present great charges on the town the scarsity & dearnes of all manner of provisions & the want of all manner of trading, wee are not able to lend the same', and instead a loan of £70 was passed on to him.[56] The deal planks and nails in the town were commandeered and the gates blockaded by workmen employed at the town's charge. Coals and candles were supplied to the courts of guards set up around the town. By 12 September the effects of this expenditure, the constant demands for more money, along with the 'eateing upp our meadows and the takeing and wasting our hay, the taking away our kine and horses', caused the town to petition the governor for relief. Seven days later a leaguer arrived and began to take away the pews in St Mary's, and levied £140 on the town to support itself. The council had the courage to refuse the sum and voted £100 instead.[57]

The county as a whole soon had to pay for the siege there and for the siege of Pontefract which had also declared for the king's doomed cause. A £10,500 levy was imposed on the county to pay for it by the county committee on 1 October 1648. Bridlington was paying for the bulwarks at neighbouring Scarborough. Constable Richard Lycock had to travel there on 3 November to sort out the money. Townswomen Judith Frost, Mary Dyneley, widow Hudson and Hoskin's wife produced 18s 3d worth of bedding for the leaguer and this still was not enough, for the constables had to buy a mattress at Scarborough to make up the assessment. It took Thomas Jackson two journeys to get the bedding to Scarborough.[58]

By January the common hall at Scarborough was describing the town as 'almost utterly ruined' in a petition for billeting arrears due from the six months before Boynton changed sides to be offset against the monthly tax assessment. Once the siege was over the war damage had to be attended to. St Thomas' was in ruins and to be pulled down, the lead and wood was to be recycled to repair St Mary's. The school house was demolished by Boynton and its stone was to be sold, the profits going to St Mary's repairs. The Ferrers aisle of the church was to used as the school.[59] Fortunately the new governor was sympathetic to the town, and declared that he would lay down his commission 'rather than stay to see the town quite impoverished and ruined'; he offered to loan 3s a week to each soldier to enable them to pay their billeting charges in houses where they were welcome.[60]

In north Yorkshire, close to the border with Lancashire, the upheavals had been great. The Court Baron of the communities of Carlton, Kirkby Malham, Airton, Hanlith, West and East Maleham had apparently been disrupted by the war, commencing again in 1648. From the late 1630s the villages had been the property of John Lambert of Carlton. In 1648 Lambert was a major general in the New Model Army and was to fight at the Battle of Preston. The courts were dealing with regular business when they recommenced and there is no overt sign of the contemporary upheavals. Many of the cases which appeared over the next three years dealt with unpaid debts; at least some of these were linked to the general economic effects of the wars. In 10 January 1650 William Younge sued the heirs of Thomas Knowles of Maleham for 10s lent to Knowles in 1645 along with damages (or in effect interest) of 5s. Robert Parker had lent John Bentham of Kirkby Malham £1 19s 10½d in 1646. He claimed 10s damages, but had to settle for a grey mare distrained by the bailiff in lieu of the whole sum and interest. There were other equally minor offences to examine: Robert Kinge of Kirkby Malham's carbine barrel and gunlock had somehow come into the possession of Thomas Squire and his son Thomas in 1648. Kinge demanded their return and 30s damages. The Squires were found guilty of holding onto the gun parts and fined 2s. By 1651 there was one very clear sign that the Commonwealth existed: the language of the court minutes, which were generally partly in Latin, were being almost wholly written in English.[61]

In Upton, Nottinghamshire, there would appear to be no evidence of open dissatisfaction with the progress of events after the first Civil War, principally because there is no evidence of rebellion in the area during 1648–9. If individual small group protests, leading to breaking the law, did occur we cannot tell. Upton accounts do in places refer to people being escorted to the Quarter Sessions, or to a JP, but the most likely place for detecting any sort of protest would be the Quarter Sessions. However, the minutes for these stopped in October 1642, and although we know they were taking place again from Easter 1646, the minutebooks do not commence again until 1652. During this most exiting and frightening time, the Upton accounts demonstrate a remarkable return to some of the normal functions of local government. The Leet court had occasionally met during the war, but as early as March 1646 the alehouse licences were being checked again. On 4 April 1646, whilst the siege at Upton was still continuing, Quarter Duties, for the relief of the poor prisoners were once again collected; the postmaster was collecting horse levies again by July. The religious climate was changing though, and whilst tithes were still collected to support the incumbent, the form of worship changed back in May 1646 when 2s was paid for a copy of the new Directory of Worship, the mildly Presbyterian liturgy drafted by the Westminster Committee of Divines.

Upton was still faced with problems caused by the war: there were large numbers of displaced persons passing through the village, comprising defeated Royalists, straggling parliamentarians, Protestant refugees from Ireland, and those rendered homeless by the war. There were backlogs of unpaid rebates from taxes to be paid to those who had supplied goods to the armies besieging Newark. The high level of taxes and the ancillary costs resulted in the 1646 total disbursements remaining very high, at £140 8s 0d. We cannot tell because of damage to the account book what the financial toll was in 1647 and 1648, although it is clear that the same sorts of payments and levies persisted. George Stanton's recorded total of £50 1s 11d for 1648 levies may be a partial record; if not then it represents a significant fall. The amounts for 1649 did show a dramatic fall from the 1646 disbursements, although an increase on Stanton's 1648 total of some £31 0s 2d. One feature of the dysfunction of the war was the continued passage through the town of displaced people. In 1649, the numbers of Irish refugees continued at a high level with sixteen Irish women, one Irish child and a man and sixteen 'companies' of unspecified Irish people passed through the village. Additionally, there were seventeen disabled people, eight children and 24 discharged soldiers. Fifteen more single people of unrecorded gender and six 'companies' of unspecified poor people passed through Upton and were given small sums of money which totalled £2, or 3 per cent of the community budget.[62]

The year 1649, which saw the execution of the king and the establishment of the Republic, saw little change in Upton. The lower levels of state functions continued almost unchanged, and the regiments raised for the 1648 war were disbanded, at the charge of the villages. The continuing war in the British Isles still intruded, during the first three months of the year the siege at Pontefract drew resources from Upton, and the army taxes remained high to fund the war in Ireland, which became the central concern of the Republic's military forces from August that year. In 1650 the continued costs of war, firstly in Ireland and then against Charles II's Scottish Army, combined to keep the village's disbursements at a high level: they totalled £77 19s 0d, and the village fell into arrears, as Constable Richard Kitchen had only collected £73 7s 7d. The continuing wars of the English Republic, in Ireland and Scotland and then in England too in 1651, prevented any return to financial stability and security in that year. The knock-on effects of displacement and destruction also kept costs high, with a constant stream of refugees and maimed soldiers passing through the village. It is likely that the total disbursements for 1651 would have been at a high level. Even though the last half page of accounts is missing the total up to that point was already £112 1s 5d, a 53 per cent increase on the year before, although still not as high as the later years of the first Civil War.

Isaac Archer was a young boy during the Civil Wars. He was born in 1641 at South Elmham in Suffolk, and at the age of six, between the wars, his family moved to Halstead. His father was a minister with a parliamentarian reputation and when Royalist soldiers made their way to Colchester in 1648 through Halstead, they asked for his father 'and threatened that if they could find my father, to chop him as small herbs for the pot'. The family had fled as soon as the Royalists approached: his father was hiding in a field with another man, under a pile of faggots, whilst Isaac, his mother, brother and three sisters also ran a mile and a half to another field where they hid before making their way to Coggleshall, where parliamentarian soldiers were stationed. The cavaliers ransacked the Archer home. Isaac's father had left a bundle of cash in the library in the home so that any soldiers would see it, take and leave the books behind. It seems that neither the books nor the money were taken.

Isaac's mother, brother and younger sister died shortly after the second Civil War. When Halstead could no longer afford to pay for William Archer's ministry, the family moved to Colchester, and young Isaac began mixing with boys his father did not approve of and so was boarded out at Halstead school. His father married again and Isaac's new (step) brother's hobby got Isaac into new trouble. He used to embellish pictures by sticking silk to them with isinglass and he seems to have done this with a picture of Charles I. William Archer came upon the picture and, 'I know not why, with a knife cutt out his head in the picture.' The young Isaac related a garbled version of the story to his friends in Colchester on a school holiday. This caused unwanted fame for his father, before the mistake was explained.[63]

Mr John Clopton, a distant relative of the politician Simonds D'Ewes, kept a diary through the revolution, from the siege of Colchester in the summer of 1648, to March 1651.[64] It would be an overstatement to suggest that the outside world did not intrude upon Mr Clopton's world at Little or Great Wratton near to Suffolk's border with Essex, but not much of one. He began this diary on 4 May 1648 when the Essex petition, one of the precipitants of the second Civil War in England, was sent up to Westminster to criticise the general level of taxation and to ask Parliament to re-open negotiations with the king prohibited by the Vote of No Addresses passed in January 1649 once the Engagement had become public knowledge.[65] Clopton remarked near the end of his diary on Oliver Cromwell's victory at Dunbar on 3 September 1650. However, the sense of Clopton's diary is of distance, surprising given that war and revolution happened around him, just a few miles away at Colchester, and not too far away in London itself. Distance was not purely geographical. The tone of Clopton's diary is set straight away. On the day the petition was sent forth he noted that it was a cold day. When, just over three weeks later, Clopton went to defend his cousin bailiff Bluster who was accused of joining the mutineers at Eye, before the Suffolk committee at Bury St Edmunds, it was, he noted a fine day. As the rebellion in the county got under way and Clopton was swept up in the military preparations, he never forgot to record the weather. At Bury St Edmunds riots broke out on 12 May when maypoles were raised and voices raised in support of the king. It was all over with little trouble and as 'the mutiny waxt' the weather was 'faire and very hot' with 'much thunder in the afternoon'.[66] At the end of the month, rioting began again, this time at Newmarket, and Clopton's friend and employer Sir Thomas Barnardiston, MP and committee member for Suffolk since 1642, had to spend the duration of this mutiny at Bury St Edmunds and had to send 'three of his men this night to Newmarket to surprise 7 or 8 of the malignants that were [had been] in Bury which surrendered ... '.

Clopton noted then that it 'rayned all night'. Two days later when the Royalists seized county gentry at Chelmsford, the day was described as 'letching'. The siege of Colchester may have passed with little event for Mr Clopton, but

Barnardiston and his father Sir Nicholas were summoned by Fairfax to attend the leaguer during June and other people had no choice but to take notice. At Messing, Essex, soldiers had stayed for twelve weeks. The constable was given 6d a week because he had so much work to do, and £58 8s 3d was spent on food for the soldiers and their horses. The eight trained bandsmen were kept under arms for 13 weeks and a day, another £36 16s, and a further number of men had to be hired as well. Spades, shovels and mattocks were supplied to the army, at the charge of £2 12s. In all the village was faced with a bill of over £200, which would have required more than eight rate collections.[67]

Mr Clopton spent much of the second Civil War going about his usual business and playing 'shove groat at Mr Lambes'. He did note assiduously some of the details of the sermons preached by Samuel Fairclough the rector of Kedeston. Fairclough had been noted as early as thirty years earlier for his non-conformity, although he had found a place at Barnardiston and then Kedeston for most of the intervening years. He was to dedicate a book *The Saints' Worthiness* to Lady Barnardiston in 1653. During July 1648 Fairclough's sermons appear to have been based on the theme of the builder on sand and the builder on rock which he preached on 7, 12 and 16 July and again on 3 September 1648. What exactly Fairclough was hinting at was unclear; it is unlikely that he was suggesting that the Royalist plots were founded on sand and more likely that he was suggesting that Parliament's initial policy of appeasement with the defeated king had laid unsound foundations for a settlement. Fairclough's later attempts to encourage celebration for Commonwealth victories suggest that he thought that the death of the king had been important in securing firm foundations. Fairclough may have continued the theme into the middle of October when Clopton referred to him preaching 'his former text' at a time when the parish elders discussed the nature of the sacrament.[68]

The diary entries for November and December are much briefer, but entries expanded again in January. However, there was no mention of the preparations for the king's trial, nor later of the trial itself which occupied so much of the month in London. Only at the last moment did Clopton write: 'A hard froste & extreme cold … A little before supper we saw a diurnal yte news yt the King was sentenced to dy this night I pd Mr Watsone his 5L for my black mare.'

The king was actually dead, as Clopton heard the next day: 'A hard frost … we had news this day from London of k Charles his beheading before white hall the tuesday before I was at my farme the after noon … '[69]

Fairclough began repeated preaching on the theme of Jesus' admonishment of the Disciples in Luke 22, in particular Simon's offer to accompany Jesus unto death. This could be read as his attempt to inspire his congregation to follow the new England established in the wake of the king's execution. The effectiveness of such exhortations are in doubt. The new regime's defeat of the Levellers at Burford in May was greeted with no enthusiasm in Clopton's parish: Clopton noted that the Day of Thanksgiving was 'kept of very few'. Indeed he and his wife were preoccupied by the re-building of the house which 'that day lay open in many places where carpenters had pulled it down', they did not go to church.[70] Again on 1 August 1649 as Cromwell made ready to embark for Ireland, Parliament called a day of fast to crave success.

> Some hereabouts called it Crumwells fast. few hereabouts present, but Mr Burwell his text for let thine enemies perish oh god: text he first made use of at the foaregoinge thanksgiving for ye Armies victory againsyt ye levellers my workmen went this day I went to church in ye morning[71]

Clopton's own preoccupations during these frantic months seldom coincided with the political world. For much of the time he was concerned with the improvements to his house, the administration of his estate and the weather.

The money for the Colchester siege had been raised very quickly and naturally Essex villages bore the brunt. By 1652, many of them had not been paid, and they brought this to the attention of the Quarter Session court. The JPs decided that they should meet within their divisions to receive the accounts from the villages which had not yet been paid.[72] The Essex courts were also, like other sessions during the 1650s, dealing with maimed soldiers' pensions, such as that of John Sapsard who claimed to be unable to earn a living. War-widows like Susanna Stringer, whose husband had died in the Scottish campaigns, were also claiming pensions. Susanna was awarded 40s a year paid quarterly for her and a child, even though she was working.[73]

In London the new state was sensitive to being attacked verbally in public, but it may have proved difficult to convince a jury that such attacks were serious. Charges laid against Paul and Mary Williams alleged that they had said that Fairfax, Cromwell and Thomas Pride were 'all sonnes of whores' and that they hoped 'to see their downefall, which is the satisfaccion we look for'. For this they were found guilty. Yet on the potentially more dangerous charge of attacking the new regime, they were found not guilty. It was alleged that the couple had declared that

> there is nowe a High Court of Justice sett upp to destroy the Royall Party, but we did hope to see those that did belonge to that Court would soone be cutt off or hanged, And that all those that belonged to the Parliament, Councell of State and the High Court of Justice are rogues and murtherers of the late King.

On this charge the jury refused to take them seriously.[74]

One thing that did concern the Middlesex courts was the number of masses being held in London during the early years of the Republic. Masses seemed to be held at Covent Garden, St Martin's in the Field, Westminster, St Giles', St James' in Holborne. There were also still unacceptable Protestant practices to be dealt with. Elizabeth Sorrell and her daughter Elizabeth were probably early

Unitarians, for on 12 June 1651 they were bound over for 'diverse erroneous damnable and blasphemous opinions against the Holy Trinity'.[75] Unlawful forms of religious worship were not alone in being regarded as unacceptable practice, and several witchcraft cases were tried in the same period, but here again, despite the dangerous times which had a few years earlier seen the execution of numerous women in East Anglia, the Middlesex juries remained unconvinced of the seriousness of the affairs. On 20 November 1649 two widows, Elizabeth Smyth and Dorothy Bromall, were tried for practising witchcraft against Jane Gwynne who had developed a wasting disease. Both women were found not guilty at the trial.[76] In February 1651, Elizabeth Lanam, a married women, was charged with bewitching John Cooke, but she too was found not guilty.

Richard Baxter, the minister of Kidderminster, was not sanguine when he recalled the execution of the king. Just like Henry Guthrie in Scotland, Baxter blamed Cromwell, whom he knew personally, as a sort of *éminence grise*. He believed Cromwell mislead what he called 'the democratical party', meaning the Independents and the Vanists (adherents of Sir Henry Vane the Younger), into thinking that he intended a democratic regime. Baxter believed Cromwell had controlled everything, from the flight of the king from Hampton Court to Pride's Purge to the trial. He had even stayed at Pontefract to make it look as if it was the work of Parliament as a whole. The death of the king was evidence of the 'severity of God and the mutability and uncertainty of worldly things and the fruits of a sinful nations provocation', for it gave hope to papists and 'hardened thousands against the hope of their salvation'.[77]

Like John Clopton, Baxter referred in his writings to the fast days and thanksgivings ordained by what he later referred to as the Rump Parliament. He would not conduct the thanksgiving services and moreover he prevented the people of his congregation (he says town and parish) of Kidderminster from taking the oath of loyalty to the Commonwealth too. Instead of offering prayers for the success of the army in Scotland, Baxter sought to exhort soldiers and officials to understand that in the Scots they were not fighting cavaliers, but 'godly men'. In the spring of 1651 details of a Royalist plot emerged in London. The tentacles of the plot reached throughout the country according to the chief informer Tom Coke, but the centrepiece was to be an attack on the Council of State and Parliament. Many of those named by Coke as principal actors were Presbyterian ministers including Christopher Love: it was Love on whom the fury of the state was turned. It was from his house that communications were entered into with the exiled prince. Love was tried and after a politically inspired delay executed just as the Scottish army under Charles Stuart approached Worcester. Baxter suggested that he was seen as an adherent of Love and his plot, but the divine was too cautious for that, even if the Royalists thought him a likely supporter. When he was asked to go to Worcester when Charles II was there with the Scots army in late August 1651, Baxter pleaded ill-health. He confided in his readers later:

And being not doubtful of the issue which followed, I thought if I had
been able, it would have been no service at all to the king, it being so
little on such a sudden that I could add to his assistance.

A nimble piece of footwork which would serve to dance to a new tune after
1660.[78]

Yet for many people who could not yet distance themselves from the actualities of war and the post-war world coping with the vicissitudes of the times had
to be as practical if not as literary. In Surrey at Elstead levies for the armed
forces fluctuated in the year of the revolution before settling at £26 8s 4d a
quarter from May onwards. The accounts still referred to the money as being
raised for Fairfax, although they acknowledged that he was now a lord, until June
1650 when he was actually superseded by Cromwell. Immediately the records
changed and the levies were now 'for the steat'.[79] By this time the levies had
fallen to £24 18s 4d a quarter, but there was also a levy for the 'Malishria'. The
quarter beginning 28 September 1650 fell to £16 13s 2d, but this was only a
temporary respite, for the war against Charles Stuart entailed higher payments
and on 8 January 1651 the levy for four months came to £44 8s 5d or over £133
a year, representing a 26 per cent increase on the previous year. This high rate
was to continue for a year, before it fell again to around £100. This only lasted a
year, for in 1652 a new levy of around £136 a year was reintroduced and this
continued until October 1654 when the rate again fell to around £100 a year.
Whether this marked a final fall, as it might well have done cannot be explored
as the accounts ended at this point. Throughout these accounts only two entries
dealt with things other than county garrisons or state taxes. Even one of these,
an entry for 5s for Trained Band weapons, referred to as 'state arms', was military. The other was for money for the gaol and house of correction in February
1652. There are notes on the collections of tithes recorded at the beginning of
this series of papers but the general impression these papers give is of obsession
with the war and its impact on the community of Elstead.

In 1649 Anne Clifford, a woman in her mid-fifties, journeyed into the northwest of Yorkshire. She was returning to Skipton Castle for the first time since she
was about ten weeks old. It was also the first time since Skipton Castle, a former
Royalist garrison, had been slighted. The castle had during the century of peace
previous to the war been redeveloped into a palatial home, although a core of
the medieval castle had remained to become the central strong point of the
garrison. This part had been destroyed by demolition teams in the early months
of 1649. Anne Clifford had inherited the lands of the Clifford family in 1644,
but the wars had prevented her return until now. She went on a progress around
her properties, many of them ruined by age or war, consciously viewing the
lands she had been cheated of since her father had bequeathed them to his
brother, not her, 36 years earlier.[80] She began almost immediately to rebuild her
properties, despite the fact that Skipton had been destroyed by Parliament's

command. Her work on Appleby Castle was soon of benefit to the Republic, for in 1651 as the 'Warres was hott in Scotland',

> So as then manie places of Westmerland and especially my Castle of Aplebie was full of soldiers what laye here a great part of the Summer. But I thank God I received no harme or Damage by them, nor by the King and his Armie who that August came into England and within six or seven myles of Aplebie Castle.[81]

She also added that the war had prevented there being any assizes held that summer in the northern circuit. This was a major upheaval, for unlike the southern circuits the northern judge only travelled the courts once a year. By July 1653, Anne had completed the re-roofing of Caesar's Tower at Appleby and the middle-wall construction began in 1651 was also completed and new stables begun, just in time for the lodging of assize judges Pulseton and Parker, since during the Commonwealth the high sheriffs were responsible for lodging and feeding the judges.[82]

At Scarborough, the physical scars were still being mended. The charnel house, which was used as the schoolhouse, had been pulled down by Governor Boynton when he changed sides in 1648. In early February 1649 it was decided that instead of rebuilding it the remains were to be sold off to benefit the general town stock. And the ruined St Thomas' church was to be demolished to repair the badly damaged St Mary's, used as a gun emplacement during the first Civil War. A week later it was decided that part of St Mary's was to be converted to school use using the money from the charnel house stone.[83] The financial charges of the new state continued to mount. Money amounting to £11 a month for the levies had to be collected in the town and those who had lodged soldiers had to present their tickets in order to claim the money due to them. Yet whilst this new normality continued in the city, Scarborough was periodically reminded that it was, in one respect at least, on the front line of the war being perpetuated by the exiled Royalists. In the autumn of 1649 the Scarborough ship *Amity* was captured by a Royalist ketch. In March 1650 further proof of their own vulnerability fell into the hands of the Scarborough authorities. Captain Nicholas Marriner of the frigate *St George* had been commissioned to destroy, 'sinke or fire' all ships in rebellion against Charles II. It was not his ship but a hoy from King's Lynn which Marriner had captured at Blakeney which ended up aground on the sands after being sent to Jersey in the charge of David Sward, Irishman John Heylin, Fleming Bastian de Master and Dane John Peeters. The crew of the hoy, the *Mary and Thomas*, had been told that Cromwell's Irish campaign had been a disaster and Prince Charles restored. Within days there was a fight just off Scarborough. Robert Coleman of Yarmouth led his fishing boat laden with soldiers and local sailors out of the harbour in an attack on a 'man o' war' (actually a dogger-style fishing boat) which was in Filey Bay. The volunteer party captured the ship and took its crew prisoner after a fight in which Colman was injured.[84] That such an effort was mounted, and with the willing support of fishermen from the town as well as from Coleman's own crew, suggests that there was frustration with the continuation of the war. Royalist boats were seen as a direct threat to the livelihood of fishermen and inshore traders on the East coast, and it was perhaps a sort of seaborne clubman attitude, rather than political persuasion, which inspired this attack. Past sea wars were also being relived in 1650. The capture of the Royalist pirate Brown Bushell inspired a large-scale court case that year. Part of the charges mounted against him concerned his hand in Sir Hugh Cholmely's handing over of Scarborough to Henrietta Maria and the Hotham's role in this. Witnesses from Scarborough, who had been a party to discussions between Bushell and Cholmely, were examined by Luke Robinson the town MP on 18 July 1650, and then summoned to Westminster for the trial in the following September. Yet the piracy continued, the Scarborough coal boat Goodwill was captured on the way to Boston just of the Humber by an armed hoy, and sent on to Jersey.[85]

In Peel on the Isle of Man the accounts kept for 1651 by Robert Kenyon show how much the upheavals of the period interfered with the normal duties paid by estate holders. There are seventeen recorded levy payments that year. Of these, two payments of 6d and 5d were to the overseers of the poor, one of 3d may have been to the churchwardens, one of 3s was to pay what was still termed the king's rent and one payment of 4s 6d went to pay the grain ships. The other twelve payments, totalling £1 8s 2½d, were for military affairs. In other words over 75 per cent of the taxation outlay was to pay for the regime. Some of this went in monthly tax or gould payments made in February, March, May, July, August, September and October. Other payments were for the war in Ireland, victuals and hay.[86]

The collapse of authority and respect for that authority is clear in many areas. The proliferation of sects may have been partly responsible for the failure of people to use familiar and traditional rites and traditions. At Odiham in north-east Hampshire, the role of the Church as recorder of the rite of passage had fallen into decline. People no longer ensured that the clerk recorded the baptisms of their children. With a fatalistic tone Thomas Hooker, the clerk throughout the wars, knew he would be blamed at a future date.

> Their will com a time that men will com to serch in this boole for the names of their children and in Regard that they cannot find there names here writen let them not balme me for it but looke upon theam selves for since the wars began in this land there have been many that have been baptised that I never knew of nether had I any notes of them never to the last. I know the blam will be laid upon me[87]

Other religious consequences of the previous years' of confusion were not acceptable to many people. George Fox was travelling around the country preaching to those who would listen. At Mansfield Woodhouse, Fox was fallen on by people:

> in a great rage, struck me down, and almost stifled and smothered me; and I was cruelly beaten and bruised by them with their hands, Bibles, and sticks. Then they haled me out, though I was hardly able to stand, and put me into the stocks where I sate some hours.

On this occasion the JP set Fox at liberty, but when he did the people chased Fox out of town with pistols.[88]

There were other reckonings too. The county of Bedfordshire was told on 5 January 1653 that it owed £13,184 13s 1½d in unpaid taxes to the Exchequer. There was also the problem of free quarter. The second Civil War had resulted in the practice being once more imposed on the county. The billets or credit notes, issued to the householders who lodged soldiers, had not been redeemed by 1651; they amounted to £2,443 9s 9d, which, the county was told, would be repaid, if they sent taxation arrears within six months.[89]

The personal difficulties caused by the first war in England had not been solved or eased by the second. Anne Gryffyn of Birmingham had been married to the sort of man who had given Birmingham its parliamentarian reputation during the first Civil War when it resisted Prince Rupert in April 1643. Anne's husband had served under Captain Melville at Northampton before being killed. Anne and her two children had no income. Birmingham had been ordered to pay 20d a week to the family, but at Easter 1648 the money had ceased. The Michaelmas sessions ordered the overseers of the poor and the churchwardens to present their reasons at the monthly Coleshill meeting of the JPs. There was then no immediate satisfaction for the Gryffyns. The other inhabitants had, within months of Anne's plea, represented themselves as hard-done-to with regard to their taxation levies, complaining that the levies were unequally applied.[90] One of the problems with court records is that sometimes they give only tantalising details. A veteran parliamentarian soldier, Thomas Hawton, married Joan Andrewes of Lemington Hastings sometime during 1644. When the war was over he returned to Lemington Hasting where Joan lived with her mother, the widow Joan Andrewes. Thomas moved in too. The rest of the village for some reason took umbrage and tried to break up the household. At Michaelmas 1649 the court ordered the town to leave them alone, as the three supported themselves and had no money from the town for their support.

Ireland

The Engagement threw the alliances in Ireland into great confusion. In the north-east George Monck, commander of the English forces, was faced with more problems than most. He had trouble with his Presbyterian soldiers and his Scottish allies on the eve of the second Civil War. The Engagement had obliged

Charles I to tacitly accept the Presbyterian Church, even if he had not had to sign the Covenant himself. The commissioners who had brought him to sign the agreement and the faction in the estates which supported their action, led by the Marquis of Hamilton, pressed the Scottish people into believing that the Engagement was the only way of defending the Kirk and keeping alive the hopes of united Presbyterian Churches in Scotland, England and Wales. In Ulster the Scots forces were genuinely divided. They were asked to support an Engagement with the king whom they had known to be in league with the Confederation against which they alone had fought for much of the period since September 1643. Even so, about 1,000 of them had crossed the Irish Sea to join with Hamilton's invasion of England. Even in the wake of the defeat at Preston, there remained an important element who opposed the separatist drift of affairs in England. In late March 1649 Monck was presented with a petition asking him to adhere to the Covenant and to defend religion, king and country. More specifically, the Scottish officers presented five demands. First, that he sign the Covenant. Second, that he sign the officers' declaration of opposition to Fairfax and Cromwell 'who have endeavoured to establish and impious toleration'. Third, that he declare himself in favour of first principles: that he was still fighting in defence of the king and Parliament and for the Protestant religion. Fourth, it demanded that he refuse to obey the orders of the 'usurped power' at Westminster and stressed the desire for the election of a 'free parliament' in England. Monck was also petitioned not to undertake any military action on behalf of the state, without consulting a council which should include captains chosen by the regiments. Finally he was asked to supply his regiments with arms and ammunition. The delegated officers presenting Monck with the petition were instructed to gain Monck's agreement to these demands if he wanted the officers and men to remain under his command. An answer was to be returned by the weekend after 30 March. Presented along with the army petition was another on behalf of the country which pressed similar demands, but which included references to arrangements for quartering in the future. The petition also expressed the desire for taxation money raised in England to be sent to Ulster. Monck responded to the latter petition positively, as it did not specifically call for him to challenge London. But with the army petition he was more circumspect. He accepted that he was still fighting for the Solemn League and Covenant as in point one, points four and five, and he put the council of officers in place. He refused points two and three. Although he did suggest that he might adhere to points two and three if the government in England challenged the Covenant or challenged the property rights of the army commanders or the British settlers in Ireland, Monck, always a shrewd politician, recognised where power lay and from where the potential to defeat the powerful alliance building up against him rested.[91] Monck's terms were accepted by many in the army, although he made it possible for those who wished to leave the army to do so with their goods unharmed, if they paid a year's cess for the place where they had resided. The council of war still rankled at Monck's adherence to the government in England and the hardline Covenanters could not be satisfied, especially as the line coming from Edinburgh grew more conciliatory towards Prince Charles. Open divisions before the end of the year resulted in fighting. In December Monck was able to write to Major George Rawdon congratulating him on his defeat of the 'bluecaps' – the Covenanters – and instructing him to deprive rebellious Scots landholders, the lord of Ars, Sir James Montgomery, Colonels Trevor and Hamilton included, of their estates. His defiance of the Covenant was now open, he instructed Rawdon to suffer no Scots ministers to preach in that country again.[92]

Action against the Scots who had settled in the province since 1642 continued in the following year. English forces captured Belfast in October 1649 and the 800 Scots families were expelled. Around the same time Sir Charles Coote captured Coleraine. In November the Scots were defeated by Coote and Venebles near Lisnagarvey, and in the following month they marched towards Carrickfergus. On 13 December Carrickfergus was captured and 'most of the Scots that had planted their families there' were expelled.[93]

In Leinster, the 1 August 1649 fast John Clopton referred to may have been seen by some as very effective. On the very next day, the forces assembled by the allied Confederates and Royalists outside Dublin were defeated at Rathmines by Michael Jones and his garrison. Forcing his way to Baggotrath south of the city, Jones drove himself between sections of the allies and managed to defeat the large army which had been assembled for an assault on Dublin. In the aftermath of the battle, English troops returned to the city across the ground where the Royal Canal now runs, through present-day Portebello, to an inn, where wounded horses were tended to in the stables. The inn, now on the corner of Charlotte Street and Camden Street has been called for this reason the Bleeding Horse. At present the pub sign carries the date 1649.[94] Jones' victory allowed him to clear first the south of the city of the defenders whilst on successive days the English forces constructed a ring of defence around the city protecting the land route from Ringsend to Dublin. This allowed Cromwell to use the outer port as a bridgehead for his troops when they landed. The New Model Army when it arrived established its reputation quickly. Cromwell initially marched northwards and on 11 September stormed Drogheda. He then returned southwards, marched through Leinster and on 12 October stormed Wexford from where he moved on into Munster.

The alliance of Confederation and Royalists had again involved Patrick Archer's resources in Ormond's cause. He provided the united Irish and Royalist alliance with £3,035 19s 6d for arms and munitions in 1650 and provided Ormond with £205, all at an interest rate which had netted £1,025 by 1656. Archer had also provided £563 of tobacco for the armies that year and £260 worth of gunpowder.[95]

On the south coast at Youghal the defeat of Lord Taffe at Knocknanuss lessened the threat to the city. In August 1647 had Inchiquin ordered the mayor to strengthen the city walls, reminding the mayor 'there have not been any public tax being lade thereon for the space of one year'. Stabling for the English Munster forces had also been prepared in the town during October, on the eve of victory.[96] In 1645 Lord Inchiquin had taken his forces over to the side of the English Parliament, abandoning the cessation negotiated by Ormond and the Confederation; in 1648 he had a second change of heart and took the town into the alliance camp. Upon Cromwell's approach along the south coast, Youghal and Cork surrendered and the town received troops from Cromwell's army sent by sea and again returned to English control. Ann, Lady Fanshaw, wife of Richard Fanshaw a secretary to Charles I and then to his son, was in Cork when it changed hands, and she recounted the story in the memoirs she wrote in 1676 for the benefit of her son. Sir Richard had been sent to Ireland to represent the king and for six months the Fanshawes had stability in their lives which they had not known for years, during their crossing and re-crossing of the English Channel after the first Civil War. This life came to an end in August when Cromwell landed and as he approached along the south coast, Cork suddenly became dangerous. One midnight in early October Ann was awoken by cannon fire and gathered her family around her. Sir Richard had gone to the naval base at Kinsale during the day. What followed was more disturbing: 'Hearing lamentable shrieks of men, women and children, I asked at the window the cause. They told me they were all Irish, stripped and wounded, turned out of the town.' The town had been seized for Cromwell. With clear presence of mind, Ann wrote a report for her husband and had a servant lowered over the wall of the Red Abbey where they lodged, whilst she gathered papers and money, and bundled up these in clothes and linen. At about 3a.m. Ann and two servants went into Cork market-place by taper-light and passed through the armed crowds gathered there. Making her way to Colonel Jeffries, the garrison commander who had led the capitulation, she persuaded him to grant her a pass out of the town. Armed with this, Ann's party made their way out of Cork and travelled to Kinsale.[97] From there, Richard and Ann made their way around the coast, attempting to obey Charles' orders to go to Spain with their papers. It took some weeks to find a boat, but in January 1650 they risked the plague in Galway to meet a vessel there. Plague had broken out in July 1649 claiming the lives of many 'commons and tradesmen'; many others had fled. Richard and Ann were greeted by a merchant who referred to the state of the town with the words, 'You are welcome to this desolate city, where you now see the street grown over with grass, once the finest little city in the world.' The couple stayed in Galway for a few weeks waiting for a ship bound for Malaga. In February:

> we left that brave Kingdom fallen in six or eight months into a most miserable sad condition, as it hath been many times in most king's reigns. God knows why, for I presume not to say. But the natives seem to me a very loving people to each other, and constantly false to strangers ... [98]

By 1651 Youghal was suffering; in September townsmen complained that sickness in the town and the Royalist pirates from the Scilly Isles were damaging trade. They further suggested that the £20 per month charged on the town's liberties be dropped and that the £40 on the town itself be reduced; it was not so much that this sum was a problem, it was that there were ancilliary charges, such as the firewood and candles required by the town guards which increase the amount considerably. The County Cork committee of revenues agreed in principle and the liberties were freed. The town was reassured that the rest of the money would be reduced as soon as it was practical. Not until February 1653 were the charges for wood and candles removed.[99]

From 1648, John Bellew of Willestone, County Louth, one of the prominent rebels in the county, sided with the alliance. In 1646 he had commanded an artillery train guard in Preston's army. In 1648 he raised a company of foot which Ormond later believed had a fighting strength of 100 men. The only company roll names just 45 men, 15 of whom were sick and wounded. The company was overwhelmingly Catholic Irish, with a few possible English-Irish names amongst them. The company fought at the Battle of Rathmines, and Bellew was taken prisoner in the battle, but released by late September, perhaps because Michael Jones had no room to keep prisoners. Bellew, possibly reunited with his company, moved on to Terroghan Fort in County Meath. Upon the surrender of this fort Bellew was allowed to make his way to Kilkenny. He ended his military career with the surrender of Kilkenny.[100]

Daniel O'Donovan of Castle Donovan, County Cork raised two companies of foot for the alliance, he also attempted to recruit more of the confederates and 'oppress' those who refused. One was commanded by Captain Murrough O'Donovan, his brother, and was part of Colonel Hennesey's Regiment of Foot. Like John Bellew's company this company was at the siege of Dublin in 1649 where Murrough O'Donovan was killed. The second company was part of Colonel O'Driscoll's regiment led by Richard O'Donovan who was likewise killed when the company formed a foraging detachment. For all of which service O'Donovan was said to have 'contributed his best endeavour to the furtherance of our service'.[101]

Although the fourteenth-century Statutes of Kilkenny, which had aimed at racial segregation to protect the 'purity' of the English, were regarded to have failed, the notion of possible racial corruption had not disappeared. On 11 May 1651, Henry Ireton issued an order forbidding intermarriage between his army and the Irish women and Catholics. Officers could be cashiered and men flogged for disobedience.[102]

The continued military occupation of Dublin was being felt throughout the city. From 1649 in St John's parish army officers were regularly serving as parish officers, and two of the auditors for 1650 were army officers: Captain Mitchell and Ensign Palfrey, with Mitchell appointed to applot the Parson's levy from April 1649.[103] The year 1650 was a difficult one in the parish: the number of burials increased to 22 from a recorded annual average of four since 1646.

Nicholas Eddis of Wood Key, once a sidesman of the Church alongside tailor Patrick Landers, buried a child that year. John Butcher and his wife of Winetavern Street died, as did Mr Walter and Mrs Floyde of Fishamble Street, along with two army officers. The high death rate continued during the next year too, with several families hit hard. The wife and child of former mayor Smith died on Wood Key, and Henry Finch of the same street suffered the same way. Richard Kitchen of Winetavern Street lost a son and a daughter. John Browne also on Wood Key lost three children; Joseph Waterhouse on Winetavern Street, two. Captain Mitchell and four children at Mr Barrane's, also possibly on Winetavern Street, were recorded at one burial. Four of Alderman Hutchinsons servants died too. In all at least 41 burials were recorded in the parish, showing a ten-fold increase on 1646–8.[104]

Instructions for the monthly tax in Ulster show how the Commonwealth administered the Irish provinces in ways which mirrored England and Wales. The province was alloted a levy of £5,430 to be collected each month for six months from 1 November 1651. This levy was divided between the nine counties, with the bulk falling on Antrim (£1,500), and Donegal (£1,249), with Tyrone contributing only £100 a month. There were some minor adjustments: the barony of Farrar was omitted from the Louth collection, but the barony of Trough was added to Tyrone to facilitate even this small collection. The levy was to be assessed on lands, tenements, hereditaments, rents, profits, goods and chattels. A complaints and appeals system had to be established. Refusers were to be sequestered until they could be properly fined and the fines could not exceed £40 or 28 days in prison. Records of the applotment and the names of those paying the taxes were to be kept. Leinster was similarly levied, to a total of £4,800 a month, with the bulk falling on east Meath (Meath) and Dublin City and county (£200 and £800 respectively). There were additional levies, such as 1,140 barrels of bread levied on Westmeath. Despite rebel strongholds in the county 400 to 500 barrels might be raised from Longford the order optimistically noted.[105]

In Munster rebel incursions curtailed the areas from which tax could be raised, so orders for taxes related to the 'Precinct of Limerick' and likewise for Cork, Clonmel and Waterford were made. South Leinster was also dealt with separately, with the precincts of Kilkenny and Wexford being given special attention. Levies in Connacht seem to have been restricted to the three counties of Mayo, Roscommon and Galway.[106]

Potential troublemakers were being removed in other ways, whilst the Catholic leaders were executed outright, for example, Ever MacMahon, the Bishop of Clogher and Henry O'Neill, or held for trial like Phelim O'Neill, the common soldier was being shipped out of the country. Christopher Mayo was warranted to raise 3,000 foot from the former rebel armies to fight for the king of Spain. This was not really a foreign policy issue, except that France harboured the exiled Stuarts and their defeated clan; the real point was to get the Irish soldiers out of the country as quickly as possible. To ensure that Mayo did not just drop them off anywhere, his warrant bound him on a surety of £20,000 not to take the Irishmen anywhere else. Other Irish people were being shipped out of the country too. They were not offered such generous terms. Warrants were issued to Bristol merchantmen to ship vagrant men, women and children to the West Indian colonies.[107]

7

CONQUERED NATIONS: REPUBLICAN AND RESTORATION SCOTLAND AND IRELAND, 1653–61

On 20 April 1653 the purged remnant of the Parliament which had first sat in November 1641 was dispersed. The first commonwealth government which had replaced the monarchy was brought to an abrupt end when the commander of the army, Oliver Cromwell, and a handful of soldiers entered Westminster and expelled the MPs. For some months Parliament with slow deliberation had been constructing the framework for a new Parliament to replace itself. It had decided the date of its own demise: 3 November 1653, thirteen years since the Long Parliament had first assembled. The slowness in setting the terms of the new elections frustrated the army. Cromwell held the army back from expelling Parliament until he too tired of the painful process.[1] The Commonwealth itself continued for another eight months during which a nominated assembly called the Little or Barebone's Parliament met.[2] When this assembly, the first at Westminster to incorporate MPs from Ireland and Scotland, dissolved itself the Commonwealth ended. The dissolution on 12 December was engineered by radical MPs from the army angered by Parliament's failure to deal effectively with army finances and the war with the Dutch which had begun in May 1652. The *coup* was well prepared and the MPs had a new constitution to hand. The Instrument of Government was largely the work of General John Lambert, and based in part on the work of the rump of the Long Parliament, but also on the 1647 *Heads of the Proposals* and even the Leveller's *Agreement of the People*. It established the Protectorate. From 15 December, when the constitution was accepted, the Republic of the four nations was governed by a lord protector and a Council of State assisted by elected parliaments. On 16 December Oliver Cromwell was appointed lord protector, a title given in the fourteenth and fifteenth centuries to caretaker managers of the kingdom during the minority or other enforced absence of the monarch. This strangely temporary sounding title was, Gerald Aylmer suspects, a prelude to the offer of the crown to the office's incumbent.

The Instrument lasted for three and a half years. War with the Dutch ended in April 1654 and the Glencairn Rebellion in the Highlands was put down in the following September, the same month as the first Protectorate Parliament opened at Westminster. Relations between the executive and Parliaments were often problematic as, despite Cromwell's injunctions the MPs continued to debate the nature of the constitution. Indeed at the instigation of the second Protectorate Parliament the Instrument was replaced by the Humble Petition and Advice. At the heart of this new constitution was an attempt to recreate an hereditary head of state, even if Lord Protector Oliver were to reject the title of king. The Humble Petition also introduced a second house into Parliament. In practice creating the new chamber was problematic and did nothing to ease the relationship between MPs and the executive. Cromwell sent his Parliament into recess in June 1657 and dismissed it the following January. Cromwell died on 3 September 1653 having appointed his son Richard as his successor, as he was entitled to do under the provisions of the Humble Petition. The revamped Protectorate lasted only until May 1659 when the army refused to co-operate with the second protector.

Looking back over the past three and half centuries it is easy to see the Republic in a variety of lights. It can be seen as either a brilliant but doomed period of political enlightenment or experiment, or as a terrible period of military dictatorship. Unlike Scotland and Ireland and even Wales, for England at least the Republic was home-grown and can be studied in the luxury of this light rather than having to think of it as a polity enforced by foreign invaders. There is less material generated in the local communities for the Republic than there is for the Civil War period. It would seem that there was a concerted attempt to rebuild stability in political and economic terms, despite some aspects of the Republican regime being uncomfortable and awkward to live with. Some actions of the government were heavy-handed responses to Royalist plots and risings which interrupted attempts to create stability.

Ireland and the Protectorate

When the Protectorate was established in December 1653 it was assumed that the four nations of the British Isles would now be governed as one. England, Ireland, Scotland and Wales would all be represented at Westminster by the unicameral assembly established by the new constitution. Although formal acts of union were in place from April 1652, covering the unification of Scotland and England, there was no comprehensive act on the statute books covering the relationship between England and Ireland. The situation in Ireland was still somewhat in flux under the terms of the Settlement of Ireland Act of 12 August 1652. This was born out of the conflict between two sources of authority. On one side there were the Republicans initially in charge of Irish affairs, who had sought to proceed gently with the lost souls of Ireland to drag them from their religious ignorance into the true twin lights of Protestantism and Republicanism. On the other side there were the army leaders who like Cromwell regarded the Catholic Irish and Old English as apostates.[3] By 1652 it was the army view which won out and the settlement was fairly punitive because of their influence.

Unlike Scotland, there was no political class or structure intact after twelve years of war which could be recognised by the Protectorate state. Moreover, there was little in the way of a political class with which the Protectorate could work. Government was in the hands of English and Welsh men sent over to administer Ireland in the wake of the Cromwellian conquest.

After the battle of Scarrifhollis in 1650, the war in Ireland ended without any cataclysmic final battle, but in a series of guerrilla conflicts and sieges. In the face of the brutal treatment of some remaining garrisons and the parliamentarian advance on Enniscorty which was accompanied, the Venetian secretary, Lorenzo Paulucci reported, by the burning of corn and houses, the towns remaining in Confederation or Royalist hands began to look for terms.[4] By surrendering the final bastions of the alliance, Irish men and women sought to preserve what they could of their property and possessions. In face of later dispossessions during the plantations the terms of these surrenders were frantically dragged up before the commissioners for Irish affairs. The political solution as far as Ireland was concerned was an Act for the Settlement and part of this legislation dealt with the enemies of the new regime and its predecessors. The Irish were divided into ten categories or 'qualifications'. The first five qualifications, which included those who had been involved in the 1641 rebellion and subsequent fighting against the English state, Jesuits, those who supplied food, plate and arms voluntarily and those who still refused to surrender were to be punished by death and confiscation of property. The latter five qualifications would lose their estates.

Naturally, putting these terms into practice was not simple and several examples can be found to demonstrate the problems faced by Irish Catholics and the administrators. For instance, several Galway merchants, Martin Blake Fitwilliam and former sheriff Andrew Bodkin amongst them, were involved in one such battle with the commissioners in 1652 and 1653 over their holdings in the Liberties of Galway. Galway city had been the last alliance stronghold to surrender, having succumbed to a siege by Edmund Ludlow and Sir Charles Coote in April 1652. Initially the terms granted to the town had been generous. Only a few inhabitants involved in the 1642 incidents, including Kirwan's seizing of the merchant ship in the bay, were denied indemnity. The other inhabitants were allowed to remain in the town and to keep their estates and houses, with the proviso that if they sold property one third of the sale value was to be given to the state. They would also lose one third of their estates in the rest of Ireland. The council in Dublin thought that Coote had been too generous in his offer and tried to rescind the terms before they were ratified, but failed to get the necessary dispatches to Coote in time.[5] Even so the council tried to introduce further qualifications into the terms, only to see them comprehensively rejected by the town. However, the taxation set upon the town was so high that it drove many of the inhabitants out, leaving an increasing burden to fall on those who remained. By the end of the 1652 many of the remaining citizens were complaining of their inability to pay. Martin Blake FitzAndrew, who seemed to be absent from the town that year, and Andrew Bodkin, submitted a petition setting forth the debts owed to them by a wide range of people, amounting to £1,700 sterling; the repayment term of the debt 'had long since expired' and the debtors had refused to pay.[6] Creditor pressures elsewhere were also responsible for Galway's plight: debts owed to English corporations which had loaned money for the campaign in Ireland caused the Commissioners for Irish Affairs to continue to question Galway's generous surrender terms and to evade them where possible. They suggested that the Irish and Anglo-Irish be removed from Galway and transplanted to other parts of Connacht. One concession was that they would lose only one-third of their estates, rather than the usual two-thirds, in acknowledgement of the terms Ludlow had granted. By 30 October 1655 this had become a firm proposal for the removal of all Catholic Irish people from the town and this seems to have included those of Anglo-Irish descent and rebel properties in the town were to be used as compensation for the inhabitants of Gloucester for losses they had sustained during the siege in 1643. It was this to which the petitioners responded. They believed, according to the surrender terms they had accepted, that they had preserved their 'private estates of houses house rooms lands mortgages and interest within the towne of Galway libertyes – and fishing thereof'. A surviving heavily corrected rough draft of the petition was drawn up apparently after the commissioners had declared themselves not satisfied by the petitioners former explanations of the treaty.[7] The petitioners by now seemed to have lost hope of remaining in Galway and refer to their proposed removal. What they appear to have hoped for was the retention of the full value and extent of their estate in their allocation of new land. The petitioners stressed their connections with the interests of the new masters. In a statement containing a very brief disingenuous explanation of the recent 'lapse' the petitioners attempted to display their true loyalty to the process of Anglification in Ireland:

> [We] who have uppwards of four hundred yeares preserved the English interest in this Corp[or]ation not withstanding the severall rebellions in this nation, till the Late General distraction, to wch submission wee were goaded out of our desire to comply...

Almost as an afterthought the petitioners also asked that their monthly taxation be suspended

> which payments we are unable to satisfie, being totally destroyed, in our p[er]sonal fortunes caused by the length of these warres, decay of trade, the present problems and so many late payments by us made and other ingagements of Common seales and otherwise due uppon the sd Town

As with all other transportees, Martin Blake FitzAndrew had to provide details of his estate as it had existed on the eve of the rebellion and of subsequent purchases to the court at Athlone which was responsible for local transplanting arrangements. One third of his estate was in Galway town: two houses, one of which was ruined, and Blakes Castle at the quay end of the High Street. The castle is still there two doors down from McDonagh's chipper. The remaining two-thirds were a series of interests in land around County Galway and in County Mayo.[8] The petitions to the commissioners were unsuccessful, for one third of the estate, equal to the Galway portion, was adjudged forfeit at Athlone Court which adjudged the qualification of the person under the Act for the Settling of Ireland and Loghrea Court which allocated the lands in Connacht, had assigned appropriate replacement estates. On 23 July 1657 Blake had been granted 425 acres in Killinmore, Killinbegg and Ballagh in Belclare and Tuam parishes. Martin seems not to have let any loyalty he later claimed to have to the house of Stuart interfere with business. He purchased further lands, 112 acres in Bunnona and Garriduffe in Anaghdowne parish from the initial grantee Walter Cheevers. Cheevers was of the eighth qualification which covered people not constantly loyal to Parliament between 1 October 1641 and 1 March 1650. Martin also obtained 75 acres in Toberneglogh in Dunmore barony which had originally gone to Ullick carra Burke, a man from the seventh qualification which covered those who had borne arms against Parliament as regular soldiers. Both of these estates had clearly been sold on once before Blake came into possession of them, for he claimed to have bought them from Robert Forestall, Walter Blake and Sir Robert Blake.

In County Cork the national origins of Munster's small landholders is revealed by the documents relating to the transfer of land ownership. Richard Gogin's lands at Adamstowne and Tullig in the Barony of Kerricurrihy were given over to parts of Captain William Pelham's company of foot from Cromwell's own regiment.[9] The initial new owners were Edward Baker, Captain Thomas Welstead and Lieutenant Matthew Scott. In late November these lands were sold to Nicholas King and Richard Covett or Lovett, described variously as being of Cork City and Adamstowne, for £195 4s 2d. The list of 17 tenants on the lands contains Irish, English and Welsh names.[10] Within this document is evidence of the colonial processes which had taken place in Ireland over the previous 70 years. The so-called Cromwellian settlement is here revealed as the latest phase in a process by which land was taken from the Gaelic Irish and given or sold to those who followed successive waves of conquest and confiscation.

Some landholders simply refused to conform to the settlement. Confederate and alliance supporter Daniel O'Donovan of Castle Donovan refused to deal with the English usurped power. The English then blew up two of his castles and siezed the rest of his estate, 'burning killing and destroying all that came in their way'. Despite this he refused any of the land offered to him in Clare and Connacht.[11] John Bellew of Willistone, County Louth, saw affairs likewise. After his release from Dublin after the battle of Rathmines, he had taken up arms again and joined the garrison at Terroghan. When the governor surrendered the fort he was offered the freedom to enjoy his estates if he renounced his cause and lived quietly. Bellew and Sir Robert Talbot, 'the only people of estates we know of [in the garrison]' refused. Bellew moved on to Kilkenny, where he was incorporated in the terms of the capital when it surrendered to Cromwell on 27 March 1650. In 1656 the commissioners adjudged Bellew's case. His lands in the county were judged to be worth £1,200 per annum; in addition he held £50 per annum worth of fishing rights. The commissioners at Athlone and Loughreagh allocated Bellew estates and fishing rights, at one third of the value of the Louth estates, in County Galway. Bellew refused despite being threatened with death.[12]

John Talbot retained control of his Malahide estates until 1652 when he assisted a messenger of Charles Stuart to reach safety. Miles Corbet, one of the original commissioners for Irish affairs and a regicide, personally took possession of Malahide Castle. Talbot was initially imprisoned, but food shortages meant that efficient land managers were required, and again Talbot regained custody of the estate and produced food for Dublin. In 1654 the Talbots were ordered to Connacht. Talbot himself was classed as being in one of the first five qualifications and thereby liable to death and confiscation, but his submission to the Lords Justices in 1642 and his subsequent service to Dublin left him in limbo. The family were sent to Connacht, but there were no lands allocated to them and so they lodged at Loughrae awaiting something from the court of allocations. Talbot was allowed to return to Malahide in spring 1655 to sell the estate's produce that he had planted and he took the opportunity to visit the shrine at Port Marnoch to pray for his salvation.[13]

Other men clearly had a lot of explaining to do to try and win peace with the new regime. Depositions were once again being taken at Dublin to confirm and enhance the accusation made in the original deposition statements of the early 1640s. One set of inquiries dealt with William Esmond of Johnstowne near the garrison of Duncannon in County Wexford. Investigation revealed evidence against Esmond which showed that he had not fled to the Duncannon fort for protection or offered help as his loyal neighbours had. But this was only a minor charge, further evidence was more damning. According to William Stafford, Esmond had been a Confederation county committeeman. He had also willingly contributed and probably organised financial and arms levies and actively assisted the Confederation's forces at the siege of Duncannon fort whilst it was being defended by William's own uncle Lord Esmond.[14]

Transportation to the West Indies proved impossible for some. In October 1654, Lord Power of Canaghmore asked to be relieved of the burden because he was 'distracted and destitute of mind'.[15] Widow Ellinor Butler was allowed to return to her County Waterford home with her cattle and 'helpless' children from Connacht.[16] Anne White, a widow of Wexford, applied for leave to stay in her home. Colonel Richard Lawrence, governor of Waterford supported her request, he had observed her charitable work in the town for four or five years and commented 'and if any of her religion might live in any garrison none [were] more deserving than she'.[17] Unfortunately the records end at this point, but it is clear from this case that the regime's officials on the ground were able to make distinctions between individuals covered in blanket terms by the state.

There were other categories of Irish people who did not fall into the terms of transportation to Connacht. On 14 September 1653, an order was made to transport 250 'women of the Irish nation above twelve years of age and under forty-five' and 300 'men above twelve and under fifty' to New England. The order was applied to the area within 20 miles of Cork, Youghal, Kinsale, Waterford and Wexford. Captain John Vernon was employed by the Commissioners of Ireland to find the means. He went to Bristol and contacted Alderman David Sellick, a slave dealer in the port, and set up the necessary means. The following year 'all wanders, men and women' were to be rounded up in the vicinities of Carlow, Clonmel, Wexford, Ross and Waterford for the same purpose.[18] In County Galway, the governor of Galway city, Colonel Stubbs, gained a fearsome reputation for seizing county people in night-raids and selling them into slavery in the West Indies.

Land cleared of Catholic and Royalist owners was needed to pay off the soldiers but also as a return on the investment of the adventurers who had as much as twelve years before advanced money to pay for the reconquest of Ireland. Also it was desirable to fully lay before the new state the full extent of the colonial property, and in June 1654 the administration began to catalogue the nation in a massive civil survey. The extent and ownership of land was examined by commissioners in twenty-seven of the thirty-two counties. Five Connacht counties had been surveyed back in the 1630s when Sir Thomas Wentworth had attempted to create plantations in the province and this was considered suitable for the present purpose. Commissioners were appointed from proprietors and collectors of the revenue in counties, although some served for more than one county in a province. They were to collect the information passed on by juries, appointed for each barony, of local, dependable men who called witnesses and, if necessary, trod the bounds of lands. There were other problems in compiling the survey: in the Kildare barony of Narragh and Reban it proved impossible to compile information on the value of the tithes because 'most of the inhabitants of the aforesd Barrony of Narragh & Reban wch have knowen the same are either dead or transported into Connought'. The same was true of Killcullen.[19]

In certain areas the survey gives an indication of the level of damage caused to the physical structures of the country. For instance in the Wexford survey barony of Ballaghkeen out of six castles, five were in ruins, of eight mills seven were ruined, and of eight stone houses recorded only one was tenable. In the barony of Shillbyrne of 33 castles, eight, around a quarter, were in ruins, of nine mills, two, again a similar proportion, only three of five weirs were in working order, and most of the churches were damaged.[20] In County Kildare the surveyors noted that valuable properties had been ruined since the rebellion. A stone house at Cartown worth £200 in 1640 was now ruined and worth only £60. The castle at Confy was now worth only half its 1640 value because it was in ruins. Lady Allen's castle at Killadowne was ruined and worth only £40, one fifth of its pre-war value.[21]

Some places remained undamaged, such as Clontraf, where rebels had tried to inveigle sailors to cut the anchor ropes of boats in the bay; and the castle (the nineteenth-century version of which is now a public house) remained standing despite Sir Charles Coote's raid in December 1641 when he had particularly targeted this, the home of George King. George King had fled at the beginning of the rebellion, but his castle with its barn, dove house and orchard was still worth £300.[22]

Scotland and the Republic

It had been argued that Cromwell and his military colleagues' attitudes towards Scotland eased the way for at least the outward appearance of a union of equals between Scotland and the Republic of England and Wales.[23] As shown in the previous chapter, Cromwell put this into practice by hoping to discuss affairs with erring brothers such as Archibald Johnston. The Act of Settlement of 21 April 1652 was not punitive towards Scotland, proscribing only 24 former enemies.

The conquest of the British Isles was extended to the extremes on 28 January 1652 when troops were sent to the Orkneys; the previous months had seen the occupation of Ross, Sutherland and Caithness. By this time the unification of Scotland and England was under way. Archibald Johnston of Wariston's dire predictions for Scotland based on the allocation of Scottish lands to principal English officers, Lambert, Monck, Whalley, Okey and Alured, had not materialised. Plans for political annexation mooted in October 1651 had been turned instead to 'A Declaration of the Parliament of the Commonwealth of England' concerning the Settlement of Scotland. In effect this was to be a tender of incorporation put to the Scottish people for their approval through their representatives at a specially assembly of delegates from the 89 constituencies, although sixteen did not send delegates. There was really little option but to accept the proposal, and whilst most did so with little enthusiasm, nine constituency representatives expressed enthusiasm and Orkney and Sheltand expressed determination to make it work.[24] For Archibald Johnston, the union of the Commonwealth and Scotland was marked in his eyes by the storms which broke out the night it was declared. He likened 21 April 1652, the day of the public proclamations of union, to the day the Five Articles of Perth were ratified by the Estates in 1621.[25]

The unity of the isles did not please all of the English either. For one person, J. Emerson, stationed on Orkney, these particular isles were not Christian or habitable:

> Unchristen'd Isles, borrowing their generall name
> From smoaky Orcus. Did Dame Nature ever
> Unmake herself, create a chaos? never,

Nor can there ever such a product bee
Found out in Bacon's Natural Historie

This vitriolic poem, *The Character of Orkney* contains a long litany of complaints about Orkney women, cheese, milk, children in general, hygiene, the method of pulling wool rather than shearing the sheep, and similarly uprooting corn rather than scything or sickling it. The conquest of Orkney made Cromwell more famous than Caesar, argued the author, but not for a really positive reason:

… butt, itt might bee said,
Had wee nott conquer'd Orknay, Cromwell's story
Had cleart noe more of honour in't, and glory
Then Caesar's; butt with this conquest fell
Under his sword, The forlorne hope of Hell.

This poem, Emerson claimed he had written in his cave, the Otter's Hole, 'in the third month of my banishment from Christendome, September 9, 1652'.[26]

A second poem deals with mainland Orkney and again commented unfavourably on the natural history of the isle. Commenting on the similarity between the island's name Pomonia, and Pomona the 'Patronesse of Fruit', Emerson instructs his reader not to expect

A wood, a copse, a tree that is nott greene
Att every season of the flitting yeare.

This poem aping a natural history, repeats many of the criticisms of the *Description*, and concludes:

Thus ends Pomonis' praise, which well might vie
With all the world, was not Scotland nott soe nigh.[27]

Robert Overton, commander of the army in Scotland, issued instructions to the garrison at Orkney to forbear molesting the inhabitants of the islands, and to leave their cattle, horses or sheep.[28] Certainly a later author, B.H. Hossack, believed that the unwilling visitors had given the Orkadians lessons in husbandry. Whilst some other have thought that the English presence brought legal and agricultural benefits, the costs were high. There was a permanent garrison in the islands, and the contribution to the Monthly Maintenance of £10,000 imposed on Scotland drained over £150 a month from the islands.[29]

The political regime established by the Instrument of Government continued the principles established by the nominated Little or Barebones' Parliament which preceded it during 1653: Scotland would be represented at Westminster by a small number of MPs. As a result the south-west was assigned just one MP for the eight burghs previously represented in the Estates: the single election was to be held at Glasgow.[30] Irvine had lost any meaningful presence in national government, yet was beset by problems caused by the national uncertainty. Beds in garrisons had to be paid for, over and above the normal levies imposed upon the burgh. It would appear that these costs were having implications for the normal obligations of the town. The schoolmaster Hew Ross had been employed in April 1652 at the princely sum of 40 merkis (marks) a year. By 12 December 1656 he had been paid only 20 merkis in total. 'I will be forced to goe out of the towne a beggar' he complained. For which 'present conditioun' the town grudgingly paid him another 20 merkis.[31]

During the mid-1650s Lady Anne Halket began to record her meditations which included reflections on the execution of the king. The sin of that execution rested upon the Scottish people for not being so thankful of God's mercies as they should have been: 'it was thy sin and mine & not his own which was his loss our prayers for him was not so fervent & so full of faith as was required'.[32] Anne hoped that things would change:

> for my child I hope thou shalt live to see that promise made good of having our rulers restored & our kings and queenes made nursing fathers and mothers to preserve the purrity of the church wch is now rent and divided by Scisme herisie & error ...

Anne was one of those people for whom twenty years seemed to dull the edge on the differences between the religious factions, it 'may make you cry to see difference 'tween those who support Christ' for she believed like the Aberdeen doctors before her that both Presbyterians and bishops agreed on the fundamentals and that this broad agreement was more important than the divisions. Anne warned her child in the memorials to be wary of Covenant and not to make 'religious prtence the ground of schisme or rebellion in church or state as i feare to[o] many hath done'.[33]

Anne's belief may have been mirrored to some extent by the thoughts of Alexander Jaffray, although the response of the Aberdonian was different. Alexander Jaffray's conversion from convinced Presbyterian to Independent meant that he was considered sympathetic to the conquered regime, and in March 1652 as the union was proposed, Jaffray was offered the post of director of the Chancellery and in June the following year he was selected as a member of the Barebone's Parliament in Westminster; one of only five Scottish members. Although he appreciated meeting the Godly men assembled there, 'I can say little of any good we did at that Parliament: yet it was on the hearts of some there.' Thereafter, having turned down a judgeship offered by Cromwell, Jaffray returned to Edinburgh to resume his duties as director of the Chancellery, living there six months when the courts were in session and at Aberdeen with his family for the other half of the year. In 1656 the family moved to Edinburgh.[34] By 1654 Jaffray's questioning of the path of God began to lead him to an association with what was to become the Quaker movement. As yet this was a small group in Scotland but proto-meetings had been held in the south in the occupying forces from 1653 onwards. When Quakers from England did reach Scotland most remained well south of Aberdeen where Jaffray and his band of friends had established their independent gathering.

As a result of this drift Jaffray's diaries become more and more spiritual in composition, detailing his thoughts on commentaries he read, on a case of incest he had heard in court, and less and less about the intrusion of the outside political world into his understanding of God's purpose. This was the period that he back-filled his 'diary' to, putting in the details of his previous life and selecting those parts which seemed to him to confirm that God had a special purpose for him. The published version of his diary was heavily edited by John Barclay in the 1820s and 1830s, and Barclay edited out sections which in the early parts dwelt on meditations of God's purpose and some family details.[35]

George Fox arrived in Scotland in via Caerlaverock, on through Dumfries and into the Highlands in the autumn of 1657. As soon as he arrived ministers raged against him in the 'steeplehouses' and informed the council in Edinburgh of his presence. Not only was he opposed by Presbyterians, but other sects in Edinburgh and Leith came to openly dispute with Fox – the Baptists were 'very rude'. The Presbyterians succeeded in having Fox summoned to Parliament House where his keeping of his hat on his head was questioned. 'I told him I had been before the Protector with it on.' Nevertheless, the council refused to listen to him and ordered him out of the country. Fox did not go immediately, and whilst staying with friends in Edinburgh he wrote to the council to try and persuade it to change its decision. It does not appear that the councillors, whilst troubled, rescinded their decision, but Fox, looking back noted that some of them were soon banished themselves at the end of the decade. He also claimed to be able to perceive that George Monck's character was submerged by his being subservient to Oliver Cromwell.[36]

In the meantime, in the west of Scotland the synod of Argyll was caught up in trying to reform society in the Isles and the former MacDonald lands in its remit. The captain of Clanranald was censured for not ensuring that the Kirk had regular diets and because priests and papists appeared to be coming into his territory. The threat from papists was both an internal and external problem for the Synod. In Edinburgh in 1650, John Nicoll recorded that Lord Linton had been excommunicated in 1650 for marrying the excommunicated Catholic widow of Lord Seton.[37] In Argyll, on the one hand were those who were coming into the Clanranald territory. Priests and Jesuits were believed to be coming from Ireland in 1655 to spread the heresy. On the other hand, there were the papists who already lived there. Anna McDonald was one. The threat from the Roman Catholic Church was considered so dangerous and so pervasive that conversing with papists was risky. In June 1654 the Lockhead meeting of the synod decided that no one should speak to Anna or to any excommunicated papist. The decision was announced the following Sunday in the Kirk. Civil magistrates were asked to punish anyone who spoke to her and the synod would see to spiritual 'condigne censure'. The only exceptions should be family, grudgingly recognised as having 'natural ties'.[38]

In order to firmly establish the reformed faith, the synod discussed the provision of Gaelic language catechisms. In May 1654 the questions were examined for their usefulness and by October 1655 the first catechism had been so successful a further 2,000 were ordered from the printers at a cost of 250 merkis. In October 1654 the lack of tutors skilled in what the synod referred to as the Irish language was noted and the ministers discussed raising a fee so that David Simpson could take up a post. A year later, as the new batch of catechisms were sent for, the synod again discussed the shortage of Gaelic speaking ministers in Kintyre. Mr John Thompson 'ane hopefull young man' was asked to take up a post as soon as he had finished his studies. The synod then decided that as psalm singing was so beneficial in spreading the Word, the lack of Gaelic versions was depriving the Gaelic speakers of the 'benefit and refreshing comfort'. The task of setting the psalms of David was set on foot. This was not an easy task and two years later it was still not complete, and in May 1657 the tasks were reallocated to try and secure 100 translated psalms by the October session. The first 52 were well on their way but three ministers were set to work on numbers 53–100. Notwithstanding these difficulties it was decided to examine the translation of the Bible into Gaelic too. This was a task which had been considered many years earlier; the ministers knew that some sections had been translated and these were to be searched for. By May 1658 only the first 50 psalms had been completed, but they were not suitable, the syllabication had not worked when translated from Scots to Gaelic so the two translators were sent with their work to Kintyre to consult two of the fittest ministers to carry out the task, David Simpson and John McMarques.[39]

The synod had a range of other social issues to deal with as the war had dislocated society considerably. There was a plethora of widowed women wishing to remarry, but the synod was worried about the veracity of their widowhood. Gorrie McNeill had taken drastic action when she wanted to remarry: she and her intended husband went to Ireland because the Kirk would not accept proof of her husband's death during the war in Ireland in the 1640s. Norrie had gone to Ireland with her husband but had returned to Scotland probably after reports of his death had reached her. In her attempt to secure proof she returned to Ireland to talk to soldiers who had been with her husband when he died. The third visit was for her second marriage, which in October 1652 the synod decided to accept. The problem was particularly acute on the Isle of Colonsay where there was no resident minister. Women there took the boat to Mull and Islay to marry only to be met with the refusal of ministers because they could not vouch for their widowed status. There was concern in the Isles that the women were testifying for each other and thus might be conspiring to cover up marriages which were not ended. The synod realised that this was not a realistic approach, for as the minutes put it this resulted in 'by which many fornicators was in the cowntrey, and, thowgh willing to marie, cold not gett the benefite thereof, many children unbaptised'. The synod appointed two men, one of them the baillie of Collonsay, to give the certificates required.[40] Men too had to sue for the same. Soldier George Orrock could not obtain sufficient proof of his single status because his profession had left him with no fixed abode from which to secure the testimony of trusted men. He and Anna McNeill had taken the matter into their own hands too and they lived together. The spiritual purity of the synod's approach had to give way again to practicalities. Provided the couple repented of their sinful cohabitation, someone could be got to swear for their general good character and provided George swore solemnly before the synod, then they would be married 'for preventing of mor sin'.[41]

Members of the synod thought that Marie McInnesker of Clachandisard had been raped. They were not actually supposed to be concerned with this, their remit was morality. Marie had an illegitimate child and at the sixth session of the Provincial Assembly at Killmichell in May 1655, they were determined to find the father. The most likely man was Neill McInlych. Several witnesses, his fellow soldiers and Marie's mistress were certain that it was him. Even McInlych admitted that 'he was struling with her that same night'. The mistress said that 'she had enowch adoe to keep the said Neill from her and that shee pulled him off by the feet'. Marie swore that she had been with no other man and the synod believed her and appointed that the child be baptised. They then added 'a letir to be writtin to my Lord Marques to cause take some cowrse with him, he being guiltie in a certain kind of rapt'. This is an unusual decision, given that it was generally accepted that conception could not take place outside of consensual sex. Nevertheless the evidence of the mistress and McInlych's admission that he struggled with Marie seem to have overborne this presumption. The synod of Argyll revealed itself to be very flexible in its approach to the society of the Highlands.

One thing noticeable as a trend was the decline in cases of adultery and fornication dealt with by the synod. Numbers in 1652 and 1653 remained low at three and four cases respectively. However in 1654 and 1655 the number of offenders named in the court grew rapidly to 13 and 24 respectively (18 men and 12 women). It was clear that the two crimes were a part of the synod's attempt to correct the disorder in society created by the war and revolution, to change the attitude of God towards his Covenanted people. Most offenders, if they acknowledged their guilt, would be ordered to apologise and acknowledge their fault publicly, and serious offenders like Angus McMarques, a fiddler and serial adulterer, could be excommunicated. There were also cases of incest to be considered and these cases all went hand in hand with the problems of ascertaining the suitability of marriages in the Isles. Society appears to have been perceived as being under reconstruction, with the synod as the master builder. Following the transfer in early 1656 of such cases to civil authorities, adultery and fornication soon ceased to be major concerns; in 1656 the number of cases fell to five, to two a year later and four in 1658. Angus McMarques was an exception, his itinerant life allowed him to have sexual relations with two women, one of who he lived with in Kilmodan and later, after a relapse into adultery, in Killespickerill. He continued bumping the statistics by making several appearances to try and have his excommunication relaxed.[42] There would seem to have been a general view that society in general was going to the dogs. Less specific issues bothered the synod. When not plagued by women and men of suspicious morals, by papists, Jesuits and Irish priests, there were always jugglers to worry about. Such people were classed with the usual collection of vagabonds and gangrels (vagrants); they and those who harboured them should be censured.[43]

For the 'Englishes' stationed in Scotland the country proved a worrying place. Captain Robert Baynes wrote to his brother Captain Adam Baynes, a future MP, at that time in Aberdeen, about commissions for his officers in June 1654. This was at the height of the Earl of Glencairn's Highland rebellion when John Middleton had taken over military affairs, and even in the coastal region there were 'many parties of the Enemy in this Country raising forces, so that I believe (when got together) will be a considerable party'.[44] There was a considerable number of the Baines family in the country, for Adam was accompanied by his sister and a cousin, John Baines, was a commissary with Monck's forces based at St Johnston's when Robert penned his letter. The period of Monck's campaign is outlined in a series of letters. The campaign was taken to the Highlands in the hope of forcing Middleton into open conflict. Scotland was garrisoned as Monck tried to fence-in the rebel forces. Baynes was involved in the march. He commented on the effects of this war on the area through which he passed:

> We have not found man, woman, or child at their homes, all being either in homes or in remote places with their cattle. At their return they will have new houses to build and corn to seek, which will be a means to quiet them, or nothing.

In other words the 'Englishes' destroyed what they found to deprive Middleton's army of supplies and support for as he later wrote in the same letter:

> but it's believed that what is already done, and will be done ere winter, will make the Country weary of Middleton and he of the Country, for at his return into the parts where we have been, he will find litte to live upon: and so must either disperse, starve, or come into the Lowlands where we shall deal with him.[45]

Rumours that the policy was having the desired effect reached Baynes by 10 July, when he related Middleton's alleged frustration to his cousin Adam. After his defeat at Dalnaspidal nine days after this letter, Middleton became less and less involved in the leadership of the rebellion and it reverted to Glencairn, but the English policy continued for some weeks. On 5 August Baynes commented on the land around Montieth:

the marches being very small because of the plenty of grass and corn we find in these parts which it is our business to destroy that the enemy may be incapable of giving or taking any entertainment hereabouts, it being a place wholly against us.

On 13 August Baynes wrote commenting on the state of the land at Lough Catteron where he was and the attitudes he and his colleagues had to the people he met. It was clear that he regarded them as uncivilised and this no doubt eased his conscience with regard to the treatment meted out to them. He was:

sojourning in a country possessed wholly with enemies, yea, such people as do seldom acknowledge any Lord. Formerly they denied us assess-ments, and their Lords their rents; but now they may plead some excuse, for we have done what we possibly can to disable them, having eaten and spoiled most of their corn, burnnt their houses, and made prizes of what cattle or horses came within our reach, and that not of a few; so that now they will have very much ado to rub out a living for themselves, being wholly disabled to entertain any of their friends. This morning, we are on our march to Aberfoyle, where we shall make what spoil we can.

The 'Englishes' were not the only ones destroying the homes and fields of the Highlands, Baynes added 'With the Enemy and we together, the people of the hills may yet in time repent their bargain; such houses as the Enemy themselves dare not keep they burn, least we should use them.'

Four days later, Baynes wrote from Aberfoyle:

We shall next week leave the field: our burning and sending to Barbadoes hath put such a fright into the Enemy, that many of them – and some of good esteem – are solicitous to come in and life peaceably at home. Some of them will go beyond the sea.[46]

There was not only the lay people to deal with: the ministers of the southern Highlands were not wholly in support of the regime, and a fast established by the government for 11 October 1654 met with resistance.[47] This was only part of a wider dispute. The ministers in the area where Baynes was based 'declared against the late Ordinance of his Highness and Council (empowering Mr Galaspy and 20 with him to settle the Ministry in Scotland), and have voted it a great sin [for] Mr Galaspy to procure such an ordinance'.[48] Galaspy was Patrick Gillespie, principal of Glasgow University, appointed by Cromwell and the refusal to co-operate with him faded once the Glencairn rebellion was over and the Kirk agreed that its ministers should abide by the rule of the government. Robert Baillie had identified Gillespie as a problem for the Kirk in 1650 and his views seem to have been justified by this action. It was clear that Gillespie had been forward not only in fomenting the Union, but also in conniving in the destruction of the General Assembly whose work he was now taking over.[49] In November 1656 the Synod of Argyll, from the same area where Baynes had encountered such opposition to the Protectorate settlement, was passing on its thanks to Gillespie for his advice and 'former courtesies', the first of several such solicitations.[50]

The Edinburgh notary, John Nichol, commented on this state of affairs in the wake of the Highland campaign.

> This yeir the povertie of the land daylie increst, by ressoun of the inlaik of tred sand traffick, both be sea and land, the peppill being poore and under cess, quarterings, and uther burdinges … Sindrie of the gude rank, alsweill nobles, gentrie, and burgessis, denuncit to the horne, their escheittis takin, their persones wairdit and imprissoned, and detenit thairin till their death. Bankruptes and brokin men throw all the paites of the natioun increst.[51]

The dearth and poverty was not as universal as Nichol, from his Edinburgh home, believed; it was more regionalised and in places it could be temporary. In any case price rises were a benefit to some and Scotland had its share of people who were well placed to benefit from the state of affairs, even if they had sympathies with the defeated cause. In Perthshire the 1650s saw price fluctuations which induced George Kinneard of Rossie Priory into seeking the most advantageous deals in Edinburgh. Robert Preston acted as his agent and supplies us with details of how prices were rising in 1656 at Haddington, south east of the capital. In April that year oats were fetching £5 and beare (barley) £8 a boll, peas were at 8 merks a boll and wheat fluctuated above and below the price of beare. 'It is expected by all that the pryces will yet rise' wrote Preston, yet five weeks later they remained at the same level.[52] In the months marked by the Glencairn rising Preston saw the selling of Kinneard's victuals as most important, and he may have perceived Kinneard's expenditure with some concern. When Kinneard bought footwear, Preston responded: 'I have delyvered to your serveand a peare of black boots bot Indeed I doe not approve of your sending for suche comodities at this tyme of danger: when ye may be sufficiently privigded at Dundie.' Whether Preston was concerned at the expenditure, for Edinburgh boots must have cost more, or whether he as concerned that this public purchase might be misconstrued in a known opponent of the regime we cannot be certain.[53]

By 1655, Nichol in Edinburgh had become worried about something other than prices, and here his customary balance and desire to eschew controversy could not still his Presbyterian heart:

> In this moneth of Januar 1655, and in sindry uther monethis preceiding, and mony monethis following, their rai up great numberis of that

damnable sect of Quakeries: quha, being deludit by Sathan, drew mony away to thair professioun, both men and women, sindrie of thame walking throw the streitis all naikit except thwir schirtis, crying, 'this is the way, walk ye into it'.[54]

Although at the time there appears to be no written record, Kinnaird was harbouring similar disgust and storing up his venom for those who acquiesced in toleration.

For Baillie the enemy of the Covenanted people was clear. It was the Scots themselves because they had allowed the great divisions of Remonstrant and Protester to develop. He wrote to Sprang on 19 July 1654 that the Remonstrancers would bring about more damage to the Kirk than would the English. Through these divisions, the men who had been prominent in recent Scottish history were pushed out of affairs. Argyll, although having submitted to the regime, despite his son's adherence to Glencairn's rising was 'almost drowned with debt in friendship with the English, but in hatred with the countrey'; Loudon 'lives like ane outlaw about Atholle'. Others, former Royalists and former Covenanters were prisoners in England. In their place 'Our Criminal Judicatories are all in the hands of the English, our Civile Courts in their hands also ... The Commissariat and Sherriffs Courts are all in the hands of English sohours.'[55] This was a period of great heart searching for Baillie and he began to put down his explanation of defeat on paper in his letters to William Sprang. At the centre of the division that had defeated the Scottish nation he placed family rivalry between Argyll and Hamilton, who between them had 'undone the Isle'. His hopes of the Glencairn rising so soon dashed were expressed with a little more caution, but he began to think that Charles II was to blame for not following up the rising in person or with foreign aid. His battles with Gillespie continued at a local level as well as national. In late 1658 Gillespie attempted to cover the expenses incurred during his national duties away from Glasgow University, using the excuse that as he did so he had attempted to win funds for the college. Baillie was prepared to admit that the principal had spent a good deal of money and that he could perhaps deduct expenses from the additional income he had generated, but not from the university rental income. Baillie was out-voted at faculty level. He disparaged Gillespie's learning which led him to make Latin prayers and disputations in 'a jolly way', but he could see that Gillespie was a shrewd self-publicist. When Gillespie proposed Secretary Thurloe for chancellor he was really doing so because James Sharpe, former bishop of Stirling, was trying to use Thurloe to lever Gillespie from his position of influence. Baillie made sure that Thurloe was informed of the reasons, only for Gillespie, upon Thurloe's refusal, to get the faculty to make himself vice chancellor.

On the eve of the collapse of the protectorate, Baillie's description of Scotland makes interesting reading. He continued, for Sprang's benefit, his catalogue of the fall of the old nobles and he berated the Union. 'The Countrey lies very quiet; it is exceddingly poor; trade is nought; the English hes all the moneyes.' The peace was remarkable. For all the rumours flying about after Cromwell's death 'crying out of the Devill and an Northerne armie', Baillie could write, 'We were feared for trouble after his death, but all is settled in peace.'[56]

Restoration

When Richard Cromwell was nominated his father's successor, it was the first peaceful governmental change since 1625. Unfortunately Richard had been isolated from political factions until recently and this, instead of just making him independent, also had the effect of divorcing him from any political support. Attacks on the structure of the Protectorate and his inability to manipulate the army left Richard powerless, and the Protectorate collapsed in Spring 1659. The ensuing attempts to find stability left the country floundering and created fears of renewed war or revolution, undoing any of the positive effects of the Republican peace. By 1660 sections of the population were happy to contemplate the restoration of the monarchy. When in March 1660 the remains of the Long Parliament, representing, of course, only England and Wales, dissolved itself and set in train the process of electing a constitutional assembly, or Convention Parliament, to decide the form of the future state, few expected anything but a monarchy.

Restoration in Ireland

The Restoration was a time for reassessing political and personal relationships. Some of the Irish transportees could claim that they had been able to survive a meagre existence without actually removing to the new estates. Others had a harder job in asserting their loyalty to the restored monarchy; Martin Blake Fitwilliam submitted his claim to the commission established by Charles II for recompense. Charles had announced that all those who had lost Galway estates should have a restoration of their own: but only extended to the 1652 promises. Some men deemed more deserving might receive more. Sir Charles Coote, now raised to the title of Earl of Mountrath was put in charge of seeing to these arrangements. Martin had lost only a third of his estates because rather than being subject to the list of qualifications established to assess complicity in the rebellion, he had claimed benefit of the surrender terms of Galway. In the dispute over the original terms which had seemingly guaranteed possession of their estates, a group of merchants to which Blake belonged had claimed affinity with the colonial process being driven forward by the commissioners for Ireland. Just as the commissioners were setting forth to make Galway an English town, Martin and the others had claimed that that had been what their families had been doing for 400 years.[57] Now after the Restoration, Blake had to claim that he had done nothing willingly offensive towards the new regime. He claimed he had been forced by 'meere necessity' to attend the courts of qualification at Athlone and of allocation at Loughrea during the 1650s.[58] The phrase 'meere necessity' being very close to his attempt to justify his actions during the rebellion to the English commissioners in 1655 when he said that he had been goaded out of his desire. However his claim that 'he hath alwayes been inoffensive in his deportm[en]t & ever faithful & loyall to his Matie & suffered much for adhering to his Royal government and authority ... ' sits uneasily with his earlier claims and with the alacrity with which he not only took up his new estates of 425 acres apportioned to him, but swiftly added 187 acres bought from other transportees to them. Details of these estates he submitted for consideration.

Others had far less to obscure: Daniel Donovan of Castle Donovan in County Cork was one of these. Donovan had been involved in the Rebellion, but had in 1648 accepted the Ormond Peace and tried, he later alleged, to get other Confederates to join with him. He had fought for Charles I and II and as a result his estate had been taken from him. He had not accepted the transportation or the lands in Clare which he seemed to have been offered.[59] For this he was regarded worthy, and evidence was taken from Lord Kingston and the Earl of Drogheda in March 1661 to this effect. As a result, the O'Donovan estates were to be restored even if they were in the hands of adventurers rather than soldiers. Any rents held by the Exchequer from his estate's sequestration were to be returned to his son Daniel.

In County Louth a similar case emerged. John Bellew of Willistowne had raised troops for the Confederation and Royalist alliance, for which, along with his part in the rebellion and Confederation activities, he was deprived of his estates. Bellew had fought for the Ormond–Confederation alliance after 1648, and this service he played up in his petition to Charles II. He referred to his imprisonment after the Battle of Rathmines and to the fact that his pay was still, a decade later, in arrears.[60] Bellew never took up his allotted lands in Connacht at the courts of Athlone and Loughrea and refused to do so under the pain of death, he claimed. The investigation proved his petition to be correct and restitution was made. By 1661 most of his estates in Louth were in the hands of the king, and these were duly returned in March that year.[61] However, some estates were not returned until very much later. Bellew was still fighting for restoration of lands in 1666, when he again petitioned Ormond for complete restitution.[62]

It took John Talbot eleven years to regain his estates. Indeed only at his death in 1671 were all the Talbot lands reunited. When Miles Corbet fled to Europe Talbot moved back into Malahide Castle. However, Talbot was compromised like many others by having remained on his estates after Ormond had Dublin in 1647 and by his Catholicism. This put him in particular difficulties when Charles II acknowledged the titles to lands held by both the adventurers of 1642 and the soldiers settled in Ireland during the 1650s. These conflicting claims resulted in a situation where the Talbot estates were allocated and reallocated eight times in 20 months by the court established by the Act of Settlement.

Patrick Archer of Kilkenny and Waterford was easily able to demonstrate his felicity to the cause of Charles I and II. Undoubtedly he had been in rebellion in the early 1640s but he had used his position as a merchant to service the joint Confederation and Royalist cause even when the relationship between the two had been uneasy. The furnishing of a ship and guarantees in 1645 when setting forth the Scottish expedition of Antrim and MacColla, had been a great help. His loans to the allies in 1650 and continued financial assistance to Charles Stuart during the next decade had also been appreciated. His claim for recompense could not be ignored. Ormond supported Archer's cause, and Charles II based his response entirely on the lord lieutenant's advice; the payment of £5,883 19s 6d was ordered from the customs of Ross and Waterford.[63] Archer may have been a little put out that despite Ormond having vouched for his being a 'very honest man', he was not immediately repaid of the money loaned to Ormond's successor the Earl of Clanricarde, because the papers were missing. Also in the same county, Henry Draycott proved his worthiness for restoration to the rectory of St Leonards in the liberty of Dundalk, although it took him until September 1663 to prove his case.[64] In some cases the lands given to soldiers were bought up by existing landowners. Edward Dayley, an English soldier, hung onto his land at Templecarrig, Drimmyne, Newtown in Counties Dublin and Wicklow until 1663. On 15 September that year he sold some them to the Earl of Meath of Templecarrig for £350 and lease others to the earl for life.[65]

Restoration in Scotland

One notable exception to Alexander Jaffray's concentration on his inner history in the later stages was the death of Oliver Cromwell. This news reached Jaffray in Aberdeen on 14 September 1658. It was interpreted as a communication from God

> There being also, at this time, very sad evidences of the Lord's anger against this land, *by unseasonable weather, so that the fruits of the earth are threatened to be destroyed*; this thought of the abuse of so much peace and plenty, as formerly we have been enjoying, did much continue on my heart – and that we were, in the righteous judgement of God, to be exercised with famine and war, and a *sharper trial to pass over such as fear the Lord, than they had ever yet met with*; especially their unthankfulness for the peace we have been enjoying these years by-gone.[66]

Amid these doom-laden prognostications, Jaffray's first volume of diaries breaks off artificially as the remainder of the volume is now missing. He took up the history of God's providence towards Scotland again in a new book which began with entries for two years hence.

By the later 1650s Archibald Johnston of Wariston was now embroiled in the business of the Protectorate and his involvement in the establishment of the Humble Petition and Advice had been unpopular in some parts of Scotland.[67]

The death of Oliver Cromwell was to end this although he retained his position as clerk register of Parliament. Archibald was warned that he had many enemies in the new Parliament called by Protector Richard.

He argued against the recall of the Long Parliament, but the army officers were not listening to him. In August Archibald was appointed to chair the council of state, and he used the position to further Scottish interest by ameliorating tax levies in the country.[68] He was soon to be embroiled in discussions on the new status of the union with Scotland, fending off suggestions that the legal framework of the two nations be unified.

In Scotland, the later 1650s saw Angus McMarques' name reappear in the minutes of the Argyll synod. The fiddler's repentance during the late 1650s had taken two years to secure his release from the excommunication imposed in May 1655. By October 1657 his penitence was communicated to the synod and investigated. It took two years for him to be rehabilitated and made aware of his sins, but by October 1659 he was released from his excommunication and the news communicated throughout Argyll. It was not a meaningful repentance. By May 1660 he had relapsed and appears to have been guilty of the rape of a sick poor women for which he was passed on to the civil authorities.[69]

In general the last years of the Republic and the Restoration saw McMarques as an exception, there were no cases of fornication or adultery brought before the synod in 1659. This is because the responsibility for adultery was taken over by the civil courts, but even so two men, one of them the fiddler, and a woman appeared so charged in 1660. The following year no one was brought forward for these offences although there was a case of incest. The last year of the Republic had seen a matter of great concern. The Humble Petition and Advice, as well as its governmental clauses, had included the establishment of broad religious toleration. Robert Baillie, in a letter to Robert Douglas on 11 April 1659 wrote that he had seen the petition and saw it as the work of the Remonstrants and he saw problems with it. First, the petition by being addressed to the lord protector seemed to acknowledge the role of a supreme magistrate in Kirk affairs. Second, the petition by concentrating on the damage to the Covenant done by toleration seemed to indicate that the Kirk was less concerned with the damage done by other things. Third, the petition condemned a toleration which was in practice before the submission of the Humble Petition and Advice, and was the attack on this one clause an attack on the whole constitution? Fourth, the attack on the clause is an attack on the religion of the leading English and Welsh politicians, who would be unlikely to be sympathetic, but might if not attacked, limit toleration. Fifth, would a commissioner sent to London to deliver the petition really be a Remonstranter agent furthering their demands, and finally would those members of the Glasgow synod who did not want to send a petition have to contribute to the expenses of the commissioner if there was a vote to send one?[70] Naturally the Presbyterian synod at Argyll was aghast, but it was not under the thrall of Patrick Gillespie, like its Glasgow counterpart. When a 'correspondent from Glasgow' asked the senate to join the Supplication opposing the clauses dealing with toleration, then being drafted to present to the new Lord Protector Richard Cromwell, Oliver's eldest son, the synod revealed that it was well aware of the state of national politics. At the meeting on 25 May 1659 they responded 'as things now stand the synod thinks the same not to be needfull'.[71] There was no longer a protector and as the Protectorate had fallen, so had the Humble Petition and Advice. There was still important work to be undertaken in the Argyll region. The word was not yet fully accessible, but the first fifty psalms translated into 'Irish' were now complete and in print. The next fifty would be ready by the next session in October. The Irish language Bible was also a project being pursued into the Restoration.[72]

As the life of the Protectorate slipped away, unwelcome ghosts of the past surfaced in Irvine in the form of bad debts. Lord Protector Richard sent a demand on 31 March for money due to the Edinburgh government for the August and September 1650 monthly maintenance which had not been paid; Irvine owed £152 and Ayr £180. The town had to send representatives to show why. On the back of the demand, an excuse was scribbled to the effect that a good deal of money had been paid over directly to military forces during those distant months which had seen the defeat at Dunbar.[73] A day later merchant Adam Fullerton presented a bill for £100 which he had lent the burgh in June 1647 towards a levy of £500 to pay for the Duke of Hamilton's regiment. He was referring to what was at the time the Earl of Lanark's horse. Lanark was the brother and heir to the Marquis and later Duke of Hamilton; he succeeded to the Hamilton title after his brother's execution in England. The second duke died of wounds after Worcester. The regiment of horse was quartered south of Glasgow from late 1646 into the Spring of 1647. Fullerton petitioned to get back the capital sum and ten years annual rent or interest. The burgh decide only to pay the capital sum and refused subsequent requests for the full debt to be paid.[74] John Galt followed suit and submitted a schedule of old debt on his and his wife's behalf. Between them they had supplied beer and provided spades for the garrison at Eglington. They had supplied horse shoes and made bread for the Association forces and quartered Colonel Cotlar's men. Galt had also rebuilt the chimney on Irvine's tollbooth. In all he claimed that the town owed him £46 19s 8d. The burgh scaled down all of the charges and knocked the quartering duties from the total completely, paying him £32 19s 4d only. This was not really a fair recompense for such a wait for the Western Association; references show that Galt had waited, like Fullerton, for almost ten years for these payments.[75]

The last days of the Republic in Scotland were recorded by Baillie in a letter to Sprang in late 1659. 'Scotland's condition for the tyme is not good: exhaust in money; dead in trade; the taxes nearly doubled.' Archibald Johnston of Warriston was the only representative of the country in the Council of State established by the Rump, and he was therefore responsible for the discussions about the new terms of Union which would be settled only after the nature of 'the government of England, to which we are to be united' had been settled.[76] The state of the economy seemed to echo the prognostications of Alexander Jaffray after the death of Oliver Cromwell. Jaffray visited Monck at the end of October 1659, but declined to explain his purpose in his memorial. Instead he meditated on whether he would be seen to approve of Monck's 'way and acting', which he did not. The visit and its consequent worries demonstrated for Jaffray the way to avoid giving the wrong public appearance. It was a significant time; Jaffray lamented the breaking of Parliament 'and less clearly, the Prince broken that brake them, and yet more liekly to break in pieces one another'. The identity of the 'prince' that broke them is unclear but it could be a reference to Lambert. Other candidates include Richard Cromwell and Charles Stuart.[77] Jaffray was still worrying on 21 November whether or not it would be right for him to visit Monck on the eve of his march into England in case he might thereby lend his support to actions of which God disapproved. It appears that Jaffray was loosing confidence in taking any action, because he was taking so much time in trying both to identify God's will and win the approval of others. When he did commit himself to refusing to sign a bond calling for peace after long deliberation, it landed him in prison at the Edinburgh Tolbooth. He had objected to clauses censuring the extreme Presbyterians in western Scotland, not because he approved of their actions, but because he disapproved of the censure. He was in prison for four months from 20 September 1660 to 20 January 1661. He felt at times that the lord chancellor, the Earl of Glencairn was keeping him there for malicious reasons, and deliberately misconstruing his attitude to the Bond as treasonable. Once again the imprisoned Jaffray was rescued by Thomas Middleton, just as once he had been in 1645 whilst a prisoner of the Royalists. The by-now Earl of Middleton pressed Jaffray's case in the Estates and secured his release on a bond of £20,000 Scots.[78] He used some of his liberty to visit other prisoners in Edinburgh, including those he had broken with after his post-Dunbar conversion and members of the Resolutioner party arrested because they had presented the king with a reminder that he had signed the Covenant. It is not clear whether being told by Jaffray that he had been right all along about the mistake of sticking to a national church brought much comfort to anyone, especially not to James Guthrie who he visited and who was executed for his part in reminding the king of former oaths and his book *The Causes of God's Wrath upon the Nation*, which included offering the king the Covenant as a cause of Scotland's damnation. Jaffray's troubles were not over, for the reintroduction of an episcopacy with the aim of exterminating the Kirk in its Presbyterian form, was as intolerant of Quakers as was the re-established church in England.

At the Restoration Captain Baynes, once commissary to Monck's forces in the Glencairn rebellion, was receiver general in Scotland, and living at Leith. His views about Monck's actions were recorded in a letter to his cousin Adam Baynes, an MP for Appleby in Westmorland under the patronage of Lady Anne Clifford. He hoped that the conflict between Monck and the English forces under Lambert would end. Robert Baynes, Adam's brother was at that time in Newcastle in the centre of the potential conflict. John hoped that

> we may have in the nations a lasting authority and government estab-
> lished, that justice and judgement may run down our streets, and there
> may be no crying out because of violence and oppression; and that all
> hopes of the common Enemy may be buried in the dust, and all good
> men and lovers of the peace of these nations may embrace cordially
> and rejoice in the welfare and property of others. But, oh! I am
> doubtful yet how things will go; some material differences yet appear,
> and I am a little afraid will not be easily decided.[79]

John Baynes was not drifting out of step with his cousins. Robert was displaced from command because of his association with Lambert, and in the Parliament of early 1660, Adam seemed to be expressing Royalist opinions, whilst John hoped that Royalist hopes would 'vanish as a cloud and be shame to them'.[80] It was not to be, for one of those Royalist men who pinned their hopes on Monck at least was going to overturn Baynes' hopes if he could.

If the prospect of the Restoration was a time for recrimination, then George Kinnaird was a man of his time. As Monck prepared to set off southwards with his army to effect the restoration of a free Parliament, Kinnaird laid the grounds for his own restoration; although he actually suggested that he was working for the 'well being of this poore natione'. Kinnaird has been identified as a man principally concerned with order and at this point, therefore, he was perhaps concerned with stability and whoever provided it.[81] Monck was identi- fied as the best hope for such stability and Kinnaird sent him a lengthy and in places repetitive fifteen-point plan of action.[82] Kinnaird was principally concerned to ensure that Monck left the garrisons of Scotland in trustworthy hands, particularly his own Perthshire, and that the government or administra- tion of the country should be similarly managed. Owners of Highland castles should be imprisoned before the army left the country. Kinnaird was suggesting that the widest possible spectrum of opinion should be marshalled behind Monck's projected march into England, to allow for any possible outcome to the march. Whilst the hopes of those willing 'to spend the last drop of there blood with you for the freedome of the people you being ther stare and hopes', Monck should not 'trust too much to your new modeled men an the anabaptistical party nor there oaths'.

Much of the advice concerns the unnamed 'he' or 'him' whose military friends were with him in one shire, and who was the likely candidate to seize castles and take advantage of the unpaid soldiers in the country and the Highland chiefs. Monck should declare him a traitor. Kinnaird's petition had ensured that when Monck called representatives of the burghs and shires to meet with him on 15 November, it was George who was chosen to represent Perthshire at Edinburgh. However, when new representatives were to be chosen to meet Monck at Berwick on 12 December Kinnaird was initially opposed within his county.

By May Kinnaird was in London and his star had begun to rise. He quizzed his colleague Robert Preston about the minor posts in the administration of Scotland. Preston sent him details of the positions in the court of exchequer which had existed before the revolution. Kinnaird seemed to have expected them to revert to monarchical form even when he had written to Preston, probably in April 1660. Preston revealed that the court had been staffed by paid civil servants during the Republic or 'since the English came here', previously the posts had been unpaid. He went on in a later letter to tell Kinnaird that the posts were all likely to be empty soon as all the members of the court were appointed by Oliver or Richard Cromwell. Preston discussed the nature of the offices of burgh and county administration, adding in the later letter that if Kinnaird wanted to be sheriff of Perth, could he put in a word to get Preston the shrievalty of Edinburgh.[83] Kinnaird and Preston were also preparing information to stab the office holders in the back. Kinnaird had asked for the names of knaves and Preston responded. Robert Gordon was such a knave, he had 'eased the supplication for Quakers Anabaptists and Independents and [had] petitioned for a vast toleration and liberties none deserves sooner to be termed one than he … '. Preston was not above naming his and Kinnaird's close associates 'a man I cannot profess love unto, it is ouir unhappie goddsonne Matthew Brisbane presenter of Signatories in Exchequer and he is one of the clerks of Exchequer. … '. He added 'Do in this as you think good'.

The days that Francis Masterson, looking back from the end of the century, would call 'the Happie restauratione of King Charles ye Second' brought danger to all as well as opportunity.[84] John Nicol the notary recorded the Restoration in Edinburgh. As well as the official ceremonies at the Mercat Cross on 14 May, which were done with 'all solempniteis requisite', there was the less solemn celebration:

> dancing about the fyres, and using all uther takins of joy for the advancement and preference of thair native King to his croun and native inheritance. Quhairat also, thair wes much wyne spent, the spoutes of the croce ryning and venting out abundance of wyne, placed thair for that end; an the magistrates and councell of the toun being present, drinking the Kinges helth, and breking numberis of glasses[85]

For Mastereson of Parkmilne, aged then only 18, the Restoration brought opportunity – within five years he was a sheriff-deputy in Clacmannanshire – and was therefore as propitious as it was for Kinnaird, who was himself within two years MP for Perthshire and a peer before Charles II had died. But as well as for poor godson Matthew Brisbane, the Restoration brought peril for others. John Maitland, the Earl of Lauderdale, associated with Charles II since he had gone to Scotland in 1650, had a past to live down. He had been linked from the first with the Covenant and then with the Solemn League and Covenant for which he had been a commissioner in London during the Civil War. His position in Four Nations politics changed as the positions of others shifted, and he had been associated with the Engagement. From the early years of the Restoration he was accused of being in league with the Marquis of Argyle, who was being used as the scapegoat for the revolution in Scotland and he was, with less justification accused of being a correspondent of Henry Ireton, widely vilified as the progenitor of the regicide. Of the accusations about him and Argyle, Lauderdale wrote to Archbishop Sharpe, 'they should have no more notice taken than the barking of dogs. It seems I have my large share of the scourge of tongues. If these be the fees of my office I could have spared them as well as I have done other fees.' The accusations about Ireton were less sanguinely dealt with, and a clearly perturbed Lauderdale responded 'that is a black fals calumnie wthout shadow of trueth; for I was so farre from keeping correspondence or wryting letters to Ireton as is alledged that I doe not remember that I ever saw him in my whole life until I saw him hanging on the gallowes at Tybourn. And I am sure that I never wrote line to him, nor receavd line from him since I was borne'.

In a different way too John Baynes had a past to live down. He had risen to be receiver general in Scotland, but he saw in the Restoration his potential downfall. At the solicitation of his cousin Adam, he signed the address to the new king along with the commissioners for the Government of Scotland and the very judges that Kinnaird was simultaneously determined to undermine. Baynes still held affection for Lambert, even though he had opposed his actions in late 1659 and in the same letter that he wrote of his quickly adopted 'faithfulness to his Majesty', he expressed his hope that 'his Majesty has granted [Lambert] a pardon, and has thoughts of kindness to him: I wish it be so.' However, Baynes knew he and the other governors in Scotland were now wholly at the mercy of what Monck could secure for his former agents.[86]

For John Nichol, obviously ignoring the fate of Argyll, the Restoration years were good ones:

> At this tyme our gentrie of Scotland did luik with such gallant and joyfull countenances, as if thai haid bene the sones of princes; the beastes also of the feild, did manefest Godies goodnes towardis this kingdome: and it wes the joy of this kingdome, quhich for samony yeiris hath bene overcloudit, and now to sie thame upone brave horses, pransing in thair acustomat places, in telting, ryneing of races, and suchlyke[87]

That something dramatic had happened in the wake of the Restoration could not escape his attention for, with some incredulity, Nicol recorded the public and official celebrations on St Andrew's (30 November) Day in 1662. 'This being a novaltie, I thoght guid to record, becaus it was nevir in use heirtofoir since the Reformatioun.'[88]

At the end of his discussions of the events of the revolution and Civil Wars, when looking back on his life in the first decades of the eighteenth century, Bishop of Salisbury, Gilbert Burnet wrote 'Thus we have passed through the times of public ruin and confusion, and now we are entering upon a more regular history, and a scene of action more delightful.'

At that time he was seventeen. Gilbert Burnet, nephew of Archibald Johnston of Wariston, and Richard Baxter the Presbyterian divine in England both considered Andrew Sharpe to be a man of the moment. Baxter, he and Lauderdale were soon engaged in establishing what they believed to be the prospective king's credentials. Burnet saw Sharpe in a different light. Sharpe had been financed by the Resolutioners with the expectation that he would further the Presbyterian Kirk. Burnet commented wryly that Sharpe, soon to be Archbishop of St Andrews, showed his true colours very quickly and 'his character for perfidy and dissimulation became detestable'. By then they were enemies, for Burnet was a latitudinarian; Sharpe began to destroy the very fundamentals of the Church which he had once been paid to represent. The prospective king was not to escape Burnet's censure, for he proved not to be beyond 'the levities of youth and extremities of pleasure'. The Restoration brought with it a 'spirit of extravagant joy … which was soon attended with all manner of profaneness and immorality'.[89]

The Venetian secretary, Francesco Giavarina, wrote on 21 April 1662, as the Restoration began to consolidate its work. Presbyterians, whom he grouped with the Sectaries whom Presbyterians hated, were in a state of 'extreme mortifaction'. The Solemn League and Covenant was burned and all papers on the subject taken from the public archive and consigned to the flames.[90] For one of the principal figures in the beginning of the revolution, the tables rapidly turned. Archibald Johnston returned to Scotland at the end of March 1660 partly because he feared for his life. He was initially hopeful that Charles II's promise of oblivion would apply to Scotland and to himself. He read it eagerly when it was brought into Scotland on 8 May 1660. Six days later his hopes appeared dashed; when he spoke to Lord Loudoun he found that he and Argyle 'was tou hayted men'. His wife was urged to hold a bonfire, perhaps to blend in with the crowd. Archibald himself was reminded of the celebrations in Scotland when Charles went there in 1650. He prayed that the these 'bonfyres [were kept] from kendling a fyre of blood and warre in thes nations, as the uthers did'. He was not calmed by the 'great ryot, excesse, extravangancy, superfluicity, vanity, naughtinesse, profanety, drinking of healths; the Lord be merciful to us'. Four days later he found that he was blamed for all the blood shed in Scotland and that many wanted his life. On 16 July a warrant was issued for his arrest and the life of a fugitive began.[91]

REPUBLIC AND RESTORATION
IN ENGLAND AND WALES,
1653–61

The Republic in England and Wales

Cromwell's expulsion of the Long Parliament in April 1653 led Dorothy
Osborne, the 26-year-old daughter of a former Royalist governor of Guernsey,
to consider the political ironies of the past twelve years. She wrote to William
Temple,

> If Mr Pym were alive again I wonder what he would think of these
> proceedings, and whether they would appear as a great a breach of the
> Privilege of Parliament as the demanding the five members. But I shall
> talk treason by and by if I do not look to myself; tis safer talking of the
> orange-flower water you sent me[1]

Demonstrating the awareness of the dangers of political commentary which Mr
Clopton and Walter Powell showed in their diaries, Dorothy reverted to avoiding
recording her political thoughts. Of course in this instance this was more of a
joke with her parliamentarian lover William Temple than a serious attempt to
cover her thoughts.

In his attempt to forestall any unforeseen eventuality Richard Baxter set out
in his autobiography an image of himself as a clear-sighted man. We left him
dodging any involvement with Charles II at Worcester. He continued his narrative with an ever-more elaborate assertion of Cromwell's political skill. Cromwell
did not go for a direct push for the throne, but 'allowed' everyone, particularly
the army, to grow tired of democracy. So even after the expulsion of Parliament
in April 1653, Cromwell set up the Little Parliament, as part of this grand
design. Of course Baxter did 'in open conference declare Cromwell and his
adherents to be guilty of treason and rebellion … '. But 'I did not think it my
duty to rave against him in the pulpit, not to do this so unseasonably and impru-
dently as might irritate him to mischief.' This leaves us in some doubt as to how
open these conferences were. Baxter went on to state that he thought on the
whole Cromwell had a design 'to do good in the main'. It is almost an unresolved conflict contained in one paragraph, the traitor who intended good.

Baxter tries to explain that he thought that this would all be in vain, partly because Cromwell might be doing it for his own reasons to make the people love him, and also because it was an usurpation and when the rightful ruler was restored, Cromwell's good acts would be swept away because they were associated with it. This tortured argument, of course allowed Baxter to justify his collaboration with the Protectorate state's actions where they suited him, without opening him up to charges of collusion.[2]

It seems evident in the Upton in Nottinghamshire constables' accounts that the Battle of Worcester brought a degree of stability in England and Wales which had not been seen for some 14 years. The Upton accounts provide an important sequence of village accounts throughout the protectorate and early Restoration years.[3] Through them we can examine the process of administration in rural England and tentatively assess something of 1650 life. Although there are some figures missing for 1652, there is a clear dramatic fall in the village's outlay, recorded sums add up to only £58 18s 1d, a dramatic fall from the previous year's partial total of over £112. The following year they increase again to a post-Civil War peacetime rate of £75 19s 5d, but then in 1654 they fall again to £66 7s 9d. In 1655 the drop is dramatic, to only £34 13s 7d. The latter years of the Republic saw Upton's levies and disbursements running at a lower charge than for over 15 years, from a peak at £41 18s 7d in 1656, to £27 1s 4d in 1657, £21 0s 10d in 1658 and £30 11s 10d in 1659: a rough average of £26 a year, compared with an average of around £94 for the previous five (1649–54). The Restoration of the monarchy forced levy totals up again, to £42 1s 1d in 1660 and for the first five recorded years of the restored monarchy an average of £33.

Even a glance at the accounts will tell us something about the state of the nation during these years. With the onset of war in England and Wales in 1642 the number of entries and pages used in the accounts per year increased dramatically. In 1641 about six and a half pages sufficed. In 1644 they numbered 13 pages, in 1649 about 10. By the 1650s the numbers fell, to 8 in 1652, and just over 3 in 1657. This is a purely visual impression, but it is confirmed by counting the transactions that the constable made. In 1641, a busy if peaceful year, William Gill needed to make only 97 disbursement transactions. At the height of the war in 1644, Jane Kitchen and William Chappell recorded about 266 individual payments, in 1649 John Parlethorpe recorded 185. Even in 1652, John Shearcroft recorded 160 transactions, but by 1657 William Gill recorded only 62.

The same may well have been true of estate accounts too. A long way from Upton, at Peel on the Isle of Man, by 1657 the Kenyon estate accounts were showing a decline in the prominence of the Republic's taxation. The year's accounts complied by George Edge were no longer dominated by state levies as they had been six years earlier. True, the level of monthly taxation was roughly similar, even slightly increased to 3s 8d as opposed to the 3s 4d of 1651, but of 16 payments, only six payments covering monthly tax in Peel, Halton and

Shoughlaige-e-Cairne, were for monthly tax. What stands out most clearly from these figures is the lack of military 'extras'. The state was imposing regular taxation only.[4]

It is generally argued that the execution of the king, and the revolution which that entailed in England, had no popular support. Lady Fairfax made exactly that point during the king's trial. Consequently, by this argument the Republic was forced on the people by the army. On the other hand we know little about what the people wanted, although they probably wanted stability. Traditionally stability involved king and Parliament, therefore, we could argue, king and Parliament was what the people wanted. However, such an argument involves forgetting that to some people, because the king was untrustworthy he could not represent stability. Without a Parliament during the 1630s Charles I had taxed them illegally, and taken away common rights in massive swathes of countryside, such as down in the south-west of England, and in the Hatfield Chase and Isle of Axholme area of Nottinghamshire and Lincolnshire for example. Moreover, until Charles had been rendered bankrupt and powerless by the military defeats of 1640, he had intended to rule without parliament. The last period of rule by king and Parliament, 1640–2 had been marked by mutual distrust and by the king's attempt to find a means, either a plot hatched by his own army, or by employing the forces of Scotland or Catholic Ireland, by which to overthrow his Westminster Parliament. In other words, settlement through king and Parliament was in 1649 an illusion, especially as the king had no intention even then of accepting the consequences of his defeat. It would be gross historical arrogance to argue that some of the ordinary people of this country did not realise that. Some of them, therefore, may well have accepted the Republic as a means to an end, the end being stability – the chance to rebuild their lives, economies and communities. That Charles II was able to command the loyalty of so few in his invasion of 1651 suggests that this may be the case. The interruptions of war, either waged by the Republic against Ireland or Scotland, and also the Dutch, prevented any such stability. Continued war would be unwanted, and resented: much the reaction to the invasion of Charles II.

The Upton accounts show that this perception can be justified. Once the wars came to an end the demands on the community both financially, and in the time and burden upon the functionaries, lessened markedly. Thus stability returned to Upton, and the Battle of Worcester was indeed a 'Crowning Mercy'. At the same time, there was very little change in the way things ran at local level. Major elements of pre-revolutionary stability or normality remained: constables still took their oaths before the JPs, who still presided over Quarter Sessions. There they still dealt with petty crime and passed on more important crimes to the assizes. They also dealt with community responsibilities, such as the reconstruction of Muskham Bridge in 1653, the attempt to make the Lord of Kelham keep up his obligations to maintain Kelham Bridge, and the repair of the Leene Bridge in 1655. In Nottinghamshire, the personnel on the bench, or at least some of them, had changed, but there was continuity; the Hutchinsons, the

Pierrepoints and the Millingtons were still represented. Emphasising a continuity something similar to that noted in Staffordshire's 1655 commissioners for the peace by John Sutton. There, over a fifth of the shire's commissioners were from families expected to hold county office in pre-war years.[5]

In the middle of the decade, following the Royalist risings in the south-west led by Colonel John Penruddock, England was divided into regions presided over by major generals assisted by the commissioners referred to above. These men were the closest to a manifestation of military dictatorship that England experienced during the Republic. They were also the most unpopular manifestation and had a existence of only a few months. In these few months the major generals were insinuated into local government, Edmund Whalley took up a place on the Nottinghamshire bench. Below the JPs the chief constables were still in place, as was the postmaster, still imposing tasks and duties upon the constables, the former collecting quarter duties for the same purposes as under a monarchy, the latter still requiring contributions towards mounts for the postal service. There were new phenomena, such as the continued assessments which had their origins within the war, and the excise office too. In both cases traditional functions were wound up with both. The chief constable was responsible for collection of the assessments from the petty constables, and the excise office examined the alewives – Upton's brewers – and their licences and products. The Leet court too still met on Twentie day and St Thomas' day.

The majority of business in the accounts for the 1650s would have been recognisable to anyone familiar with pre-war accounts. There were strangers passing through, and hurried attempts to get pregnant travellers out of the parish bounds before they gave birth. Travellers were still required to have certification legitimising their journey, only this time they could be related to trips to the Council of State in England, or issued by the lord protector such as those given to 'tooe gentlemen there wives one child & one servant' and 'Eight criples men woomen and Children which came forth of St Thomas Ospital in London to goe to Whitby in yorkshire … '. At Addlethorpe and Ingoldmells in 1656 approximately 15 per cent of the village stock was spent on 80 travellers. These travellers were varied, but at least 34 (42 per cent) were from Ireland: another 18 (22 per cent) were sailors and 9 (11 per cent) were disabled travellers.[6] In central Lincolnshire at South Kyne, the number of travellers declined dramatically after 1653 and the costs had correspondingly fallen to around 4 per cent of village stock.[7]

The tentacles of the new regime could reach into the personal lives of the people of Upton, especially those of doubted loyalty. Penruddock's rising, whilst confined to a skirmish outside Salisbury prison followed by a two-day man-hunt, had far-reaching consequences beyond prompting the inception of the major generals' rule. The state began to compile a list of the potential enemies. Constables in each parish were to send in a return of those in their parish who had born arms against the Parliament. Those for the hundred of Blackburn still exist.[8] The returns are now bound together in a small book. The entries are subdivided into Delinquent Papists, meaning Roman Catholics who had fought for the king; Papists who had not taken up arms; and Delinquents which referred to Protestant Royalists. This was varied at Ribchester and Dillworth to a list of those who bore arms and a list of recusants who never bore arms. John Grave of Pendle forest's original return is included, and it suggests that the recorded returns were made at meetings in the county when the recusants were registered in the presence of the major general of the region on 28 January 1656.

Grave listed 152 names of 'such as I have heard are Recusants'. Poor labelling makes it impossible to be certain of the category of 37 of his named men, but it appears that not all of those he had been told were recusants were indeed so. Twenty-seven men were simply labelled delinquent, but 77 were listed as recusants and 37 as recusants in arms. Some of the named men were too young to have been involved in the wars at all: John Bradley of Henbrough was labelled 'under age' and John Barkes of Sailbury was noted as 'was taken away by his father at 10 yeares old, & came back whin 13 weeks and bond himself aprentize to a weever'. On the Lincolnshire coast constables in the twin settlement of Addlethorpe and Ingoldmells also had to deal with the former Royalists. Samuel Parker and William Woodes had to pay for their copy of the warrants for the 'late kings partie to put in Bonds at Spillsby' on 4 April 1656.[9]

For some families the decade was a constant struggle in which Penruddock's foolery was a minor distraction. In County Durham the Forcer families of Harbourhouse in Durham spent the 1650s trying to accomodate themselves to the new regime. Jane Forcer was a Roman Catholic widow classed as a delinquent living on a fifth of her husband's estate for the early years of the Republic. The family estates in the nearby villages of Kelloe and Northwash had been confiscated by the Treason Trustees and subsequently bought by John Rushworth and Gilbert Crouch. In 1652 Jane's Harbourhouse property was finally discharged from further levies.[10] John Forcer also of Harbourhouse spent the 1650s keeping quiet. He had fought for Charles I in the Civil Wars. His estate had been sequestrated as a result. The 1659 act of banishment worried him and he sought a testimonial from the leading figures of Durham. They all signed a document confirming that John had 'well demeaned himself in quiet and peacfull manor' and that he had done nothing 'injurous to Commonwealth or state'.[11] Within 5 miles of the former Forcer estate at Kelloe the Salvins were also trying to remain at peace with the new regime. They ensured that they obtained a copy of the 1653 Act of Parliament for Compounding with Delinquents, probably because they had been caught out before a couple of years earlier by Commonwealth legislation which had threatened to overturn their previous composition arrangements. In early 1654 Gerrard must have complained to Oliver Cromwell that he was now infirm. Cromwell wrote to the county high sheriff reminding him that he was not to impress for jury services anyone over 70 or who was continually infirm. The sheriff had named Salvin for assize jury service and when he had refuse had distrained property as a punishment. Cromwell ordered the sheriff to pay back all the confiscated money without delay.[12]

Whilst the Salvins may have at least outwardly accepted the Republican state, others were not prepared to allow their grievances to lie hidden. John and Deborah Machon were determined to renegociate their position within the new state. They had tried to get the back allowance due to Deborah from the Sherburn Hospital which amounted to one fifth of the hospital income since 1645 when it had been taken out of their charge. Ten years later it seems that the payments were behind hand if paid at all. A lengthy inquiry had established by 1650 that Deborah Machon was entitled to the money. John Machon also launched a renewed campaign for reinstatement as master of Sherburn Hospital.[13] Fenwicke, his replacement, was obliged to level charges at Machon, which related to events before the war as well as the specific war related charges, most of which related to the goods of the hospital which would have paid for the repairs that Fenwicke had had to fund during the previous ten years. Machon was accused of being master at two hospitals, Sherburn and Lichfield, a contravention of Elizabethan legislation. The war charges were more damaging.

Machon was accused of supplying money to the Earl of Newcastle, working on Royalist committees acting against parliamentarians selling timber and giving plate to the Royalist cause, as well as his desertion of the hospital in 1644. The charges were very specific, naming the plate, the other belongings of the hospital Machon had given to the Royalists and the names of the men in whose company Machon fled. Machon was stung. He compiled a reply in verbose, smugly composed (and quite boring) legal pedantry. He was allowed to hold two posts because the remuneration was so small. In any case the statute Fenwicke had referred to stated that the master should be a minister, which Fenwicke as a Newcastle tradesman clearly was not. Machon declared that he only gave money, timber, plate and other income to the Earl of Newcastle as had everyone else, because he was threatened with imprisonment if he did not; he had never been a committeeman; he had not verbally attacked parliamentarians, the evidence for this he asserted was purely hearsay. On the charge that he drove the hospital's cattle from their grazing in spring 1644, Machon claimed he did so only to keep it out of the hands of both the Army of the Solemn League and Covenant and the Northern Army during the days they faced each other near Durham, just before the Battle of Selby. His flight from Durham was purely on health grounds, he did so alone and he went to Richmond only until he was well.[14] Machon counter-claimed that when he took over the mastership in 1635 the hospital lands had been alienated and the income thus lost, therefore he had had to pay for repairs himself. In order to secure compensation for his loss he was prepared to acknowledge that Fenwicke was the master, but only from the date of the letters patent which had only been issued in 1650. By 1657 the Machons had forced a compromise. Fenwicke would pay £60 per annum to the Machons from the hospital income, if they left him to hold the office.[15] It seemed as if all could now rest and the course of the hospital run quietly.

For some people the Republic was a period not of development, but of Restoration. By 1655 Anne Clifford was rebuilding the church at Skipton. The steeple had been demolished during the first Civil War as the leaguer had closed in on the garrison. In October she moved into the inhabitable part of Skipton castle and began 'to make the rubbidge to be carried out of the old Castle at Skipton, which had layn in it since it was throwne downe and demolished in December 1648 and the January following'. This was dangerous, especially as her grandson Lord Tufton had been arrested on suspicion of being involved in the Royalist rising that year, and she was warned that Cromwell was likely to be displeased. She replied 'Let him destroy my Castles if he will, as often as he levels them I will rebuild them, so long as he leaves me a shilling in my pocket.'[16] And so she did and the refurbished castle was again used by the state. Lady Anne was also attempting to rebuild the networks of relationships of her Pembroke inheritance. Her letter to Evan Edwards in Flint who had been in the household of the earl her husband provides an example of this restorative work. Anne had heard that Evan was ill, but she consoled him: 'I know you have soe wise and well tempered a minde ... that you re able to beare that and all other worldly inconveniences with patience.' Anne looked forward to seeing Edwards, and of course he would have to go to Skipton to see her. After wishing him happiness, Anne added:

> I desire you to pardon mee for nott writting all this letter to you with my own hand when I would have done butt that I have this day bin troubled with a fitt of the Winde.[17]

The Republic could impinge on all aspects of life. Marriages could now be conducted through a JP rather than through the Church. In August 1653 Dorothy Osborne thought that involving JPs could prevent marriage: 'tis a new form for it that sure will fright the country people extremely for they apprehend nothing like going before a Justice; they say no other marriage will stand good in law'. She declared that it would stop her marrying, 'In conscience I believe the old one is the better for my part I am resolved to stay till that comes in fashion again.' She did not really let it stop her marrying the love of her life: she married William Temple in December 1654.[18] Not did it really frighten others. Henry Stowe and Jane Dodgson of St Bees in Cumberland were married in such a way on 10 November 1657. William Thompson of Thorneflatt was the officiating JP and the couple made their way to him there. Three witnesses went with them and signed the certificate.[19]

For other people the Republic was not so benign, and their dealings with JPs or judges were not part of an ordinary way of life. Isaac Atkinson of Wichling in Kent gave vent to his dislike of the Protector in the wake of the Penruddock rising:

The lord Protector is a rogue, a robber and a thief. Within a year and a half he will have a bullet in his arse, or else (here he held one of his ears for dramatic effect) I will give the ears from my head.

He was committed to the assizes by the Grand Jury at Maidstone on 17 March 1656.[20] Thomas Bennett of All Hallowes was similarly unimpressed with the regime. He believed that Cromwell was a fool. He was accused of calling his dog Cromwell and 'my Lord Protector' and implying that Cromwell was as powerless to deal with him as was the dog. The protector had established a regime of 'rogues, knaves and thieves … and that the justices of the peace are fools'. Bennett claimed somewhat less understandably that Cromwell had been over-thrown by a 'simple cuckoo' at Maidstone Assizes.[21]

In Stanstead, Essex, John Milton a blacksmith was similarly unimpressed. When he saw a group of wealthy travellers during late 1655, he was said to have remarked 'These are Parliament rogues, and I am fain to work hard by the sweat of my brows to maintain such Parliament rogues as these are.' He turned to Richard Hubbert and accused him of being one of Cromwell's bastards and said that the regime would not last long. At Wimbish in the same county about five months later Christopher Emberson, a labourer, accused Cromwell of murdering the king. He too believed that the regime would fall 'and I shall see it speedily'.[22]

Isaac Archer of Colchester in 1655 was now fourteen years old and was going through a spiritual change. Archer classed himself as a petty thief and a loner. He began to refer at this point in his biographical sketch to his stutter which kept him away from other boys. He began to 'have some serious thoughts Godwise'. He also began to think in terms of going to college and on to a career in the Church. William Archer objected to his son's ambition, perhaps because he was worried about his stutter. Isaac also suggested that his father was concerned that 'not knowing how long these times of libertye might last'. The religious world of the Republic was complex with the Presbyterian Churches established in the mid-1640s embattled by a range of independent congregations and Anglican survivalists. The worrying question as far as William Archer may have been concerned was not whether or not his son should go into the Church, but in which Church would he be safest from the vicissitudes of the political world. So instead, with commercial accumen, William apprenticed Isaac to a linen draper. It was a short-lived career, as Isaac was not big enough nor strong enough to do the job, and anyway the draper's business collapsed. Isaac got his wish after the failure of the drapery business, and entered Trinity College, Cambridge on 29 October 1656. His thoughts on God were not all-consuming, and Isaac caught 'the pox of a girl in Petty Cury'. Being cured of this re-focused his mind and 'Now Oh my God how good wert thou to me when I knew not the danger to my self.' This warning was heeded and Isaac seems to have spent the next three years as a diligent scholar.[23]

The wars which carried on into the 1650s continued to wreck the lives of people in Essex. Some of them tried to seek at least some form of financial recompence: Elizabeth Ward was given 20s in hand and then 20s a year in quarterly payments to replace her husband's income. He had been killed in Ireland in the campaigns launched in 1649. Yet some people were claiming for long past wars, Thomas Butcher was wounded when he served in the Eastern Association Army, yet it was January 1655 before he was given a pension. Susan Collenson's husband had served with the Earl of Essex, but he seems to have been killed or gone missing, because, as she put it to the same sessions, he had 'never since retorned unto her'.[24]

In July 1655 the Essex courts also made a declaration regarding a current concern, the Quakers who had been moving about the county. All constables in the villages were ordered to arrest any wandering persons to stop them from spreading their 'damnable opinions' and from seducing people from their proper allegiances. They were also to arrest anyone who disrupted services in churches.[25] Concerns in Warwickshire had an older ring to them. There was a disturbing tendency for 'idle and vain people' to erect maypoles and may bushes. The 1655 Easter sessions prohibited not only the erection of poles but also morris dances and other 'heathenish practices' at Henley in Arden. A year later the national orders for the suppression of undesirables, sturdy beggars, rogues and vagabonds, took up a considerable amount of time in the county. Not only were county officials ordered to deal with such people, but the JPs listed the types of people to be stopped, scholars, seafarers without licences, palmists, physiognomy and 'other crafty sciences', jugglers, tinkers, pedlars and petty chapmen were to be prevented from wandering and begging. In the same county the wreckage of war-blighted lives also had to be dealt with, such as when at the January 1655 Quarter Sessions Ann Toms claimed a pension, for her and her three children after the recent death of her husband, a soldier at Warwick garrison.[26]

In London, the Protectorate regime was unpopular with some. There was a market for the kind of verses which magistrates suspected William Seywell of writing. His verses were 'scandelous and trayterous' attacks on Cromwell. John Tyne was also accused of similar sentiments; he was brought before the court for scandalous words against the commonwealth and the protector in early 1656. Fulham victualler Robert Plumstead turned violently on William Newman. Newman, and the army, Plumstead said, were murderers who had murdered the king 'theire hands were soe dipt in blood they could not wash it off'. The charges against George Sanderson were probably not really related to his politics. He was accused of living incontinently with Margaret, that he had converted someone to popery, and that he had an evil life and conversation. That he was 'an enemie of this Common Wealth' seemed an unnecessary addition. There were the usual concerns that the authority of the state could be impugned by attacks on minor officials, a worry of pre-revolutionary estates. When Christopher Stankes laughed at watchman William Weller and asked 'who made you one of my lord protectors' fools?' it was not just blacksmith Weller's pretentions he mocked, but the protector's. When Edward Matthews of Middle Temple took the protector's name in vain, it was not an attack on the state, but an attempt to cozen money out of George Tomson of Chancery Lane, by forging an order from Cromwell demanding money.[27]

In Denbighshire the institution of the Protectorate caused local military figures, enemies of Sir John Trevor and his correspondent John Peck, to battle firmly for place. In the summer's hiatus, Peck told Trevor: 'Captain Ball and the Wrixham party are knocking their heads together to put out most of the old justices of the commission of the peace where I am one and to put in new ones.'

At the creation of the Protectorate the army men were even more active:

> heare is a great change in Wrixham since my Lord General wais maid protector for they are all like men metamorphyss. Captaine ellis was on Thursday last to a met us at Wrixham but was pvented by reason of his ague. I heare he intends to put in for Flintshier as their representative and thinkes his being Custos Rotulorum will be a means to further his purpose ... [28]

For most people in the county and the neighbouring areas there were more pressing concerns. In April 1654 plague struck Chester and caused the abandonment of the assizes there. By September cattle yields were 'so poor', rye and wheat prices had also been affected by low yields across Denbighshire, and Trevor's tenants claimed poverty when it came to Michaelmas rent collection.[29]

The Restoration in England and Wales, 1658–62

In Scotland Alexander Jaffray had seen the death of Cromwell as potentially dangerous. In England and Wales the succession of Richard Cromwell was apparently welcomed. Boroughs threw civic parties to accompany the proclamations of Richard and these proved popular events.[30] However, by 1660 after the upheavals following Richard's succession and then his displacement in May 1659, there was a willingness on some people's part to contemplate the return of the monarchy. When Charles Stuart signalled his willingness to return many welcomed the Restoration. But there were people who felt betrayed, who most probably did not think that God had turned on them as Major General Harrison did and instead ascribed the problem to human failings.

The end of the Republic was foreseen by the Venetian secretary, who wrote on 13 June 1659 that the grandees and the middling sort could not 'submit and never will be ruled by base and vile folk as they are now, so it is to be feared that they will be constantly involved in dissensions and confusion'. This he put down to the country being used to a monarchy and therefore it could never settle down. Within six months, the country seemed to be moving towards a Restoration of the monarchy heralded by a demand for a free Parliament. The Venetian secretary commented at the end of January that London and Exeter, once grouped together by Henrietta Maria as centres of rebellion, were demanding a new assembly. Exeter's recorder had written to the Speaker of the

Commons to procure hearing for their petition 'for the maintenance of the rights and the privelidges of the nation so that the people may not be forced to take other steps'.[31]

At Scarborough the confusion of the summer months of 1659 could have been alarming. The militia was to be prepared, and new lists of eligible persons compiled. Luke Robinson appeared too busy to reply to their letters, claiming that the Royalist rising led by Presbyterian George Booth in Cheshire had given him too much work in Parliament. Former Royalist gentlemen, Tritram Fish, John Hixon, Richard Bilborough and Francis Sollit, were arrested on 8 September in case they had any involvement in Booth's rising and then released on bond. The attempts to find some firm basis for national finances did make their way to Scarborough. At 8 o'clock in the evening of 29 September Parliament's request for information about brewers of beers, ciders and perrys who would be liable to pay excise taxes arrived in the town. Even in the Republic's last days, Scarborough was reminded of the £21 14s it had to contribute towards the three months' levy of monthly pay for the British Isles of £100,000. The Restoration made no immediate difference to this aspect of Scarborough life; the assessment instructions sent to the town in late September 1660 were exactly the same as the last Republican levy even though now it was part of only £70,000 across England.[32]

In the late 1650s Upton was as much at peace with itself as it would have been before the 1640s. Its self-regulating community functions, like its legal and administrative obligations to the wider state, were operating smoothly. If there was discontent, it was certainly quiescent. Some historians regard the Restoration as being something in which the common people had an important part. It is undeniable that the apprentices of London and their counterparts in other towns, howled down the remnants of the Republic in late 1659 and 1660. Just as fervently in May 1660 they cheered and celebrated Charles II, the bringer of stability and peace. However, as Professor Ronald Hutton has pointed out recently, this howling and cheering only occurred once the Republic itself had tottered and divided. Professor Hutton argues that much of the blame for the fall of the Republic can be laid at the feet of Cromwell's attempts to structure a broad-bottomed government consensus, by employing men of different political outlooks.[33] In the end this led to a polity whose only glue was the loyalty or friendship of the individuals who comprised it to Cromwell. With Cromwell dead, the glue holding the Republic together dissolved, and chaos again ensued. The howling crowds may have raged at instability and uncertainty; by the end of 1659 chaos and the Republic were apparently one.

For John Machon in County Durham it truly was a Restoration. The sixteen-year battle against the two John Fenwickes at the Sherburn hospital appeared to be finally over. His petition to Charles II on 3 March 1661 was met with success. Two days later the Bishop of Durham announced that Machon was to be rein-stated and John Fenwicke's mastership, judged illegal on the grounds not only that he was an adherent of Parliament and then of the protectorate, but that as a tradesman, not an ordained minister, he was ineligible for the position. The awkward questions about Machon's own past, and about his agreement to the deal worked out in 1657 were sidestepped, and Fenwicke's charges about Machon's illegal use of hospital property were forgotten; well almost. Machon was not one to let a fallen man go unkicked. He immediately launched a suit against Fenwicke for damages to the hospital property during the sixteen year intermission, and for not adhering to the agreement of 1657.[34] If the Civil War had been a period which allowed personal scores to be settled then so was the Restoration. In many ways this marked only a continuation. Machon had been a litigious master before the war, when he had sued for unpaid tithes, and his dismissal in 1645 had given him an alternative career as litigant, so why should we expect the Restoration to stop him?

The Restoration brought hope to many others and Sir Edward Hyde wrote of the welcome the king received in the capital: 'all the ways from Dover thither being so full of people and exclamations as if the whole kingdom had been gathered. ... In a word, the joy was so inexpressible and so universal.' In one month, thought Hyde, all the miseries of twenty years of war and rebellion were swept away.[35] Hyde was soon to be raised to the peerage for his loyalty to the monarchy. One of his erstwhile opponents, Bulstrode Whitlocke, noted the mixture of reactions. One of Charles I's judges was arrested and the others had their goods sequestrated. Bonfires were lit and bells rung when the king's intentions were known in the city and 'Divers maids of the city petitioned the lord mayor for leave to meet king in white clothes' on 25 May. There was a darker side, on 7 May Parliament passed legislation to prevent tumults and on the 10th 'someone was committed for speaking treasonable words against the king'.[36]

The Venetian secretary wrote on the eve of the king's return that he had seen bonfires and toasts to the king's health had been drunk in the streets.[37] Sir John Barrington bubbled over with joy. He and his family took up lodgings at Mr Snowe's in Cheapside just to see the king's entry into the city. Once there he bought sack to celebrate and even contributed 3s to buy faggots for one of the street fires. Although the family returned to their Essex home a day later, Sir John was back in London promenading in Hyde Park eating cherries, currants and strawberries with his children.[38]

Many miles to the north, in Westmorland, Lady Anne Clifford, Countess of Dorset and Countess of Pembroke, in 1659 saw her rebuilt castle at Skipton and her other houses, Brougham Tower and Appleby Castle filled again with soldiers during the summer. Yet Anne recorded her pleasure at the state of the castle, 'in part well finished and better than I expcted it could have bin'. In the following Spring Anne recorded the 'happie Parliament' which brought back the king. As her son-in-law the Earl of Northampton had been imprisoned in the wake of Booth's rebellion it must have been with some relief that she referred to the settlement and to Monck's armie as the 'Happy Instrument' which had engineered the Restoration. She too also mentioned the king's triumphant entry into London.[39] Ann, Lady Fanshawe's account referred to the crowds which greeting the king. 'So great were the acclamations and numbers of people that it reached like one street from Dover to Whitehall.' When Charles arrived in London her enthusiasm bubbled over: 'the hearts of all men in this kingdom moved at his will'. But the year which followed was one marked by 'the great hurry of the business I was then in, and perpetual company that resorted to us, of all qualities, some for kindness, and some for their own advantage'. Ann's Restoration was tinged with sadness, for as a result of the 'great hurry' Ann miscarried three sons born during two hours of labour.[40]

The Venetian secretary, Francesco Giavarna, wrote that there were popular retributions taken out against the conveniently dead. Within a month of Charles entering London he saw an effigy of Cromwell hung out of a Whitehall window with a rope around its neck and 'spared no act of contempt and ignominy'. Oliver Cromwell's name, he commented 'and memory are increasingly cursed by the people'. In October he referred to the assembling of the three distinct Parliaments, 'so things are returning to their pristine state'.[41] Giavarna believed that the Anabaptists were declining in influence and noted that attempts were being made to capture their hero John Lambert. The Anabaptists were 'numerous and mortal enemies of the monarchy'.[42]

Richard Baxter went to London in April 1660 to participate in the Restoration. The Earl of Lauderdale and Baxter discussed establishing the king's credentials as a Protestant, and disturbing reports had been coming in from France. Baxter also was called upon to preach to Parliament on its day of fasting on the eve of the invitation to the king to return to his throne. He also preached at St Paul's on the city's day of thanksgiving. Baxter too noted the excitement at the king's return. The 'expectations of men' he wrote, 'were various'. There were, he noted too, expectations that the Presbyterians who had assisted in bringing in the king would receive 'a reward'. Baxter received one, he was appointed chaplain in ordinary to the king.[43] George Fox also had high hopes, for the king set at liberty many Quakers imprisoned during the later years of the Protectorate. He saw this as part of the Divine justice executed on Oliver Cromwell. Fox believed that after Dunbar Cromwell had declared that if he did not remove tithes 'let him be rolled into his grave with infamy'. That tithes remained in place was the cause, Fox felt, of Cromwell's being disinterred and hung lifeless from the Tyburn gallows and 'rolled into his grave with infamy'.[44] This was to be short-lived optimism.

For many people the Restoration must have been unwanted. The existence of such people worried the government and this caused ripples which lapped against those not personally involved in any action against the state. In January a group of those people for whom acquiescence to a state so clearly opposed to God's divine will was not an option, openly tried to create the kingdom of God on earth. Led by Thomas Venner, a fifth monarchist, a small group of men sized St Paul's before fleeing the city. For George Fox, Venner's rising was an unmitigated disaster. Fox was in the city when the rising broke out and was woken by the cries of 'Arm! Arm!' The consequences were quick to make themselves felt at

Whitehall the next day: 'They looked strangely at me there.' Within a week Quakers in London were arrested at their meeting houses and Fox himself was arrested by troopers, only to be rescued by Richard Marsh, a gentleman of the king's bedchamber. The next morning he was again at Whitehall, this time under escort.

Like Penruddock's rising in 1655, Venner's fight in London had far-reaching consequences. In the north of England the wake of Venner's rising caught up Fox's followers. George Middleton and William Spencer wrote to Sir Phillip Musgrave, the governor of Carlisle and inveterate Royalist. In their letter of 13 January, six days after the rising, they referred to 'that unsatisfied enemy' who had called upon all of those who would 'fight king Jesus his Battle'. More specifically the two men were concerned that there were only too many in Cumberland who were prepared to fight for King Jesus. Amongst the Quakers, Anabaptists and Fifth Monarchy men were those 'privie to yt wicked disigne and insurection' and they had sent out several orders 'for apprehending and securing all such persons as are aformencioned'.[45] They set about it with gusto, perhaps building on the relative intolerance which had been displayed in the far north-west towards Quakers.[46] Within ten days, they had sent to Musgrave at Carlisle Castle a collection of the unsatisfied. Musgrave believed that the two men and their associates had acted correctly, but he began to suspect that they may have been over-zealous and couched some cautious suggestions in terms of expense. Instead of keeping the Trained Band horse out at all times, he suggested putting the burden onto the communities. He further advised that they follow the example of others: do 'what I heare is done in all other pts of England, namly that command be given for strong night watches to be kept in every town and these be required to examine all that shall travel or rid in the night and to give an account of them as you shal direct'.[47] Musgrave was in line with central government which had realised that Venner was acting with only a very small clique, and which by 25 January had begun to order the release of many of the prisoners.[48] Fox, Margaret Fell and Thomas Moore worked on the king, and presented him with lists of Quaker prisoners throughout the country. It had been an expensive business for the state and the counties as well as for their agents. In October 1661, the Essex Quarter Sessions met with a petition from a constable of Burneham for 36s in expenses he had incurred carrying the Quakers to prison at Colchester.[49]

At Bedford the victory of the freemen obtained after the Civil War was ended before the Restoration of the monarchy was more than three months old. There were new instructions issued for the election of the mayor and council (the thirteen) on 29 August 1660. Just over a year later it was made explicit. The acts which had reformed the council in favour of the freemen were all repealed. Once again they were not automatically called burgess and lost burgess rights. The act declared that the democratisation of the 1650s or more specifically the 'infringements of custom' were rectified.[50] As a result Bedford corporation pushed its relentless way towards the domination by an oligarchy which marked the development of urban government in England during the latter half of the seventeenth century.

Across the country too other features of the pre-revolutionary days reappeared. The Venetian secretary wrote that legislation had been passed to prevent people holding markets in church yards and cemeteries.[51] The people were distanced from their courts as Latin returned to the papers of the Quarter Sessions and the borough courts. At York the last complete entry in English, dated 4 May 1660, dealt with the large-scale riot at the mayor's house at the end of March 1660. About a hundred people had burst into Republican Mayor Christopher Topham's house near Ouse Bridge.[52] Just one week after the court sat and heard evidence from 15 people, the same mayor proclaimed Charles II.[53] When the court next sat in August the proceedings were chiefly in Latin. The business in the courts reflected the changing circumstances. Around the country peace was being made with the Stuarts. Oxford's councillors from a city with perhaps less to be ashamed of than many, sent its 'abhorrence of the murther committed upon the late King and expressing theire Duty and Loyalty to his Majestie that now is'. That same day, 14 May, the council continued its work, sending

> a humble gratulacon and petition to the Kings most excellent Majestie expressing theire greate joy in his Majesties being brought by the greate and righteous God to the lineall and lawefull inheritance of his Crownes and Kingdomes, their utter abhorrence of that barbarous and inhumane parracide comitted upon Our late Soveraigne Lord, of the tender of theire Duty and allegiance to His Majestie[54]

So full of this good effort was the council that it even offered a vote of thanks to the recorder for 'his trouble in drawing up the petition'. Not everyone was prepared to let the Restoration pass by unremarked. Matthew Barnard came to the attention of the York court in early 1661. He had said

> That five and twenty of the Parliament House was sent to the Tower and that the king went with a list of their names and that the Duke of York puld the speaker out of the chaire, and that the King would have drawne his sword but was hindered by his nobles.

A scandalous tale of little importance were it not to coincide with Venner's rising and coming as it did on the nineteenth anniversary of Charles I's attempt to seize the five members. For his tale Barnard was committed before being later released on surety for good behaviour.[55] Barnard was not alone in his distaste for the new regime. At the July sessions Ralph Constable was accused of spreading similar rumours, although he may have been innocent as his accusers were reluctant to appear before the court. In October Richard Smith was accused of turning on George Monck, now elevated for his role in bringing about the

Restoration. Smith was accused of uttering 'scandelous and reproachful words against George, Duke of Albemarle, and one of his Majesty's Privy Council'.[56] In Leicester the very day of the king's entry into London was the occasion of a court case over the Restoration. A day earlier William Dawes, son of the town's sergeant at mace, Hugh Dawes, had referred to the new coat of arms being painted in St Martin's church. When his mother Jane was told that it would do her good to see the new work, William within hearing of the conversation retorted 'it would do the Devill good to see them'. That same day between eleven o'clock and noon William had seen another royal coat of arms. This time it was a drawing on a piece of paper fastened to Christopher Norrice's door. William, incensed at this display of triumphalism, picked up a stone or clod of earth, Norrice was not sure which, and threw it at the offending image.[57] In Kent, shoemaker Simon Oldfield of Canterbury begged to differ from the opinion such as that offered by Oxford Council. Contrary to the notion that Charles I had been cruelly or inhumanely murdered, Oldfield said in public hearing on 10 December:

> king Charles the first had a faire and legall tryall and those persons that were lately executed for the same were executed and suffered wrong-fully. And the king is noe more head of the Church then I am. And I was allwayes against Kingly Government.[58]

He was not alone in his frustration. Later that same month a sailor, John Watson, originally of Stepney, but now in Milton, declared, 'The king prays and goes to Mass twice a day and a blood sucking crew there is of them.' Watson's attack on the king and the nobility earned him two successive days in the pillory for two hours at a stretch with a notice declaring his fault pinned over him and detention at the king's pleasure thereafter. Edward King, another shoemaker, of Westerham was in agreement. He was said to have declared that 'If I could have my opportunity, I would be the death of the king.' However, although the Grand Jury agreed that there was enough evidence to pursue the accusation, Edward King who could have been guilty of encompassing the death of the king was only found guilty of uttering the more cryptic phrase:

> There are thirty thousand men of our judgement at an hour's warning, and within quarter of a year here will be the biggest fight that ever was known in England … Divide the land in four parts, and the third part will be for us; and there will be thirty thousand in arms if need shall be.

Whilst this may well have presented the somewhat frightening notion that there was a great underhand conspiracy afoot, something similar to the fears which had gripped the new governors a year earlier, King was not taken too seri-ously. He was fined £10 and held in prison until he paid up. Others, if not making rash public statements, refused to acknowledge the new regime. Roger

Ellis, Ralph Young, Thomas Ewer, Thomas Arkinsoll and Edward Moorecocke refused in early 1661 to take the oath of allegiance to the king. All were described as Sectaries or Anabaptists.[59] These men were all soon to be joined in their resistance to the oaths of the new regime by those who wanted to preserve the religious rights they had fought for over the previous twenty years. The Kent Assizes were soon dealing with those who began to disobey the legislation re-establishing the Church of England. At the Maidstone sessions at the end of July 1661 two ministers, Nicholas Thoroughgood of Monkton and Ephraim Bothell of Hawkshurst were presented for not using the Book of Common Prayer. Bothell was also indicted of 'uttering perverse opinions in contempt of the Book of Common Prayer' on several occasions. Bothell was presented again the following March for several instances of not using the book. This time he was in the company of Matthew Dary of Plaxtol.[60] Conventicles of dissenting sects were found to exist at Deptford, Teyham, Wrotham, Rolvenden, Brasted, Sevenoaks and Sundridge within the next few months. This form of disobedience affected all types of people, sailors, yeomen, shoemakers, blacksmiths, potters, carpenters, tailors millers, glaziers, ships' carpenters, ropemakers from Deptford, labourers at Teynham, knights, gentlemen, clerks, labourers and bricklayers at Wrotham and mercers, yeomen, clothe workers, broadweavers and carpenters at Biddenham.[61]

The Middlesex courts too soon had to deal with those for whom this was no 'happy restoration'. Robert Lockyer uttered words against 'the King's majesty' in early 1661. Edward Medburne, a glazier from Wapping, said

> if he met the king hee would run his knife into him to kill him, and that hee did not care that he were hanged for it himselfe, and did wish that the King and Generall Monk were hanged together, and that he would spend that day five shillings for joy.

Dorothy Phillips of St Sepulchres and John Tyler, a joiner of St Martin in the Fields, both said that Charles II was a 'bastard'. Abraham Johnson uttered 'treacherous words'. Husband and wife, Edward and Alice Jones had declared 'It was the King's time now to raine, but it was upon suffrance for a little time, and it would be theres agine before itt be long.' Richard Cheltham said that he 'hoped to meet the Kinge at the gallows'. Lambert was not forgotten in these dark days; William Cox had declared 'my Lord Lambert deserved the Crowne and to be King better than King Charles II'. Alice Hatton and John Nickson both maligned the king and his dead father. Margaret Osmond believed like Simon Oldfield of Canterbury that Charles I had had a legal trial and she hoped that his son would be gone within a year. The Headborough of Stepney, John Drew, thought the new king 'poore and beggarly'. William Fenne wanted to run his rusty sword into the king's heart. A private meeting held in September 1661 at Wapping heard Wentworth Day and Matthew Chaffee speak 'treasonable and seditious words'.[62] The government also through these courts began to round up the disaffected like John Hobert and John Tossier. It also began to hear of things undertaken before the Restoration and to hold them against the speakers. Thomas Willis, vicar of Twickenham, was thrown out for preaching against the prince and the rebels in Booth's rising. He also said on the eve of the Restoration 'Wee thanke God for delivering us from that bloody family.' He meant the Stuarts, but God spat in his face just as surely as he spat at Major General Harrison. That bloody family, defined by Jaine Blunstone of Whitechapel as 'the Great Whore of Babilon, the son of a whore and … a rogue' had returned. By the beginning of 1662, the numbers of angry and frustrated people being hauled before the JPs declined, but instead the frequenters of illegal conventicles began to appear. As in Kent they were a mixed group: tailors, chandlers, tobacco-pipe makers, gardeners and glovemakers. At one meeting on 24 February 1662 the arrested group included widows Mary Smith, Elleanor Simcock, Mary Light, Hannah Lash, Susan Carnall, Anne Graves, spinster Katherine Drake and ten unaccompanied married women.[63]

At York too, as elsewhere, it was time to deprive the parliamentarian injured veteran soldiers of their allowances. This also applied to the widows and orphans of these soldiers. On 22 March 1661, Mrs Isabel Anlaby and her children were deprived of their money pension of 2s 6d a week first granted in March 1652. This was the same day that George Heslewood 'a soldier lamed in the service of Charles I' was granted 6s 8d immediately and 26s 8d a year thereafter from 'the lame soldier's money'. Of course it was a good time to practise deceit and the council was aware that the unscrupulous may well pass themselves off as loyal veterans of Charles I too. So on 13 January 1662, John Robinson was granted only an interim payment of 10s because 'the Court not being satisfied where he first took up arms'.[64]

In Warwickshire the maimed soldier treasurers were reconstituted at the second – the Michaelmass – sessions of the Restoration. They were ordered, however, to pay 'such soldiers (as he useth to pay) their pensions as aforesaid and to forebear to pay any more until they have urther order from this court'.[65] Fewer Warwickshire people were brought to court for attacking the king and the Restoration. Exceptions included Humphrey Beeland, John Tombes and Richard Woodward who were caught distributing seditious and scandalous books attacking the monarchy.[66]

The Essex sessions were dealing with the same issues. Former Royalist soldiers were now putting in petitions to the sessions for payment. There were also more complex cases like that of John Merriman who had served with Monck, and now could be regarded as loyal to the restored monarchy. There was also the case of Edward Hart of Felsted who had been ruined financially during the siege of Colchester. He was awarded £5 out of the maimed soldier money.[67] In April 1651 the JPs cleared up the problem of the parliamentarian maimed soldiers. They paid off 32 of them, 16 received 30s and 16 received 20s in 'full Compensacon of all pencons for the future'. A world had turned upside down.

Isaac Archer, the new diligent student at Trinity, Cambridge, had graduated towards the end of the Protectorate's life. His father had given up his work as a lecturer in Colchester shortly after the death of his second wife. Isaac won a scholarship in 1659, and this became interpreted as another mark of God's interest in Isaac. However, he also became more and more obsessed with seeking proof of election but this became entwined with a fear of death, and embroiled with an obsessive need to avoid sin. As the Restoration became reality, Isaac became recognised as a 'factious spirit' at college, although he claimed that his attacks on the principles of monarchy were undertaken to heighten his powers of disputation. Nevertheless, whilst content with the secular Restoration, Isaac was not happy with his prospects if the 'bishops did get the upperhand'. In 1660 Isaac began to attend conventicles and was one of those discomforted by Venner's Rising, which closed down the legal outlets for nonconformity. Isaac refused the Three Articles, but his circumspect opposition enabled him to get a living in the Isle of Ely where he used the Book of Common Prayer as prescribed. This resulted in arguments with his father who felt that his son had conformed to the Church. Isaac drifted further from the tenets of the Church throughout the 1660s as he moved from Ely to Amington and to Chippenham in Cambridge. He was invited to preach at Wichen by Henry Cromwell, but discussions with his father resulted in Isaac resigning his living and giving up his post at Wichen, and thereafter his dislike of the prayerbook increased. In 1672 after the Declaration of Indulgence, Archer, whilst remaining in the Church of England, licensed his home for Presbyterian worship. His would appear to be the story of a man born and educated in the revolutionary period in the freedom of those years. A man forced to conform to a society which was to him, as to many others, not a Restoration, but an imposition.[68]

AFTERWORD

We return to a man with whom in many ways we began. Perhaps surprisingly, Archibald Johnston's later diary was similar to that of Lady Anne Clifford. For much of her diary this woman, for whom a personal Restoration began before the second Civil War had been fought, looked back over the years. She enumerated the dates on which she had stayed in whatever house she was currently resident in, or recalled the events of past years on dates when she compiled her diary.

As his 'brave new world' finally crumbled Johnston did something similar. On 13 August 1659, as the Republic began unravelling, Johnston discussed with his wife the changes they had experienced since 1637. His mind returned to the themes of recent history: the Bishop's Wars; the Solemn League and Covenant; the Committee of Both Kingdoms on which he had served; and his post as clerk of the registers in Scotland which held until the English threw him out of office in 1650. He reflected on his enforced retirement from then until 1657 when summoned, by Cromwell, to serve in Parliament at Westminster. When he looked back, his mind played on the many changes of circumstances which he and his country had undergone as a result of the wars begun in '1639' and continued through

> '40, '44, '45, '46, '48, '49, '50, and aye since under the Inglishes, so that heyther the publyk nor my particular hes continewed in an certain condition for 3 yeirs togither except thir last 7 yeirs in captivetye … It troubles me to forthink of the dangers and ruynes I forsee. … [1]

Whether or not he foresaw the Restoration of the monarchy, he was ruined by what followed.

Clifford was trying to establish a coherent narrative for her life to explore the reasons for her existence, by searching for the patterns within. Her personal war against the injustice done to her by her father needs explanation. For Johnston, he was searching for the meaning of God's will. That caused him to look at the national picture and to reflect upon his role within it, but he was nonetheless faced by a present which he could not fathom without constantly reconstructing his and Scotland's past. Clifford and Johnston were not alone in creating their personal and national chronologies. As people across the four nations began to atone for their actions, tried to reclaim lost money, or as they bemoaned the turn of events, chronologies in constables' and churchwardens' and overseers' accounts, and in diaries and memorials, were constructed, reconstructed, regretted and perhaps revised. Some, like John Clopton or Walter Powell, had edited their lives' record as they recorded it. Missing out direct connections to events they considered too dangerous to identify strongly with. Or like Dorothy Osborne, self-censoring the political or social comments in her letters to William Temple through literary slaps on the wrist or through humour. Other people had their experiences edited for them. The countless numbers submitting claims for recompense to the Westminster Exchequer, to the Estates' Committee for Accounts and Monies all had their statements formalised, assessed and re-assessed. Even so, clues to experience turn up in them. Were these simple tallies then their use would be very limited, especially because of the problems associated with the rounded up and convenient recorded total sums. But instead they contain details and snippets of narratives which taken together allow for exploration of the wider aspects of the Civil Wars and revolutions.

Many others did not remove central events through self-censorship, nor were they censored out by others. The wars, rebellions, revolutions and their fears were recorded in diaries like Elizabeth Jekyll's, or used as vehicles for spiritual and personal reassessments like Alexander Jaffray's meditations. Some records put the wars at the forefront. Pleas for pensions by ex-soldiers such as Richard Eastbourne at the outset of the troubles, or war-widows like Elizabeth Ward near their end, or the financial records of communities such as Crathie, or individuals, like Patrick Archer seeking recompence or compensation, do this. The wars and revolutions prompted or caused their writings and naturally provide the core.

It may be argued that this makes these people poor witnesses. Clopton and Powell provide few details at times; Jaffray and Johnston refocus the wars and thus distort the events to fit their spiritual needs, Osborne jokes, and others omit. Yet the absences, the spaces and the gaps in diaries bear witness too. They demonstrate what had to be left out and thus betray reactions, retractions and withdrawals. This helps us to perceive what contemporaries thought would betray them. Reading these omissions, as much as the detail provided elsewhere by others, gives us an understanding of the range of experiences people underwent, physically and mentally. Showing us not only what it was dangerous to live through but also what it was dangerous to record.

There are many more experiences which can be found. This brief work only scratches the surface of the total experience of the wars. Other memorialists such as Lucy Hutchinson, or diarists like Bulstrode Whitelock can be drawn upon, there are many more accounts in the English and Welsh Exchequer papers and vast numbers of 1641 Depositions to be consulted, each containing narratives of physical and mental experiences centred upon war and revolution

and the individual. Yet these personalised narratives do not provide an alternative history, any more than the Aberdeen Doctors' attempt to stop the Covenant
provides a launch-pad for counter-factual history. This is all the same history.
Constraining history into a grand narrative provides nothing more than a convenient package to be used as an introduction. The narratives here are part of
what follows that introduction.

NOTES

1 THE ABERDEEN DOCTORS AND HISTORY

1 A. Johnston of Wariston (1911) *Diary of Sir Archibald Johnston of Wariston 1632–1639*, vol. 1, Edinburgh: Scottish History Society, p. 265.

2 J.G. Fyffe (ed.) (1928) *Scottish Diaries and Memoirs, 1550–1776*, Stirling: Eneas Mackay, p. 122.

3 Ibid., pp. 137–8

4 D.H. Fleming (1925–6) 'Scotland's Supplication and Complaint against the Book of Common Prayer (otherwise Laud's Liturgy) The Book of Canons and the Prelates, 18 October, 1637', *Proceedings of the Society of Antiquaries of Scotland*, vol. 60.

5 Fyffe (ed.), *Scottish Diaries*, p. 138.

6 Johnston, *Diary*, pp. 385, 393, 395.

7 For an excellent discussion of the Aberdeen issues see D. Stevenson (1990) *King's College Aberdeen, 1560–1641: From Protestant Reformation to the Covenanting Revolution*, Aberdeen: Aberdeen University Press. The details of the debate are taken largely from this account.

8 D. Stewart (1984) 'The "Aberdeen Doctors" and the Covenanters', *Records of the Scottish Church History Society* 22, part 1, p. 35.

9 Ibid., p. 37.

10 N. Ferguson (ed.) (1997) *Virtual History: Alternatives and Counterfactuals*, London: Picador, Introduction, *passim*.

11 Ibid., pp. 19, 23.

12 Ibid., J. Adamson, 'England without Cromwell', p. 95.

13 Ibid., pp. 99.

14 K. Jenkins (1991) *Re-Thinking History*, London: Routledge, p. 7.

15 Ibid., pp. 26, 70.

16 R.J. Evans (1997) *In Defence of History*, London: Granta, p. 74.

17 E. Hobsbawm (1997) *On History*, London: Century, p. 271.

18 M. Phillips (1996) *All Must Have Prizes*, London: Little Brown, pp. 171–3.

19 Evans, *In Defence of History*, p. 242.

20 Herodotus (1996) *Histories*, Wordsworth: Ware, pp. 154, 334.

21 Vincent (1995) *An Intelligent Person's Guide to History*, Duckworth, pp. 36–7, for example.

22 Fergusen (ed.), *Virtual History*, p. 64.

23 This is taken from D. Sutton (1982) 'Radical Liberalism, Fabianism and Social History' in R. Johnson, G. McLennan, D. Schwarz and D. Sutton (eds) *Studies in History Writing and Politics*, London: Hutchinson, p. 16; it refers to P. Clarke, *Liberals and Social Democrats*, Cambridge: Cambridge University Press, 1979, pp. 1–4.

24 Ibid., pp. 9–10.

25 Evans, *In Defence of History*, p. 184.
26 J. Stuart (ed.) (1871) *Extracts from the Council Register of the Burgh of Aberdeen, 1625–1642*, Edinburgh: Scottish Burgh Records Society, pp. 133–5, 137.
27 Ibid., pp. 140–1.
28 Ibid., pp. 160.
29 Ibid., pp. 131–3.

2 UNDER OCCUPATION: THE NORTH OF ENGLAND, 1640–8

1 M. Ashcroft (ed.) (1991) *Scarborough Records, 1600–1640*, Northallerton: North Yorkshire Record Office, p. 339.
2 F. Barber (ed.) (1879) 'On the West Riding Sessions Rolls continued', *Yorkshire Archaeological and Topographical Journal* 5, 20, pp. 386–8.
3 E. Gillett and K.A. MacMahon (1980) *A History of Hull*, Oxford: Oxford University Press, p. 167.
4 Barber, *West Riding*, pp. 385–400.
5 G.F. Warner *et al.* (1893) *Miscellany of the Scottish Historical Society (First Volume)*, Edinburgh: Edinburgh University Press, p. 111.
6 C.H. Firth (1906) 'Ballads on the Bishops' Wars 1639–42', *The Scottish Historical Review* 3, 11, April, pp. 260–71.
7 Ashcroft, *Scarborough Records*, pp. 352–3.
8 Ibid., pp. 396, 398.
9 Ibid., pp. 395–6, 397.
10 Ibid., pp. 398, 400.
11 West Yorkshire Archive Service (WYAS), Vyner Ms 5755/C.4/15.
12 Northumberland Record Office (NorthRO) ZSW 7/ 32, 33
13 NorthRO, ZSW 7/29, 31.
14 NorthRO, 1966/1–3.
15 Ashcroft, *Scarborough Records*, pp. 7–8 for Scarborough and Falsgrave.
16 York City Archives, B36, pp. 74f.
17 Ashcroft, *Scarborough Records*, pp. 15–16
18 Ibid., p. 17.
19 Public Record Office (PRO), SP 28/190.
20 Joseph Lister (1860) *The Autobiography of Joseph Lister of Bradford, 1627–1709*, Bradford: Abraham Holroyd, p. 8.
21 See Andrew Hopper (1997) *"The Readiness of the People": The Formation and Emergence of the Army of the Fairfaxes, 1642–46*, York: Borthwick Institute, p. 8 and *passim*.
22 Gillett and MacMahon, *Hull*, pp. 170–1.
23 Lancashire County Record Office (henceforth Lancs RO), DDHo 352.
24 York City Archives, B36, pp. 79f.
25 Ibid., pp. 84f.
26 VCH North Yorkshire, vol. 2, pp. 214–16, 137–8.
27 PRO SP28/189 Notebook of North Riding Payments, pp. 13, 15, 17ff.
28 WYAS, Vyner Ms 5756, C48.15.
29 VCH, *Yorkshire North Riding*, vol. 2, pp. 309–14, 286–2, 383–5.
30 R. Hutton (1996) *Stations of the Sun*, Oxford: Oxford University Press, p. 386.
31 WYAS, TN/PO 2BI.
32 Ibid.
33 Ashcroft, *Scarborough Records*, pp. 17–20.
34 Ibid., pp. 32–3.
35 Ibid., p. 32.
36 Ibid., p. 22.

37 Ibid., p. 23.

38 Ibid., pp. 44, 65, 97.

39 Derbyshire County Record Office, D258M/34/10, pp. 3–5ff.

40 Ibid., p. 52.

41 Ibid., p. 43.

42 Ibid., pp. 44, 46–7.

43 VCH East Riding, vol. 2, pp. 44–69.

44 Bridlington Town Chest: Constables Accounts. I am grateful to the present Lords Feoffees for their generous permission in allowing me access to these papers in 1993.

45 P. Newman (1981) *The Battle of Marston Moor*, Chichester: Anthony Bird, p. 22.

46 Ashcroft, *Scarborough Records*, pp. 58–9.

47 Ibid., p. 63.

48 Ibid. pp. 68–9.

49 Gillett and MacMahon, *Hull*, pp. 166, 173.

50 Yale University, Beinecke Library, Osborn Ms b221, pp. 5f. Thanks are due to Elizabeth Clarke for this reference.

51 Gillett and MacMahon, op. cit., pp. 173, 175.

52 PRO, SP28/189.

53 Fieldhouse, J. (1972) *Bradford*, London: Longman, pp. 60–63; Hanson, T.W. (1968) *The Story of Old Bradford*, East Ardesley: SR Publishing.

54 See J. Priestley (1883) *Some Memoirs touching the Family of the Priestleys written, at the request of a friend by Jonathan Priestley*, Surtees Society, vol. 77; and Hopper, op. cit., p. 8.

55 Lister, op. cit., p. 15.

56 Hanson, 1916, p. 254

57 Hopper, op. cit., pp. 17–18.

58 Hanson, op. cit., pp. 151, 158–9, 160.

59 PRO, SP28/153; Newman, op. cit., pp. 26–7.

60 Durham County Record Office, D/Sa/E585.8.

61 Durham County Record Office, D/Sa/F176.1, 176.2.

62 Durham County Record Office, D/Sa/F176.3, 176.4.

63 Durham County Record Office, D/Sa/F176.6, 176.7

64 C. O'Riordan (1987) 'Thomas Ellison, the Hixon Estate and the Civil War', *Durham County Local History Society and the Civil War* 39, pp. 3–5.

65 Ibid., pp. 5–6. and CCC, p. 1180.

66 Durham County Record Office, D/Sa/G585.4.

67 Durham County Record Office, EP/DU SO 118.

68 PRO, SP28/153.

69 E.M. Furgol (1990) *A Regimental History of the Covenanting Armies*, Edinburgh: John Donald, pp. 186–7.

70 Ibid., pp. 184–5.

71 Morrill (1974) *Cheshire, 1630–1660*, Oxford: Oxford University Press, p. 77.

72 Morrill refers to British Library, Harleian Mss, 2126 for the Edisbury Committee.

73 M. Bennett (1997) *The Civil Wars in Britain and Ireland 1638–1651*, Oxford: Blackwell, p. 218.

74 Lancs RO, DDF 5

75 Durham County Record Office, D/Sa E585.28; Furgol, op. cit., p. 166.

76 WYAS, TN/PO 2B III.

77 PRO, SP28/153.

3 EXPERIENCING REBELLION IN IRELAND, 1641–9

1 A. Clarke (1986) 'The 1641 Depositions' in P. Fox (ed.) *Treasures of the Library*, Dublin: Trinity College Library, pp. 112–18.

2 Trinity College Dublin Library (TCD) MS812 Kilkenny and Carlow is a good example of an indexed volume.

3 M. Perceval-Maxwell (1979) 'The Ulster Rising of 1641 and the Depositions', *Irish Historical Studies* 31, 82, September, p. 145.

4 Clarke, 'The 1641 Depositions', p. 112.

5 N. Canny (1993) 'The 1641 Depositions as a source for Social History: County Cork as a Case Study' in P. O'Flanaghan and C.G. Buttimer (eds) *Cork: People and Society*, Dublin: Geography Publications, pp. 213–48.

6 TCD, Ms 839, pp. 95, 96, 98, 99, 102ff.

7 TCD, Ms 839, Tyrone, pp. 1ff.

8 TCD, Ms 839, Donegall, pp. 132, 134ff.

9 TCD, Ms 834, Monaghan, pp. 92ff.

10 Ibid., pp. 95, 123ff.

11 TCD, Ms 834, Louth, pp. 1, 3ff.

12 TCD, Ms 839, pp. 95f., 102.

13 Ibid., Ms 839, pp. 132ff.

14 TCD, Ms 834, Monaghan, pp. 81, 82ff.

15 Ibid., pp. 196, 198, 202ff.

16 TCD, Ms 839, Tyrone, pp. 4f.

17 TCD, Ms 834, Monaghan, pp. 56, 92.

18 TCD, Ms 834, Monaghan, pp. 78f.

19 TCD, Ms 834, Louth pp. 6f.

20 TCD, Ms 839, Tyrone, pp. 132f.

21 TCD, Ms 834, Louth, pp. 18f.

22 TCD, Ms 829, Limerick, pp. 310f.

23 TCD, Ms 834, Monaghan, pp. 81f.

24 TCD, Ms 834, pp. 6f.

25 TCD, Ms 830, pp. 136f, her story is recounted in T. Fitzpatrick (1903) *The Bloody Bridge and Other Papers Relating to the Insurrection of 1641*, Dublin: Sealy, Bryers & Walker, pp. 259–60.

26 NAI, M1121/1/1, LXXXXVII, e, pp. 108f.

27 C. Dillon (ed.) (1995–6) 'Cin Lae Ui Mheallain: Friar Mellon's Journal', *Duiche Neill* 10, p. 171.

28 Ibid., p. 145.

29 Ibid., p. 156.

30 Ibid., p. 149.

31 TCD, Ms 837, Down, pp. 38, 155, 157ff. See also Fitzpatrick, *The Bloody Bridge*, pp. 107–10.

32 TCD, Ms 830, pp. 24f.

33 J. Casaway (1984) *Owen Roe O'Neill and the Struggle for Catholic Ireland*, Philadelphia, PA: University of Pennsylvannia Press, pp. 103–4.

34 TCD, Ms 3395, Genealogy of the House of O'Reilly, pp. 66, 77ff.

35 Dillon (ed.) 'Father O'Mellan Journal', p. 167.

36 Bennett (1997) *The Civil Wars in Britain and Ireland*, Oxford: Blackwell, p. 95.

37 TCD, Ms 834, Louth, pp. 22f.

38 Bennett, 1997, p. 94.

39 J. Byrne (1997) *War and Peace: The Survival of the Talbots of Malahide 1641–1671*, Dublin: Irish Academic Press, pp. 37–44.

40 National Archives, Ireland (NAI) M981/1/4 Esmonde Papers; N. Furlong (1987) 'Life in Wexford Port, 1600–1800' in K. Whelan (ed.) *Wexford: History and Society*, Dublin: Geography Publications, p. 156.

41 TCD, Ms 812, Carlow, pp. 6, 15, 17, 18, 19, 45ff.

42 TCD, Ms 812, Kilkenny, pp. 32, 197, 232–3ff.

43 TCD, Ms 829, Clare and Limerick *passim*.

44 TCD, Ms 828, Kerry, pp. 203, 205, 206, 213, 215, 219, 230 and 245ff.

45 TCD, Ms 830, Galway, pp. 140, 142ff.

46 TCD, Ms 830, Roscommon, pp. 2, 39ff.

47 TCD, Ms 809, Dublin, pp. 128f is one example of the investigation of a soldier.

48 Ibid., pp. 95f.

49 Ibid., pp. 164, 166, 168, 170ff.

50 Ibid., pp. 180–96ff. Lenman's deposition suggts that Cox's house was on New Street, but this does not make geographical sense in terms of the chase.

51 Ibid., pp. 214, 216ff; Byrne, op. cit., 1997, p. 37.

52 TCD, Ms 831, Mayo, pp. 143f.

53 TCD, Ms 829, Limerick, pp. 262, 310ff.

54 TCD, Ms 820, pp. 234, 261ff.

55 TCD, Ms 831, pp. 2f.

56 Ibid., pp. 182f.

57 TCD, Ms 821, Tipperary, pp. 12f.

58 TCD, Ms 829, pp. 341ff, told to Anne Etone.

59 TCD, Ms 811, Wicklow, pp. 135f.

60 TCD, Ms 829, Limerick, pp. 183f.

61 TCD, Ms 831, Leitrim, pp. 4, 10ff.

62 TCD, Ms 820, pp. 219, 234ff.

63 E. Razzell and P. Razzell (eds) (1996) *The English Civil War: A Contemporary Account*, London: Caliban, p. 280.

64 TCD, Ms 811, Wicklow, pp. 135f.

65 TCD, Ms 829, Limerick, pp. 310f.

66 Ibid.

67 NAU, M7051(10).

68 TCD, Ms 820, pp. 15ff.

69 Ibid., pp. 219, 312ff.

70 TCD, Ms 829, pp. 125ff.

71 TCD, Ms 811, Wicklow, 40, Edward Deane's testimony.

72 TCD, Ms 831, Leitrim, pp 5f.

73 TCD, Ms 812, pp. 44f.

74 TCD, Ms 812, pp. 248, 251, 255, 263ff.

75 TCD, Ms 828, pp. 190, 203ff.

76 TCD, Ms 183.

77 Ibid., pp. 230, 232, 241ff.

78 J. Hardiman (1985) *History of Galway*, Dublin: Galway Connacht Tribune, pp. 108–22 (first published 1820); J. Lowe (ed.) (1983) *Letterbook of the Earl of Clanricarde*, Dublin: Irish Manuscripts Commission, pp. 2–5.

79 TCD, Ms 830, pp. 2–3ff.

80 Ibid., pp. 3v f.

81 TCD, Ms 830, f136. The account is given in full in Fitzpatrick, *The Bloody Bridge*, pp. 259–60.

82 TCD, Ms 831, Leitrim, pp. 105f.

83 Ibid., pp. 112f.

84 TCD, Ms 834, pp. 79f.

85 TCD, Ms 811, pp. 23f.

86 TCD, Ms 834, pp. 53f.

87 NAI, M2450, Treasury Orderbook of the Lord Justices and Council, vol. 1, pp. 129ff.

88 Historical Manuscripts Commission (1903) *The Papers of the Marquis of Ormond*, New Series, vol. 2, London, p. 173.

89 A dryfat is a barrel for dry goods, a gaberd was a boat used for inland navigation. NAI, M2450, vol. 2, pp. 465ff.

90 NAI, M1071/3/1.

91 D. Stevenson (1994) *Highland Warrior*, Edinburgh: Saltire Society, pp. 113–14. Stevenson tackles the question of which ship or ships were sunk or destroyed at Mingary. He concludes that neither the Irish frigate, the *Harp*, accompanying the merchant ships, nor the *Jacob* were sunk on that day, although one Flemish ship was captured, but that one Irish vessel and the other Flemish ship were captured on 10 August.

92 NAI, M1071/3/1.

93 NAI, M981/1/14, Esmond papers relating to the surrender of Duncannon.

94 Representative Church Body Library, Dublin (RCBL); Vestry Book, St John's Parish (transcripts).

95 C. Lennon (1995) 'Dublin's Great Explosion', *History Ireland* 3, 3, August.

96 Dublin City Archives (henceforth DCA), Cess Book, 1647–1649.

97 RCBL, Vestry Book, p. 258.

98 DCA, Cess Book, pp. xxvi–xxix, 1ff.

99 Ibid., 109–111.

100 RCBL, Vestry Book *passim*; Bennett, *Civil Wars*, pp. 199–200.

101 I must thank Sam Ratliffe, a former postgraduate student at Nottingham Trent University who worked on the Dublin Cess material with me during 1997.

102 RCBL, Vestry Book, pp. 252, 258, 280ff.

4 THE SCOTTISH EXPERIENCE OF THE WARS IN THE FOUR NATIONS, 1638–48

1 S. Adams (1997) 'The Making of the Radical South West: Charles I and his Scottish Kingdom 1625–1649' in J. Young (ed.) *Celtic Dimensions of the British Civil Wars*, Edinburgh: Edinburgh University Press, p. 53.

2 A. Johnston of Wariston (1911) *Diary of Sir Archibald Johnston of Wariston, 1632–1639*, vol. 1, ed. G.M. Paul, Edinburgh University Press, pp. 324–6.

3 Baillie, vol 1, pp. 64–5.

4 Johnston, *Diary*, pp. 368–9.

5 A. Hopper (1997) *The Readiness of the People: The Formation and Emergence of the Army of the Fairfaxes, 1642–46*, York: Borthwick Institute, pp. 78–9; Baillie, p. 110.

6 Hopper, *Readiness*, pp. 89, 96.

7 Ibid., p. 98.

8 National Library of Scotland, Ms 5070 Erskine Murray Papers, pp. 63–4ff.

9 Razell and Razell (eds) *The English Civil War*, vol. 1, p. 238.

10 Ibid., p. 96.

11 For perspectives on the war-time levies and fiscal structures see D. Stevenson (1972) 'The Financing of the Cause of the Covenanters, 1638–51' *Scottish Historical Review* 51, 152, October.

12 I.D. Whyte (1995) *Scotland Before the Industrial Revolution*, London: Longman, p. 119.

13 A.C. O'Dell and K. Walton (1962) *The Highlands and Islands of Scotland*, Edinburgh: Thomas Nelson, pp. 52, 108.

14 J. Nicholson, pp. 7–8, 13, 16.

15 Ibid. pp. 44, 60–2, 65.

16 Ibid., pp. 110, 124, 155–6. One boll is equal to 6 bushels or 48 gallons.

17 Ibid., pp. 156–8, 165–7.

18 Razzell and Razzell, *Civil War*, pp. 206, 236, 237.

19 Ibid., vol. 2, pp. 25, 29.

20 Scottish Record Office (SRO), PA 14/1, pp. 25, 37, 43, 61, 66, 68ff.

21 Ibid., pp. 3, 48, 60, 72ff.

22 Ibid., pp. 271f.

23 Ibid., pp. 7f.

24 J. Strawhorn (1986) *The History of Irvine*, Edinburgh: John Donald, see chapter 3 *passim*.

25 J.S. Dobie (ed.) (1890) *Muniments of the Royal Burgh of Irvine*, Edinburgh: Ayrshire and Galloway Archaeological Association, vol. 1, p. 98; vol. 2, p. 56.

26 D. Stevenson (1996) *King or Covenant? Voices from Civil War*, East Linton: Tuckwell Press, p. 42.

27 J. Fyffe (ed.) (1928) *Scottish Diaries and Memoirs*, Stirling: MacKay, p. 146.

28 D. Stevenson (1994) *Highland Warrior, Alasdair MacColla and the Civil Wars*, Edinburgh: Saltire Society, pp. 95–8.

29 Dobie (ed.) *Muniments*, vol. 1, p. 101.

30 Stevenson, *Highland Warrior*, p. 101.

31 Dobie (ed.) *Muniments*, vol. 1, pp. 102–3.

32 Stevenson, *Highland Warrior*, p. 203.

33 Ibid., pp. 205–6.

34 Dobie (ed.) *Muniments*, vol. 2, pp. 58–9.

35 Ibid., p. 70.

36 Ibid., vol. 1, p. 103, vol. 2, p. 69; Stevenson, *Highland Warrior*, p. 199.

37 Dobie (ed.) *Muniments*, vol. 2, pp. 7–13.

38 J. Stuart (ed.) (1972) *Extracts From the Council Register of the Burgh of Aberdeen 1643–1747*, Edinburgh: Scottish Records Society, p. 12.

39 A. Jaffrey (1856) *Diary of Alexander Jaffrey*, Aberdeen: George & Robert King, pp. 47–9, 155.

40 Stuart (ed.) *Extracts From the Council Register*, p. 29.

41 Ibid., pp. ix–x.

42 Ibid., p. x, citing the eye-witness account of John Spalding.

43 Jaffrey, *Diary*, p. 156.

44 Ibid., pp. 50–2, 157.

45 Ibid., p. 53.

46 Ibid., pp. 52–4.

47 Ibid., pp. 145–6.

48 Baillie, II, pp. 182–5.

49 Ibid., pp. 262–5.

50 Ibid., p. 362.

51 Ibid., pp. 370–1.

52 Ibid., pp. 386–7.

53 SRO, PA 7/6, 209.

54 SRO, PA 7/6, 171, 172.

55 SRO, PA 7/6, 21.

56 SRO, PA 7/6, 173.

57 SRO, GD176/389.

58 E.M. Furgol (1990) *A Regimental History of the Covenanting Armies*, Edinburgh: John Donald, pp. 197, 220, 287.

59 SRO, PA7/6, 170.
60 I have also dealt with Crathie in my earlier work (1997) *The Civil Wars in Britain and Ireland*, Oxford: Blackwell, pp. 194–6.
61 SRO, PA 7/6 162.
62 I argued this in *The Civil Wars in Britain and Ireland*.

5 EXPERIENCING WAR IN WALES AND ENGLAND

1 Razzell and Razzell (eds), *The English Civil War*, vol. 2, pp. 219, 222, 236.
2 Clwyd Record Office, Hawarden, D/6/3275.
3 Ibid. Woodds to Trevor, 4 June 1642, 23 July 1642 and 6 August 1642.
4 Ibid., Woodds to Trevor, 9 February 1643.
5 Ibid., Woodds to Trevor, 9 March 1643.
6 Ibid., Woodds to Trevor, 23 October 1643.
7 National Library of Wales (NLW), unpublished 'Calendar of Owen of Clenennau', p. 16.
8 Clwyd Record Office, D/GW/2145.
9 Gwent Record Office, D/PA 111.1 Panteg Parish Register.
10 Gwent Record Office, D/Pa/86.1 *passim* and pp. 87f.
11 A.H. Dodd (1971) *Studies in Stuart Wales*, Cardiff: University of Wales Press, p. 85.
12 Glamorgan Record Office, D/DFV/122.
13 Clwyd Record Office, D/HE/874 and 875, D/HE/464.
14 I have dealt with this in 'Dampnified Villagers: Taxation in Wales During the First Civil War', *Welsh History Review* 19, 1, June 1998.
15 PRO, SP28/251.
16 NLW, Ms 17088A, Diary of Walter Powell. The diary has no pagination, entries are grouped under the year and by date. See the entries for 19 and 20 January and 13 and 14 February.
17 I have dealt with these papers in *The Civil Wars in Britain and Ireland*, pp. 189–92.
18 NLW, Ms17088A, entries under 1642.
19 Ibid., entries for 1643.
20 Ibid., entries for 1644.
21 Ibid., entries for 1645.
22 Bennett, *Civil Wars in Britain and Ireland*, pp. 234–5; Morrill (1999) *Revolt in the Provinces*, London: Longman, pp. 174–5.
23 NLW, Ms17088A, entries for 1646.
24 Ibid., entries for 1648. See Chapter 6 for the 1648 rebellion.
25 Clwyd Record Office, D/6/3275 Woodds to Trevor, 22 and 23 August 1646.
26 Ibid., Woodds to Trevor, 22 August and 13 November 1646.
27 Ibid., Woodds to Trevor, 22 and 29 October 1647.
28 Ibid., Woodds to Trevor, 28 November 1646.
29 Ibid., Woodds to Lady Tirringham, 15 January 1647.
30 Ibid., Woodds to Trevor, 29 May, 29 October and 5 November 1647.
31 Dodd, *Studies in Stuart Wales*, pp. 79–81.
32 Glamorgan Record Office, D/DFV/123. J.F. Rees, *Studies in Welsh History*, Cardiff: University of Wales Press, 2nd edn, 1965, p. 78.
33 Razzell and Razzell (eds), *Civil War*, pp. 197, 245.
34 Historical Manuscripts Commission, *Records of Exeter*, London: HMSO, p. 208.
35 Historical Manuscripts Commission, *Fourteenth Report*, Appendix, part 8, p. 188.
36 S.M. Bond (1974) *Worcester Order Book*, Worcester: Worcestershire Historical Society, pp. 358, 357, 361, 362–4, 366.
37 Ibid., p. 370. This is the true figure, the town miscalculated it as £117 15s 4d.

38 Ibid., pp. 377–8

39 For assessments of the Worcestershire clubmen see Morrill, *Revolt in the Provinces*, pp. 132–51; G.A. Lynch 'The Risings of the Clubmen in the English Civil War', unpublished M.A. thesis, Manchester University, 1973; Hutton (1982) *Royalist War Effort*, London: Longman, pp. 159–65; and his article in *Midland History* 5, 1979–80, 'The Worcestershire Clubmen in the English Civil War'.

40 Bond, *Worcester Order Book*, pp. 390–2.

41 Ibid., pp. 411–12, 415–18, 419, 421.

42 PRO, SP28/187.

43 Worcestershire Record Office, 850, Salwarpe Papers BA 1054/2, Bundle D4.

44 Gloucestershire Record Office, D261 E2.

45 M. Coate (1963) *Cornwall in the Great Civil War*, Truro: Bradford Barton, pp. 357–9.

46 Ibid., pp. 366–8.

47 Ibid., p. 369.

48 Devon Record Office, 32.484./10/56.

49 The best account of the region's experience remains C. Holmes (1974) *The Eastern Association and the English Civil War*, Cambridge: Cambridge University Press.

50 A.C. Edwards (ed.) (1952) *English History from Essex Sources, 1550–1750*, Chelmsford: Essex Record Office, pp. 78–9.

51 Essex Record Office (ERO), D/P 75/5/1.

52 For the county as a whole see R.W. Ketton-Cremer (1970) *Norfolk in the Civil War*, Hamden, CT: Archon.

53 Norfolk Record Office PD254/112, pp. 1–2ff.

54 Norfolk Record Office. PD219/126.

55 For those interested in exploring this theme, the principle works are those in foot-note 40 and P. Gladwish (1985) 'The Herefordshire Clubmen: A Reassessment', *Midland History* 10.

56 S. Osborne (1994) 'The War, the People and the Absence of the Clubmen in the Midlands, 1642–1646', *Midland History* 19, pp. 85–104.

57 Staffordshire County Record Office, D1454/2.

58 Nottinghamshire Archive Office (NAO), PR2130, Edwinstowe Constables Accounts, pp. 12f.

59 Staffordshire Record Office, D3712/4/1, Mavesyn Ridware Parish Book.

60 R.S. Shaw (1976) *History and Antiquities of Staffordshire*, Ilkley; 1st published London, 1798–1803, vol.1, p. 60.

61 Staffordshire Record Office, D3539/2/1, Biddulph Parish Book, np.

62 Lichfield Cathedral Library, Ms 24, The True and Perfect Account of the Expenses of Collonell Richard Bagott; Lichfield Joint Record Office, D30 LIIIB, Contributions to the Garrison in the Close.

63 NAO, PR1710, Upton Constable' Accounts: published as M. Bennett (ed.) (1995) *A Nottinghamshire Village in War and Peace: The Accounts of the Constables of Upton*, Nottingham.

64 NAO, PR1529, Coddington Constables' Accounts Levies, np.

65 NAO, PR1531, Coddington Constables Accounts, 1641–1769, np.

66 NAO, PR5767, Thorpe Constables' Accounts, np.

67 M. Bennett (1985) 'Royalist War Effort', chapter 2, or 'Contribution and Assessment: Financial Exactions in the First Civil War, 1642–1646', *War and Society* 4, 1. They could cross Trent Bridge on the occassions which they captured the fort there. The Toton rentals show that the Royalists could reach this are of the county on these occasions. NAO, D35/5.

68 See for example the Lady Martha Button (or Dutton), NAO, DD 4P 55/49. This account actually refers to Devonshire. At Powick in Worcestershire Margaret

Staunton was promised payment of 2s.10d a week for quartering one man, Public Record Office, SP 28/152, Accounts of the Constables of Powick, p. 4.

69 Leicestershire County Record Office (LRO), DE1965/41, Belton Constables', Churchwardens' and Overseers' Accounts, np.

70 LRO, DE25/60, Waltham on the Wolds Constables' Accounts, pp. 68f.; DE720/30, Branston Constables' Accounts, p. 62.

71 LRO, DE 2461/135, Preston Civil War Receipts.

72 LRO, DE730/3, The Papers of Abel Barker, pp. 49, 50ff.

73 Ibid., pp. 52f.

74 B. Couth (ed.) *Grantham During the Interregnum: The Hallbook of Grantham, 1641–1649*, pp. 30–1.

75 NAO, PR1710, pp. 24f.

76 NAO, PR5767.

77 Historical Manuscripts Commission (1888) *The Manuscripts of his Grace the Duke of Rutland*, Twelfth Report, Appendix Part IV, I, London: HMSO, pp. 460–1; C. Carlton (1992) *Going to the Wars: The Experience of the British Civil Wars, 1638–1653*, London: Routledge, p. 94.

78 Ibid., pp. 35, 40.

79 NAO, PR1710, pp. 24–7ff.

80 Historical Manuscripts Commission (1930) *Report on the Manuscripts of the Late Reginald Rawdon Hastings*, 4 vols, London, vol. 2, p. 128.

81 Ibid., p. 132.

82 British Library, Additional Manuscripts, 18922, pp. 47f.

83 William Salt Library, Stafford, Salt Manuscripts, 481, 547.

84 NAO, DD294/1.

85 J. Nichols (1804) *The History and Antiquities of the County of Leicester*, 4 vols, Leicester, vol. 3, part 2, Appendix 4, p. 39.

86 LRO, D730 Barker Mss, vol. 4, pp. 15, 20ff.

87 NAO, PR 1710, pp. 40ff.

88 S. Porter (1984) 'The Fire Raid in the English Civil War', *War and Society* 2, 2.

89 NAO, DDN 122. This state of affairs lasted into the next decade, with only slight and inconsistent recoveries.

90 L. Hutchinson (1806) *Memoirs of the Life of Colonel Hutchinson*, London: Longman, Orme, Rees and Brown, p. 262.

91 NAO, PR1710, pp. 49f.

92 A.C. Wood (1971) *Nottinghamshire in the Civil War*, Wakefield: SR Publishing, p. 120; 1st published Oxford: OUP, 1937.

93 Bennett (ed.)(1995) *A Nottinghamshire Village*, Nottingham: Thornton Society, p. xxvii.

94 Couth, *Grantham During the Interregnum*, p. 150.

95 Staunton Hall Family Papers, 34/16, Account Book of Lieutenant Gervase Hewit.

96 Osborne, 'The People, the War', pp. 99–100.

97 R. Hutton (1982) *The Royalist War Effort*, London, pp. 148, 156.

98 Derbyshire County Record Office, D258M/34/10, pp. 3–5ff.

99 R. Hutton (1979) 'The Worcestershire Clubmen and the English Civil War', *Midland History* V.

100 Bennett, 'The Royalist War Effort in the North Midlands', pp. 165–7.

101 S.C. Ratcliff and H.C. Johnson (eds) (1936) *Warwick County Records*, Warwick: Warwickshire County Council, vol. 2, p. 46.

102 Ibid., p. 117.

103 For work on Warwickshire see A. Hughes (1987) *Politics, Society and Civil War in Warwickshire, 1620–1660*, Cambridge: Cambride University Press, chapters 5, 6 and 7 in particular; also see P. Tennant (1992) *Edgehill and Beyond*, Stroud: Alan Sutton.

104 Hughes, *Politics, Society and Civil War*, pp. 256–7.

105 Ibid., p. 256.

106 Tennant (1996) *Stratford upon Avon During the Civil War*, pp. 130–1.

107 Ibid., p. 132.

108 Ratcliff and Johnson (eds) *Warwick County Records*, p. 135.

109 Ibid., p. 156.

110 Carlton, *Going to the Wars*, p. 347.

111 Ratcliff and Johnson, *Warwick County Records*, pp. 158, 161, 163, 179–80.

112 Tennant, op. cit., p. 43.

113 G.H. Fowler (ed.) (1936) 'The Civil War Papers of Sir William Boteler, 1642–1655' in *Bedfordshire Historical Society*, vol. 18, Apsley Guise, pp. 4, 39.

114 Ibid., p. 9.

115 Ibid., p. 8.

116 Bedfordshire Record Office, TW 959.

117 Fowler, 'Civil War Papers', p. 37.

118 Bedfordshire Record Office, TW964.

119 Bedfordshire Record Office, TW953.

120 Hampshire Record Office, 44M69/E6/162; Calendar of the Committee for Compounding, Part 3, pp. 2372–3.

121 Ibid., part 4, p. 2533.

122 Surrey Record Office, EL 12/1/6.

123 Ibid., pp. 1f reverse.

124 Ibid., pp. 2f reverse.

125 Ibid., pp. 2f.

126 G. Hampshire (ed.) (1983) *The Bodelian Library Account Book 1613–1646*, Oxford: Oxford Bibliographical Society, pp. 133–4.

127 Ibid., pp. 138–9.

128 Ibid., p. 150.

129 J.C. Jeafferson (ed.) (1974) *Middlesex County Records (Old Series)*, London: Greater London Council, vol. 3, p. 74.

130 Ibid., p. 80.

131 Ibid., p. 82.

132 Ibid., pp. 87–8.

133 Ibid., pp. 92, 94, 179.

134 Razzell and Razzell (eds), *Civil War*, pp. 29, 84, 108, 120.

135 Jeafferson (ed.) *Middlesex County Records*, vol. 3, pp. 80–1, 84, 88, 90, 93, 94–5.

136 Ibid., p. 99.

137 D.J.H. Clifford (ed.) (1990) *The Diaries of Lady Anne Clifford*, Stroud: Sutton, p. 95.

6 THE REVOLUTIONARY PERIOD, 1648–53

1 B. Manning (1992) *1649: Crisis of the Revolution*, London: Bookmarks.

2 This a paraphrase of part of the last sentence in *Revolt in the Provinces*, London: Longman, 1999, p. 208.

3 R. Garlick and R. Mathias (eds) (1990) *Anglo-Welsh Poetry 1480–1990*, Bridgend: Seren, pp. 70–2.

4 Ibid., pp. 83, 84.

5 NLW, Ms 17088 A Diary of Walter Powell, entries for 1648.

6 Ibid., entries of 1649.

7 Ibid., entries for 1651.

8 Ibid., entries for 1652 and final pages.

9 Glamorgan Record Office, D/DFV/124.

10 J.F. Rees (1965) *Studies in Welsh History*, Cardiff: University of Wales Press, 2nd edn, pp. 1121–2, 149–51, 153–8.
11 Glamorgan Record Office, D/DFV/125.
12 PRO, SP28/251 Pembrokeshire bundle.
13 PRO, SP28/251 Cardiganshire bundle.
14 B.J. Charles (ed.) (1967) *Calendar of the Records of the Borough of Haverfordwest, 1539–1660*, Cardiff: University of Wales Press, pp. 89–91.
15 Ibid., pp. 97, 99–100.
16 Ibid., pp. 100–12, 117.
17 Clywd Record Office, D/6/3276. See Chapter 4 for Trevor's corrsespondence with Samuel Woodds.
18 Clwyd Record Office, D/6/3276. Peck to Trevor, 17 September and December 1649.
19 Ibid., Peck to Trevor, 17 August 1650, 21 August and 7 September 1652.
20 J.S. Dobie (ed.) (1891) *Muniments of the Royal Burgh of Irvine*, Edinburgh: Ayrshire and Galloway Archaeological Association), vol. 2., pp. 73–4; E.M. Furgol (1990) *A Regimental History of the Covenanting Armies*, Edinburgh: John Donald, pp. 171–2, 269–71.
21 Ibid., pp. 247, 292; Dobie, *Muniments*, vol. 2, p. 74–5.
22 Ibid., vol. 1, p. 104.
23 Scottish Record Office, GD/561/2, ii, iii, v, vi, vii.
24 Baillie, III, pp. 43–9.
25 M. Wood (ed.) (1938) *Extracts From the Records of the Burgh of Edinburgh*, Edinburgh: Oliver and Boyd, vol II, p. 152.
26 Baillie, III, pp. 50–3.
27 Scottish Record Office, GD16/36/12.
28 Scottish Record Office, PA7/9, 162 *passim*.
29 J.G. Fyffe (ed.) (1928) *Scottish Diaries and Memoirs*, Stirling: Mackay, pp. 151–2.
30 Ibid., pp. 152–3.
31 Baillie III, pp. 66–7.
32 A. Jaffray (1856) *Diary of Alexander Jaffray*, ed. John Barclay, Aberdeen: George & Robert King, pp. 55–6.
33 Ibid., pp. 60–3, 157–63.
34 Ibid., pp. 195, 212, 232, 233, 245, 250, 254.
35 J.D. Marwick (ed.) (1881) *Extracts of the Records of the Burgh of Glasgow*, Glasgow: Scottish Burgh Records Society, pp. 182, 189, 194, 195.
36 Ibid., pp. 196, 197.
37 Ibid., pp. 207, 208, 211, 212.
38 A. Johnston of Wariston (1919) *The Diary of Sir Archibald Johnston of Wariston*, vol. 2, ed. D.H. Fleming, Edinburgh: Scottish History Society, pp. 11, 26.
39 Ibid., pp. 40, 62.
40 W. Calverley-Trevelyan (ed.) (1856) *Letters from Roundhead Officers in Scotland Chiefly Addressed to Captain Adam Baines*, Edinburgh: Bannantyne Club, pp. 1–2, 18.
41 Ibid., p. 31.
42 Ibid., p. 36.
43 Fyffe, *Scottish Diaries*, p. 178.
44 Ibid., p. 179, 183–4.
45 For an assessment of how this fits into the pattern of relations between republicans, Cromwell and Scotland and Ireland see S. Barber, 'Scotland and Ireland under the Commonwealth: A Question of Loyalty' in S.G. Ellis and S. Barber (1995) *Conquest and Union: Fashioning a British State, 1485–1725*, London: Longman, pp. 195–222.
46 Johnston, *Diary*, vol. 2, p. 46.

47 Ibid., pp. 132–3, 137; Barber, 'Scotland and Ireland Under the Commonwealth', p. 214.
48 Baillie, III, pp. 106–10.
49 Scottish Record Office, GD124/13/5.
50 Scottish Record Office, GD196/331.
51 Razzell and Razzell (eds), *The English Civil War*, vol. 3, pp. 317, 351.
52 See John Morrill's reassessment of this in *Revolt of the Provinces*, 1999, pp. 204–8.
53 WYAS, TN/PO 2B IV.
54 Lancs RO, DDPt 1.
55 Lancs RO, DDPt 1.
56 Ashcroft (1991) *Scarborough Records*, pp. 117–19.
57 Ibid., pp. 120–1.
58 M. Edwards Ingram, *The Manor of Bridlington and the Lords Feoffees*, Bridlington, p. 55.
59 Ashcroft, *Scarborough Records*, pp. 126–7.
60 Ibid., pp. 128.
61 Lancs RO, DDMA Boxes 9, 17.
62 For the village context see M. Bennett (1995) *The Constables' Accounts of Upton, 1640–1666*, Nottingham: Thoroton Society. The proportion of village income increases to 5 per cent if the monthly pay is removed from the community budget.
63 M. Storey (ed.) (1994) *Two East Anglian Diaries*, Woodbridge: Boydell Press, pp. 1, 44–50.
64 ERO, D/DQs 18, Clopton's Diary.
65 R. Ashton (1994) *Counter Revolution: The Second Civil War and its Origins*, London: Yale, pp. 142–3.
66 ERO, D/DQs 18, pp. 1ff, 36, 37.
67 A.C. Edwards (ed.) (1952) *English History from Essex Sources, 1550–1750*, Colchester: ERO, p. 84.
68 ERO, D/DQs 18, pp. 41–3ff., 45, 51, 57.
69 Ibid. pp. 69–70ff.
70 Ibid., pp. 85f.
71 Ibid., pp. 88f.
72 D.H. Allen (1974) *Essex Quarter Sessions, 1652–1661*, Chelmsford: Essex County Council, p. 6.
73 Ibid., pp. 7, 14.
74 J.C. Jeaffreson (1974) *Middlesex County Record* (Old Series), London: Greater London Council, p. 192.
75 Ibid., pp. 193, 200, 201,204.
76 Ibid., pp. 191.
77 Baxter, R. (ed.) (1985) *The Autobiography of Richard Baxter*, ed. N.H. Keeble, London: Dent, pp. 63–4.
78 Ibid., pp. 65–7.
79 Surrey Record Office, EL 12/1/6, pp. 3f.
80 D.J.H. Clifford (ed.) (1990) *The Diaries of Lady Anne Clifford*, Stroud: Sutton, p. 100.
81 Ibid., p. 113.
82 Ibid., pp. 118–19.
83 M. Ashcroft (1991) *Scarborough Records*, Northallerton: North Yorkshire Record Office, p. 127.
84 Ibid., pp. 155–8, 179.
85 Ibid., pp. 165–9, 174.
86 Lancs RO, DDKe 11.
87 Hampshire Record Office, 47M81/PR1.
88 N. Penney (ed.) (1924) *The Journal of George Fox*, London: Dent, p. 27.

89 G.H. Fowler (ed.) (1936) 'The Civil War Papers of Sir William Boteler, 1642–1654', *Bedfordshire Historical Record Society*, vol. 18, Apsley Guise, p. 37.

90 I.S.O. Ratcliff and H.C. Johnson (eds) (1936) *Warwickshire County Records*, Warwick: Warwickshire County Council, pp. 215, 228.

91 Historical Manuscripts Commission, *Papers of Reginal Rawdon Hastings*, vol. 2, London: HMSO, pp. 356–9.

92 Ibid., pp. 359–61.

93 J.T. Gilbert (1880) *A Contemporary History of Affairs in Ireland from 1641–52*, Dublin: Irish Archaeological and Celtic Society, vol. 3, pp. 160–1.

94 K.A. Kearns (1996) *Dublin Pub Life: An Oral History*, Dublin: Gill & Macmillan, pp. 18, 52, has however, conflicting evidence. A modern photograph shows the pub with the date 1649; but an older photograph shows clearly the date 1710.

95 NAI, M1071/3/1.

96 R. Caulfield (ed.) (1878) *The Council Book of Youghall*, Guildford, pp. 263, 268–9.

97 A. Fanshaw (1907) *The Memoirs of Ann Lady Fanshaw*, London: Bodley Head, pp. 53–4.

98 Ibid., pp. 62–3; Historical Manuscripts Commission (1885) *Tenth Report*, London: HMSO, p. 500.

99 Caulfield, *The Council Book of Youghall*, pp. 290, 297.

100 NAI, M1121/1/1, LXXXXiiii, pp. 94–6ff.; LXXXXV, pp. 90f; K. Harvey (1998) *The Bellews of Mount Bellew: A Catholic Gentry Family in Eighteenth Century Ireland*, Dublin: Four Courts Press, p. 28.

101 NAI, M7051 (10).

102 NAI, M4974, Caulfield Ms, The Volumes, n.p.

103 RCBL, Vestry Book, p. 302.

104 Ibid., p. 315.

105 National Library, Ireland, Ms 11959, pp. 17–19, 29ff.

106 Ibid., pp. 34, 35, 36, 42ff.

107 British Library, Additional Manuscripts, 32093, pp. 275ff. National Library, Ireland, M 4974 Caulfield papers, n.p.

7 CONQUERED NATIONS: REPUBLICAN AND RESTORATION SCOTLAND AND IRELAND, 1653–61

1 R. Hutton (1990) *The British Republic*, London: Macmillan, pp. 24–5.

2 See Gerald Aylmer's excellent analysis of the Nominated Assembly or Little Parliament in *Rebellion or Revolution*, 1986, Oxford: Oxford University Press, pp. 159–62.

3 Barber (1995) 'Scotland and Ireland under the Commonwealth', *passim* and pp. 215–17.

4 Razzell and Razzell (eds), *The English Civil War*, vol. 4., pp. 87, 91.

5 J. Hardiman (1820) *History of Galway*, Dublin; repr. Galway: Connacht Tribune, 1985.

6 NAI, M6935, Bally Glunin Papers, Parcel 31/64, a.

7 NAI, ibid., Parcel 31/64, b.

8 NAI, ibid., Parcel 1/1.

9 NAI, M1095, Dennis Family of County Cork Papers, 1/ 2/2.

10 Ibid., 1/2/3, 1/2/4, 1/2/5.

11 NAI, M7051 (10).

12 NAI, M1121/1/2, LXXXXV, pp. 89, 90ff., 99, LXXXXVi, pp.101–2.

13 A. Bryne, 1997, pp. 45–6.

14 NAI, M981/1/4 Esmond papers, No.2.

15 NAI, 4974 Caulfield Mss, n.p.

16 Ibid.

17 Ibid.
18 NAI, M4974 Caulfield Mss, The Volumes, np.
19 R.C. Simington (ed.) (1952) *The Civil Survey*, vol. 8, Dublin: Stationery Office, County of Kildare, pp. 78, 97.
20 R.C. Simington (ed.) (1953) *The Civil Survey*, vol. 9, Dublin: Stationary Office, County of Wexford, pp. 78, 193–4.
21 Simington, *Civil Survey*, Kildare, pp. 7, 13, 23.
22 R.C. Simington (ed.) (1945) *The Civil Survey*, vol. 7, Dublin: Stationery Office, p. 176.
23 Barber, 'Scotland an Ireland under the Commonwealth', pp. 200, 211, 214.
24 F.D. Dow (1979) *Cromwellian Scotland*, Edinburgh: John Donald, pp. 30–2, 35, 40–2, 44.
25 A. Johnston of Wariston (1919) *Diary of Sir Archibald Johnston of Wariston*, vol. 2, ed. D.H. Fleming, Edinburgh: Scottish History Society, p. 167.
26 J. Emerson, *Poetical Descriptions of Orkney M.DC.LII*, pp. v, xvii, *passim*.
27 Ibid., pp. xix, xxvii.
28 The Orkney Library, D29/7/3.
29 B.H. Hossack (1900) *Kirkwall in the Orkneys*, Kirkwall: William Peace & Son, pp. 83–5.
30 J.S. Dobie (ed.) (1890) *Muniments of the Royal Burgh of Irvine*, Edinburgh: Ayrshire and Galloway Archaeological Association, vol. 1., p. 106.
31 Ibid., vol. 2, pp. 76–7.
32 National Library of Scotland, MS6489, pp. 32ff.
33 National Library of Scotland, MS6489, pp. 228–9ff., 233
34 A. Jaffray (1856) *The Diary of Alexander Jaffray*, Aberdeen: George & Robert King, p. 66–8.
35 The archivist at Aberdeen City Archives believes that there are inconsistent ommissions and that in comparison with the manuscript the published version is 'far from complete'. Personal Communication. Letter 9 March 1998.
36 Penney (ed.) *Journal of George Fox*, pp. 154–8
37 J. Fyffe (ed.) (1928) *Scottish Diaries and Memoirs*, Stirling: MacKay, p. 183.
38 D. MacTavish (ed.) (1944) *Minutes of the Synod of Argyll 1652–1661*, Scottish History Society, vol. 38, Edinburgh: Edinburgh University Press, pp. 39, 69, 109.
39 Ibid., pp. 40, 58, 93, 98, 105, 177, 198.
40 Ibid., pp. 18–19, 129.
41 Ibid., p. 70.
42 Ibid., *passim*, and pp. 53, 59–60, 77–8, 81, 91–2, 150, 163.
43 Ibid., p. 41.
44 W. Calverley-Trevelyan (ed.) (1856) *Letters from Roundhead Officers Written from Scotland and Chiefly Addressed to Captain Adam Baines*, Edinburgh: Bannantyne Club, p. 72.
45 Ibid., p. 78.
46 Ibid., pp. 91, 92.
47 Ibid., pp 102.
48 Ibid., p. 105.
49 Baillie III, pp. 176–7, 194–5.
50 MacTavish, *Minutes of the Synod of Argyll*, pp. 143, 198, 204.
51 Fyffe, *Scottish Diaries*, p. 179.
52 Perth and Kinross Record Office, Rossie Priory Papers, Ms 100, 1099, 1100.
53 Perth and Kinross Record Office, Ms 100, 1099.
54 Fyffe, *Scottish Diaries*, p. 180.
55 Baillie, pp. 249–51.
56 Ibid., pp. 286–7.
57 NAI, M6931 Bally Glunin Papers, Parcel 31/64, b.
58 NAI, M6931, Parcel 1/1.

59 NAI, M7051 (10).
60 NAI, M1121/1/2, Bellew papers, pp. 109ff., LXXXXVIII.
61 Ibid., pp. 111ff.
62 Ibid., LXXXXVII, 104, LXXXXVIII, f.111.
63 NAI, M1071 Archer Papers, 3/1.
64 NAI, M1004, Pike-Fortesque Papers, 1/1.
65 NAI, Calendar of the Papers of the Earl of Meath, A/1/157. A/1/158.
66 Ibid., pp. 119–20.
67 A. Johnston of Wariston (1940) *Diary of Sir Archibald Johnston of Wariston*, vol. 3, ed. J.D. Ogilvie, Edinburgh: Scottish History Society, p. 86.
68 Ibid., pp. 132.
69 D. MacTavish (ed.) (1944) *Minutes of the Synod of Argyll, 1652–1661*, Edinburgh: Edinburgh University Press, pp. 163, 195, 202, 219.
70 Baillie III, pp. 392–5.
71 Mactavish, *Minutes*, p. 193.
72 Ibid., pp. 198, 210–11.
73 J.S. Dobie (ed.) (1890, 1891) *Muniments of the Royal Burgh of Irvine*, Edinburgh: Ayrshire and Galloway Archaeological Association, vol. 1, p. 106.
74 Ibid., vol. 2, p. 78.
75 Ibid., pp. 86–7.
76 Baillie, III, p. 428.
77 Jaffray, *Diary of Alexander Jaffray*, p. 124.
78 Ibid., pp. 127–30, 133–8.
79 W. Calverley-Trevelyan (ed.) (1856) *Letters from Roundhead Officers Written from Scotland and Chiefly Addressed to Captain Adam Baines*, Edinburgh: Bannantyne Club, p. 152.
80 Ibid. pp. 152–3, 154.
81 F.D. Dow (1979) *Cromwellian Scotland*, Edinburgh: John Donald, p. 254.
82 Perth and Kinross Record Office, Ms 100, 1001.
83 Perth and Kinross Record Office, Ms 100, 1002i and ii.
84 G.F. Warner *et al.* (eds) (1893) *Miscellany of the Scottish History Society First Volume*, Edinburgh: Edinburgh University Press, p. 467.
85 Fyffe, *Scottish Diaries*, p. 181.
86 Calverly-Trevelyan, *Letters from Roundhead Officers*, pp. 156–7.
87 Fyffe, *Scottish Diaries*, p. 181.
88 Ibid., p. 182.
89 T. Stackhouse (ed.), *Bishop Gilbert Burnet: History of his Own Times*, London: Dent, p. 32.
90 Razzell and Razzell (eds), *The English Civil War*, vol. 5, p. 298.
91 Johnston, *Diary*, vol. 3, pp. 180–4.

8 REPUBLIC AND RESTORATION IN ENGLAND AND WALES, 1653–61

1 E.A. Parry (n.d.) *Letters from Dorothy to Sir William Temple*, London: Dent & Son, p. 78.
2 N.H. Keeble (ed.) (1985) *The Autobiography of Richard Baxter*, London: Dent, pp. 69–70.
3 NAO, PR 1710, or see M. Bennett (ed.) (1995) *A Nottinghamshire Village in War and Peace: The Accounts of the Upton Constables*, Nottingham: Thoroton Society, pp. 75–126.
4 Lancs RO, DDKe 11.
5 J. Sutton (1998) 'Cromwell's Commissioners for Preserving the Peace of the Commonwealth: A Staffordshire Case Study' in I. Gentles *et al.* (eds) *Soldiers, Writers and Statesmen of the English Revolution*, Cambridge: Cambridge University Press.
6 Lincolnshire Archive Office, Addlethorpe and Ingoldmells, Par 12, np.
7 Lincolnshire Archive Office, South Kyme, Par 12, np.

8 Lancs RO, QDV 11.
9 Lincolnshire Archive Office, Addlethorpe and Ingolmells Par 12, np.
10 CSPD, p. 2632
11 Durham Record Office, D/Fo/40
12 Durham Record Office, D/Sa/176.13i, 14, 15,
13 Durham Record Office, S/Sh/.H/950, 954, 958, 961.
14 Durham Record Office, D/Sh.H/945, 946
15 Durham Record Office, S/Sh.H/966, 970
16 D.J.H. Clifford (ed.) (1990) *The Diaries of Lady Anne Clifford*, Stroud: Sutton, pp. 101, 125.
17 Flint Record Office, D/HE/477.
18 Parry (ed.), *Letters from Dorothy to Sir William Temple*, p. 136.
19 Cumbria Record Office, D Lons W9.
20 J.S. Cockburn (ed.) (1989) *Calendar of Assize Rolls: Kent Indictments*, London: HMSO, p. 242.
21 Ibid., p. 281.
22 A.C. Edwards (ed.) (1952) *English History from Essex Sources, 1550–1750*, Colchester: ERO, pp. 87–8.
23 M. Storey (ed.) (1994) *Two East Anglian Diaries*, Woodbridge: Boydell Press, pp. 51–2.
24 D.H. Allen (ed.) (1974) *Essex Quarter Sessions Order Book*, Colchester: ERO, pp. 53, 55, 59.
25 Ibid., p. 88.
26 S.C. Ratcliffe and H.C. Johnson (eds) (1937) *Warwick County Records*, Warwick: County Record Office, vol. 3, pp. 254, 271–2, 310–11.
27 J.C. Jeaferson (ed.) (1974) *Middlesex County Records*, London: Greater London Council, pp. 228, 240, 258, 261, 270.
28 Clywd Record Office Ms D/6/3276, Peck to Trevor, 17 June 1653 and 10 January 1654.
29 Ibid., Peck to Trevor, 18 April and 29 September 1654.
30 R.R. Hutton (1985) *The Restoration: A Political and Religious History of England and Wales*, Oxford: Oxford University Press, pp. 21–2.
31 Razzell and Razzell (eds), *The English Civil War*, vol. 5., pp. 153, 209.
32 M. Ashcroft (ed.) (1991) *Scarborough Records, 1641–1660*, Northallerton: North Yorkshire Record Office, pp. 257–9, 261, 263.
33 These references to Hutton's work all come from Hutton (1985) *The Restoration: A Political and Religious History of England and Wales 1658–1667*, Oxford: Oxford University Press, pp. 118–23.
34 Durham Record Office, D/Sh.H 979, 980, 981.
35 Clarendon, Earl of, *History of the Rebellion*, vol. 6, pp. 233–4.
36 Whitlocke, *Memorials*, vol. 4, pp. 411–13.
37 Razzell and Razzell (eds), *The English Civil War*, vol. 5, p. 232.
38 Edwards (ed.) *English History*, p. 95.
39 Clifford (ed.) *Diaries of Lady Anne Clifford*, p. 142, 144.
40 Fanshawe, *Memoirs*, pp. 95–6.
41 Razzell and Razzell (eds), *The English Civil War*, vol. 5., pp. 250, 263.
42 Ibid., p. 234.
43 Keeble (ed.) *Autobiography of Richard Baxter*, pp. 142–6.
44 Penney (ed.) *The Journal of George Fox*, pp. 192–3.
45 Cumbria Record Office (Carlisle), CMBE Box 32, Bundle 3, George Middleton and William Spencer to Sir Phillip Musgrave, 13/1/1661.
46 See for instance the treatment of Quakers in Kendal in neighbouring Westmorland in C.B. Phillips (1988) 'Colonel Gervase Benson, Captain John Archer, and the corpora-

tion of Kendal, 1644–c1655' in Gentles *et al. Soldiers, Writers and Statesmen*, 1988, pp. 197–201.

47 Cumbria Record Office (Carlisle), CMBE Box 32, Bundle 3, Sir Phillip Musgrave to 'Gentlemen', 13/1/1661.

48 Hutton, *Restoration*, 1985, p. 152–3.

49 Allen (ed.) *Essex Quarter Sessions Orderbook*, p. 203.

50 G. Parsloe (ed.) (1949) *The Minute Book of Bedford Corporation, 1647–1664*, Luton: Bedfordshire Historical Record Society, pp. 138, 149–150.

51 Razzell and Razzell (eds), *The English Civil War*, vol. 5, p. 294.

52 York City Archives, F7 Quarter Sessions Minute Book, 1638–62, p. 437.

53 P.M. Tillot (ed.) *The City of York*, London: Oxford University Press, 1961, p. 191.

54 M.G. Hobson and H.E. Salter (eds) (1933) *Oxford Council Acts 1626–1665*, Oxford: Oxford University Press, p. 259–60.

55 York City Archives, F7, pp 452, 453, 472.

56 Ibid., pp. 478, 490.

57 H.E. Stocks (1923) *The Records of the Borough of Leicester*, vol. 4, Cambridge: Cambridge University Press, p. 465.

58 J.S. Cockburn (ed.) (1995) *Calendar of Assize Records, Kent Indictments*, London: HMSO, pp. 23–24.

59 Ibid., p. 11, 57.

60 Ibid., p. 27, 44.

61 Ibid., pp. 62, 64, 77, 78.

62 J.C. Jeaferson (1974) *Middlesex County Records*, London: Greater London Council, 2nd edn, pp. 302–9.

63 Ibid., pp. 311–12

64 York City Archives, F7, pp. 322, 469, 470, 501.

65 S.C. Ratcliff and H.C. Johnson (eds) (1938) *Warwick County Records*, Warwick: Records Committee of Warwickshire County Council, vol. 4, p. 130.

66 Ibid., p. 143.

67 Allen (ed.) *Essex Quarter Sessions Order Book*, p. 175.

68 Storey (ed.) *Two East Anglian Diaries*, pp. 11, 15, 21, 25, 64–9.

AFTERWORD

1 A. Johnston of Wariston (1940) *Diary of Sir Archibald Johnston of Wariston*, vol. 3, ed. J.D. Ogilvie, Edinburgh: Scottish History Society, pp. 131–2.

BIBLIOGRAPHY

Primary Manuscript Sources arranged by Record Office

Bedfordshire County Record Office

TW836 Levy for Collection of Money to Repay the constables for Biddenham
TW 895–1014, Papers of the late Charles Trevor-Wingfield

Bodleian Library

Ms Dugdale 19, A register of Docquets of all Letters Patent and other Documents ...
    from 23 January 1643 to 11 June 1646.

Bridlington, The Bayle

Papers belonging to the Lords Feoffee
Constables Accounts, 1633–53
Billeting Lists 1–8
Cesses and Levies
Receipts, 1643–8
Receipts, 1644

British Library

Additional Mss: 29548, ff7–9, Commissions addressed to Sir Christopher Hatton
Harleian Mss: 986, Notebook of Richard Symonds
Stowe Mss: 155, f7, letter of Thomas Leveson to constables of Burton and Tothill

Cambridgeshire County Record Office

P46/1/1 Comberstone Parish Register
P53/12/1 Croyden cum Clopton Accounts, 1651–1818
P145/5/1 Stretchworth Churchwardens' Accounts

R58/5/3 Maynard Collection, vol. 3

Cheshire County Record Office

DFI 192 Church Lawton Constables Accounts (transcript of Harleian Ms 1943)
P109/13 Church Lawton Constables Lists

Clwyd County Record Office

D/DM/223/139, Letter of Charles I to the Sheriff of Flint
D/GW/2145, Civil War Notices
D/GW/B/1020 Letters of Civil War News
D/HE/ 462–78, Papers and letters of Evan Edwards
D/HE/ 874–5 Edwards Papers

Cornwall County Record Office

P19/9/1–25, St Breock Constables' Accounts

Cumbria Record Office: Cumberland

CB/ME Box 32/3 Letters and Papers Sir Phillip Musgrave
D Lons W9 Sandwich Bundle 77 item 23 Certificate of William Thompson JP of the marriage of Henry Stowe and Jane Dodgson

Derbyshire County Record Office

D 803 M29 Copybook of Sir George Gresley

Devonshire County Record Office

3248A/10/56–7 Okehampton Constables Disbursments 1642–4

Dublin City Archives

MR/15 Cess Book 1647–9 (1648–50)

Durham County Record Office

D/FO/ Testimonial of John Forcer's Good Behaviour 1659
D/Sa/C5 Salvin Papers
D/Sa/E585.6 Salvin Estate papers
D/Sa/F176–7 Salvin Sequestration Papers 1645–59
D/Sh.H/937–81 Papers concerning John Machon

EP DU SO 118 Durham St Oswald Parish Register
EP/Ga SM 4/1 Gateshead St Mary's Minutebook, 1626–78

Essex Record Office

D/DQs 18 Clopton's Diary 1648–51
D/P 75/5/1 Waltham Holy Cross Churchwarden's Accounts
D/P 232/8/1 (MF 38) Great Easton (Much Eaton) Parish Books
Q/S Ba 2/65 Quarter Sessions Bundles. Pay petition midsummer 1647

Gloucestershire County Record Office

D640/ L6-7 Parliamentary Tax Levies in Hartpury
P338/C0/1/1 Tortworth Tythingmen's Accounts
P338/CO/1/2 Tortworth Constables' Accounts
P343/VE/2/1 Twyning Parish Book

Glamorgan Record Office

D/DFV/122–125, Fonmon Papers

Gwent County Record Office

Misc. Mss 253–8 Letters of Charles I to Sheriffs of Monmouth
Misc. Mss 648 Letter-Book of Richard Herbert D.L.
D/Pa 30.1 Bryngwyn Parish register
D/Pa/86.1 Chepstow Parish Church Registers 1595–1694
D/PA 111.1 Panteg Parish Register

Hampshire Record Office

44 M69/E6/162 Exchequer Court papers Re: Sir Thomas Jervaise
47M81/PR 1 Odiham Parish Register

Hertfordshire County Record Office

D/P12/9/1 Baldock Assessments for Constables' rates
D/P17/12/1, Bengeo Churchwardens', Overseers', Constables' and Surveyors' Formal
    Accounts, 1646 to early eighteenth century
D/P26/10/1 Bushey Rate Book 1632–49
D/P71/5/2. Little Munden Constables Rate Assessments
D/P89/12/1, Sacombe Parish Officers Accounts 1613–1733
D/P110/5/1 Thundridge Constables Accounts 1622–75
Off. Acc. Cheshunt Constables Accounts, 1631–92

Huntingdonshire County Record Office

2661/5/1, Buckden Parish Book 1627–1714
2735/9/1, Great Staughton Parish Constables' Accounts

Kilkenny Corporation Archives: Baras Cille Cainnis

CR/J/41 Account of Mr Peter Shee 1645
CR/K/58 Order of Provincial Council of Leinster
CR/K/59 Petition of William Nash 1644
CR/K/62 Petition of John Quidihye

Lancashire County Record Office

DDF 5 Farington of Worden Papers A True and Perfect Book all Rates and Taxations concerning the County of Lancaster
DDHo 352 De Hoghton of Hoghton Papers Instructions from Lord Byron
DDKe 11 Kenyon Papers Accounts 1621–59
DDMa Boxes 9 and 17 Court Baron of Malhamdale
DD Pt 1 Petre of Dunkenhelm Papers Levies 1648
PR 2597/1 Latham Constable's Order for collection of money 1650
QDV II Returns in Blackburn Hundred of Papist Delinquents

Leicestershire County Record Office

DE625/60 Waltham on the Wolds Constables' Accounts 1608–1706
DE 670/14 Edmondthorpe Constables' Accounts
DE 720/30 Branston Constables' Accounts
DE 730 Barker Mss
DE1605/56 Stathern Constables' Accounts
DE1965/41 Belton Constables and Churchwardens' and overseers Accounts 1601–1739
DE 2461/135 Preston (Rutland) Receipts
PR/1/45/8 Will of Joseph Willmore Gt, of Ashby de la Zouch

Lichfield Cathedral Library

Ms Lich 24, A True and Perfect Account of the Expenses of Col. Richard Bagot

Lichfield Joint Record Office

D 30 LIII B, Contributions to the Garrison in the Close

Lincolnshire Archive Office

Addlethorpe and Ingoldmells Constables Accounts 1637–84

ANC XII/A/5 Commission for the maintenance of a regiment to Lord Willoughby
ANC XII/A/6 Commission to Lord Willoughby for a regiment of horse
ANC XII/14 Commission of Array
South Kyme Constables' Accounts 1639–85
ASW 2/59/15 Scotton Assessment 1654
Misc Don 310 Diary of John Archer 1645

National Archives, Ireland

M981/1/14 Esmonde papers relating to the siege of Duncannon
M1004/3/1/1–2 (Pike-Fortesque papers), Grant of land in Co. Louth
M1071/3/1–2 papers relating to Patrick Archer
M1095/1/2/2–5 (Dennis family papers) Papers relating to Kerricurrihy and Kinsale, Co. Cork
M1121/1/1–2 Bellew of Louth Papers
M 2450 Treasury Orders of the Lord Justices, 2 vols, 1642.
M4974 Caulfield Papers
M6935 (Ballyglunin papers), Parcels 1, 1 and 31, 64, 73, Papers relating to the estates of Martin Blake FitzAndrews
M7051 (10) Order for the Restoration of Daniel O'Donovan

National Library, Ireland

Ms 345 Plunkett Mss, A Treatise of Account of the War and Rebellion in Ireland
Ms 758 Copies of Documents Relating to Government, Finance and Administration, 1650–6
Mss 856–7 Transcrpts of Documents by J.T. Gilbert
Ms 11,959 Transcripts of Commonwealth Records Formerly in the Public Record Office of Ireland

National Library of Scotland

Ms 5070 Erskine Murray Correspondence 1604–50
Mss 6489–93 Meditations of Anne, Lady Halket

National Library of Wales

LL/MB/17 Results and orders of his Majesty's Commission of Array 1643–4 (Glamorganshire)
Mss 17088A Diary of Walter Powell of Llantilio, 1603–54
Mss 17091E Letters and Papers Addressed to Walter Powell
Plymouth Deeds:1368–9, Petition of people of Flint and John Byron's reply.

Norfolk County Record Office

PD100/258 Diss Constables' Accounts, 1635–49
Pd 144/70 Fersfield Constables' Accounts, 1606–1706
PD 219/126 East Harling Constables' Accounts, 1617–92
PD 254/112 Carelton Rode Constables' Accounts, 1621–72
PD 437/83 Hardwick Constables' Accounts 1589–1720

Northumberland Record Office

NRO 1966 Three letters from the Scottish Commissioners, 1641
ZSW 6
ZSW 7

Nottinghamshire Archive Office

DD39/5 Toton Rentals, 1626–45
DD4P 55/49 Billeting Charges in Devon
DD294/1 Petition of the Vale of Belvoir
PR1531 Coddington Constables' Accounts. 1641–1769
PR1710 Upton Constables' Accounts, 1640–66
PR2130 Edwinstowe Constables' Accounts
PR5767 Thorpe Constable' Accounts
PRMW 13/2 Accounts of William Dand

Orkney: Kirkwall Library

D005/1/6/2 Letter of Oliver Cromwell re: Nichols Aitkin
D029/7/3 Order to officers 1652

Oxfordshire County Record Office

Ms DD Par Wheatley b5, Overseers Accounts, 1638–61
Ms DD Par Spelsbury d5, Churchwardens' and Overseers' of the Poor Accounts, 1525–1707

Perth and Kinross Archive Office

Ms 100 Rossie Priory papers: pieces 1000, 1009, 1101–3,
Public Record Office (Chancery Lane)
SP 28/152 Exchequer Papers, Cambridge to Cumberland
SP28/153 Exchequer Papers, Derbyshire to Essex
SP28/161 Exchequer Papers, Lancashire to Lincolnshire
SP28/174 Exchequer Papers, Northumberland to Shropshire
SP 28/187 Exchequer Papers, Westmoreland to Worcestershire

SP28/189 Exchequer Papers, Yorkshire and Wales

SP28/ 190 Exchequer Papers, Associated Counties Misc.

SP28/194 Contributions for Distressed Protestants in Ireland 1642

SP28/251 County Committee Papers

SP63/263, 53 Excise and Other levies (Ireland)

SP64/264, 31 Account Book of the Court of Revenue of the Catholic Confederacy, 1644–7

Representative Church Body Library, Dublin

Vestry Book, St John's Dublin (transcripts)

Scottish Record Office

B9/12/8 Burntisland Council Minutes

Airlie Muniments

GD16/25/14 Commission to the Earl of Kinghorne and Committee of War, Forfar

GD16/36/12 Barony Papers of Cortachy 1649–50

GD16/50/37 Committee at Forfar letters to Lord Airlie

GD16/50/39 Court of Corsmiln orders re: soldiers

GD16/50/45 Levies on Oban

GD16/50. 60–5, Committee of war exactions 1651

GD16/50/82 nos 1–11, Paper of Lord Ogilvy collecting tax arrears in England

Sinclair of Mey Muniments

GD96/561, 1–17 Papers of the Committee of Caithness

Marr and Kellie Muniments

GD124/10/388 Levies on the Shires

GD124/17/9 Receipts and other financial documents

GD124/17/12 Rents and Debts, 1650

GD124/17/15 Losses of the Earl of Marr

GD124/17/208 Receipt of Lord Erskine 1650

Henderson of Fordell Muniments

GD172/1500 Receipt of John Fletcher

GD172/1509 Receipt of John Dickenson

GD176/389 Inverness Committee of War Discreet againt the Frazers

GD190/195 Levy of Transport money and Arms on Holme

GD196/331 Extract in Favour of John Drummond of Lenoch

BIBLIOGRAPHY

Hamilton Muniments

GD406/1/1237, 2156, Letters
Parliamentary Papers
PA7/6 Supplementary Papers regarding loan and taxt
PA8/2 Charges of Loan and Taxt
PA11/1 Committee of Estates
PA 11/3 Committee of Estates
PA 11/4 Committee of Estates, Register, March 1645–March 1646
PA11/5 Parliamentary Papers
PA14/11 Register of the Committee for Common Burdens
PA16/3/2/5 The Account of Sir Alexander Hepburne August 1643–March 1645

Somerset Record Office

PAM 835 Petition of th Inhabitants of Trull

Staffordshire Record Office

D3451/2/2 Pattingham Parish Book
D3539/2/1 Biddulph Parish Book
D3712/4/1 Mavysn Ridware Parish Book

Staunton Hall

Family Papers 34/16 Account book of Lt. Gervase Hewet

Suffolk Record Office (Bury St Edmunds)

FL522/11/22 Bardwell Accounts
HA525/1/1/1–5 Warrants to the constables of Chelworth

Surrey Record Office

EL12/1 Elstead Parish Records: Accounts

Trinity College, Dublin Library

1641 depositions:

Ms 809 Dublin
Ms 811 Wicklow
Ms 812 Carlow and Kilkenny
Ms 820 Waterford
Ms 821 Tipperary

Ms 828 Cork (part) and Kerry
Ms 829 Clare and Limerick
Ms 830 Roscommon and Galway
Ms 831 Mayo, Sligo and Leitrim
Ms 834 Louth and Monagham
Ms 839 Tyrone, Derry and Donegall
Ms 844 Orders of the Commissioners for Ireland
Ms 3395 Genealogy of the House of Reilly of East Bresney

West Sussex Record Office

Add Ms 15216 Receipt for levies for Henry Haukes at Midhurst 1648

William Salt Library, Stafford

Salt Mss 48/49 Minute Book of the County Committee at Stafford
Salt Mss 479–564 Civil War Letters

Wiltshire County Record Office

GD/1/40 Notes of Goods and Chattels taken by force from Salisbury Citizens
413/502 Rate for Maintenance of Fairfax's Army

Worcestershire County Record Office, St Helen's Worcester

850 Salwarpe BA 10/54/2 Bundles B, D, E and F

Yale University: Beineke Library

Osborn Mss b221 Elizabeth Jekyll Misc
Osborn Mss b233 Jane Cavendish Misc
Mss l.b. 701, 702, 705 Letters of Elizabeth More

York City Archives

B36 City of York House Book
F7 Quarter Sessions Minute Book 1638–62

Yorkshire

North Yorkshire County Record Office (readers here are expected to use the microfilm
    versons of documents – hence the Mic numbers)
PR/KMZ/ 2/2 (Mic 1204) Kikby Malzeard Churchwarden's Accounts, 1576–1655
PR/Mas/ 3/1/1 (Mic 995) Masham Parish Churchwarden's Accounts, 1542–1677

PR/OUL/2/1 (Mic1462/0341) Little Ousburn Churchwarden's Accounts
PR/TH/ 3/1/1 (Mic 1611) Thirsk Churwarden's Accounts, 1630–83
PR/TW/3/1 (Mic1161) Thornton Watless General Register, 1574–1722
Scarborough Borough Records, Mic 1320/906, /918, /1083, /1085, /1144, /1208

West Yorkshire Archive Service: Leeds District Archives

Calverley 82 Memorandum and Account Book of Overseers, 1633–1724
TN/PO/2b/I–IV Civil War Assessments and Disbursements for the Armies for Whorlton
Vyner Mss 5755, 5757, 5813 Various Warrants and Assessments for Fountains Abbey Estate

Printed primary sources

Anon (nd) 'Church Lawton Accounts', *The Cheshire Sheaf*, Series 3, vols. 56 and 57.
Ashburnham, J. (1830) *A Narrative of His Attendance on King Charles*, London: Payne & Foss.
Ashcroft, M. (ed.) (1991) *Scarborough Records, 1600–1640*, Northallerton: North Yorkshire Record Office.
—— (ed.) (1991) *Scarborough Records, 1641–60*, Northallerton: North Yorkshire Record Office.
Baillie, R. (1841–2) *The Letters and Journals of Robert Baillie 1637–1662*, 3 vols, ed. David Laing, Edinburgh: Bannantyne Club.
Baker., W.T. (ed.) (1900) *Records of the Borough of Nottingham 1625–1702*, Nottingham: Nottingham Corporation.
Baxter, R. *The Autobiography of Richard Baxter*, ed. N.H. Keeble, London: Dent, 1974, 1985.
Bennett, M. (ed.) (1995) *A Nottinghamshire Village in War and Peace: The Accounts of the Constables of Upton 1640–60*, Nottingham: Thoroton Society.
Bond, S.M. (ed.) (1974) *The Chamber Order Book of Worcester, 1602–1650*, Worcester: Worcestershire Historical Society.
Bruce, J. (ed.) (1967) *Calendar of State Papers: Domestic, Charles I*, Lichtenstein: Kraus Reprint.
Byrne, J (1997) *War and Peace: The Survival of the Talbots of Malahide 1641–1671*, Dublin: Irish Academic Press.
Calverley-Trevelyan, W. (ed.) (1856) *Letters from Roundhead Officers Written from Scotland and Chiefly Addressed to Captain Adam Baines July MDCL-June MDCLX*, Edinburgh: Bannantyne Club.
Caulfield, R. (ed.) (1878) *The Council Book of the Corporation of Youghal*, Guilford.
Charles, B.J. (ed.) (1967) *Calendar of the Records of the Borough of Haverfordwest, 1539–1660*, Cardiff: University of Wales Press.
Clanricarde, Earl of (1983) *Letter-Book of the The Earl of Clanricarde 1642–47*, ed. J. Lowe, Dublin: Irish Manuscripts Commission.
Clarendon, Earl of (1888, 1992) *The History of the Rebellion and Civil Wars in England*, ed. W.H. Mackay, Oxford: Clarendon Press.
Clifford, A. (1990) *The Diaries of Lady Anne Clifford*, ed. D.J.H. Clifford, Stroud: Alan Sutton.

Cockburn, J.S. (ed.) (1995) *Calendar of Assize Records: Kent Indictments Charles I*, London: HMSO.

—— (1989) *Calendar of Assize Records: Kent Indictments 1649–1659*, London: HMSO.

—— (1995) *Calendar of Assize Records: Kent Indictments Charles II, 1660–1675*, London: HMSO.

Cope, E.S. and Coates, W.H. (eds) (1977) *Proceedings of the Short Parliament of 1640*, London: Royal Historical Society.

Cranford, J. (printer) (n.d.) *The Souldiers Catechisme Composed for the Parliaments Army, 1644*, London: Cresset Press.

Dobie, J.S. (ed.) (1890, 1891) *Muniments of the Royal Burgh of Irvine*, 2 vols, Edinburgh: Ayrshire & Galloway Archaeological Association.

Erickson, J. (ed.) (1964) *The Journal of the House of Commons, 1547–1900*, New York: Readex Microprint.

Everitt-Green, M. (ed.) (1967a) *Calendar of the Committee for Compounding*, Lichtenstein: Kraus Reprint.

—— (1967b) *Calendar of the Committee for the Advance of Money*, Lichtenstein: Kraus reprint.

Firth. C.H. (ed.) (1899) 'Journal of Prince Rupert's Marches', *English Historical Review* 13.

Firth, C.H. and Rait, R.S. (eds) (1911) *Acts and Ordinances of the Interregnum*, London: HMSO.

Fitzpatrick, T. (ed.) (1903) *The Bloody Bridge and Other Papers Relating to the Insurrection of 1641*, Dublin: Sealy, Bryers & Walker.

Fleming, D.H. (1923) 'Scotland's Supplication and Complaint against the Book of Common Prayer … ', *Proceedings of the Society of Antiquaries of Scotland*, vol. 60.

Furgol, E.M. (1990) *A Regimental History of the Covenanting Armies*, Edinburgh: John Donald.

Fyffe, J.G. (ed.) (1928) *Scottish Diaries and Memoirs, 1550–1776*, Stirling: Eneas Mackay.

Gardiner, S.R. (ed.) (1889, 1979) *The Constitutional Documents of the Puritan Revolution*, Oxford: Clarendon Press.

Gibson, J.S.W. and Brinkworth, E.R.C. (eds) (1977) *Banbury Corporation Records, Tudor and Stuart*, Banbury: Banbury Historical Society.

Gilbert, J.T. (ed) (1879–80) *A Contemporary History of Affairs in Ireland from 1641–1652*, 3 vols, Dublin: Irish Archaeological and Celtic Society.

Graham, E., Hinds, H., Hobby, E. and Wilcox, H. (eds) (1989) *Her Own Life: Autobiographical Writings by Seventeenth-Century English Women*, London: Routledge.

Hampshire, G. (ed.) (1983) *The Bodelian Library Account Book 1613–1646*, Oxford: Oxford Bibliographical Society.

Hanson, T.W. (ed.) (1916) 'Three Civil War Notes', *Halifax Antiquarian Transactions*.

Hassall, T. (1989) *The Parish Register and Tithing Book of Thomas Hassall of Armswell*, ed. S.G. Doree, Cambridge: Hertfordshire Record Society.

Historical Manuscripts Commission (1901) *First Report*, London: HMSO.

—— (1874) *Second Report*, London: HMSO.

—— (1885) *Tenth Report*, London: HMSO.

—— (1891) *Thirteenth Report*, London: HMSO.

—— (1895) *Fourteenth Report*, London: HMSO.

—— (1899) *Report on the Manuscripts of the Marquis of Ormond*, London: HMSO.

—— (1902) *Report on the Manuscripts of the Marquis of Ormonde, New Series*, London: HMSO.

—— (1914) *Report on Manuscripts in Various Collections*, vol. 7, London: HMSO.

—— (1916) *Report on the Records of the Borough of Exeter*, London: HMSO.

—— (1930) *Report on the Papers of Reginald Rawdon Hastings*, London: HMSO.

Hobson, M.G. and Salter, H.E. (eds) (1933) *Oxford Council Acts, 1626–1665*, Oxford: Oxford University Press.

Hogan, J. (ed.) (1930) *Letters and Papers Relating to the Irish Rebellion*, Dublin: Stationery Office.

Hopper, A. (1997) *"The Readiness of the People": The Formation and Emergence of the Army of the Fairfaxes, 1642–46*, York: Borthwick Institute

Howells, B.E. (ed.) (1967) *A Calendar of Letters Relating to North Wales, 1533–c.1700*, Cardiff: University of Wales Press.

Hutchinson, L. (1806) *Memoirs of the Life of Colonel Hutchinson*, London: Longman, Orme, Rees & Brown.

Jaffray, A. (1856) *Diary of Alexandar Jaffray, Provost of Aberdeen, One of the Scottish Commissioners to Charles II and a Member of Cromwell's Parliament*, ed. John Barclay, 3rd edn, Aberdeen: George & Robert King.

Jansson, M. (ed.) (1984) *Two Diaries of the Long Parliament*, Stroud: Alan Sutton.

Johnson, D.A. and Vaisey, D.G. (eds) (1964) *Staffordshire and the Great Rebellion*, Stafford: Staffordshire County Council.

Johnston of Wariston, A. (1911, 1919, 1940) *Diary of Sir Archibald Johnston of Wariston*, 3 vols, ed. G.H. Paul, D.H. Fleming and J.D. Ogilvie, Edinburgh: Scottish History Society.

Kearns, K.A. (1996) *Dublin Pub Life: An Oral History*, Dublin: Gill & Macmillan.

Kenyon, J.P. (ed) (1966) *The Stuart Constitution*, Cambridge: Cambridge University Press; 2nd edn 1986.

Lister, J. (1860) *The Autobiography of Joseph Lister of Bradford, 1627–1709*, Bradford: Abraham Holroyd.

Lockyer, R. (1959) *The Trial of Charles I*, London: Folio Society.

Luke, Sir Samuel (1950–3) *Journal of Sir Samuel Luke*, 3 vols, ed. I.G. Phillips, Oxford: Oxfordshire Record Society.

MacTavish, D.C. (ed.) (1943, 1944) *Minutes of the Synod of Argyll*, 2 vols, Edinburgh: Edinburgh University Press.

MacTavish, D. (ed.) (1944) *Minutes of the Synod of Argyll 1652–1661*, Scottish History Society, vol. 38, Edinburgh: Edinburgh University Press

Mahaffy, R.P. (ed.) (1901) *Calendar of State Papers Relating to Ireland in the Reign of Charles I, 1633–47*, London: HMSO.

—— (1903) *Calendar of State Papers Relating to Ireland in the Reign of Charles I, 1647–60*, London: HMSO.

—— (1926) *Calendar of Wynn of Gwydir Papers, 1515–1690*, Aberystwyth: National Library of Wales.

Marwick, J.D. (ed.) (1881) *Extracts of the Records of the Burgh of Glasgow, 1630–1662*, Glasgow: Scottish Burgh Record Society.

Morley, H. (ed.) (1891) *Character Writings of the Seventeenth Century*, London: Routledge.

Newcastle, Margaret Cavendish, Duchess of (n.d.) *Memoirs of William Cavendish Duke of Newcastle and Margaret His Wife*, ed. C.H. Firth, London: Routledge.

Nicholson, J. (ed.) (1855) *Minutebook kept by the War Committee of the Covenanters in the Stewartry of Kircudbright 1640–1*, Kirkudbright: Nicholson.

Parry, E.A. (n.d.) *Letters from Dorothy to Sir William Temple*, London: Dent & Son.

Parsloe, G. (ed.) (1949) *The Minute Book of Bedford Corporation 1647–1664*, Streatley: Bedfordshire Historical Society.

Penney (ed.) (1924) *The Journal of George Fox*, London: Dent.

Pennington, D. and Roots, I. (eds.) (1957) *The Committee at Stafford*, Stafford: Staffordshire Historical Collections.

Prall, S. (ed.) (1968) *The Puritan Revolution, A Documentary History*, London: Routledge & Kegan Paul.

Ratcliff, I.S.O. and Johnson, H.C. (eds) (1936) *Warwickshire County Records*, Warwick: Warwickshire County Council.

Razzell, E. and Razzell P. (eds) (1996) *The English Civil War: A Contemporary Account*, 5 vols, London: Caliban.

Rushworth, J. (1657–1701) *Historical Collections*, 7 vols, London.

Simington, R.C. (ed.) (1938) *The Civil Survey: County of Limerick*, vol. 4, Dublin: Stationery Office.

—— (1945) *The Civil Survey: County of Dublin*, vol. 7, Dublin: Stationery Office.

—— (1952) *The Civil Survey: County of Kildare*, vol. 8, Dublin: Stationery Office.

—— (1953) *The Civil Survey: County of Wexford*, vol. 9, Dublin: Stationery Office.

Stevenson, D. (1982) *The Government of Scotland under the Covenanters, 1637–1651*, Edinburgh: Scottish History Society.

Stocks, H.E. (ed.) (1923) *Records of the Borough of Leicester, 1603–89*, Cambridge: Cambridge University Press.

Storey, M. (ed.) (1994) *Two East Anglian Diaries, 1641–1729, Isaac Archer and William Coe*, Woodbridge: Boydell Press.

Stuart, J. (ed.) (1846) *Minutes of the Committee for the Loan Monies and Taxations of the Shire of Aberdeen*, Spalding Club Miscellany, vol. 3.

—— (ed.) (1871–2) *Extracts from the Council Register of the Burgh of Aberdeen*, 2 vols, Edinburgh: Scottish Burgh Record Society.

Symonds, R. (1859) *Diary of the Marches of the Royal Army*, ed. C.E. Long, London: Camden Society.

Taylor, L.B. (ed.) (1950) *Aberdeen Council Letters* , vol. 2, Oxford: Oxford University Press.

Terry, C.S. (ed.) (1917) *Papers Relating to the Army of the Solemn League and Covenant, 1643–7*, 2 vols, Edinburgh: Edinburgh University Press.

Verney, F.P. (ed.) (1970) *Memoirs of the Verney Family during the Civil War*, London: Tabard Press.

Warner G.F. and others (eds) (1893) *Miscellany of the Scottish History Society*, vol. 1, Edinburgh: Scottish History Society.

Whitlock, B. (1853) *Memorials of English Affairs from the Beginning of the Reign of Charles I to the Restoration of Charles II*, Oxford: Oxford University Press.

Wilson, J. (ed.) (1983) *Buckinghamshire Contributions for Ireland 1642 and Richard Greville's Military Accounts 1642–45*, Buckingham: Buckinghamshire Record Society.

Wood, H. (ed.) (1919) *A Guide to the Records Deposited in the Public Record Office of Ireland*, Dublin: HMSO.

Wood, M. (1936, 1938) *Extracts from the Records of the Burgh of Edinburgh*, 2 vols, Edinburgh: Oliver & Boyd.

Secondary sources

Books

Adair, J. (1973) *Cheriton, 1644, The Campaign and the Battle*, Roundwood Press, Kineton.

—— (1983) *By the Sword Divided*, London: Century Press.

Anderson, M.S. (1988) *War and Society in Europe of the Old Regime, 1618-1789*, Leicester: Leicester University Press.

Ashley, M., (1992) *The Battle of Naseby and the fall of King Charles I*, Stroud: Alan Sutton.

Ashton, R. (1978) *The English Civil War Conservatism and Revolution*, London: Weidenfeld & Nicolson.

—— (1994) *Counter Revolution: The Second Civil War and its Origins*, New Haven, CT: Yale University Press.

Atkin, M. and Laughton, M. (1992) *Gloucester and the Civil War*, Stroud: Alan Sutton.

Aylmer, G.E. (1986) *Rebellion or Revolution: England from Civil War to Restoration*, Oxford: Oxford University Press.

—— (1972) *The Interregnum: The Quest for a Settlement*, London: Macmillan, London.

—— (1975) *The Levellers in the English Revolution*, London: Thames & Hudson.

Barclay, C. and Besly, E. (1994) *A Little Barrel of Ducatoons: The Civil War Coinage of Yorkshire*, York: Yorkshire Museum

Baskerville, S. (1993) *Not Peace But a Sword: The Political Theory of the English Revolution*, London: Routledge.

Bennett, M. (1984) *Lord Loughborough, Ashby de la Zouch and the English Civil War*, Ashby de la Zouch: Ashby Museum.

—— (1990) *Travellers' Guide to the Battlefields of the English Civil War*, Exeter: Webb & Bower.

—— (1995) *The English Civil War*, London: Longman.

—— (1997) *The Civil Wars of Britain and Ireland, 1638–1653*, Oxford: Blackwell.

Berresford-Ellis, P. (1975) *Hell or Connaught! the Cromwellian Colonisation of Ireland, 1652–1660*, London: Hamish Hamilton; Belfast: Blackstaff Press, 1991.

Birkenhead, Earl of (1938) *Strafford*, London: Hutchinson.

Blackmore, D. (1990) *Arms and Armour of the English Civil War*, London: Royal Armouries.

Blackwood, B.G. (1978) *The Lancashire Gentry and the Great Rebellion 1640-1660*, Manchester: Chetham Society.

Brown, K.M. (1992) *Kingdom or Province: Scotland and the Regal Union*, London: Macmillan.

Brunton, D. and Pennington, D.H. (1954) *Members of the Long Parliament*, Cambridge, MA: Harvard University Press.

Byrne, J. (1997) *War and Peace: The Survival of the Talbots of Malahide*, Ballsbridge, Irish Academic Press.

Canny, N. (1987) *From Reformation to Restoration, Ireland 1534–1660*, Dublin: Helicon.

Capp, B. (1989) *Cromwell's Navy*, Oxford: Clarendon Press.

—— (1994) *The World of John Taylor the Water Poet*, Oxford, Clarendon Press.

Carlton, C. (1992) *Going to the Wars: The Experience of the British Civil Wars, 1638–1651*, London: Routledge.

Casaway, J.I. (1984) *Owne Roe O'Neill and the Struggle for Catholic Ireland*, Philadelphia: University of Pennsylvania Press.

Clarke, H.B. (1995) *Irish Cities*, Cork: Mercier.

Cliffe, J.T. (1984) *The Puritan Gentry*, London: Routledge & Kegan Paul.

—— (1969) *The Yorkshire Gentry*, London: Athlone Press.

Coate, M. (1963) *Cornwall in the Great Civil War*, Truro: Bradford Barton (reprint of 1933 edition).

Coleby, A.M. (1987) *Central Government and the Localities*, Cambridge: Cambridge University Press.

Collinson, P. (1988) *The Birthpangs of Protestant England*, London: Macmillan.

Cope, E. (1987) *Politics without Parliaments*, London: Allan & Unwin.

Corish, P. (1981) *The Catholic Community in the Seventeenth and Eighteenth Century*, Dublin: Helicon.

Crawford, P. (1979) *Denzil, First Lord Holles*, London: Royal Historical Society.

Cronne, H.A, Moody, T.W. and Quinn, D.B. (eds) (1949) *Essays in British and Irish History in Honour of James Eadie Todd*, London: Frederick Muller.

Cust, R. and Hughes, A. (eds) (1989) *Conflict in Early Stuart England*, London: Longman.

Davis, J.C. (1986) *Fear, Myth and History: The Ranters and the Historians*, Cambridge: Cambridge University Press.

Donald, P. (1990) *An Uncouncelled King; Charles I and the Scottish Troubles, 1637–41*, Cambridge: Cambridge University Press.

Donaldson, G. (1990) *Scotland: James V–James VII*, Edinburgh: Mercat Press (originally published 1965).

Dow, F.D. (1979) *Cromwellian Scotland*, Edinburgh: John Donald.

Duffin, A. (1996) *Faction and faith, Politics and Religion of the Cornish Gentry Before the Civil War*, Exeter: Exeter University Press.

Durston, C. (1989) *The Family in the English Revolution*, Oxford: Blackwell.

Eales, J. (1990) *Puritans and Roundheads, the Harleys of Bampton Bryan and the Outbreak of the English Civil War*, Cambridge: Cambridge University Press.

Edwards, A.C. (ed.) (1952) *English History from Essex Sources, 1550–1750*, Chelmsford: Essex Record Office.

Edwards, R.D. (1973 and 1991) *An Atlas of Irish History*, London: Routledge.

Eley, G. and Hunt, W. (eds) (1988) *Reviving the English Revolution: Reflections and Elaborations on the Work of Christopher Hill*, London: Verso.

Ellis, S.G. and Barber, S. (eds) (1995) *Conquest and Union: Fashioning a British State, 1485–1725*, London: Longman.

Erickson, A.-L. (1993) *Women and Property in Early Modern England*, London: Routledge.

Evans, R.J. (1997) *In Defence of History*, London: Granta

Everritt, A. (1969) *The Local Community and the Great Rebellion*, London: Historical Association.

—— (1973) *The Community of Kent and the Great Rebellion 1640–1660*, Leicester: Leicester University Press.

Ferguson, N. (ed.) (1997) *Virtual History: Alternatives and Counterfactuals*, London: Picador

Fieldhouse, J. (1972) *Bradford*, London: Longman.

Firth, C.H. (1992) *Cromwell's Army*, London: Greenhill (first published 1902).

Fissel, M. (1994) *The Bishops' Wars: Charles I's Campaigns against Scotland*, Cambridge: Cambridge University Press.

Fitzpatrick, P. (1988) *Seventeenth Century Ireland: The War of Religions*, Dublin: Gill & Macmillan.

Fletcher, A. (1981) *The Outbreak of the English Civil War*, London: Arnold.

Friedman, J. (1993) *Miracles and the Pulp Press during the English Revolution*, London: University College London press.

Gardiner, S.R. (1988) *History of the Commonwealth and Protectorate 1649–1656*, Adlep: Windrush Press (originally published 1903; 1988).

—— (1991) *History of the Great Civil War*, 4 Vols, Adelstrop: Windrush Press (originally published 1893).

Garner, A.A. (1972) *Boston and the Great Civil War*, Boston: Richard Key.

Gentles, I. (1992) *The New Model Army in England, Ireland and Scotland, 1645-1653*, Oxford: Blackwell.

Gentles, I., Morrill, J. and Worden, B. (1998) *Soldiers, Writers and Statesmen of the English Revolution*, Cambridge: Cambridge University Press.

Gibson, A.J.S. and Smout, T.C. (eds) (1995) *Prices, Food and Wages in Scotland 1550–1780*, Cambridge: Cambridge University Press.

Gillespie, R. (1985) *Colonial Ulster: The Settlement of East Ulster, 1600–1641*, Cork: Cork University Press.

—— (1991) *The Transformation of the Irish Economy, 1550–1700*, Dublin: Economic and Social History Society of Ireland.

—— (1995) *Cavan: Essays on the History of an Irish County*, Blackrock: Irish Academic Press.

Gillett, E. and MacMahon, K.A. (1980) *A History of Hull*, Oxford: Oxford University Press.

Gilligan, H.A. (1989) *The Port of Dublin*, Dublin: Gill & Macmillan.

Gregg, P. (1961) *Freeborn John: A Biography of John Lilburne*, London: Harrap.

Grimble, I. (1993) *Chief of Mackay*, Edinburgh: Saltire Society (originally published 1963).

Guttery, D.R. (1950) *The Great Civil War in Midland Parishes: The People Pay*, Birmingham: Cornish Bros.

Hainsworth, R. (1997) *The Swordsmen in Power: War and Politics under the English Revolution*, Stroud: Sutton.

Handcock, W.D. (1991) *The History and Antiquities of Tallaght*, Dublin: Anna Livia Press (originally published 1879).

Hanson, T.W. (1968) *The Story of Old Halifax*, East Ardesley: S.R. Publishing (originally published 1920).

Harvey, K. (1998) *The Bellews of Mount Bellew: A Catholic Gentry Family in Eighteenth Century Ireland*, Dublin: Four Courts Press.

Hibbard, C. (1983) *Charles I and the Popish Plot*, Chapel Hill: University of North Carolina.

Hill, C. (1975) *The World turned Upside Down*, Harmondsworth: Penguin (originally published 1972).

—— (1979a) *God's Englishman, Oliver Cromwell and the English Revolution*, Harmondsworth: Penguin (originally published 1970).

—— (1979b) *The English Revolution*, London: Lawrence & Wishart (originally published 1940).

—— (1986) *Puritanism and Revolution*, Harmondsworth: Perigrine.

—— (1993) *The English Bible and the Seventeenth Century Revolution*, London: Allen Lane.

Hobby, E. (1988) *Virtue of Necessity, English Women's Writing 1649–88*, London: Virago.

Hobsbawm, E. (1997) *On History*, London: Century.

Holmes, C. (1974) *The Eastern Association in the English Civil War*, Cambridge University Press.

—— (1980) *Seventeenth Century Lincolnshire*, Lincoln: History of Lincoln Committee

Hossack, B.H. (1900) *Kirkwall in the Orkneys*, Kirkwall: William Peace & Son.

Houston, R.A. and Whyte, I.D. (eds) (1989) *Scottish Society, 1500–1800*, Cambridge: Cambridge University Press, Cambridge.

Hughes, A. (1987) *Politics, Society and Civil War in Warwickshire*, Cambridge: Cambridge University Press.

—— (1992) *The Causes of the English Civil War*, London: Macmillan.

Hutton, R.E. (1990) *The British Republic*, London: Macmillan.

—— (1982) *The Royalist War Effort*, London: Longman.

Jenkins, G. (1991) *Re-Thinking History*, London: Routledge.

—— (1992) *Protestant Dissenters in Wales*, Cardiff: University of Wales Press.

—— (1993) *The Foundations of Modern Wales*, Oxford: Oxford University Press.

Jones, C., Newitt, M., and Roberts, S. (1986) *Politics and People in Revolutionary England: Essays in Honour of Ivan Roots*, Oxford: Blackwell.

Jordan, D.E. (1994) *Land and Popular Politics in Ireland: County Mayo from the Plantation to the Land War*, Cambridge, Cambridge University Press.

Kearney, H.F. (1989) *Stafford in Ireland: A Study of Absolutism* Cambridge: Cambridge University Press (originally published 1959).

Kelsey, S. (1997) *Inventing a Republic: The Political Culture of the English Commonwealth*, Manchester: Manchester University Press.

Kenyon, J.P. (1988) *The Civil Wars of England*, London: Weidenfeld & Nicolson.

Kenyon, T. (1989) *Utopian Communism and Political Thought in Early Modern England*, London: Pinter.

Ketton-Cremer, R.W. (1970) *Norfolk in the Civil War*, Hamden, CN: Archon.

Lee, M. (1985) *The Road to Revolution, Scotland under Charles I 1625–1637*, Chicago, IL: University of Illinois Press.

Lindley. K. (1982) *Fenland Riots and the English Revolution*, London: Heinemann.

Liu, T. (1986) *Puritan London, A Study of Religion and Society in the City Parishes*, Newark, DE: University of Delaware Press.

Lloyd, H.A. (1968) *Gentry of South West Wales, 1540–1640*, Cardiff: University of Wales Press.

Lockyer, R. (1989) *The Early Stuarts*, London: Longman.

MacInnes, A.I. (1991) *Charles I and the Making of the Covenanting Movement, 1625–1641*, Edinburgh: John Donald.

Mac Cuarta, B. (ed.) (1993) *Ulster 1641, Aspects of the Rising*, Belfast: Institute of Irish Studies.

MacCurtain, M. and O'Dowd, M. (ed.) (1991) *Women in Early Modern*, Edinburgh: Edinburgh University Press.

Malcolm, J. (1983) *Caesar's Due: Loyalty and King Charles, 1642- 1646*, London: Royal Historical Society.

Manning, B. (ed.) (1973) *Politics, Religion and The English Civil War*, London: Edward Arnold.

—— (1976) *The English People and the English, 1640–1649*, London: Heineman.

—— (1992) *1649: The Crisis of the English Revolution*, London: Bookmarks.

Manning, R.B (1988) *Village Protest: Social Protest and Popular Disturbances in England, 1509–1640*, Oxford: Oxford University Press.

McGregor, J.F. and Reay, B. (eds) (1984) *Radical Religion in the English Revolution*, Oxford: Oxford University Press.

McKerral, A. (1948) *Kintyre in the Seventeenth Century*, Edinburgh: Oliver & Boyd.

Mitchison, R. (1990) *Lordship to Patronage Scotland, 1603–1745*, Edinburgh: Edinburgh University Press.

Moody, T.W., Martin, F.X. and Byrne, F.J. (eds) (1991) *A New History of Ireland*, Vol. 3, Oxford: Oxford University Press.

Moran, G. and Gillespie, R. (ed.) (1996) *Galway, History and Society*, Dublin: Geography Publications.

Morrill, J. (1974) *Cheshire, 1630–1660*, Oxford: Oxford University Press.

—— (1976) *The Revolt of the Provinces*, London: Longman; repr. 1980.

—— (1982) *Reactions to the English Civil War*, London: Macmillan.

—— (ed.) (1990) *Oliver Cromwell and the English Revolution*, London: Longmand.

—— (1991) *The Impact of the English Civil War*, London: Collins & Brown.

—— (1992) *Revolution and Restoration: England in the 1650s*, London: Collins & Brown.

—— (1993) *The Nature of the English Revolution*, London: Longman.

—— (1999) *The Revolt in the Provinces: The People of England and the Tragedies of War, 1630–1648*, London: Longman.

Newman, P.R. (1981) *The Battle of Marston Moor*, Chichester: Anthony Bird.

—— (1981) *Royalist Officers in England and Wales, 1642–60*, New York: Garland Press.

Nichols, J. (1804) *The History and Antiquities of the County of Leicester*, 4 vols, Leicester.

Nolan, W. and McGrath, T.G. (eds) (1985) *Tipperary: History and Society*, Dublin: Geography Publications.

Nolan, W. and Power, T.P. (eds) (1992) *Waterford: History and Society*, Dublin: Geography Publications.

Nolan, W. and Whelan, K. (eds) (1990) *Kilkenny: History and Society*, Dublin: Geography Publications.

Nolan, W., Roynayne, L. and Dunleavt, M. (eds) (1995) *Donegal: History and Society*, Dublin: Geography Publications.

O'Dell, A.C. and Mackintosh, J. (eds) (1963) *The North-East of Scotland*, Aberdeen: British Association.

O'Dell, A.C. and Walton, K. (1962) *The Highlands and Islands of Scotland*, Edinburgh: Thomas Nelson & Sons.

O'Dowd, M. (1991) *Power Politics and Land, Early Modern Sligo 1568–1688*, Belfast: Institute of Irish Studies.

O'Flanaghan, P. and Buttimer, C.G. (eds) (1993) *Cork: History and Society*, Dublin: Geography Publications.

Ohlmeyer, J. (1993) *Civil War and Restoration in the Three Stuart Kingdoms. The Career of Randal MacDonnell, Marquis of Antrim, 1609–1683*, Cambridge: Cambridge University Press.

—— (ed.) (1995) *Ireland, From Independence to Occupation, 1641–60*, Cambridge: Cambridge University Press.

Peace, W. (1905) *Peace's Orkney and Shetland Almanac* Kirkwall.

Percival-Maxwell, M. (1994) *The Outbreak of the Irish Rebellion of 1641*, Dublin: Gill & Macmillan.

Phillips, M. (1996) *All Must Have Prizes* , London: Little Brown.

Porter, S. (1994) *Destruction in the English Civil Wars*, Stroud: Alan Sutton.

—— (ed.) (1996) *London and the Civil War*, London: Macmillan.

Priestley, J. (1883) *Some Memoirs Touching the Family of the Priestleys Written, at the Request of a Friend by Jonathan Priestley*, Surtees Society, vol. 77.

Proudfoot, L. (ed.) (1997) *Down: History and Society*, Dublin: Geography Publications.

Quintrell, B. (1993) *Charles I*, London: Longman.

Rees, W. (1951) *An Historical Atlas of Wales From Early to Modern Times*, London: Faber & Faber.

Reeve, J. (1989) *Charles I and the Road to Personal Rule*, Cambridge: Cambridge University Press.

Richardson, R.C. (1988) *The Debate on the English Revolution Revisited*, London: Routledge.

—— (ed.) (1992) *Town and Countryside in the English Revolution*, Manchester: Manchester University Press.

Roberts, S.K. (1985) *Recovery and Restoration in and English County Devon Local Administration*, Exeter: University of Exeter.

Russell, C. (ed.) (1973) *The Origins of the English Civil War*, London: Methuen; repr. 1984.

—— (1990) *The Causes of the English Civil War*, Oxford: Oxford University Press.

—— (1991) *The Fall of the British Monarchies, 1637–42*, Oxford: Oxford University Press.

Sanderson, J. (1989) *But the Peoples' Creatures The Philosophical Basis of the English Civil War*, Manchester: Manchester University Press.

Seaver, P. (1985) *Wallington's World; A Puritan Artisan in Seventeenth Century London*, Stanford: Stanford University Press.

Sharpe, K. (1992) *The Personal Rule of Charles II*, New Haven, CT: Yale University Press.

Shaw, H. (1968) *The Levellers*, London: Longman.

—— (1976) *History and Antiquities of Staffordshire*, Ilkley (1st published London, 1798–1803).

Sherwood, R.E. (1992) *The Civil War in the Midlands*, Stroud: Alan Sutton.

Sims, A. and Andrews, J.H. (eds) (1994) *Irish Country Towns*, Cork: Mercier.

—— (1995) *More Irish Country Towns*, Cork: Mercier.

Sommerville, J.P. (1986) *Politics and Ideology in England, 1603–40*, London: Longman.

Spence, R.T. (1992) *Skipton Castle in the Great Civil War*, Skipton: Skipton Castle.

Stephens, N. and Glasscock, R.E. (eds) (1970) *Irish Geographical Studies*, Belfast: Queens University.

Stevenson, D. (1973) *The Scottish Revolution, 1637–44*, Newton Abbot: David & Charles.

—— (1977) *Revolution and Counter-Revolution in Scotland, 1644–1651*, London: Royal Historical Society.

—— (1988) *The Covenanters*, Edinburgh: Saltire Society.

—— (1990) *Kings College, Aberdeen 1560–1641: From Protestant Reformation to Covenanting Revolution*, Aberdeen: University of Aberdeen.

—— (1994) *Highland Warrior, Alasdair MacColla and the Civil Wars*, Edinburgh: Saltire Society (originally published 1980).

—— (1996) *King or Covenant? Voices from the Civil War*, East Linton: Tuckwell Press.

Stevenson, J. (1990) *Two Centuries of Life in Down, 1600–1800*, Dundonald: The Whiterow Press.

Stone, B. (1992) *Derbyshire in the Civil War*, Cromford: Scarthin Books.

Stone, L. (1965) *The Crisis of the Aritocracy*, Oxford: Clarendon Press.

—— (1977) *The Causes of the English Revolution*, London: Routledge & Kegan Paul.

Strawhorn, J. (1985) *The History of Irvine, Royal Burgh and New Town*, Edinburgh: John Donald.

Tennant, P. (1992) *Edgehill and Beyond: The People's War in the South Midlands, 1641–45*, Stroud: Alan Sutton.

—— (1996) *The Civil War in Stratford-upon-Avon, Conflict and Community in South Warwickshire, 1642–1646*, Stroud: Alan Sutton.

Tillot, P.M. (ed.) (1961) *The City of York*, London: Oxford University Press.

Toynebee, M. (1973) *Strangers in Oxford: A Sidelight on the Civil War*, Chichester: Phillimore.

Trease, G. (1979) *Portrait of a Cavalier, William Cavendish, First Duke of Newcastle*, London: Macmillan.

Underdown, D. (1973) *Somerset in the Civil War and Interregnum*, Newton Abbot: David & Charles.

—— (1985) *Revel, Riot and Rebellion: Popular Politics and Culture in England, 1603–60*, Oxford: Clarendon Press.

—— (1992) *Fire from Heaven: Life in an English Town in the Seventeenth Century*, London: Harper Collins.

—— (1996) *A Freeborn People: Politics and the Nation in Seventeenth Century England*, Oxford: Oxford University Press.

Victoria County Histories (1904, 1908) *History of the County of Bedford*, vols 1 and 2, London: Institute of Historical Research.

—— (1968) *A History of Yorkshire: North Riding*, vol. 2, London: Institute of Historical Research (originally published 1923).

—— (1971) *Hertfordshire*, vols 1–4, London: Institute of Historical Research, (originally published 1902, 1908, 1912, 1914).

—— (1971) *A History of Worcestershire*, vol. 4., London: Institute of Historical Research (originally published 1924).

—— (1974) *A History of Huntingdonshire*, vol. 2, London: Institute of Historical Research (originally published 1932).

—— (1974) *A History of Yorkshire*, vol. 3., London: Institute of Historical Research (originally published 1913).

—— (1974, 1976, 1979) *A History of Yorkshire: East Riding*, vols 2–4, London: Institute of Historical Research.

—— (1978, 1982) *A History of Cambridgeshire and the Isle of Ely*, vols 6 and 8, London: Institute of Historical Research.

Warner, T. (1992) *Newark: Civil War and Siegeworks*, Nottingham: Nottinghamshire County Council.

Wedgwood, C.V. (1961) *Thomas Wentworth: First Earl of Strafford A Revaluation*, London: Jonathon Cape.

—— (1983a) *The King's Peace*, Harmondsworth: Penguin (originally published 1955).

—— (1983b) *The King's War*, Harmondsworth: Penguin (originally published 1958).

—— (1983c) *The Trial of Charles I*, Harmondsworth: Penguin (originally published 1964).

Wenham, P. (1970) *The Great and Close Siege of York*, Kineton: Roundway Press; republished as *The Siege of York*, York: Jonson, 1994.

Whelan, K. (ed.) (1987) *Wexford: History and Society*, Dublin: Geography Publications.

Whyte, I. (1979) *Agriculture and Society in Seventeenth Century Scotland*, Edinburgh: John Donald.

—— (1995) *Scotland Before the Industrial Revolution*, London: Longman.

Williams, G. (1993) *Renewal and Reformation: Wales, c.1415–1642*, Oxford: Oxford University Press.

Withers, C.J. (1988) *Gaelic Scotland*, London: Routledge.

Wolffe, M. (1997) *Gentry Leaders in Peace and War: The Gentry Governors of Devon in the Early Civil War*, Exeter: University of Exeter Press.

Wood, A.C. (1971) *Nottinghamshire in Civil War*, Wakefield: S.R. Reprint (originally published 1937).

Woolrych, A. (1966) *Battles of the English Civil War*, London: Pan.

Wormald, J. (1981) *Court, Kirk and Community*, London: Edward Arnold.

—— (ed.) (1991) *Scotland Revisited*, London: Collins & Brown.

Wroughton, J. (1992) *A Community at War: The Civil War in Bath and North Somerset*, Bath: Lansdown Press.

Young, J.R. (ed.) (1996) *The Scottish Parliament 1639–1661*, Edinburgh: John Donald.

—— (ed.) (1997) *Celtic Dimensions of the British Civil Wars*, Edinburgh: John Donald.

Young, P. (ed.) (1964) *Newark upon Trent, the Civil War Siegeworks*, London: HMSO.

—— (1967) *Edgehill: 1642 The Campaign and the Battle*, Kineton: Roundway Press.

—— (1970) *Marston Moor 1644: The Campaign and the Battle*, Kineton: Roundway Press.

—— (1985) *Naseby 1645: The Campaign and the Battle*, London: Century.

Journal Articles

Adamson, J.S.A. (1990) 'The Baronial Context of the English Civil War', *Transactions of the the Royal Historical Society*.

Barber, F. (ed.) (1879) 'On the West Riding Sessions Rolls continued', *Yorkshire Archaeological and Topographical Journal* 5, 20.

Barnard, T.C. (1990) 'Crises of Identity Among Irish Protestants, 1641–85', *Past and Present* 127, May.

Baskerville, S., (1993) 'Blood Guilt in the English Revolution' *The Seventeenth Century* 7, 2, Autumn.

Beats, L. (1978) 'The East Midland Association, 1642–44' *Midland History* 4.

Bennett., M. (1986) 'Contribution and Assessment: Financial Exactions in the First Civil War 1642–46', *War and Society* 5, 1.

—— (1988) 'Dampnified Villagers: Taxation in Wales During the First Civil War', *The Welsh History Review* 19, 1.

—— (1992) 'Between Scylla and Charybdis: The Creation of Rival Administrations at the Beginning of the English Civil War', *The Local Historian* 22, 4.

—— (1997) ' "My Plundered Townes, My Houses Devastation": The Civil War and North Midlands Life, 1642–1646', *Midland History* 22.

—— (1997) *The Civil Wars in Britain and Ireland 1638–1651*, Oxford: Blackwell.

Braddick, M. (1991) 'Popular Politics and Public Policy: The Excise Riot at Smithfield in February 1647 and its Aftermath', *Historical Journal* 34, 3.

Bradley, I. (1989) 'Gerrard Winstanley, England's Pioneer Green', *History Today* 39.

Canny, N. (1973) 'The Ideology of English Colonisation from Ireland to America', *William and Mary Quarterly* 30.

—— (1986) 'Protestants, Planters and Apartheid', *Irish Historical Studies* 25, 98, November.

Cotton, A.B. (1977) 'Cromwell and the Self Denying Ordinance', *History* 62.

Davis, J.C. (1990) 'Fear, Myth and the Furore: Reappraising the Ranters', *Past and Present* 129, November.

Dillon, C. (ed.) (1995–6) 'Cin Lae Ui Mheallain: Friar Mellon's Journal', *Duiche Neill* 10.

Dodd, A.H. (1948) 'Wales and the Second Bishops' War', *Bulletin of the Board of Celtic Studies* 12.

—— (1952) 'Anglesey in the Civil War', *Transactions of the Anglesey Antiquarian Society*.

—— (1954) 'Civil War in East Denbighshire', *Transactions of the Denbighshire Historical Society* 3.

Dore, R.N. (1961) 'Sir Thomas Myddleton's Attempted Conquest of Powys, 1644–5', *Montgomeryshire Collections* 57.

Dore, R.N. and Lowe, J. (1961) 'The Battle of Nantwich', *Transactions of the Lanchashire and Cheshire Historical Society*.

Durston, C. (1987) 'Signs and Wonders and the English Civil War', *History Today* 37, October.

Eames, A., (1955) 'Seapower and Caernarvonshire 1642–60', *Transactions of Caernarvonshire History Society* 16.

Ensberg, J. (1966) 'Royalist Finances during the English Civil War', *Scandinavian Economic History Review* 14, pt 2.

Fleming, D. (1981–2) 'Faction and Civil War in Leicestershire', *Transactions of the Leicestershire Archaeological and Historical Society* 57.

Fowler G.H. (ed.) (1936) 'The Civil War Papers of Sir William Boteler, 1642–1655,' *Bedfordshire Historical Society*, vol. 18., Apsley Guise.

Fox, P. (ed.) (1986) *Treasures of the Library*, Dublin: Trinity College Library.

Gillespie, R. (1985) 'Mayo and the Rising of 1641', *Cathair Na Mart* 5.

Gladwish, P. (1985) 'The Herefordshire Clubmen: A Reassessment', *Midland History* 10.

Gratton, M. (1984) 'The Military Career of Richard, Lord Molyneux, c.1623–54', *Transactions of the Lancashire and Cheshire Historical Society* 134.

Hardiman, J. (1985) *History of Galway*, Dublin: Galway Connacht Tribune, (first published 1820).

Hazlett, H. (1938) 'The Financing of the British Armies in Ireland: 1641–9', *Irish Historical Studies* 1.

Hughes, A. (1982) 'Warwickshire on the Eve of Civil War: A County Community?', *Midland History* 7.

—— (1985) 'The King, the Parliament and the Localities during the English Civil War', *Journal of British Studies* 24, April.

Hutton, R.E. (1979–80) 'The Worcestershire Clubmen in the English Civil War', *Midland History* 5.

—— (1980) 'The Failure of the Lancashire Cavaliers', *Transactions of the Lancashire and Cheshire Historical Society* 129.

—— (1981) 'The Structure of the Royalist Party', *Historical Journal* 23, 3.

Jones, J.G. (1970) 'Caernarfonshire Administration: Activities of the Justices of the Peace', *Welsh Historical Review* 5.

—— (1972) 'Aspects of Local Government in Pre- Restoration Caernarfonshire', *Transactions of the Caernarfonshire Historical Society* 33.

Kaplan, L. (1970) 'Steps to War: Scots and Parliament, 1642–3', *Journal of British Studies* 9.

Laurence, A. (1992) 'Women's Work and the English Civil War', *History Today* 42.

Lennon, C. (1995) 'Dublin's Great Explosion', *History Ireland* 3, 3.

Mack, P. (1982) 'Women as Prophets during the English Civil War', *Feminist Studies* 8, 1.

Makey, W.H. (1969) 'Elder of Stow Liberton, Canongate and St Cuthbert's in the Mid-Seventeenth Century', *Records of the Scottish Church History Society* 17.

Malcolm, J.L. (1978) 'A King in Search of Soldiers: Charles I in 1642', *Historical Journal* 21, 2.

McArthur, E.A. (1909) 'Women Petitioners and the Long Parliament', *English Historical Review* 24.

Ohlmeyer, J. (1993) 'The Marquis of Antrim: A Stuart Turn-kilt?', *History Today* 43.

O'Riordan, C. (1987) 'Thomas Ellison, the Hixon Estate and the Civil War', *Durham County Local History Society Bulletin* 39, December.

Osborne, S. (1994) 'The War, the People, and the Absence of Clubmen in the Midlands, 1642–6', *Midland History* 19.

Perceval-Maxwell, M. (1979) 'The Ulster Rising of 1641 and the Depositions', *Irish Historical Studies* 31, 82.

Porter, S. (1984) 'The Fire-Raid in the English Civil War', *War and Society* 2, 2, September.

Raymond, S.A. (1980) 'Glamorganshire Clubmen, 1642–46', *Morgannwg* 24.

Rees, F. (1962) 'Breconshire During the Civil War', *Brycheiniog* 8.

Roberts, A. (1985–6) 'The Depredations of the Civil War in South West Leicestershire', *The Leicestershire Historian* 3, 4.

Roy, I. (1978) 'England Turned Germany? The Aftermath of the Civil War in its European Context', *Transactions of the Royal Historical Society* 28, 5th series.

Russell, C. (1988) 'The British Background to the Irish Rebellion of 1641', *Historical Research* 61, 145.

—— (1993) 'The Scottish Party in English Parliaments, 1640–2 OR the Myth of the English Revolution', *Historical Research* 66, 159.

Stephenson, R.B.K. and Porteous, J. (1972) 'Two Scottish Seventeenth Century Coin Hoards', *British Numismatical Journal* 42.

Stevenson, D. (1972) 'The Financing of the Cause of the Covenanters, 1638–51', *Scottish Historical Review* 51.

—— (1990) *King's College Aberdeen, 1560–1641: From Protestant Reformation to the Covenanting Revolution*, Aberdeen: Aberdeen University Press.

Tucker, N. (1958) 'Rupert's Letters to Anglesey and Other Civil War Correspondence', *Transactions of the Anglesey Antiquarian Society*.

INDEX